"A thoughtful and comprehensive examination of the curious issue of love and money in sport." —Frank Deford, Senior Contributing Writer at *Sports Illustrated* and author of *The Entitled*

"A well-written and poignant analysis of America's stadium mess."—Andrew Zimbalist, Robert A. Woods Professor of Economics, Smith College, and author of *In the Best Interests of Baseball? The Revolutionary Reign of Bud Selig*

"If this book had been around for the Greeks to read, they would have learned that they should've billed Troy for the horse." —Molly Ivins, newspaper columnist, political commentator, and best-selling author

"The authoritative book on stadium boondoggles across the country."—*Minneapolis City Pages*

FIELD OF SCHEMES

How the Great Stadium Swindle Turns Public Money into Private Profit

Revised and Expanded Edition

Neil deMause and Joanna Cagan

University of Nebraska Press : Lincoln and London

Library of Congress Cataloging-in-Publication Data
deMause, Neil.
Field of schemes : how the great stadium swindle turns
public money into private profit / Neil deMause and Joanna
Cagan. — Rev. and expanded ed.
p. cm.
Rev. ed. of: Field of schemes / Joanna Cagan and Neil
deMause.
Includes bibliographical references and index.
ISBN 978-0-8032-6016-0 (pbk. : alk. paper)
1. Stadiums—United States—Finance. 2. Sports facilities—
United States—Finance. 3. Sports and state—United States.
I. Cagan, Joanna. II. Cagan, Joanna. Field of schemes. III. Title.
GV415.D46 2008   796.06′873—dc22   2007033590
Set in Dante MT by Bob Reitz.
Designed by Ashley Muehlbauer.

For Jordan Eli Nass-deMause
&
Finlay Cagan Patterson,
with love.

Contents

Preface to the New Edition
by Neil deMause xi

Introduction
The View from the Cheap Seats xiii

1. A Tale of Two Inner Cities 1
2. Stealing Home 27
3. Ball Barons 42
4. The Art of the Steal 62
5. Deus Ex Pizza 83
6. Home Field Advantage 103
7. Local Heroes 119
8. Bad Neighbors 136
9. Repeat Offenders 160
10. The Bucks Stop Here 182
11. Winning Isn't Everything 194
12. One Year 198
13. The Art of the Steal Revisited 225
14. Youppi! Come Home 247
15. The Perfect Storm 272
16. Saving Fenway 318

Acknowledgments 341
Notes 347
Index 389

Preface to the New Edition

Neil deMause

When we sat down to begin reporting the articles that ultimately became the first edition of this book, we were only dimly aware that we were witnessing the beginnings of an epochal shift in the sports landscape. In more and more cities, owners of sports teams were demanding new publicly financed stadiums at hundreds of millions of dollars a pop, even as local governments pleaded poverty when it came time to allocate funds for such trivialities as schools or libraries. It seemed a curious moment in the worlds of both sports and urban politics, and we set out to document it before it disappeared.

That moment was now almost twelve years ago, and the little trend that we noticed then has become a massive industry. No one keeps reliable figures on how much taxpayer money goes to building new homes for sports teams—though this book details some of the best guesses—but it's certainly now in the neighborhood of $2 billion a year. The reasons given are largely the same: Sports subsidies are good for economic development, the old place is obsolete, you'll lose your team if you don't build one. And, as we explain here, they're still almost entirely bogus—as when, for example, Florida Marlins team president David Samson declared a series of "firm" deadlines for state legislators to approve a stadium deal, and then, when no cash was forthcoming, simply waited a year and tried again.

This newly expanded edition of *Field of Schemes* picks up where the previous one left off, with four new chapters that investigate some of the most notable stadium and arena controversies of the new millennium. Chapter 13, "The Art of the Steal Revisited," covers the tricks of the trade of stadium seekers, and how they've changed (and more often, haven't) over the years. Chapter 14, "Youppi! Come Home," details what baseball business writer Doug Pappas dubbed the Stadium Extortion across North America Tour that Major League Baseball conducted as it sought to wring maximum profits from the orchestrated demise of the Montreal Expos. Chapter 15, "The Perfect Storm," recounts the blizzard of new-stadium deals that hit New York City in the new millennium, with a public price tag of more than $2 billion. And chapter 16, "Saving Fenway," is the story of that rare group of citizen activists who took on the combined power of the sports industry and the local political establishment, and won.

In addition, annotations have been added to the original chapters of this book, bringing their stories into the present day—so if you're wondering how Cleveland's new stadiums look as an economic-development project more than a decade down the road, you'll find out here. (Hint: not good.)

The little story that we stumbled across more than a decade ago turns out to be one of the defining themes of our political culture: How one big-money industry has manipulated democratic institutions to boost its own profits. The stories in this book are not just about sports, or even tax money, but ultimately about something more fundamental: Who does our government serve, and why?

Introduction

The View from the Cheap Seats

Back in the dim, distant past, when the Earth was new and the Carolina Hurricanes were still the Hartford Whalers, we knew little about the world of sports-franchise roulette. We probably were about as informed as any regular newspaper reader or ESPN junkie—namely, we knew that sports teams seemed to be moving to new cities, or at least threatening to do so, at an alarming pace. Those that stayed put were more often than not rewarded with new sports palaces with odd corporate names like the TWA Dome and the Pepsi Center. We might have wondered, too, whether these new sports facilities were really worth the hundreds of millions of public dollars being spent on them. And we might have questioned, in idle conversation, the wisdom of spending such exorbitant amounts of money on behalf of private interests while so much of what we knew and loved about U.S. cities was falling apart.

Mostly, all we knew back then, in the fall of 1995, was that the Cleveland Browns were no more.

Each of us had a long history as a sports fan. Joanna grew up in Cleveland, singing the Browns Christmas song in sixth-grade choir and generally confident in the notion that football and Sunday afternoons would forever go together. The announcement in November 1995 that longtime owner Art Modell was yanking the team away to Baltimore stunned locals. If this could happen to one of the most devoted fan bases in the country, it could happen anywhere.

Suddenly, the topic of team relocation and stadium construction seemed to deserve greater scrutiny. Local taxpayers had handed over hundreds of millions of dollars for a new baseball stadium for the Indians—should they have done the same for the Browns? And at what point was it fair for a beleaguered populace, facing a neglected educational infrastructure and a continued urban exodus, to say "enough is enough; we deserve to have sports teams *and* a successful school system"?

For Neil, meanwhile, growing up a Yankees fan meant riding the subway to the newly renovated ballyard in the Bronx thirty times a year, to sit in $1.50 bleacher seats with a crowd more diverse than you'd find most anywhere in a rapidly polarizing city: Latino families from the surrounding neighborhoods, members of the rap group Grandmaster Flash and the Furious Five, a Japanese newspaper reporter who happily gave up her press-box seat to sit with the real fans, and an elderly cowbell-wielding man named Ali, who commuted from his native Puerto Rico every baseball season to watch his team in action.

But being a Yankees fan also meant weathering New York Yankees owner George Steinbrenner's recurrent threats to move the team to the swamplands of neighboring New Jersey. Yankees games became poignant, with the fear that ours could be the last generation to share in this sudden camaraderie. Meanwhile the city, pleading poverty, doubled the subway fare, while Steinbrenner, pleading poverty, redoubled his threats while quadrupling bleacher ticket prices. But it wasn't until a new mayor slashed social services to the bone while endorsing Steinbrenner's demand for a new midtown sports palace that the full extent of the story became clear: What was it about sports teams that allowed them to find public money where the public couldn't?

Like other sports fans of long standing, we had worried over the yearly ritual of watching our teams declare their intentions to move to another city unless bribed with a new stadium or a new lease. As journalists concerned with urban issues, we wondered about the wisdom of city governments spending millions of dollars on these stadiums at a time when public housing, libraries, and schools were being dismantled at an unprecedented pace. Perhaps, we thought, there was a story in that.

What we found was more than a mere story. For one thing, the scale of the public subsidy was not millions of dollars, as we had thought, but *billions*—an expected $11 billion over the course of the 1990s, with no signs of slowing down.

We also discovered that the popular notion of the villains and the heroes in the battle over sports-franchise blackmail was upside-down. Although newspapers had portrayed the public as unthinking fans who demanded their elected officials keep teams in town at any cost, we instead found hundreds of citizen activists who had been fighting city by city for years to stop public money from going to private profit. Corporate welfare, they called it, and understandably so. Meanwhile, the local politicians who had pleaded that they had no choice but to give in to sports owners' demands turned out to be eagerly lining up to build sparkling new luxury boxes—where they then happily attended games as the owners' special guests. As one fed-up city resident told us, "They're not public servants. They're corporate servants."

This book began because we were frustrated with free-agent franchises demanding money as the price of their loyalty. But this is far more than a sports story: It's also a story of deceptive politicians, taxpayer swindles, media slants, the power of big money, and most of all, a political system that serves the rich and powerful at the expense of the average fan, the average taxpayer, the average citizen.

The more we learned in researching this book, the more apparent it became that the most important partner in the new stadium tango has been left out for far too long. Average citizens are the ones paying for the cost of new sports facilities—in public subsidies, in tax revenue lost, in public spaces taken over for private gain, in disillusionment with the democratic process, and in the loss of sheer enjoyment at being a spectator at a pro sporting event. We spoke with heartbroken sports fans who couldn't imagine life without their team, and neighborhood activists just struggling to make ends meet. One outraged citizen, questioning the whole concept of public money going to sports facilities, wondered aloud if his love of bowling meant he should get state money to build new bowling lanes.

Another vowed never to patronize the monolithic stadium his once-beloved home team was set to build. All were willing to open their memories, their homes, and their lives to our inquiries and curiosity.

We remain overwhelmed and moved by the stories these people had to share. Yes, this is the tale of the Art Modells and George Steinbrenners of the world, but more than anything it is the average citizen's story: the story of people across the country saying "enough is enough" with corporate welfare in all its many forms.

We ultimately tracked the roots of the sports-stadium swindle back in time to the construction of the railroads in nineteenth-century America, and into the corridors of local power politics in a hundred towns across the United States and Canada. But the story of the swindle really begins on the night it first broke through to public consciousness: a cold spring night in a Maryland suburb, when a fleet of moving vans crept away in the dead of night—stealing a city's football team away, and forever changing the way we think about sports, urban politics, and the future of the American city.

1 A Tale of Two Inner Cities

It is simply unconscionable that cities are forced to succumb to blackmail by pro football and baseball. You should not capitulate to blackmailers. You don't deal with hostage situations. You don't deal with terrorists. I put these teams in the same category. —*Maryland state senator Julian Lapides*

It was late on the night of March 29, 1984, when a dozen moving vans backed up to the football training complex in the Maryland suburb of Owings Mills and took the Baltimore Colts away.

Since 1953 the Colts had been an institution as fundamental to Baltimore's self-image as crab cakes or Edgar Allan Poe. Now, overnight, this symbol of the city was to be reborn as something called the Indianapolis Colts and disappear forever into an indoor football stadium in the American heartland.

A few spectators gathered in the rain to watch as the worldly belongings of Baltimore's football team were loaded up for the six-hundred-mile drive west. The movers, imported from Indianapolis by Colts owner Robert Irsay for the occasion, packed away helmets and pads, file cabinets and film projectors, as Pinkerton guards kept onlookers at bay.

"It's unbelievable, the callousness of this man," Colts fan Brian Yaniger told a crowd of assembled reporters. "Just because he has a couple of bucks, he can tear a whole city down on his whims."

The Colts' move was hardly the first time a pro sports team had switched cities. In 1958, after all, the Dodgers had famously fled Brooklyn, and six of the National Basketball Association's inaugural eight teams had moved from their original homes by 1963. The first great era of sports-franchise migration ran from 1952 until 1968— when the Kansas City (née Philadelphia) A's ended their two-decade westward flight by settling in Oakland. In the interim, more than a dozen sports franchises took up new residences.

But those were different times. Jet travel had abruptly made bi-coastal leagues a reality, and the great population shifts away from the urban centers of the Northeast to the suburbs and the Sunbelt had opened up new markets for pro sports. By the time the Colts took flight, the major sports leagues had already expanded into most of the attractive locations, and franchise shifts had become rare. Before the Oakland Raiders moved to Los Angeles in 1982, no established football team had switched cities in two decades. Baseball hadn't seen a move in twelve years; basketball and hockey had undergone unprecedented expansion but little franchise movement since the early '70s. Sports fans in Baltimore, like their counterparts across the nation, had grown secure in the expectation that their team would still be there to cheer on next year.

Besides, the team's absentee owner, Robert Irsay, had just been handed $25 million in city-funded stadium improvements to quiet his earlier threats to leave town. And the team was moving to Indianapolis, of all places—a city no larger than Baltimore, with only a single major-league team to its name, the fledgling Indiana Pacers basketball club—a prototypical hick town derisively nicknamed India-no-place.

The Colts' move, clearly, was something new and frightening: a team leaving its home of three decades not for lack of support (the Colts had continued to attract large crowds in its last years in Baltimore), but solely for the lure of greater profits. "If the Colts can be moved that way," wrote *New York Times* sports columnist Dave Anderson following the team's midnight flight, "any other franchise area in any sport can wake up some morning to find itself without a team."

They were prophetic words. The Colts' move may have seemed an anomaly at the time, but in retrospect it was the dawn of an era. In 1984, corporations large and small were learning as never before how to supplement profits by extorting money from their home-towns under threat of moving across the country or overseas. The sports industry may have come late to this game of "corporate wel-fare," as it came to be known, but it soon had adopted the tactic for its own. Whereas a manufacturing plant could win perhaps tens of millions of dollars this way, the final tab for a single sports subsidy could run as high as half a billion dollars.

The Colts' sudden move led to a series of events far beyond any-thing that could have been imagined that spring night. By the time the dust had settled, another football team had been taken from its diehard fans, and two cities had undertaken the building of four new stadiums, leaving taxpayers in two states to pay close to $1 billion in construction costs. The resulting transfer of public funds into private pockets would lay claim to public schools and fragile urban neigh-borhoods, leave democratic checks and balances in shambles, and enrich a handful of owners—real-estate barons and wealthy indus-trialists—by hundreds of millions of dollars. The flight of the Balti-more Colts may have seemed like the end of the world for the team's fans, but for sports owners, it was the beginning of a lucrative dream that has yet to end. Before long, Cleveland, another urban center similarly struggling to survive the shifting industrial landscape of the 1970s, would be drawn into the musical-chairs game of relocating sports teams and earmarking public funds for stadium construction. Within a decade, nearly every major city in the nation was being asked to mortgage its future to the sports industry, and Robert Irsay was beginning to look less like a singular demon than the harbinger of a scam of historic proportions.

It all started, inauspiciously enough, with the Hoosier Dome.

Take the Money and Run

The idea was first floated in the mid-1970s by business and political leaders in Indianapolis. The local government had already poured more than $400 million into a decade's worth of downtown office blocks and hotel complexes; a new domed football stadium, they proposed, would complement the city's convention center as the centerpiece of a hub of sports-based tourism. Construction of the Hoosier Dome was under way by 1982, its $78 million price tag financed by a 1 percent county-wide tax on food and beverages and $30 million in grants from two local foundations.

Indianapolis had a state-of-the-art domed stadium rising in its city center, but it still had no team. Dome boosters had assured city leaders that the NFL would place an expansion football team in Indianapolis once construction was complete. By 1982, however, it had become clear that the football league was in no hurry to expand—thanks in part to an ongoing lawsuit over the Raiders' move to Los Angeles the previous year. Furthermore, it was looking more likely that, once expansion did arrive, the NFL would favor booming Sunbelt cities such as Phoenix and Jacksonville over Indianapolis. Articles started appearing in financial publications with such headlines as "Will Indianapolis' Domed Stadium Become a White Elephant?"

This, clearly, would not do. So three-term mayor William Hudnut, sensing political disaster, reestablished an old contact he had made back in 1977, when the dome was still just a set of blueprints: He called Robert Irsay, owner of the Baltimore Colts. And he offered him a deal.

A Chicago industrialist who had made his fortune in sheet metal, Irsay had bought the Colts in 1972 and watched as his new team took an immediate nosedive in the standings. In 1979, with the Colts floundering on the field and in ticket sales, the team's owner demanded that the city pay for $25 million worth of improvements to twenty-five-year-old Memorial Stadium, which the Colts shared with the Baltimore Orioles baseball team. If not, he intimated, he would take his team elsewhere.

The city capitulated to the Colts' owner's demands, but still Irsay's eye wandered. By 1984 his flirtations had focused on Indianapolis, where Hudnut was offering a low-rent lease on the new dome to entice the team to relocate. Baltimore city officials, scrambling to keep the Colts in place, countered with an offer of a $15 million loan and a city-backed guarantee on ticket sales. But even as they held out this gold-plated carrot to Irsay, city leaders also readied an unprecedented stick: They asked the state legislature to consider condemning the team via the principle of eminent domain.

Under eminent-domain powers, local governments can condemn a private asset and then seize it, paying the former owners fair market value for their property—in this case, the Colts themselves, which would then be sold to a new, local owner. It's a tactic more often used for highway rights-of-way than for football teams; it's also one that had failed two years earlier in Oakland when the Raiders skipped town. But that case had been rejected by an appeals court on very narrow grounds, and legal experts were hopeful that the city of Baltimore would have better luck with its case.

It never got the chance. The Colts, tipped off to the city's plans, hurriedly completed negotiations with Indianapolis. And so, on March 29, 1984, while the Maryland legislature continued to debate the use of eminent domain, in came the moving vans. That afternoon, the bill to place the Colts under state control was passed, but it was a few hours too late: Courts would later rule against the seizure on the grounds that by the time the law was passed, there was nothing left for the state to seize.

The Baltimore Colts were no more. As fans grieved, local politicians plotted to obtain a replacement franchise, either through expansion or by moving an established team. And city officials across the nation braced for a new wave of demands from their own sports teams, under threat of becoming "another Baltimore."

"Mistake on the Lake"

The last thing the city of Cleveland wanted was to become the next Baltimore. It was already the first, and hopefully last, Cleveland, and that was enough of an emotional burden for even the windy town's hardiest souls. Once a thriving industrial center with dominating sports teams, Cleveland had seen its fortunes, its national image, and the reputation of its historic baseball stadium plummet over mere decades.

In 1931 the successful completion of the new sports stadium on the shores of Lake Erie was hailed as the harbinger of great things to come. Cleveland Municipal Stadium, built by the federal Works Project Administration with the hope of luring the 1932 Olympics to downtown Cleveland, was "a monument to the progressive spirit of the city's people," according to the special section of the *Cleveland Plain Dealer* devoted to the new stadium.

The city, not yet crippled under the weight of the Depression, was coming off one of its most successful economic decades ever. Cleveland had become the nation's second-largest center for automobile manufacturing, behind only Detroit. Big steel was thriving, as was manufacturing. And the brand-new horseshoe by the lake, which cost local taxpayers some $2.5 million, was the crown jewel in an economic construction plan designed to give the city even more national attention. When eighty thousand fans jammed into Municipal Stadium's wooden seats for the Cleveland Indians' first baseball game there in 1932, headline writers crowed "Depression Given Black Eye." It was there that the team reveled in its glory years of the 1940s and 1950s, when the Indians were one of the most successful teams in baseball, and their fans set attendance records that would last for decades.

Fifty years later, the stadium had assumed a very different meaning. Municipal Stadium, and the city itself, were dubbed the "Mistake on the Lake." As Cleveland struggled through a series of national embarrassments in the 1970s—from the Cuyahoga River catching on fire to the city becoming the first major American city to go into default since the Depression—the dreadful performance of the Indians, and their aging ballpark, seemed horribly symbolic of Cleveland's misfortunes. Year after cellar-dwelling year, the team was considered an embarrassment to professional baseball, and talk escalated that opposing teams dreaded the trip to frigid Cleveland Municipal Stadium, with its bitter winds off Lake Erie and its tiny crowds, cramped locker rooms, and out-of-date scoreboard.

And while many in the city turned critical eyes on the performance of the Indians, Cleveland itself was feeling the uncomfortable burn of a national spotlight that illuminated a shrinking population, deteriorating race relations, escalating poverty, and vanishing industrial jobs. The city, which had lost 23 percent of its population between 1970 and 1980, started the 1980s with its credit suspended by several Wall Street ratings agencies because of its fiscal woes.

When Indians owner Steve O'Neill died in 1983, rumors ran rampant that the financially shaky team would be sold to buyers from another state, most likely Florida. Even before O'Neill's death, league officials had come to town to announce that the Indians were very likely not long for Cleveland. Without a principal owner for the team, its future was suddenly even more precarious. And so in 1984 a new tax initiative to fund a domed stadium (domes were then in fashion—several cities had followed Indianapolis's lead) was called for, in order, it was claimed, to keep the team in the city.

The campaign for the dome was the brainchild of Cuyahoga county commissioner Vincent Campanella. Working largely without the organized support of his fellow politicians, Campanella proposed putting a domed stadium in the old Central Market area of downtown Cleveland; the new $150 million, seventy-two-thousand-seat stadium was to be entirely paid for by a countywide property-tax levy.

Emotions ran high among fans and residents throughout the dome debate. The way some locals talked, the threatened move of a sports team would tear the heart out of the city. Yet many Clevelanders questioned the fiscal sanity of forking over public dollars at a time when the town overall was struggling to reverse years of financial woe. Others were reluctant to spend a great deal of tax money on a team that had performed so abysmally for so many years. "Go Browns," a cynical graffitist scrawled on the walk to Municipal Stadium. "And take the Indians with you."

In May 1984, voters resoundingly rejected the proposal. The choice of a property tax to fund the initiative, the Indians' poor performance on the playing field, and, most important, a lack of consensus among the city's power brokers probably sent the campaign to its defeat. The effort never had the full support of then governor Richard Celeste or the city's Republican mayor, George Voinovich. Indeed, Campanella himself would later speculate that the failure of the domed-stadium tax killed his political career.

But if Campanella's mishandling of the political situation temporarily doomed the dome, the *idea* of a new stadium had plenty of support, especially from the city's powerful business community. As would become the national pattern, advertisements by dome supporters promised Cleveland taxpayers that the new stadium would result in magnificent economic dividends for the city as a whole, promises that continued after the referendum went down to a solid defeat. Soon after the initiative lost, the *Washington Post* reported, "Cleveland leaders can't ignore a study that said a dome would result in the construction of three new downtown hotels, an office building and restaurants, that 1,588 full-time construction jobs would be created; that another 6,829 permanent jobs would result; that the total annual spending impact would be $62.2 million." National and local media, the business community, and local politicians all firmly pushed the idea that a new stadium was needed for the team and for Cleveland's hopes of reestablishing itself as an important city.

And although their referendum failed, domed-stadium backers didn't give up. The Civic Committee to Build a Domed Stadium was formed, chaired by the acting chair of the Greater Cleveland Growth Association, the town's chamber of commerce. The Civic Committee would later become the Greater Cleveland Domed Stadium Corporation, which borrowed $22 million from local banks and the state to purchase a site for a new facility. Despite public opposition and construction, and financing plans that were sketchy at best, supporters were determined to plunge ahead with the stadium project.

Before Cleveland's power brokers could come up with a new pitch, however, the national sports-stadium scene irrevocably shifted—thanks in large part to events taking place back in Baltimore.

"Just Give Me the Tools"

The departure of the Colts in the spring of 1984 had an immediate impact on Baltimore politics. Seeing the outcry over the loss of one sports team, Mayor William Schaefer, who had been a steadfast opponent of spending public money on sports stadiums, abruptly became the biggest booster of a new ballpark for the Baltimore Orioles.

A success on the field and off since relocating from St. Louis in 1954, the Baltimore club landed seven first-place finishes between 1966 and 1979, and their home at city-owned Memorial Stadium was a pleasant one, nestled in a residential neighborhood of single-family homes whose rooftops were visible beyond the wooden bleachers in right and left fields. In the mid-1980s a poll of fans ranked Memorial as one of the best ballparks in the major leagues.

But for all its pastoral charm, Memorial was a no-frills ballpark, without such modern-day amenities as luxury boxes or lavish food-preparation facilities. As early as 1967, when municipalities across the country were building new concrete "dual-purpose" stadiums to house both their football and baseball teams, the owners of the Colts and Orioles had proposed such a facility for Baltimore, to be situated near the old Camden rail yards just west of downtown. In 1972 Orioles exec Frank Cashen upped the ante, proclaiming, "We are not going to be able to do anything in terms of a new long-term lease unless a stadium is built downtown." But as it became clear that no such deal was forthcoming, the Orioles continued to sign short-term leases on Memorial, and no one moved to resurrect the idea of a new facility.

Then, in 1979 local beer magnate Jerrold Hoffberger sold the Orioles to Edward Bennett Williams, a lawyer-to-the-pols from hated rival Washington DC. Many in Baltimore suspected Williams of harboring secret plans to move the ballclub to the nation's capital—a suspicion that the new owner wasted no time in using to force the city's hand on his demands for a new stadium. "For as long as the city will support the team," he told the *Washington Post*, "it will stay here"—leading to rampant speculation that he would take the team south on the pretext of low attendance. When American League president Lee MacPhail followed with a public vow of league support for a new stadium on Interstate 95 between Baltimore and Washington, the pressure built for Baltimore to prevent a repeat of the Colts' betrayal.

By 1986, when Mayor Schaefer was elected governor of Maryland, he was not just a proponent of a new baseball stadium; he had become Williams's greatest ally. The man who as mayor had declared that "unless private enterprise builds it, we won't build it" was now missing no opportunity to stump for a new state-built ballpark. Bill Marker, a local community leader who would play a major role in the stadium battle to come, recalls watching Schaefer's inaugural speech as governor: "I remember saying to friends, 'Well, let's see whether he mentions the stadium, and if so where in his speech.' And it was basically: 'Hi, Marylanders! We've gotta build a stadium!'"

Schaefer knew just where he wanted to build it, too: the same Camden Yards site that had been considered for a multi-sport facility back in the '60s. Ten years earlier, Mayor Schaefer had helped mastermind the reconstruction of Baltimore's inner harbor as the Harborplace mall-and-museum tourist mecca. Now, Governor Schaefer concluded that a stadium could only enhance the attractiveness of the city's rebuilt downtown to out-of-towners and their entertainment dollars.

To keep Williams happy, Schaefer was prepared to build the project entirely with public money, proposing two state-run lotteries with a sports theme to raise the $235 million necessary to condemn the existing industrial park on the site and to fund the construction of separate stadiums for baseball and football. (As it turned out, Schaefer had seriously underestimated the cost of clearing land for the project. The total tab would ultimately reach $410 million, plus an additional $30 million for road improvements, to be paid out of federal transportation funds.)

The plan was cemented at a memorable public hearing of the state senate in March 1987. The star attraction was Williams, who used every bit of his personal charm and political connections to sway the legislators. In attendance that day was Bill Marker, preparing to testify on behalf of his fledgling Marylanders for Sports Sanity (MASS), a hastily organized citizens' group opposing public stadium funding. His hand-drawn placards, detailing alternate proposals that MASS had calculated could keep the team in town for far less money—including having the state buy the team outright for less than the cost of a new stadium—sat unused at his feet as he watched Williams testify at length that a new ballpark was the only solution to the woes of his team, as well as those of Baltimore. The Orioles' owner, recalls Marker, was greeted as an old friend: "It was all these senators saying, 'Oh, you were my professor in law school, and you were so wonderful.'"

While Marker sat, several legislators expressed concerns about spending such a large sum on what was, after all, a private enterprise. When Williams remarked that he needed a stadium that could guarantee sales of fifteen thousand season tickets, state senator Julian "Jack" Lapides shot back, "It might be cheaper for the state to buy fifteen thousand season tickets." Williams waited for the cheers from the gallery to die down, then replied, "I didn't come here to ask for a subsidy. . . . I can make this thing go in the private sector if I get the tools."

The "tools" Williams wanted—a taxpayer-funded stadium—represented just as much of a subsidy as a direct cash grant, of course, but the state senate didn't let that stand in its way. Four weeks after Williams's testimony, the senate voted to empower the Maryland Sports Authority to build two new stadiums: a baseball park immediately for the Orioles, and a football stadium to follow once a replacement for the Colts could be lined up.

With the governor, state legislature, and mayor united behind a publicly funded ballpark, Marker and his fellow community activists had only one weapon left at their disposal. According to the Maryland state constitution, any government expenditure can be submitted to a binding public referendum. Within two weeks of the state senate decision, MASS had gone door-to-door to gather twenty-eight thousand signatures calling for a public vote. The state rejected the petitions on the grounds that the stadium-funding bill was not subject to referendum; MASS took the state to court. An initial ruling sided with the neighborhood activists. But that September the Maryland court of appeals overturned the lower court's ruling, agreeing with the state's argument that the stadium project constituted an "appropriation for maintaining the state government" and so was exempt from public vote.

"I think they lost the distinction that the state was doing it for a private enterprise," Jack Lapides later recalled of the court's ruling. "If the state were condemning the land and building the facility for a *state* football team, or a state road, or a state hospital, or a state school, then there would be justification. But I thought that their rationale was very convoluted."

Opponents screamed long and loud that Schaefer had bullied his way past the democratic process, but the deed was done. The stadium—given the cumbersome appellation "Oriole Park at Camden Yards" at the insistence of Eli Jacobs, who bought the Orioles following Williams's death in 1988—had cleared its final hurdle. On April 6, 1992, five years and $120 million worth of lottery tickets later, the new ballpark opened to a packed house. And the value of Jacobs's team, according to figures compiled by *Financial World* magazine, jumped by nearly $100 million.

At long last, the new stadium had taken its place alongside the other government-sponsored tourist attractions that now crowded the city's Inner Harbor. But as important as it was to Baltimore, Oriole Park at Camden Yards was destined to play a still more pivotal role in the history of pro sports. For the Orioles had insisted on a building that would be not an antiseptic stadium but a *ballpark*; unlike every other baseball stadium built in recent memory, this one eschewed concrete walls and symmetrical dimensions for a self-consciously quirky design that used steel and brick to sheath its luxury boxes and ad-filled video screens. From the upper-deck seats, fans were treated to vistas not of suburban parking lots but of the city skyline. In a final touch that delighted architectural critics and baseball fans alike, the right-field wall abutted an eighty-seven-year-old brick warehouse that was converted into team offices, a baseball museum, and upscale shops.

As the stadium's biographer Peter Richmond wrote, "Baltimore didn't need a new baseball stadium, but it was more than grateful for the deliverance of a national showpiece." Camden Yards, as the park would soon be known nationwide, caught the attention of every baseball team yearning for a new stadium. Fans flocked through the gates of the new "old-time" park, filling the Orioles' ledgers with unprecedented revenue, and the repercussions would be felt nationwide.

"Comeback City"

While the Orioles' new owner was lobbying for a new home in Baltimore, the hapless Indians (helmless as well after O'Neill's death) were about to see their fortunes change. Whether real or imagined, the threat of losing their baseball franchise, no matter how much the Indians had struggled, was of enormous importance to many Clevelanders. The city had witnessed, as had the rest of the country, what had happened to Baltimore's beloved Colts when another town laid down better terms. So when, two years after the domed stadium went down in defeat at the polls, the Indians were bought by brothers Richard and David Jacobs, there was a collective sigh of relief. The Jacobses (no relation to Orioles owner Eli Jacobs) were locals who had made millions in real-estate development, especially in shopping-mall construction. Significantly, they had made their fortunes in the Cleveland area and had considerable interest in downtown development projects. "Increasingly they began to make substantial investments in the city of Cleveland," explains David R. Elkins, a professor of political science at Cleveland State University, noting that the brothers purchased building after building in the downtown area. "They made some enormous changes on the physical appearance of the city."

There wouldn't be much of a grace period for Clevelanders, however, because the Jacobs brothers weren't about to give up on the idea of having a new home built for their team. The brothers had made their fortunes in an industry that had benefited tremendously for decades from Cleveland's generous tax-abatement policies, and when they bought the Indians, they argued that a central element of their successfully rebuilding the team would have to be a new home. But in a city that had already rejected public funding of a new stadium, it would take masterful manipulation to persuade the populace to fund such a project.

In 1990 the Central Market Gateway Project was formed in order to develop a new downtown stadium for the Indians and an arena for the basketball Cavaliers (who had been playing in suburban Richfield), with what was then proposed as a mix of public and private funds. The project got its title from the proposed construction site— twenty-eight acres of prime downtown real estate that was home to the city's historic Central Market. The site was one of the city's two old open-air produce and supply markets and was still an active, if somewhat neglected, neighborhood gathering spot when it was demolished in 1989 at the request of the domed-stadium supporters. For several years, as stadium backers plotted tactics, the site sat, unused, as Cleveland's inner-city residents were forced to go elsewhere to meet their shopping needs. Those same taxpayers presumably could take solace, along with the rest of the city, in thinking of the newly razed spot as the centerpiece for what had been dubbed a "comeback city."

With property taxes a proven failure with voters and politicians alike, the principal means of paying off the city bonds that would fund the new stadium project was to be a "sin tax"—a tax on alcoholic beverages and cigarette- and tobacco-related products. The Cuyahoga County commissioners, no doubt fearful of tying their own political futures to such a project, decided to put that decision to the voters—against the wishes of stadium boosters, who desperately wanted to have the county impose the tax without a costly referendum campaign. Raising $1 million from private interests, including $300,000 from both the Indians and the Cavaliers, supporters of the initiative set out to prove to Cleveland voters that a vote for the stadium was a vote for the future of Cleveland.

"Who wins with Issue 2?" blared a newspaper ad just days before the 1990 vote. "We All Do," answered the placards held by a multicultural rainbow of Cleveland schoolchildren. "Gateway will create a development that will generate $33.7 million in public revenues every year and provide: 28,000 good-paying jobs for the *jobless*; neighborhood housing development for the *homeless*; $15 million a year for schools for our *children*; revenues for City and County clinics and hospitals for the *sick*; energy assistance programs for the *elderly*." The ad went on to promise what wouldn't be taken from taxpayers' wallets or given to team owners: "No property tax; no sales tax; no income tax; no tax abatement . . . Gateway: the next chapter in our future."

The PR campaign was combined with some hardball threats from the Major League Baseball establishment. Two days before the vote, baseball commissioner Fay Vincent paid a visit to the city of Cleveland. "Should this facility not be available in Cleveland, should the vote be a negative one, we may be finding ourselves confronting a subject that we want to avoid," Vincent said. "I say to you, it would be very bad for baseball, and I am opposed to Cleveland losing its team." A *Plain Dealer* columnist laid it out for the public: "Anyone who thinks the Indians will still be playing in [Municipal] Stadium at the end of the century is nuts. They'll either be in a new stadium here or a new stadium elsewhere. Period."

The so-called Gateway initiative won a narrow victory with 51.7 percent of the vote. As with the earlier domed-stadium initiative, all but one of the twenty-one wards located within the city limits voted against the proposal.

The voting reflected a split in the local electorate, explains John Ryan, executive secretary of the Cleveland AFL-CIO. "One is the suburbanites and a couple of wards that have quite a bit of money. The other are low-income people or people that rely on the school systems. And for the most part, they are people who don't have much of a voice." The stadium vote had reaffirmed working-class and poor Clevelanders' suspicions that, when it came to matters of public policy and decision making in the city, their pocketbooks were the first to be raided (via cigarette and liquor taxes, which, like all taxes on the sale of goods, fall disproportionately on those with lower incomes), even though their concerns were the last to be addressed.

Voters had approved the proposal with the understanding that the combined cost of the new stadium and arena would run about $344 million. But that soon turned into a much greater public investment—some estimate the total cost through 1996 to be as high as $462 million, with as much as two thirds coming from the public.[1] And that cost continued to accumulate. It wasn't until late December 1996 that Gateway Economic Development Corp. signed a contract agreeing to pay, over five years, $1.6 million in overdue taxes—most of it owed to Cleveland schools.

"The arena was the real bugaboo," says Elkins. The Cavaliers played in a nearly new arena in nearby Richfield, he explains, and the team owners, Gordon and George Gund, had just refurbished that arena at their own expense. The Gunds, he recalls, "were constantly saying, 'We don't need to come downtown. We have a fine facility out at Richfield Coliseum, and if we don't have a state-of-the-art facility here in Cleveland, there's no incentive, more or less, for us to come downtown.'"

Cost overruns or not, by the spring of 1994 the Indians had their new home. (Gund Arena, for the Cavaliers, would follow that autumn.) Named Jacobs Field after Richard Jacobs offered the highest bid for the naming rights, the new stadium was directly in the Camden Yards mold—modestly sized and constructed out of lime rock to reflect local construction resources, with an asymmetrical seat layout and state-of-the-art scoreboard.

Send in the Browns

Even while some Clevelanders bemoaned a stadium seen as too big, too old, and too drafty for baseball, the town's football team continued to pack in crowds at the same location. The Cleveland Browns, owned since 1961 by multimillionaire GOP fundraiser Art Modell, were as much a symbol of NFL glory as the Indians were a baseball embarrassment. All winter long, Sunday afternoons meant packed Browns games at Municipal Stadium with a boisterous core of working-class fans who'd cheered the team on for decades. The rabid enthusiasm was symbolized by the nationally known "Dawg Pound"—the rowdy crowd of fans in the end zone bleacher seats who painted themselves in the team's orange and brown, often consumed great quantities of alcohol, and donned canine masks when the team's defensive secondary took to calling themselves the Dawgs and barking. (Arsenio Hall would immortalize this group by encouraging his late-night national television audience to bark in the same manner.)

By the mid-1980s, when the fate of the Indians was portrayed as being in severe jeopardy, the future of the Browns was never publicly questioned. But on November 4, 1995, Modell stunned the city with the revelation that he had been involved in negotiations with Maryland officials to move his team to Baltimore. Rumors had circulated for months that Modell resented the city's finding money to build the Gateway Project and the new Rock and Roll Hall of Fame while not funding renovations of Municipal Stadium. But Modell had also promised the city in 1994 that as long as he owned the team he'd never leave town, and the rumors remained just that—until November 1995.

Modell had long requested renovations to Municipal Stadium, and some were in the works. In fact, the story of his probable exodus broke the day before a scheduled vote to extend the sin tax created to fund the Gateway complex so that it could be used to pay for improvements to the Browns' home. Perhaps not surprisingly (the *Plain Dealer* ran a front-page editorial urging a yes vote), the referendum passed.

But with a lucrative offer from Baltimore in hand, Modell was not to be placated with mere stadium renovations. Three days later, the deal was official. Cries of fury came from almost every corner of Cleveland. From carefully orchestrated petition drives by the mayor's office, to spontaneous anti-Modell outbursts (at times lapsing into anti-Semitism—"They killed the wrong Jew" read one memorable homemade sign at a Browns game after Israeli prime minister Yitzhak Rabin was slain), the city reacted with passion and outrage to Modell's announcement.

There were several "Save Our Browns" rallies in the months following Modell's announcement—especially after Mayor Michael White urged Clevelanders to let the nation hear their outrage. "No Team, No Peace" was a common slogan in a surreal time in which a city saw its usually moderate mayor tirelessly campaign against one of the town's most famous multimillion-dollar residents. Concerned citizens wore orange armbands and gathered petitions, Cleveland-born comedian Drew Carey spoke at one rally, and a cottage industry hawking anti-Modell T-shirts, buttons, and bumper stickers blossomed. But the Browns left anyway, and the city reeled. It was perhaps the only time the *New York Times* has ever run a photograph of a grown man wearing a dog mask, smoking a cigar, and weeping.

As for Baltimore, after twelve years the city had finally found its replacement for the Colts, even if the new Baltimore Ravens didn't yet have quite the allure of the old club. The Browns' move also meant that Baltimore would at last have to build the new stadium that it had denied the Colts, a football-only stadium adjacent to Oriole Park at Camden Yards, at a cost of an additional $200 million in state-lottery money. For the Ravens, there was no question of paying their own way: Their new lease guaranteed the team thirty years of free rent, plus a $50 million cash relocation bonus. "As sweetheart [deals] go, call this one the Demi Moore special," *San Diego Union-Tribune* sportswriter Tom Cushman wrote, noting that a Ravens subsidiary would even rake in half the profits (plus a 10 percent "management fee") for rock concerts and other non-football events at the new stadium. The Orioles, noting a parity clause in their lease requiring that they get at least as good a deal as any football team at Camden Yards, immediately demanded free rent, too.

Baltimore had paid dearly to replace its departed football team; now it would be Cleveland's turn to ante up. The city had hoped that the renovation of Municipal Stadium that voters had approved in November would be enough to lure a new team. But when Mayor White met with NFL officials in early January 1996, he was told that the league would consider a replacement team only if there were a new stadium in place. White, following negotiations with NFL officials on the city's chances of getting a replacement football team, quickly brokered a deal to tear down Municipal Stadium and replace it with a new $220 million football-only stadium to be paid for primarily with tax money.

A populace that had just been called upon to hand over $175 million in stadium-renovation money was now going to have its wallets raided once again. And yet, with Cleveland's voters and politicians facing the very real specter of a town without football, local activists calling for a change in fiscal priorities faced an uphill battle.

Marge Misak, a longtime community activist, remembers well her sense of isolation. "There was no outcry. There were no people publicly, no politicians, no groups, that were saying, 'Wait a minute. Let's look at it. Let's question it.' It was astounding, especially in light of the fact that all the cost overruns at Gateway were coming through, and the county was coming up with more and more loans that were obviously not going to be repaid, just to finish that project. . . . It was kind of an astounding juxtaposition, because you would think that there would be questions about, 'Did we learn our lesson here?'"

Six days of debate in the Cleveland City Council culminated in a 13–8 vote in support of funding the new football stadium. The final tally was closer than many had expected. At the council hearings, recalls Misak, "One councilperson got up and talked about his neighborhood and the children, apologizing to the eight-year-olds in his neighborhood who didn't have swings to play on. In the beginning of his speech I thought, 'Oh my gosh. I can't believe this person, who is a total mayor's ally.' I'm thinking he's going to come out against this. . . ." She trails off in a laugh. "But he didn't! He apologized to all the eight-year-olds in his neighborhood and then voted to put the city general fund at risk."

By February 1996 the *Plain Dealer* could boast in its lead editorial, "The best deal possible; Cleveland is rid of Art Modell and his mediocre team, and Mayor White has helped foster a Browns rebirth." It was civic-boostering spin at an all-time peak—what had been painted as tragedy only a few short months before was now seen as the only possible way for the city to hold on to its team name and rid itself of a suddenly unpopular man at the same time. No one dared mention that the city coffers didn't have the money to fund a new stadium— Cleveland's third publicly funded new sports facility in less than a decade—or that acquiring a new team could very well mean enticing a team to bolt from yet another town.

Early reports had the Cincinnati Bengals or, ironically enough, the Indianapolis Colts being brought in to play in the new Cleveland stadium. But the Bengals soon took themselves out of the running by striking a deal for their own new stadium—paid for lock, stock, and luxury box by the citizens of Cincinnati to keep their football team in town. The March 1996 referendum that authorized that football stadium also approved a new stadium for the baseball Reds to keep them from feeling left out. And so, by the spring of 1997, plans had been laid for four stadiums in two states as a consequence of Art Modell's flight from Cleveland, itself a product of the Colts' move from Baltimore more than a decade before.[2]

Aftermath

According to today's conventional media wisdom, both Cleveland and Baltimore are cities in the midst of "renaissances," rising from the ashes of '70s decay to stand newly triumphant as urban growth centers. Credit for these rebirths is largely given to the cities' reconstructed downtowns, anchored in each case by a multimillion-dollar sports complex that draws tourists from across the country.

Indeed, it's hard to imagine how the new stadiums could have been more successful. Jacobs Field and Camden Yards sold out virtually every game from the day they opened; in 1996 and 1997 the Indians set a new baseball record by selling out the *entire season* months before opening day, leaving the team's ticket sales staff with little to do for the year but count the money. A study by the city of Baltimore found that the number of fans coming into town from outside the Baltimore–Washington region for Orioles games nearly doubled after the new ballpark was built.

As for the visions of a rising economic tide that would lift all boats, though, the story was more troubling. And so while Cleveland, under the leadership of Mayor White, has been lauded repeatedly by the national media as a classic comeback town—with its beautiful new sports facilities as key elements—life remains much the same for the city's still-shrinking urban population. In the midst of a decades-long drop in population, the percentage of Clevelanders living in poverty rose from 17 percent in 1970 to more than 40 percent by the mid-1990s. The city school system, drained of property taxes, is in shambles—only 38 percent of its students graduate high school, with only 7 percent testing at a twelfth-grade level—and was placed in state receivership in 1995. In fact, the day before the deal for a new football stadium in Cleveland was approved by the Cleveland city council, the Cleveland public school system announced it would cut $52 million over two years, laying off up to 160 teachers and eliminating interscholastic athletics from a program that Cleveland school superintendent Richard A. Boyd described as "in the worst financial shape of any school district in the country."[3]

In Baltimore the toll is harder to quantify. Because the stadiums were built with state money, there is no guarantee that the city would have reaped the benefit of alternative uses for the funds. Still, the Camden Yards complex ultimately drew more than $400 million out of the state treasury, the bulk of it coming from poor Baltimoreans who are the lottery's best customers. That's $400 million, critics charge, that could have been spent on the city's gaping chasm of needs for education or drug treatment. And the vein is now tapped out: With each new sports lottery to meet the stadiums' cost overruns, state lottery officials have seen their yield decline, leading many locals to conclude that the lottery market is simply saturated. In 1997 a plan to legalize limited casino gambling in the city of Baltimore and use the proceeds for education was shot down by Parris Glendening, Schaefer's successor as governor.[4]

As for the neighborhood activists who had opposed Camden Yards, not all of their worst fears were realized. The surrounding neighborhoods, so far at least, have neither been gentrified beyond recognition nor lost in a flood of sports-fan amenities. "They did a good job of doing a bad thing," concedes Bill Marker, looking up at the new stadium that literally casts a shadow over his mixed-income row-house neighborhood of Ridgely's Delight. True, the "historic" nature of the ballpark is more cosmetic than real; even the warehouse, without which the baseball field would, in Lapides's words, "just be sort of a blob sitting in the middle of a field," lost its northern end, lopped off to afford better views of the downtown skyline from the seats behind home plate. And the city did lose many of the one thousand manufacturing jobs provided by the twenty-six companies that had existed on the Camden Yards site, in addition to the property taxes that the food plants and other businesses had generated.

Just across the highway from the new stadiums, the black enclave of Sharp–Leadenhall is less thrilled with its new neighbors, as it continues to plead for money from the city to repair its recreation center and swimming pool amid city cutbacks. "Oh man, the city," sighs Sharp–Leadenhall Planning Committee organizer May Ringold. "It's a pity that the city's there. We need some of that federal money. We're just a small community, but we've been around since the seventeenth century. . . . If the stadium wanted to come into our neighborhood, I think they should try to help spruce up the neighborhood itself." The Stadium Authority's only offer to date: a new path through the community's playground, so that football fans could walk through more quickly on their way to the games.

Three miles to the north, in Baltimore's old sports center, the picture is more uniformly gloomy. Memorial Stadium now sits empty, save for the eight Sundays a year when the Ravens are in town, occupying the old bowl as they await their new digs at Camden Yards.[5] The residential neighborhoods around the stadium, Waverly and Charles Village, whose modest brick houses provided the backdrop for so many Orioles and Colts games over the years, have started showing the first signs of decline: "For Sale" signs sprout like dandelions along Thirty-third Street, and the shopping drag on nearby Greenmount Avenue is littered with empty storefronts. The Stadium Lounge, on Greenmount and Thirty-fourth, bears two large signs in its window: "The Stadium Lounge Welcomes the NFL Baltimore Ravens" and "Checks Cashed in a Flash."

Jack Lapides, who is quick to praise the decision to place the new stadiums downtown instead of in the suburbs, is just as quick to point out that Baltimore already had a ballpark that met the same "old-time" criteria that would later draw compliments at Camden

Yards. "The old Memorial Stadium was a perfectly valid ballpark," he says. "And it also would have kept up one of the few truly integrated neighborhoods in Baltimore, a nice middle-class neighborhood. People loved having the stadium there—many moved to the neighborhood because the stadium was there. And this was a nice draw in another part of the city, rather than putting everything in the Inner Harbor of Baltimore."

The greatest irony about these new sports palaces is that those who paid the most for them—the buyers of Maryland lottery tickets and Cleveland cigarettes—are the least able to enjoy them. Ticket pricing is steeper than in the old parks, though admittedly not quite as prohibitive as elsewhere in the country. But more important, the facilities often have fewer seats than their older counterparts, and that, coupled with a much greater number of luxury boxes and season tickets, has meant far fewer tickets available for the average fan.[6]

Jacobs Field is beautiful, agrees union activist Ryan. "One of the things that happened though, I've noticed as a lifelong Indians fan, is that the increase in prices and the decrease in low ticket prices has made the crowd much more white. Incredibly much more white.

"And with the special parking and all that, the wealthier people don't mix with the working-class people for the most part. And to me that's disturbing. If you take a look at who's paying for that [with cigarette taxes], it is more the working-class people."

The cost of a game at Camden Yards is "prohibitive for a poor family," agrees Lapides. "You used to be able to go out to Memorial Stadium and sit in a fairly decent seat for three bucks. Three bucks won't even buy you a hot dog now at the new stadium."

If city schools and low-income fans were the losers in the twin stadium deals, the undeniable winners were the owners. The Orioles, bought by Eli Jacobs for $70 million while Camden Yards was still under construction in 1989, were resold in 1993 for $173 million, appreciating a whopping 147 percent in just four years. Art Modell's football team jumped $38 million in value in one year after it left

Cleveland for Baltimore. The Indians, whose new stadium coincided with the team's first contending team in forty years, were the least-valued team in baseball in 1993, the year before Jacobs Field opened, with a value of $81 million; by 1996 the team had appreciated to $125 million, a tidy 54 percent profit in three years for the Jacobs brothers.[7]

Even if the increased attendance abates after the novelty of the new stadiums wears off, team owners can always hit up their hosts for a few renovations or lease improvements, under threat of once again taking their act on the road. "If it's not a personal toy of yours, if you are an owner and you have any fiduciary responsibility to anybody, and you *don't* demand a new facility, you're probably violating your fiduciary duty, given the way this stuff goes," notes Marker.

Fiduciary duty can rest easy. In the decade following the Colts' flight, not many owners would pass up the opportunity to levy demands on their city, or someone else's. Baltimore and Cleveland would prove to be merely the tip of the sports-welfare iceberg.

Notes

1. In 2000 the *Cleveland Plain Dealer* put the public's final tab at $470 million. Gateway project director Tom Chema later admitted of the $344 million figure: "I didn't have a clue what this project was going to cost. . . . That wasn't a real number. I didn't want to say that number. I tried to avoid saying that number; but when you are in an election campaign, you have to put a number on it."

2. The new Cleveland Browns, an expansion team bearing the old name and uniforms, took the field for the first time in 1999. The final price tag for the new football stadium: $309 million, of which $216 million came from county taxpayers.

3. In December 2004 the *Newark Star-Ledger* reported: "Today, the main streets in and around the Gateway are marked by empty office towers, vacant department stores and storefronts with 'For Lease' signs. After spending $700 million to build the nation's most extensive sports infrastructure,

this city finds itself in a familiar place: trying to fix a downtown abandoned by businesses and the middle class, with neighborhoods gripped by despair." Shortly before this, the Census Bureau had declared Cleveland to be the poorest city in the nation.

4. A subsequent study by Johns Hopkins economists Bruce W. Hamilton and Peter Kahn calculated that Camden Yards earned the state of Maryland $3 million a year in new revenues, while costing $14 million a year in construction debt. As baseball business writer Doug Pappas would later note: "All told, each dollar of extra revenue from the ballpark costs Maryland taxpayers almost $5—making Camden Yards one of the few investments worse than the lottery which financed it."

5. Memorial Stadium was demolished in 2001 and replaced by apartments and a retirement home.

6. John Christison, the former manager of the Orlando Arena, was blunt in a 2001 interview: "These things would not be practical if it were not for public money to make them happen. And my disappointment is that the public is not getting a hell of a lot for their investment. They're not getting cheaper ticket prices, certainly. The average schmuck that pays for the thing out of property tax, or whatever the case, isn't getting a bigger more comfortable seat, he's not getting warmer popcorn. What he's getting is a higher ticket price and a tougher time trying to buy a ticket to take his kids to the game. Somebody's getting fat, but it's not the taxpayer."

7. In Indianapolis, meanwhile, the Colts owners were soon threatening to pull up stakes again if a new stadium wasn't forthcoming to replace the now two-decade-old dome. After rumors that Bob Irsay's son Jim, who had taken over the reins of the franchise after the death of his father, would move the team to Los Angeles, in 2005 the Indiana state legislature approved construction of a $687 million replacement—with $635 million of the funding shouldered by taxpayers.

2 Stealing Home

It's amazing what a pretty picture you can draw when you spend other people's money. —*Houston radio station owner Dan Patrick*

If it were only in Baltimore and Cleveland that the commotion over new stadiums reached such desperate extremes, it might be possible to write the two towns off as nothing more than a couple of sad coincidences—a pair of down-on-their-luck cities trying anything and everything to remake themselves. But in city after city, from Boston to Seattle, Los Angeles to Miami, Minneapolis to Houston, the story has been the same: Team owners in the four biggest sports in the country—baseball, football, basketball, and hockey—are demanding new publicly funded stadiums and arenas and threatening to pull up and leave if they don't get them. North America is in the midst of a remarkable stadium and sports-arena building boom unlike any other in its history. And municipalities large and small are paying the price for it—in massive public expenditures and tax abatements that lead to the loss of revenue for more worthy projects, and in the dismay and heartache of dedicated fans who see their decades of loyalty and devotion trampled en route to the newest arena. Between 1980 and 1990, U.S. cities spent some $750 million on building or renovating sports arenas and stadiums. The bill for the '90s is expected to exceed $12 billion, about $7.5 billion of which will have been paid by taxpayers—and hidden subsidies could amount to billions more.[1]

By 1997 almost one half of the country's 115 major professional sports franchises either were getting new or renovated facilities or had requested them. Indeed, in an era of increased public and government reluctance to lay out public money for anything—from food stamps to the local philharmonic—the eagerness with which cities are offering up hundreds of millions of dollars to build new stadiums is mind-boggling. Welfare as we know it may be dead, but corporate welfare is alive and kicking.

There are instances from sea to shining sea, encompassing every profit-making scheme imaginable. In San Francisco, the Giants baseball team owners pushed four times for a publicly funded new stadium and were four times rejected by Bay Area taxpayers—until winning a compromise on the fifth try. In south Florida, billionaire Wayne Huizenga received a new home at taxpayer expense for his Florida Panthers hockey club after only four years of playing at Miami Arena. His cotenants, the Miami Heat basketball team, also moved to a new facility down the coast, leaving the old arena vacant just ten years after it was built. Meanwhile, Denver built a $215 million baseball-only stadium with money from a sales-tax hike in 1995 (for its new expansion franchise) and followed it up with plans to construct a brand-new football stadium to placate an envious owner. The list includes towns like Seattle, where voters rejected a proposed tax hike to fund a new home for the Mariners but were ignored by a state legislature determined to see the new stadium funded at any cost, and Minneapolis, where Twins owners requested a replacement for a fifteen-year-old facility that the city was still paying off.

A new stadium didn't always mean massive amounts of public money—until the late 1940s and '50s, most professional sports teams played in privately owned facilities built by the teams' owners with their own revenues. But that changed in the ensuing decades; by the early 1990s, 77 percent of stadiums and arenas in use were publicly owned. In the typical scenario, a municipality will float hundreds of millions of dollars in municipal bonds in order to afford the massive initial expenditure, and then pay off the bonds with increased taxes, lotteries, or even general city funds. Because of their guaranteed nature, the repaying of those costly loans has taken on a central role in many cities' budgets for years after the initial stadium deal. By shackling themselves to these massive debts (and often massive cost overruns), cities may very well have allowed the further deterioration of local schools, roads, and public services. In many cases the bond issue runs years longer than the team's lease, raising the specter of local governments, ten or twenty years hence, still having to pay off the costs of stadiums for teams that have since fled for greener pastures—or still paying off bonds on old stadiums while building new ones with even higher price tags.

Welfare by Any Other Name

For anyone who has followed the fortunes of city-development policies in recent decades, this story has a familiar ring to it. Over the past twenty years, city governments large and small have made tax breaks and other subsidies a part of their regular repertoire in the drive to keep businesses in town—or lure them to relocate from elsewhere. What some have called "the economic war among the states" has its roots in the earliest years of the country (Alexander Hamilton once got a tax abatement from the state of New Jersey for starting a business there), and helped drive much early industrial development—particularly railroad companies, which grew rich off land grants from the federal government.

It wasn't until the early 1980s, though, that the subsidy frenzy really hit its stride. As the national economy sagged throughout the late 1970s and early '80s, the country's governors and mayors became more and more desperate to retain jobs and increasingly did so by paying off companies to stay put or relocate to their region. Those years saw an explosion of local government subsidies for private investment. In 1977 fewer than half of all states provided tax incentives or public loans for private development; fifteen years later, hardly a state was without them.

In his study "No More Candy Store," researcher Greg LeRoy detailed dozens of examples of what he called "subsidy abuse." In 1994 Baton Rouge granted tax abatements worth a total of $14,372,600 to Exxon in exchange for the company's creating exactly one new permanent job. Sears accepted $240 million in land and cash bonuses from the state of Illinois just for staying put, while laying off many of its local employees. Meanwhile, the automaker BMW garnered a $150 million subsidy from South Carolina for a new car factory; then Mercedes-Benz topped BMW with a $253 million tax break from Alabama for a plant that created just fifteen hundred jobs, meaning the state had spent nearly $170,000 for each new job. Over one two-year span in the 1980s, the state of Louisiana handed out $3.7 billion in tax abatements and denied exactly zero applications.

Small cities and towns, eager to show that they could compete with the big boys, quickly leaped into the fray. In 1993 Amarillo, Texas, went on the offensive with a page from the phone companies' marketing plan: The city sent thirteen hundred checks, each worth $8 million, to selected companies around the country, offering to cash the check for any company that would commit to creating seven hundred jobs in Amarillo. The following year, tiny Rio Rancho, New Mexico, outbid towns in several neighboring states for an Intel computer-chip manufacturing plant, handing the chip maker $114 million in incentives and tax breaks even though the town couldn't afford its own high school.

As a result of the explosion of corporate subsidies, according to the Economic Policy Institute, tax breaks now dwarf all other state and local economic-development projects combined. And as LeRoy writes in "No More Candy Store," "Despite recurring predictions that the states have finally grown tired of their ruinous 'economic development civil war,' the size of incentive packages continues to skyrocket. Whereas a package worth $50,000 per job sparked debate in the mid-1980s, by the early 1990s, there were several deals worth $100,000 to $150,000 per job and one worth $350,000."[2]

In terms of the level of public subsidies, sports teams can easily hold their own with other industries. When the first wave of public-stadium building hit in the late '60s and early '70s, stadiums were $40 million affairs, a sum that could be at least somewhat offset by rent and other fees paid by the baseball and football teams that shared these hulking multipurpose facilities. By the 1990s, though, stadium costs had soared to $300 million and up. Teams were demanding separate buildings for each sport, and more expensive accommodations inside, even as rents had plummeted—to zero in some cases—allowing teams to keep all the new revenue from their stadium for themselves at the expense of their host cities. The Ravens' deal with Baltimore, in which the team pays no rent or construction costs and received a $50 million cash relocation fee, was extravagant but not unprecedented: The previous year, the Los Angeles Rams had agreed to move to St. Louis in exchange for a low rent (just $250,000 a year), while receiving all luxury-box and concession revenues and 75 percent of advertising and naming-rights fees—plus a $46 million relocation fee. (One fellow owner was moved to call it "the mother of all stadium deals.") What was once at least in part a public investment in a city's sports team had turned into an outright subsidy—and the price was getting ever steeper.

Sports stadiums and arenas don't pay for themselves—not even their staunchest advocates claim they do. Even in the 1960s and '70s, when public money was first used consistently on sports facilities, the returns on the new buildings—increased rent and advertising, higher ticket sales and concession prices—were still usually not enough to offset the millions of dollars a year in debt payments by the state or city that fronted the money. And for today's buildings, with exponentially higher costs, there is no question of making them self-sufficient.

The explanation from local officials for these subsidies has invariably been that a new stadium is needed if the team is to stay in town and that, indeed, a team in town is needed if the city hopes to make a great urban comeback or remain a "major-league city." New sports facilities are highlighted by the national media in pop analyses of a city's vitality—thus, Camden Yards and Jacobs Field are seen as symbolic of the great revitalizations of Baltimore and Cleveland, as is Coors Field of the supposed renaissance of downtown Denver. As Indianapolis mayor William H. Hudnut III told the *New York Times* right after the Colts fled to his town's new dome, "It's a wonderful thing for our community. It's a boost to the city's image nationally and to local morale as a symbol of major league status."

All for One and One for All?

When it comes time to convince taxpayers to vote for new-stadium subsidies, stadium proponents—whether team owners, local business interests, or enthusiastic politicians—don't rely just on images of an emotionally rejuvenated civic pride. Instead, their central argument has historically been that the new facility will mean an economic windfall for its host town. Building a stadium at public expense—even if the teams don't pay rent or share ticket, concessions, or parking revenues—will mean long-term prosperity *and* respect, citizens are told. It's difficult to find U.S. cities, whether large or small, even with vastly different economic bases and financial prognoses, in which sports teams and their new stadiums are not continually held up as economic bonanzas, worthy of enormous public investment and sacrifice. A new arena or stadium, it is said, can jump-start a flagging economy with millions of new fans and spin-off businesses like restaurants, hotels, and other tourist attractions.

For example, an organizer of the drive to bring the Oakland Raiders football team to the city of Sacramento in the 1980s once remarked, "The Raiders coming to Sacramento would be an event of the magnitude of the Gold Rush." And when discussing a threatened exodus of the New York Yankees from their historic stadium in the Bronx, New York mayor Rudolph W. Giuliani, while publicly lamenting any move at all, crowed that a proposed location on the West Side of Manhattan would provide a revenue stream for the city that was "off the charts."

It's a tempting offer, especially for cities that have seen other industries flee town for the suburban plains or for competing cities willing to cough up more-generous tax breaks or a more pliable labor force. But can the numbers be trusted? That's what Cleveland community activist Marge Misak took a hard look at before the 1995 vote on extending her city's sin tax, which would ultimately pay for a new football stadium.

"At the time there was a claim in the *Plain Dealer* that the mayor basically asserted that the stadium would bring $46 million in economic development to the city," Misak explains. Since the news article failed to report where Mayor White had gotten the figures, Misak went on the trail of the original source. "It turned out that it had come from an earlier study that the Growth Association, I think, of Cleveland had done. And basically the mayor's office took this number and extrapolated it for the '95 season and came up with $46 million. Over half of that money was actually the revenue that would be generated from ticket sales and concessions at the stadium. Well, all of that money goes into the owners' pockets."

There's a difference, ultimately, and an important one, between benefit to the *economy* and benefit to the *treasury*. If people buy an extra $10 million in goods (whether cans of tuna fish or baseball tickets), that's $10 million extra for the economy, but aside from any taxes it generates, the government doesn't see any money from that.

Money for Nothing

In fact, the claim that public funding of new sports facilities leads to quick and easy urban success stories is vastly overrated, say most economists. These critics charge that, by ignoring basic economic realities and crucial issues in urban planning, the pro-construction studies are left with a central premise that is almost always out of whack.

"The consulting reports are basically political documents," says economist Roger Noll, perhaps the nation's preeminent sports-finance expert and the coeditor of *Sports, Jobs, and Taxes*, an exhaustive tome from the Brookings Institution. "Usually they're supported by the people who want a stadium, and so they come up with unrealistically high numbers. Occasionally, they're supported by people who don't want the stadium, and they come up with real tiny numbers." In fact, in study after study, when reports done by local chambers of commerce and the like are thrown out, the claims of stadium boosters are resoundingly rejected.

"Given the self-serving nature of these studies," adds economist Robert Baade, the author of several definitive analyses of the topic, "I wonder if we shouldn't be looking at things a little more carefully than we are." He's devoted his efforts to doing just that. A professor at Lake Forest College in Illinois, Baade has gained national attention for his extensive examinations of the actual benefits that sports teams and new facilities do or do not bring to cities. And he, like many other economists across the country, questions the basic claims and priorities of new-stadium deals.

One of the more extensive examinations of the issue was a 1994 study Baade did for the Heartland Institute, a think tank that opposes almost any government regulation or spending. (On its board of directors are representatives from Amoco, Philip Morris, Fidelity Bank, and Procter & Gamble.) Baade looked at forty-eight cities over a thirty-year time span, examining every U.S. city during that period that had acquired either a new professional sports stadium or arena or a professional sports team (baseball, football, basketball, or hockey). His overwhelming finding was that "professional sports teams generally have no significant impact on a metropolitan economy." Because of that research, Baade's study "finds no support for the notion that there is an economic rationale for public subsidies to sports teams and stadium and arena construction. Professional sports does not appear to create a flow of public funds generated by new economic growth. Far from generating new revenues out of which other public projects can be funded, sports 'investments' appear to be an economically unsound use of a community's scarce financial resources."

Among the thirty cities with new stadiums or arenas that Baade examined, twenty-seven showed no economic impact on their local economy over a thirty-year period. In three instances—St. Louis, the San Francisco Bay Area, and Washington DC—the new facilities appeared to have *hurt* the local economy.[3]

Economists point out that even when cities do see an increase in spending because of a new stadium or the addition of a sports team, that doesn't represent new dollars flowing in to the local economy so much as expenditure substitution—money shifted from one entertainment source to another. Far from stadiums' generating new economic activity, as new-stadium proponents continually assert, the new facilities, according to Baade, at best seem to bring in dollars that otherwise would have been spent elsewhere in the immediate or general region.

"If you draw larger and larger circles away from the place where the sporting event actually occurs, it's more and more likely that you're going to have a zero-sum game," says Baade. "In the case of Wisconsin, it may well be that you're taking money away from a dog-racing track in Racine when you subsidize Brewers baseball. It may be that people who ordinarily go to the racetrack may now go up to Milwaukee to see a game at the new retractable-dome stadium. But you have to wonder about the implications for other entertainment activities in Racine."

Sometimes the issue of displaced dollars confronts stadium backers themselves. In his push for a new home for his Denver Broncos football team, owner Pat Bowlen cited the new baseball-only stadium the city had just completed as a draw that was taking away from his now-outdated facility. The local media were reporting that season-ticket sales at Mile High Stadium had been suffering since baseball's Rockies began playing at brand-new Coors Field, and Bowlen had the answer. "Coors Field is a beautiful place to see a game," he told the *Denver Post*, "Football needs those kinds of venues to stay competitive. I have to have a stadium that's as attractive as baseball['s stadium]." Thus, a city was in effect being told (much as had happened in Cleveland) that once it got the ball rolling on new-stadium construction, it would be only fair to lay out the public dollars for each and every team in town.

Mark Rosentraub, a professor of urban planning at Indiana University, also questions the displaced dollars that sporting events take in. "How much more food do people eat because of the presence of a team?" Rosentraub writes. "In other words, if a family eats dinner near the stadium or arena before a game, where did they not eat their dinner that night? . . . Sports are not only small potatoes, but those potatoes may have been someone else's before the team or stadium existed."[4]

The same goes for claims of new jobs to be had from stadium spending. Minnesota Wins!, a pro-stadium group funded by the Twins, Vikings, and local corporations, estimated that a new baseball-only stadium costing $310 million would generate an additional $35.9 million in economic activity and the equivalent of 168 new full-time jobs—prompting University of Chicago economist Allen Sanderson to remark that if the money were "dropped out of a helicopter over the Twin Cities, you would probably create eight to ten times as many jobs."

Moreover, the new jobs that are created are not necessarily cream-of-the-crop positions. "They're parking-garage attendants, they are hot-dog salespeople, they are waiters and waitresses, sometimes cooks, people who do maintenance work and repair work and cleaning," says Cleveland union activist John Ryan. "And none of them are jobs that the mayor hugs his kids and says, 'I hope you can get one of those jobs someday.'"

Rosentraub has also examined stadium boosters' promises in great detail. In a study Rosentraub did for his 1997 book, *Major League Losers*, he looked at the private-sector payrolls for all U.S. counties with at least three hundred thousand residents, and found that only .06 percent of the jobs in those counties were associated with either professional sports teams or managers. Noting that "if they were classified by their gross revenues, they would be considered small to medium-size businesses," he concludes that the economic impact of professional sports teams is actually quite small—especially compared to the size of the public subsidies, which can often run as high as $250,000 per job.

All of which raises an even larger question: If stadium-construction funds end up coming from the same civic coffers as other municipal projects' funds do, and if massive stadium deals are being given the go-ahead nationwide, what isn't getting funded instead? When Toronto built the costly SkyDome for some $400 million, the city was having trouble coming up with money for its parks department. "One city official estimated that the city needed 700 new acres of parkland to keep pace with the demand," writes Charles C. Euchner, a political science professor at the College of Holy Cross, "but the city had a budget of just $500,000 for parks acquisition. Other infrastructure needs that went begging included public transportation, housing rehabilitation, and expansion of the sewer system."

Economist Dennis Zimmerman goes a step further in emphasizing what he calls the "opportunity cost" involved in publicly funding a new stadium. "If an alternative generates $2 million of benefits net of subsidy and the stadium generates $1.5 million net of subsidy, the stadium can be viewed as imposing a $0.5 million *loss* on taxpayers, not a $1.5 million *benefit*," Zimmerman wrote in his 1996 study for the Congressional Research Service assessing, among other things, expenditure substitution in publicly funded stadium projects.

Thus, in a case such as Baltimore's construction of a new home for the Ravens, Zimmerman believes that "economic benefits were overstated by 236 percent, primarily because the reduced spending on other activities that enables people to attend stadium events was not netted against stadium spending. And no account was taken of losses incurred by forgoing more-productive investments. The state's $177 million stadium investment is estimated to create 1,394 jobs at a cost of $127,000 per job. The cost per job generated by the state's Sunny Day Fund economic-development program is estimated to be $6,250."[5]

It isn't as if these and other studies have been kept hidden from the public. In fact, during the early days of the latest debate in New York over a proposed new home for the Yankees, the Heartland Institute sent copies of its studies to city planners. Baade, Noll, Zimbalist, and others are quoted constantly and often called upon to testify at legislative hearings on the topic, and yet the frantic pace of stadium construction continues. It's interesting to see how the stadium builders themselves justify the economics of stadium construction—because if local municipalities aren't benefiting from new-stadium deals, as the research indicates, these people certainly are.

The Dirty Dozen

For a look at the stadium builders' response to the economic studies, one need only have attended the Inaugural Municipal Issuers' & Sports Franchises' Symposium on Sports Facilities Finance—a long-winded title for a conference largely devoted to reassuring those who benefit from new sports facilities that their business is alive and well. Filling the conference room at Manhattan's Grand Hyatt Hotel for the two-day conference in May 1997 was a who's who of sports-industry movers and shakers: municipal officials, stadium-authority employees, team executives, and financiers from across the country, all gathered to hear how to profit from stadium construction. Jerry Colangelo, whose sports empire had recently grown to three Phoenix-area pro franchises, was the keynote speaker. And featured on the program, along with such panels as "Remodeling vs. Building a New Stadium" and "Beyond Peanuts and Crackerjacks: Examining Unique Revenue Streams," was what looked to be the owners' long-awaited counterstrike to the Baades and Rosentraubs of the world: a panel entitled "Letting the Numbers Speak for Themselves: Public Funding and Economics." "This panel," a program note promised, "will finally answer the age-old questions, not with anecdotal opinions but with actual numbers derived from detailed studies."

With the crowd still buzzing from Colangelo's lunchtime address, James McCurdy, president of the low-minors Pioneer Baseball League, took the podium. "I'm not going to talk about numbers," he drawled. "I want to talk to you about how you think about numbers"—then he reeled off a monologue on "paradigm paralysis versus paradigm pioneers" that would not have been out of place at any motivational seminar, and that, as promised, steered clear of any economics at all. McCurdy did, however, manage a dig at economist Mark Rosentraub, calling him "the Howard Stern of the stadium business," drawing a few chuckles from the otherwise stone-faced crowd.

McCurdy's pep talk complete, Philadelphia commerce director Stephen Mullin stepped to the mike. "Are cities getting conned?" he asked. "Are sports teams worth it? Are subsidies too high?" How much benefit do stadiums really have, he asked the crowd rhetorically, then answered his own question: "I don't know, but I think it is positive."

With that, Mullin dropped the subject of economic benefits of stadiums—as did the conference as a whole, which spent its remaining hours mulling how best to get cities to go along with new-stadium plans. The only "detailed studies" presented were Rosentraub's, which were presented by panelist Joseph Passafiume of Buffalo's county government, to deafening silence from the assembled onlookers.

Cities' willingness to believe the claims of these stadium boosters, despite all evidence to the contrary, reminds Robert Baade of Pascal's Wager. "The idea was somebody asked if [French philosopher Blaise Pascal] believed in God, and he said, 'Yes, I believe in God because I can't take a chance that there isn't one.'" Baade says. "I think in some ways that resembles city attitudes with regard to this thing. I think that people who make decisions about these things say to themselves that 'we believe there is an economic impact because we really can't take the chance that there isn't one.' In part I think that's a reflection of the state of urban America."

Notes

1. The final total for MLB, NFL, NBA, and NHL facilities that opened during the 1990s was between $9.4 billion and $9.8 billion, depending on the source; add in minor-league facilities and the total would be well over $10 billion. Of this, figures compiled by the group League of Fans calculated the public cost as about $6.2 billion. By the early years of the new century, construction expenses were averaging nearly $1.7 billion a year, with more than $1 billion a year of that coming from the public.

Moreover, when Princeton researcher Judith Grant Long carefully accounted for such hidden costs as sweetheart lease deals and property-tax breaks, she estimated the 1990s public total as more than $8 billion—and in just 2000 and 2001 alone, taxpayers coughed up almost $2.9 billion for "big four" sports venues. Add in federal tax-exempt bond subsidies, which weren't included by Long, and it's fair to assume that total taxpayer expense on sports facilities now approaches $2 billion a year.

2. The mother of all corporate-subsidy deals came in 2003, when Boeing launched a twenty-state bidding war to be the site of facilities to build its 7E7 Dreamliner passenger jet. The winner: Washington State, which coughed up an unprecedented $3.2 billion in tax breaks for a plant expected to employ between eight hundred and twelve hundred workers—a rate of more than $3 million per job.

3. Subsequent studies reported similar findings. A report in 2000 by University of Maryland–Baltimore economists Dennis Coates and Brad Humphreys found that although the presence of sports teams tended to raise per capita income, the cost of building a new facility reduced wages by even more, leaving local workers at a net loss. "Our research," they concluded, "suggests that professional sports may be a drain on local economies rather than an engine of economic growth."

4. Evidence of this "substitution effect," as economists call it, has come from sports labor stoppages, where it's easy to measure what happens when a team is abruptly removed from the local economy. During the NHL lockout of 2004–05, wrote *Minneapolis Star Tribune* reporter Jay Weiner, "sales tax collection in the city of St. Paul hasn't gone down. Businesses near the

arena have suffered, but, citywide, consumers are simply spending in other neighborhoods." An investigation by Canada's CBC News during the 1994 baseball strike revealed "dramatic increases in rentals at the video store," with one Toronto comedy club manager quipping: "We really feel it would be in the best interest of entertainment in Toronto if the hockey players sat out the whole season too."

5. In 2005 Minnesota Twins exec Jerry Bell admitted to the *Minneapolis Star Tribune* that those who say stadiums do not generate economic development, "At some global level they are obviously correct. . . . I don't think the economic argument turns it one way or another, so why go there? If there are side benefits, great. If not, so what?"

3 Ball Barons

Anyone who quotes profits of a baseball club is missing the point. Under generally accepted accounting principles, I can turn a $4 million profit into a $2 million loss, and I can get every national accounting firm to agree with me. —*Toronto Blue Jays vice president Paul Beeston*

Deep Throat was always right: Follow the money. —*Sports economist Rodney Fort*

When *Financial World* magazine conducted its yearly roundup of the sports business in 1996, it advised would-be investors to keep an eye out for teams that met three criteria: "The revenues they rake in from their venues are below the average for teams in their sport, they have no definite plans to build or move into a new facility, and their leases expire by 2000 (or can be rather easily gotten out of)." Anyone buying into one of these "undervalued" franchises—the poor, stadium-less, and mobile—could see their investments skyrocket in value, the magazine advised, by levying a build-or-else ultimatum. Topping the magazine's to-buy list: the Hartford Whalers, which were projected to double in value if moved to a new publicly funded arena in Nashville.

The sports industry is relatively small by the standards of the corporate world—"about the size of the pork and beans industry," in the memorable words of former Senator Sam Ervin. But for the handful of men (and still-tinier handful of women) who own major-league sports franchises, it's very big business indeed. Since professional sports began, running a team has always been a reasonable investment, likely to earn an owner a tidy return of a few percentage points a year. In the 1980s, though, according to James Quirk and Rodney Fort's masterful study of sports economics, *Pay Dirt*, franchise values in every sport abruptly leaped upward: baseball teams by 23 percent a year, football by 19 percent, and basketball by an astounding 50 percent—meaning an NBA team bought during that decade would likely double in value in less than two years.

There's a pleasant myth that in the early days of pro sports, teams were run by gentleman owners, whose concerns lay more with performing a civic duty for their local community than with turning a profit. The story has a grain of truth—as late as the 1970s, most sports franchises were owned by independent moguls, some of whom could trace their families' ownership back to the early twentieth century—but even they kept a careful eye on the bottom line. And by the 1980s, independent owners had begun to give way to even more profit-conscious corporate ownership.

The first prominent sports team to come under corporate ownership was the New York Yankees, bought by CBS in 1964 (making the old gibe that "rooting for the Yankees is like rooting for U.S. Steel" uncomfortably close to the truth). CBS divested itself of the team in 1973 (selling it to a Cleveland shipbuilder named George Steinbrenner), but the television network was ahead of its time. By the 1990s even most wealthy individuals were being priced out of the market: With franchise values soaring past the $100 million mark, ownership of a sports franchise had passed from being a privilege of the rich to one of the super-rich.

Those reaping the rewards of the sports-value boom in recent years have included such corporate conglomerates as Disney and Time-Warner, for which a sports team is just another item in their portfolio. The independent owners who remain are those who can afford the high-stakes world of modern-day sport—billionaires like Carl Pohlad of the Minnesota Twins or Microsoft cofounder Paul Allen, who owns the Seattle Seahawks football team and the Portland Trailblazers basketball club. For those who can afford the entry fee, the payoff can be staggering.

Ballpark Figures

When discussing sports finances, the first thing to understand is that the numbers literally don't add up. Without an understanding of the inner financial workings of the sports industry, it's impossible to comprehend the most obvious conundrum of modern pro sports: Even as revenues soar to record levels, team owners invariably insist that they are losing money hand over fist. Contract negotiations with players' unions, in particular, have occasioned especially shrill cries of poverty, with management insisting that any concessions from their side of the table will plunge them into bankruptcy, or even result in teams disappearing altogether from the face of the map. "It will take a club to go belly up in order to stop this madness," Montreal Expos general manager Dave Dombrowski warned ominously just before baseball management's contract giveback demands helped spur players toward an eight-month-long strike in 1994 that cost owners hundreds of millions in lost revenues—and which was immediately followed by the leagues' decision to expand by two teams in 1998.

None of this is unexpected or unusual, especially in an industry faced with relatively powerful unions ready to leap on any scrap of profit growth to boost their own salaries. But unions and other skeptics can point to a statistic that belies the owners' poverty claims: Sale prices of teams are soaring, and even a break-even or money-losing team is likely to yield a huge financial windfall for its owners once they decide to put it up for sale. As baseball owner Bill Veeck once explained, "You don't make money operating a baseball club. You make money selling it."

When examining public subsidies, it's important to remember that not all are simple cash handouts. In fact, most corporate welfare, in any industry, comes in the form of tax breaks: special dispensations to evade local, state, or federal taxes that can save corporations or wealthy individuals millions of dollars. Whenever the federal government allows deductions for one group and not for another—for homeowners but not for renters, say, or for sports franchises but not for other businesses—the subsidy may be hidden, but it's just as real as if Congress were doling out cash from the federal treasury.

For sports owners, tax breaks have been an integral part of doing business ever since they discovered perhaps their most incredible financial gimmick, the depreciation of players. This trick was first devised in the late 1940s by the then Cleveland Indians owner Veeck, an innovator and iconoclast who at one time or another owned three different major-league baseball teams. It was Veeck who introduced some of the most popular ballpark events of his day: As a Chicago Cubs executive, he planted the ivy that to this day distinguishes Wrigley Field's outfield walls; he held the first-ever Bat Day; he built Comiskey Park's famed exploding scoreboard; and in his most famous gimmick, he sent a midget up to bat (Eddie Gaedel walked and was promptly removed for a pinch runner). It's less well known that he also claimed to have devised a plan to buy the last-place Philadelphia Phillies and import players from the Negro Leagues, five years before Jackie Robinson broke baseball's color line, but said he was blocked by league authorities. (Veeck later bought the Cleveland Indians and promptly signed the American League's first African American ballplayer, Larry Doby.) Veeck was much reviled by his fellow owners for his antics, but it was he who first discovered the accounting scheme that would change the face of the pro sports business: the notion that player contracts could be depreciated, just like industrial equipment, providing a potentially huge tax deduction for owners by turning an actual profit into a paper loss.

The sharp-eyed Veeck had noticed that a 1935 IRS ruling had allowed cash purchases of players to be written off as an expense of running a sports business—athletes could be considered just another spare part that wore out and ultimately had to be replaced. What if, he wondered, he were to treat the acquisition of a team's entire roster at the time of purchasing a team in the same way? Better still, by declaring nearly all of a team's value to reside in its player contracts, an owner could depreciate nearly the *entire* purchase price of a team over several years.

On the face of it, this argument is absurd. Most athletes, after all, *increase* in value as they gain experience, at least until age takes its toll. What's more, teams already claim the costs of player development—scouting, minor-league teams, and the like—as a business deduction, and claiming both depreciation and replacement-cost deductions is usually a sure way to raise red flags at the irs. Yet the tax agency would instead turn out to be remarkably understanding over the years. Depreciation of player contracts quickly caught on in all four major sports and was soon standard operating procedure for all teams. When Paul Beeston of the Toronto Blue Jays bragged that he could turn a $4 million profit into a $2 million paper loss, he wasn't just making a bargaining point with labor; he had an eye to the millions in tax benefits that the paper loss could earn his team.

In 1970 Rodney Fort became one of the first researchers to challenge the fiction that players were a major part of the value of a sports franchise and as such could be depreciated until the team's "value" had all but disappeared. Milwaukee car dealer Bud Selig had bought the fledgling Seattle Pilots baseball team, which had finished dead last in its only year of existence, for $10.8 million and moved them to Milwaukee, where they became the Brewers. Fort recalls how Selig's tax documents assigned a value of $10.2 million to the players themselves, meaning that fully 94 percent of the purchase price could be written off as depreciation. "I was working with Roger Noll, and we were as generous as we could possibly be in figuring out the relative value of this team to all the rest of the kinds of players in the league at the time," says Fort. "We came up with something like three million, tops. The judge read it, said, well, that's a good piece of work, but I can see no reason that Selig's choice violates the accepted rules of accounting in Major League Baseball."

With that invocation of the "accepted rules," the Veeck loophole stood—meaning team owners in the four major sports could continue to reap huge rewards from this tax break. Although its benefit was reduced somewhat by the 1986 Tax Reform Act, the depreciation bonus continues to earn teams tax savings; and if depreciation isn't enough, plenty of other loopholes remain for enterprising owners to fall back on. For one thing, they can deduct interest payments on loans they take out to buy the team; better still, owners can create dummy corporations to own their teams, lend *themselves* money, and then deduct the interest payments that the teams pay back to themselves. Team owners who have their own television stations—as franchise prices soar, more and more teams find themselves owned by media conglomerates—can sell themselves their broadcast rights at bargain-basement prices, creating yet another book loss.

The list of fiscal shenanigans is endless, including the $2 million in parking and concessions fees that Anheuser-Busch, owner of the St. Louis Cardinals baseball team, diverted to another subsidiary in 1984; and the $25 million that New York Yankees owner George Steinbrenner reportedly paid himself in the early 1980s as a "fee" for negotiating his team's cable contract. When Roger Noll was hired by the Players' Association to look into baseball's books in 1985, he determined that what Major League Baseball had claimed to be a $41 million industry loss was in fact a $25 million gain. For sports teams, Quirk and Fort conclude, "the balance sheet and the income statement simply lie in describing the financial health of the team, as they do with the typical tax-shelter operation."[1]

Why the federal government allows this kind of accounting to continue is "the ultimate unanswered question in sports," according to Fort, who continues to follow the sports industry from his position in the Washington State University economics department. But then, notes Fort, baseball's famous antitrust exemption, in place since 1922, has a similarly hazy legal footing—and a similarly cynical explanation. "The IRS is, after all, an administrative agency," he says. "And even though none of those guys are elected, the choices they make do have political impact. And so I can envision elected officials thinking, make baseball teams fifteen to twenty million bucks poorer with the stroke of a pen, in a seemingly volatile financial situation, and all hell's gonna break loose. And so the IRS is probably instructed by the political overseers not to do that."

Suite Deals

When sports owners talk about old stadiums lacking the "amenities" of the new ones, they're not speaking of high-tech scoreboards or spacious player clubhouses, though the newest buildings are flush with those as well. By and large, there's one thing that distinguishes new sports facilities from old ones in terms of profit-making potential: luxury seating.

The Houston Astrodome, which in 1966 brought the world AstroTurf and indoor baseball, was also the first stadium to offer "skyboxes," a ring of luxury suites nestled against the building's roof. Despite the distant view, they were an immediate sellout. Luxury boxes quickly became a fixture in the new public ballparks of the '70s, and by the '90s were a primary element of ballpark architecture. A luxury box in Philadelphia's Veterans Stadium (built in 1971) might be architecturally functional, enjoying such customary amenities as private elevators and separate stadium entrances. But in structure and luxurious feel it's quite clearly more than twenty years old—nothing like the lavish boxes in Cleveland's Jacobs Field, with their spectacular views of the city skyline and attention to all the modern amenities corporations have come to expect from recreational outings.

Over the course of the twentieth century, the world has been introduced to night baseball, basketball's 3-point shot, and instant replays in football and hockey, but no innovation can match the luxury box for sheer money-making power without improving either the quality of the game or the enjoyment of the average fan. Along with their cousins the "club seats"—sort of an open-air corporate suite of prime seats with expanded legroom and waiter service—luxury boxes are about money, pure and simple. By the 1990s teams were charging more than $100,000 a year for the private suites. This was money that didn't have to be shared either with the teams' municipal landlords or with their fellow owners, since all four major sports exempt suite revenue from profit sharing among teams. With upward of two hundred boxes in some of the newest stadiums, this can translate into millions more a year in team profits.

The vast new revenue streams made possible by luxury boxes, in fact, have driven much of the current wave of stadium construction, as even relatively new facilities are declared "obsolete" for shortage of suites. The stadium-building boom of the '80s and '90s was a huge boon to sports teams' bottom lines because each box took what would have been a few dozen moderately priced seats and turned them into a previously unheard-of source of income.

But luxury boxes constitute more of a subsidy than just the public money spent on building the glassed-and-carpeted enclosures themselves. The key here is the target market, which for luxury boxes—and the majority of club seats—consists overwhelmingly of corporations. When an average fan plunks down $25 for a ticket, the money comes straight out of his or her pocket, but when a corporation buys tickets, the finances work differently. Companies are able to claim sports tickets as a business-entertainment deduction, on the theory that this is a perk they use to lure clients, wining and dining them in an attempt to land business deals. Because of this, so long as a company has profits to declare the deduction against, it can rest assured that the federal government will pick up the tab for a portion of the purchase price. Team owners can then safely charge more for their boxes, knowing that corporations will happily pay higher rates if the purchase is tax-deductible.

This is a subsidy that's seldom included in figures on public spending, yet the rewards for team owners can be substantial. For example, take a stadium with a hundred luxury boxes, each selling at $80,000 a year—not at all out of the ordinary for today's lavishly appointed structures. That's $8 million that corporations spend every year on boxes, of which 50 percent is deductible, saving them about $1.2 million in federal taxes. Multiplied by the seven thousand or so luxury boxes currently in use in the United States, the luxury-box subsidy costs the federal treasury more than $80 million a year in lost tax revenue.

The size of the subsidy used to be even larger: Until the mid-1990s, 100 percent of business-entertainment expenses could be deducted, and that change to the tax code did, in fact, take a good bit of steam out of luxury-box sales. But it by no means stopped them entirely, as corporations continue to take advantage of this tax shelter; some teams, in fact, make a point of distributing brochures to their corporate clients detailing the best ways to use luxury-box purchases to reduce their taxes.

The Ten-Percent Solution

Yet another hidden subsidy lurks in stadium deals' fine print. When cities finance these projects, they do so with federally tax-exempt bonds. Since the bond buyers don't have to pay taxes on their income from these bonds, municipalities can sell them at lower interest rates. This reduces the cost to the city treasury (since it has to pay less in interest each year), but it comes at the expense of the federal treasury, which forgoes taxes on the bond buyers' profits. As a result, stadiums look cheaper than they really are, with the federal government kicking in the difference.

Tax-exempt bonds have been around ever since the introduction of the federal income tax in 1913. For decades, cities and states levied these bonds, which can be sold at a much lower interest rate because they are tax-free, generally for roads or other public works. But beginning in the 1950s, cities started using tax-exempt bonds for economic-development projects by private industry. By the early '80s, so-called private activity bonds were everywhere—amounting to nearly 80 percent of all government bonds issued, and soaking up so much capital that there was little left over for genuine public-interest projects. So Congress made a point of eliminating this subsidy as part of the 1986 Tax Reform Act, making private-activity bonds subject to the usual taxes. And in what was intended as a death blow to public-stadium deals, lawmakers specifically declared sports-construction projects to be private activity and thus taxable.

They left two loopholes, however. First, since no elected official wanted to be accused of sabotaging his or her own city's bid for a sports team, the tax-reform bill contained a grandfather clause exempting all stadium and arena projects then under way, as well as twenty-six other projects that were merely under consideration. This clause would go on to create billions more in federal subsidies.

The other loophole, though unintended by its congressional drafters, ultimately proved far more lucrative to team owners. The Tax Reform Act had redrawn the definition of private-activity bonds to be exceedingly strict: If more than 10 percent of the facility's use was to be by a private entity, and more than 10 percent of the bonds would be paid off by revenue from the private project, the bonds were considered taxable. But what if the stadium lease were drawn so that total government revenues—whether from lease payments, ticket surcharges, parking fees, or whatever—were held below that 10 percent threshold? The local government issuing the bonds would take a bath on them, for sure. But if a city's political leaders were willing to go along, teams could still have the use of tax-exempt bonds—and a guaranteed 90 percent of the resulting revenues to boot.

The difference between taxable and nontaxable bonds may sound small, but it adds up quickly. Because interest rates on tax-free bonds are significantly lower than on taxed bonds, and because interest payments wind up constituting the lion's share of the cost of a bond-financed project, stadiums can be built far more cheaply—albeit because the federal government forgoes its tax revenue on the bonds.

The lifetime federal-tax subsidy on a stadium financed with tax-exempt bonds can be as high as one third of the total cost.

New York senator Daniel Patrick Moynihan, who had helped craft the 1986 law, was appalled at how his envisioned tightening of the tax laws had been turned into the biggest loophole yet, in effect forcing cities to fund only facilities that were guaranteed money losers. "In other words," Moynihan would later explain before Congress, "non-stadium governmental revenues (i.e., tax revenues, lottery proceeds, and the like) must be used to repay the bulk of the debt, freeing team owners to pocket stadium revenues. Who would have thought that local officials, in order to keep or get a team, would capitulate to team owners—granting concessionary stadium leases and committing limited government revenues to repay stadium debt, thereby hindering their own ability to provide schools, roads, and other public investments?"

But that's exactly what cities did, in droves. Stadium rents, which had previously been used to defray at least part of the cost of a publicly built stadium, plummeted, as municipalities struggled to keep revenues below the 10 percent threshold. This, explains Maryland Stadium Authority deputy director Ed Klein, was the origin of the lease discrepancy that would cause friction between the Orioles and Ravens: While the Camden Yards baseball park (built under the 1986 loophole) could safely charge rent to the baseball team, the new Ravens football stadium could not do so without running afoul of the new limit. Instead, the Ravens were granted free rent, which immediately sent the Orioles clamoring for a free-rent deal to match. "The Tax Reform Act of 1986 was in theory supposed to put an end to these [stadium deals]," observes Roger Noll, "but all that it did was reduce the rents to zero."

Congress had created a monster. The law that was supposed to put a stop to stadium giveaways had instead caused them to metastasize. Moynihan would later try to close the loopholes he had created, but was unable to convince his congressional colleagues to pass a bill eliminating tax-exempt bonds once and for all.[2]

What's in a Name?

As if direct subsidies and tax loopholes weren't enough, there's yet another way for sports owners to make money at public expense. This is the diversion of revenue streams (in sports-business parlance, every source of cash, from tickets to popcorn to advertising signage, is considered a "revenue stream" in the team's ledgers) that would otherwise benefit the building's owners—the local government—into the owners' corporate coffers. The newest cash cow on the block is naming rights—for a fee of up to $60 million, corporations can affix their name to a stadium, guaranteeing unlimited exposure during every sports telecast or news recap.[3] And though the stadium itself may be owned by the public, the fee invariably goes straight into the team owner's pocket.

There's hardly a new stadium being built that doesn't bear a corporate moniker, from Pacific Bell Park (San Francisco) to Miller Park (Milwaukee) to Bank One Ballpark (Phoenix). Even older facilities can be renamed for a fee—San Diego's Jack Murphy Stadium, named for a renowned local sportswriter, became Qualcomm Stadium at Jack Murphy Sports Complex after a computer company kicked in $18 million; and Cincinnati's Riverfront Stadium will end its days promoting the local power company as Cinergy Field. With old stadiums, though, there's always the danger of the new name not taking (Candlestick Park's transformation into 3Com Park, for a local computer company, was short-lived, as public disdain for the new name led to the official adoption of "3Com Park at Candlestick Point" as the park's name), and besides, who wants to advertise on an aging billboard when a brand-new one can be had the next town over?

With the exception of Pacific Bell Park, privately built by the Giants, all these stadiums are publicly owned. Yet, naming fees nearly always go to pay the teams' share of construction costs and are not counted as public subsidies.

Ballparks Go Condo

Owners have likewise captured the bulk of revenues from the other great innovation in sports money making: personal seat licenses. Since the dawn of professional sports, team owners have juggled ticket prices up and down, trying to balance their desire for increased profits with their fear of alienating fans. Occasionally, there would be attempts at ticket surcharges and other hidden fees, but these extra charges seldom amounted to more than another dollar or two—until, that is, the invention of personal seat licenses (PSLS). These devices burst onto the sports scene in the early '90s as a new way of raising funds directly from the fans themselves and, in so doing, substantially raised the ante on what level of outside funding teams could demand.

The first proto-PSLS appeared in Texas Stadium, the football stadium built by Dallas Cowboys owner Tex Schramm for his team in 1968; Schramm offered forty-year "seat options," allowing fans to buy—and sell—their season-ticket rights. PSLS then disappeared for nearly twenty years before their rediscovery by Max Muhleman, a sportswriter-turned-marketer who, in 1987, stumbled upon the idea while searching for a way to raise money for a new arena that the Charlotte Hornets basketball team was hoping to finance without public funding. His solution: Sell "charter seat rights" to fans, guaranteeing them a shot at scarce season tickets in exchange for a nonrefundable fee.

"We thought as an incentive to season ticket holders who were being asked to put up forfeitable deposits that they be given what we thought every fan would always like to have—and that was essential ownership of their seats," Muhleman explained in a 1996 newspaper interview. "Instead of the team dictating who could have your seat if you moved out of town or whatever—in some cities you couldn't give the seat to your buddy and in some cases couldn't transfer your tickets to a family member if there was a waiting list—we thought it would be nice to designate these as seat rights that could be held by the original ticket buyer."

Six years later, North Carolina businessman Jerry Richardson was looking for an edge in his competition for an NFL expansion franchise. The going was rough: Other cities, like St. Louis and Baltimore, had new stadiums on the drawing boards, but Richardson had been unable to convince Charlotte to build one for him. Muhleman proposed raising $100 million for a stadium via his charter seat license gimmick.

The licenses, by now renamed "permanent seat licenses," sold out the day they went on sale. This time, the close-knit cabal of sports owners sat up and took notice. Richardson, much like Bill Veeck four decades before him, had abruptly discovered a whole new revenue stream for sports teams—all you needed was a new stadium and a few thousand fans desperate enough to get their hands on tickets to invest $1,500 or more in a PSL.

PSLS are an especially devious money-making tactic because of their hybrid nature. Not quite a ticket surcharge, not quite an investment, they can be used to lure fans into paying far more for sporting events than they otherwise would. If fans decide to give up their season tickets, they are told, they can sell their PSLS to another buyer and be out only the cost of the tickets they've already used. If they're lucky—if the team is doing well, say, and demand for tickets is high—they may even reap a profit. "It has been unfairly reported that a seat license is a surcharge on top of your season ticket, or simply a charge that you have to pay before you have a right to buy a season ticket," said Muhleman in 1996. "In fact, what you are buying is control that ordinarily rests entirely with the clubs."

It's the kind of win-win scenario that sounds more fitting for a pyramid scam than for a multimillion-dollar investment—and for good reason. PSLS are an investment, but one whose value depends entirely on the willingness of someone else to buy that "control" from you. For ten-, twenty-, or thirty-year "personal seat licenses," there is at least an expiration date built in; buyers know that the licenses will be worth little toward the end of their useful life—who wants rights to a season ticket for only a year or two? But even for so-called permanent seat licenses, such as those sold for the San Francisco Giants' new ballpark, the permanence lasts only as long as the team stays put. With teams now staying in a facility for a decade or two at most, a thirty-year PSL could end up being no more real an investment than a Ponzi scheme, with PSL owners at the time the team moves left holding the bag.

The profits from PSLs, meanwhile, almost always go directly to the teams, regardless of whether it's the team or local government that owns the seats themselves. In one of the few exceptions, the Oakland Coliseum provides an indication of some of the pitfalls of relying on fans' speculation on seat rights to raise capital for a stadium.

The Oakland Raiders had led the wave of NFL franchise relocations in the '80s, leaving behind a rabid following in Oakland for the larger market of Los Angeles in 1982. But by decade's end, owner Al Davis was already itching for a better deal. After hearing pitches from such unlikely suitors as tiny Irwindale, California, Davis focused his attentions on none other than Oakland, which had never given up hope of luring the Raiders back to their original home.

Davis's price was steep. In exchange for the Raiders' return, he would demand that twenty-two thousand new seats be added to the Oakland–Alameda Coliseum at public expense—along with two forty-thousand-square-foot clubs and 125 new luxury suites. (The resulting wall of seats would tower precariously above the rest of the bowl-shaped stadium, peering out at passing motorists like a transplanted slice of some other building entirely.) Since the city of Oakland was in no position to raise the necessary $100 million on its own, city officials turned to PSLs as their savior. Upon the Raiders' return, the city announced, anyone wishing to buy season tickets would first be required to pay a fee of up to $16,000 for a ten-year personal seat license.

But by opening day of the 1996 season, during which the Raiders would make their triumphant return by losing 9 out of 16 games, the Oakland Football Marketing Association, the nonprofit organization set up jointly by the Raiders and the city to push PSL sales, had sold just thirty-five thousand of the forty-five thousand licenses, leaving the city $35 million in the hole for the already-completed construction. The marketing association, desperate to fill the newly expanded stadium, began selling tickets without requiring a PSL purchase first—and soon enough faced the added obstacle of a lawsuit, filed by a fan who had purchased a PSL back when they were being sold as the only way to get a Raiders season ticket, and who now charged the city with fraud.

Despite the controversy, personal seat licenses—variously called permanent, preferred, premium, or charter seat licenses—continue to flourish, especially in football, where high ticket prices are already common and a short season keeps ticket demand high. In each case the main beneficiary is almost always the team; even when PSLS are used to defray the cost of building a stadium, they are generally considered part of the team's contribution toward the project.

"Private" Stadiums, Public Cost

Naming rights and PSLS are only the beginning of indirect subsidies to sports teams, which are as varied as the stadiums and arenas that they help finance. Pacific Bell Park, in addition to its naming-rights deal, is an example of yet another hidden subsidy. Though construction of the ballpark was privately financed (by PSLS, naming fees, and the private sale of taxable bonds), the cost of clearing the land for the facility will be paid for by the city of San Francisco—an additional $1.2 million a year. Other stadiums, such as the Washington Redskins' new privately built football emporium in southern Maryland, have likewise taken what's been dubbed the "off-ramp" approach to subsidies, raking in hundreds of millions of dollars in government expenditures for new highways, roads, and parking lots around the new facility. And there's always the opportunity for additional subsidy via tax breaks: When the owners of the New York Knicks and Rangers threatened to leave town in 1982, the city agreed to exempt whatever corporation controlled the team from *all* local property taxes so long as the teams stayed put—a clause that has cost the city millions of dollars in tax revenues as the land's value has soared.

As public opposition to sports giveaways grows, teams and municipal governments are growing more and more adept at playing hide-the-subsidy. Arenas are especially susceptible to this trend. A well-utilized arena can be full 365 days a year with hockey, basketball, and concerts, whereas a baseball stadium sees only eighty-one home games, and a football field is used on only eight to twelve Sundays. Because of this capacity for year-round income, as well as their smaller size, arenas are more likely to be financed with private money—ten of the thirteen sports facilities built privately starting in 1987 were arenas. But scratch the surface of even these deals and you'll find public involvement: The "privately built" Fleet Center in Boston sits atop a $100 million city-funded parking garage; Philadelphia's $217 million CoreStates Center (built next door to the twenty-nine-year-old Spectrum in 1996) included $32 million in state funds. Overall, about 40 percent of new-arena construction winds up being financed by the public.[4]

Lastly, there are always ticket guarantees, whereby localities promise to reimburse teams for unsold seats. When the San Diego Chargers football team intimated in 1996 that it was thinking of relocating when its lease expired in 2003, the city agreed to spend $76 million on renovating city-owned Jack Murphy (now Qualcomm) Stadium and adding ten thousand seats. City officials also guaranteed that, for the next ten years, at least sixty thousand tickets would be sold for each game, with the city making up any shortfall.

It was only after the deal was signed that critics pointed out an odd consequence of this ticket guarantee. Because the Chargers' renegotiated lease called for the team to pay 10 percent of ticket revenues to the city as rent, owner Alex Spanos would stand to earn 90 percent of the face value of all tickets sold, 40 percent of which he would have to give to the league as revenue sharing. For unsold tickets, however, the city had agreed to pay the team *100 percent* of the ticket price—meaning the Chargers would make more money *not* selling tickets than selling them. Since the team's lease did not limit what Spanos could charge for these tickets, the team's owner had a potentially limitless pipeline to the city treasury.

When local libertarian activist Richard Rider realized what the city had agreed to, he was aghast. "It became apparent when this came up that the city council, and we think even the city manager who negotiated the deal, didn't know what they'd done," he says. "They get their ten-year guarantee, without any control over the prices. And we're building ten thousand seats that basically nobody wants. The real reason for doing the stadium remodeling is to come up with skyboxes. But the ten thousand extra seats are seats nobody will use."

Ryder predicts that the total city subsidy could easily wipe out the Chargers' $5.5 million in yearly rent, leaving the city paying the team to play before a near-empty house.[5] "A good parallel to think of is the airline industry," Ryder continues. "One thing an airline doesn't want to fly is an empty seat. You want to sell out your industry. So they do whatever they have to do—they cut all kinds of deals; they're constantly juggling their prices trying to sell them. Well, we just told the Chargers that it's actually not important for you. In fact, it's less than not important—it gets better."

Anatomy of a Swindle

If the benefits of a major-league sports team are insufficient to repay a city for constructing a new stadium, as Robert Baade and his fellow researchers argue, they're nowhere near enough to compensate for all the various subsidies that a new stadium can earn its sports tenants as well. Take a sample stadium—say, the TWA Dome in St. Louis. Built in the early 1990s to lure an NFL expansion franchise to town (thus filling the football vacuum left when the Cardinals were lured away to Phoenix in 1988), the new dome was bypassed in favor of sites in Charlotte and Jacksonville, leaving the city desperate to lure an existing franchise to relocate. In 1996 they found one—the Los Angeles Rams—but at an astronomical cost to taxpayers.

The TWA Dome was constructed entirely at government expense, with $301 million raised by selling general-purpose bonds. That $301 million, plus interest, will be paid back at $24 million a year over thirty years; a boost in the county hotel tax will pay for about a quarter of the sum, and the rest will be paid out of the general city and state treasuries. The 113 luxury boxes and sixty-five hundred club seats will generate $1.8 million per year in tax subsidies via the business-entertainment deduction, paid for by the federal treasury. U.S. taxpayers will likewise be responsible for an additional $6 million a year in subsidies through the federal-tax exemption of the bonds. Trans World Airlines agreed to pay $1.3 million a year (plus inflation) to plaster its name on the dome, nearly a million of which will go to the Rams. Total subsidy: $1.07 billion over thirty years.

That amounts to a public cost of $36 million a year; meanwhile, the Rams' annual revenues were expected to leap by more than $15 million.[6] And according to the team's brand-new lease, if the stadium does not remain among the most lavish in football for another ten years, the Rams can then leave town for more lucrative turf—or demand further improvements.

Notes

1. A fascinating glimpse into the inner world of baseball's finances was provided in 2001, when Major League Baseball released to a congressional committee its most comprehensive itemization of team finances since the antitrust hearings of the 1950s. Among the revelations, as detailed by Doug Pappas in a seven-part series for the Baseball Prospectus Web site: Both the Atlanta Braves and the Chicago Cubs, which were owned by major media conglomerates, appeared to be charging their cable superstation siblings well below market rate for broadcast rights; $174 million in paper losses were actually depreciation charges and actually represented a tax *benefit* to owners of $60 million or more. And even as MLB claimed that player salaries were driving the sport to the brink of bankruptcy, the league's own figures showed that non-player expenses were rising faster than player salaries. The

league's claim that it had lost $519 million in 2001 despite record revenues, concluded Pappas, was "about as believable as Enron's September 2001 financial statements."

2. In 2006, as discussed in chapter 15, savvy sports owners figured out how to evade the 10 percent rule altogether, with the blessing of the IRS.

3. The new record, as of 2006: the staggering $400 million fee paid by Citigroup to affix its name to the new Mets stadium for the next twenty years. None of this money will go to New York City, the building's owner.

4. Researcher Judith Grant Long (see chapter 13) has more recently estimated that, when one includes hidden subsidies, taxpayers are on the hook for an average of 65 percent of arena costs.

5. The city of San Diego ended up paying the team $36.4 million for unsold tickets, against $42.9 million in team rent payments, before the lease was finally renegotiated in 2004.

6. Rams revenues rose $10 million the team's first year in St. Louis and kept right on rising: By 2005 the franchise was bringing in $179 million a year, up from $76 million a decade earlier. The team's estimated value, meanwhile, had soared from $193 million to $757 million.

4 The Art of the Steal

The subsidy they get is totally disproportionate to the economic benefit they bring. . . . It would ashame Jay Gould and
his fellow robber barons of the nineteenth century. Even Geng-
his Khan got sated after a while. —*Houston mayor Bob Lanier,
explaining why he had opposed public funding for a new stadium for
the Houston Oilers football team, August 1996*

The result [of not using public funds] is that we won't have any
pro sports in Houston. Things might change someday, but the
reality is that if you say [no to public subsidies] in today's market, you're below any market. —*Lanier, explaining why he was
supporting public funding for a new stadium for the Houston Astros
baseball team, October 1996*

S tadium deals can bring unprecedented riches to a sports team
owner, but city residents tend to be unenthusiastic at first. "Sure,
we love our team," is a typical response when the stadium juggernaut rolls into a new city. "But hundreds of millions of dollars for
rich owners and greedy players, when we can barely even afford to
buy books for our school kids? It'll never fly."

Yet fly it does, in city after city. Regardless of how vocal the public
opposition or how cash-strapped the municipal treasury, rare is the

local government that has just said no to the demands of its sports franchises. Before a stadium proposal hits the drawing boards, polls will show that even though people don't want to see their team leave town (no surprise), neither do they want their tax money spent to keep them; yet invariably, these *nos* turn to *yeses* by the time public referenda are held. Nearly every city has some local politicians who proclaim that public funds will be spent on a new sports facility over their dead bodies; by the time the bond issues are passed and ground is broken at the construction site, they will likely as not be the ones wielding the shovels.

This pattern has been followed in cities large and small, those run by Democrats and Republicans, by free spenders and those traditionally stingy about every penny:

- Houston Mayor Bob Lanier's disdain for the sports industry didn't stop at comparing team owners unfavorably to Mongol hordes. In the midst of Oilers owner Bud Adams's fight for a new football stadium, Lanier commissioned a study that found that the entire sports industry in Houston, plus all other events at the Astrodome, amounted to less than 1 percent of the city's economy—smaller than the total economic impact of the Houston Medical Center. In 1995 Lanier let the Oilers pack up and leave rather than accede to their demands. Yet within just a year of that team's announced departure, the city, county, and state had agreed to team up behind a $465 million construction project for new baseball and football facilities, while making plans for a new basketball arena as well.

- When the Seattle Mariners threatened in 1995 to leave town if they didn't get a new baseball stadium to replace the nineteen-year-old Kingdome, Seattle voters narrowly rejected a referendum calling for public financing for a new stadium. But state legislators, not to be deterred, held a special emergency session to authorize the $320 million in funding anyway—then raised the figure to $414 million when the Mariners complained.

- Detroit had a historic ballpark in Tiger Stadium, a thirty-year lease with its baseball team, and a 2–1 public vote against spending city funds on a new stadium. It also had a well-organized opposition that had convinced the state legislature to deny any state funds for new stadium construction. But though it took ten years and a change of team ownership to make it happen, the mayor and governor ultimately were able to find $320 million to tear down and replace Tiger Stadium—and plan a separate downtown stadium for the Detroit Lions as well.

- Four times between 1987 and 1992, San Francisco–area voters were asked to approve public money for a ballpark for the San Francisco Giants. Four times, the referendum was presented as the "last chance" to keep the team in town. And four times, the voters turned the Giants down flat. Finally, the Giants' owner, a multimillionaire real estate heir named Bob Lurie, tried to sell his team to new ownership in Tampa, only to see his own fellow owners reject the deal. The Giants were ultimately sold to local supermarket baron Peter Magowan, who decided to build a new park almost entirely with private funds, and San Francisco looked to have gotten away with standing up to stadium blackmail—until the 49ers football team demanded, and received, $100 million in public money toward a stadium–mall complex to replace Candlestick Park.

If you're a sports owner looking to have your city build you a new stadium at public expense, the obstacles can initially seem daunting: Public opposition is a given, and getting government approval can be even worse—even when elected officials are on your side, the political process can drag on for long, luxury box–deprived seasons. To smooth the path, owners and their political allies have devised a set of strategies to coerce elected officials, media reporters, and taxpayers into accepting the necessity of a multimillion-dollar subsidy for their local sports millionaire. If you're an owner looking for a windfall of public money, follow this game plan, and you, too, can pull a last-second victory from the jaws of defeat.

Step 1: The Home-Field Disadvantage

When trying to convince taxpayers of your need for a stadium, there's an obvious obstacle: You already have one. Because of this, the first step is usually the *obsolescence claim*—alleging that your old stadium is obsolete, insufficient to cater to the demands of modern fans, or even on the verge of physical collapse.

"They say, 'The old girl, she's getting old. I love that place as much as anybody, but . . .'" says Frank Rashid, cofounder of the Tiger Stadium Fan Club, which spent a decade battling two different pizza barons over the fate of the Detroit ballpark. "Whenever anybody says that, you know, watch out."

Rashid should know, because he's watched some masters of the obsolescence claim at work. In 1987, Tigers owner Tom Monaghan (also the owner of Domino's Pizza, and a leading supporter of the antiabortion group Operation Rescue) claimed that it would cost up to $100 million to effectively repair seventy-five-year-old Tiger Stadium; when Rashid's group investigated, they found the actual figure to be a mere $6 million.

At the same time, America's oldest ballpark, Comiskey Park on the South Side of Chicago—built in 1909 as one of the first steel stadiums in the country—was similarly declared obsolete. As in Detroit, the White Sox owners hired an engineering firm to study the feasibility of renovating Comiskey; the old ballpark passed every test the engineers threw at it (including piling 50-gallon drums of water in a stadium concourse to see if the floor would give way), but the study recommended tearing it down anyway. The owners also may have decided to help it along some: By many accounts, from the time owners Jerry Reinsdorf and Eddie Einhorn purchased the team from Bill Veeck in 1981, hardly a single penny was put into maintenance of the ballpark.

Several hundred miles to the northwest, meanwhile, citizens of Minneapolis could look on their neighbors in Chicago and Detroit and breathe a sigh of relief that they were through with such squabbles. The downtown Hubert H. Humphrey Metrodome might not be the most beautiful edifice in the country—Yankees manager Billy Martin once wondered aloud, after watching his fielders losing fly balls in the glare of the translucent fabric roof, how they could "name someone like Hubert Humphrey after such a dump." But at least it was new, built in 1982 to house the baseball Twins and football Vikings, costing the citizens of Minneapolis some $55 million. It was also fresh and modern, a domed stadium built at the height of dome fever—a time when St. Petersburg dome booster Richard Dodge could say, "There is something about a dome that excites people; they get more bullish on themselves and where they live. It gives them a new and positive view of themselves. They react to issues and challenges in different ways. You can say it is the pride factor." Old Metropolitan Stadium out in suburban Bloomington, roofless and unloved, was dynamited in 1985, its demise filmed for use in a disaster movie, and was replaced by the Mall of America.

Eleven years later, the fashion pendulum had swung to old-time parks like Camden Yards, and the antiseptically modern Metrodome suddenly looked positively archaic. The Twins, noting that a minor-league team across the river in St. Paul was outdrawing their club on warm summer days, decided that an unroofed stadium was what they needed after all. Or perhaps a *retractable* roof, like those tried in fellow cold-weather cities Toronto and Montreal—though the former city's dome had gone more than $300 million over budget, and the latter's was stuck permanently in the closed position. Minnesotans, who were still paying a sales-tax surcharge to finance the bonds for the old new stadium, were faced with picking up the tab for a do-over.

Shortly after the Twins presented their demands, the Minnesota Vikings football team suggested that they should get a new stadium as well.

In Houston, the Astrodome, dubbed the Eighth Wonder of the World when it was built in 1966, was abandoned by its football tenants in 1995, and the eponymous Astros demanded a new open-air downtown park the following year. Basketball and hockey arenas have been even quicker to be thrown on the scrap heap. In 1986 Denver spent $12.5 million renovating McNichols Arena—just eleven years old at the time—for the Nuggets basketball team, improving the scoreboard and adding new luxury boxes and restaurants. Eight years later, city arena manager Gary Lane was calling the boxes "spartan" and "claustrophobic," and the Nuggets were demanding a new facility.

Next door to the Nuggets, Denver Broncos owner Pat Bowlen chimed in that his football team's home, Mile High Stadium, was rusting and might fall down. "This is a serious, serious question," said Bowlen in asking for $180 million in state money toward a new stadium. "Where do we play in 1998 or 1999 if that stadium is condemned?" As in Detroit, independent engineers countered that Mile High was in fine shape; one declared that the stadium could "last indefinitely" if properly maintained. What was not in perfect shape, it turned out, was Bowlen's bank account—the owner had sold the rights to Mile High's luxury boxes some years earlier to raise some quick cash, and hoped that a new stadium would restore the millions a year in luxury-box revenue that he had sold off.

Meanwhile, the shifting sands of stadium tastes have left cities scrambling ever faster to keep up with the latest trends. The owners of the Pittsburgh Pirates, who left thirty-five-thousand-seat Forbes Field in 1970 for the publicly financed fifty-thousand-seat concrete bowl of Three Rivers Stadium, approached the city in 1996 with demands for a new publicly built facility. The new stadium should be a "thirty-five-thousand-to-thirty-seven-thousand-seat park with natural grass and no roof, bells, or whistles," owner Kevin McClatchy said. And one more thing—perhaps it could be modeled after Forbes Field?

Step 2: Faking a Move

"That isn't even on the table, on the agenda," proclaimed Philadelphia Eagles owner Jeffrey Lurie to the press corps that had assembled for the opening of Eagles training camp in 1996. Lurie, responding to rumors that the team would relocate to Los Angeles, insisted, "It's never even been discussed. It's so off the map. . . . I know it sells papers and I know. . . . I lived in [Los Angeles] for nine years and I know you can sell a story quickly by saying, 'Uh, the team could be moving to L.A.' Forget about it. The fans can feel very, very safe that this franchise will be very successful in this area."

"And," as the *Philadelphia Daily News* remarked the next day, "with those three little words—'in this area'—Lurie perked up the good listeners in the room while opening up another can of worms." Because "this area," they knew, could mean across the river to southern New Jersey, which had already offered to build a new arena for Philadelphia's basketball and hockey teams.

Successfully threatening to pick up and move a sports franchise to another city is an art form unto itself, one that you need to perform well if you're to achieve your goal. Lurie brandished a few more tricks of the stadium trade in his speech to the press that summer day in Philadelphia—he also noted how sports teams "spin off tremendous economic benefits" and warned ominously that "I'm not going to allow this franchise to get in the kind of situation Art Modell got into in Cleveland"—but with his opening words, he proved that he had mastered the basic ingredient of sports welfare brinkmanship: the *non-threat threat.*

Even the most casual follower of the sports industry can tell you that teams get their demands met by threatening to move to other cities; and yet, virtually no owners ever make that threat themselves. Those who are too direct about the threat risk getting slapped down by angry local politicians and columnists, as San Francisco 49ers president Carmen Policy found out after bluntly threatening to leave town if an upcoming stadium-funding referendum was not approved. His statements made front-page headlines and stunned even 49ers supporters—"I almost shit when I read it," gulped state senator John Burton—and Policy quickly had to back away from the overt threat.

Somewhat tempered words, like those used by Lurie, are more

effective in conveying the proper mix of hometown spirit and subtle blackmail. As Miami Heat executive Jay Cross told his fellow sports leaders following his team's successful campaign for a new basketball arena, "We never threatened. We never said we're going to leave. When people asked us what we're going to do if we don't win the referendum, we said, 'We don't know. We don't know where we're going to play. We don't have a choice. We'll have to look around.'"

The undisputed master of the non-threat threat has been George Steinbrenner, whose tenure as owner of the New York Yankees (with time off for one felony conviction for illegal campaign contributions to Richard Nixon's Committee to Re-Elect the President, and one suspension for hiring a gambler to spy on one of his players) has been little more than one long plea for a new city-financed ballpark. Despite being reviled even by many of his own team's fans as a meddling blowhard, Steinbrenner managed to put himself in position to reap an incredible $1.2 billion stadium—all without a viable threat to move.

When Steinbrenner, an heir to a shipbuilding fortune, bought the team from CBS for $10 million in 1973, it was about to move into a newly renovated Yankee Stadium (really rebuilt from the ground up), with twenty-five luxury boxes and a state-of-the-art scoreboard, all thanks to $125 million in state and city funding. The administration of Mayor John Lindsay had agreed to the reconstruction in response to threats by the team's then owner, CBS, to move the team to neighboring New Jersey.

Steinbrenner was happy with his new stadium until the early '80s, at which point he dusted off the old New Jersey threat and demanded further renovations. Although New Jersey voters showed little enthusiasm for building him a stadium, Steinbrenner's demands steadily escalated from minor renovations, to a complete "old-time" reconstruction of Yankee Stadium—with such publicly funded amenities as a new commuter rail station, an additional bridge across the Harlem River to Manhattan, and a new parking lot built by paving a nearby public park—to a brand-new ballpark in midtown Manhattan that would cost $1 billion or more.

If anything tarnishes Steinbrenner's record, it's that he has yet to get his dream stadium for his efforts. Before the start of the 1996 season, he declared that he would make a decision on where to move the team by Opening Day; he repeated these words before the start of the 1997 season, then leaked word to the press that negotiations would be put on hold until after the mayoral election, in which Mayor Rudolph Giuliani, a supporter of the $1 billion Manhattan plan, was expected to face one of two staunch stadium opponents.[1]

Unspecified threats can prime the pump of public spending, but when it comes time to win an important vote, owners invariably bring in the big guns: the sports league presidents and commissioners, who are pressed into service to warn of the consequences of a no vote. When then baseball commissioner Fay Vincent made his trip to Cleveland to warn that a no vote on the Indians stadium would mean no Indians for Cleveland, it was just one in a long string of last-minute appearances by league executives to try to pull victory from the jaws of defeat. In Houston it was National League president Leonard Coleman who delivered the dire warnings during talks on a new stadium for the Astros in 1996: "We want to do all we can to first keep a team in Houston," Coleman told reporters. "However, if we cannot strike some kind of agreement with regards to stadiums . . . I don't think we would ask a businessman to lose millions of dollars each year." Bud Selig, the Milwaukee Brewers owner who became "permanent acting commissioner" when Vincent was fired by the baseball owners, got to deliver the threat in Minnesota three weeks before that state's legislature decided whether or not to fund a new baseball stadium, declaring that "if there isn't anything on the horizon to change the economics, baseball will allow that club to move. We'll have no alternative." A week after Selig's visit to Minneapolis, American League president Gene Budig announced his support for a new stadium for the Boston Red Sox, saying, "No one is anxious to leave Fenway Park, [but] it is important here that we be realistic in terms of economics and the long-term viability of the Boston Red Sox."

Threats, of course, are easy. But the obvious question then is, will the teams really follow through if a city says no? Details are sketchy—in part because so few cities have called their teams' bluffs—but there are indications that some sports franchises' threats to hit the road may be more idle than they would have voters believe. Both the Detroit Tigers and San Diego Chargers played the threat card while in the middle of long leases that would have been difficult if not impossible to break. The Houston Astros successfully threatened a move to Northern Virginia in 1996, even though no stadium funding was forthcoming in that state, and Baltimore Orioles owner Peter Angelos was reportedly preparing to file suit against any team that tried to relocate on his doorstep.

Finding a prospective suitor, in fact, has become more and more difficult in recent years for teams looking to create leverage for a new facility at home. For years, for example, baseball owners' favorite tease was Tampa Bay, a relatively large metro area (twentieth largest in the United States) with a stadium (the publicly financed Florida Suncoast Dome, since renamed Tropicana Field in a naming-rights deal) but no major-league team. Over the years, the San Francisco Giants, Chicago White Sox, Texas Rangers, Cleveland Indians, and Baltimore Orioles had all threatened to move to Tampa if they didn't get their way; all but the Giants ultimately won new stadiums from their current hometowns.

But it is the nature of modern sports leagues to expand (thanks to the $100 million–plus fees that expansion-team owners must pony up to the existing teams to gain entrance to the major leagues), and in 1995 Major League Baseball granted Tampa Bay an expansion franchise—the Devil Rays—to begin play in 1998. With Tampa no longer on the horizon to bully their cities with, teams had to resort to such new locales as Charlotte, Sacramento, Portland, Oregon, and the Virginia suburbs of Washington DC. No one dared mention that some of these cities were not even considered worthy candidates for expansion by the leagues.

"We make fun of these 'free-agent franchises,'" says economist

Rodney Fort. "Well, if there really were such things, all of the league owners know that that's bad for business. You've got to cultivate that long-standing relationship with fans and the identity and the tradition and all that jazz." Not to mention wanting to hedge your own bets. As University of Illinois law professor Stephen Ross observed when Minnesota Twins owner Carl Pohlad was threatening to move his team, "If you're an owner and thinking, 'What are my options?' you don't want [Pohlad to move to North Carolina] because then *you* can't threaten to move there."

How the different leagues handle this tension between the desire to play the move threat and the need for stability has varied, Fort notes. Ever since Al Davis survived an NFL lawsuit and moved the Raiders to Los Angeles in 1982, the football league has approved all proposed franchise shifts without a challenge. (The league did make the Rams pay a $65 million fine for moving from a more lucrative TV market in Los Angeles to a smaller one in St. Louis, but then approved the move without a vote—and the city of St. Louis wound up paying the fee, in any case.)

"Then you look at baseball," continues Fort. "There hasn't been a move, although there have been lots of threatened moves, since 1972, when the [Texas] Rangers opened up shop.[2] I think there's two differences. One is, there's a lot more cities out there willing to host a football team. The NFL for some reason hasn't been quite as good at expanding into those places that are real viable threats to existing team hosts. Either [baseball has] been much better at it, or the owner group is so cohesive that they've watched the Al Davis episode, and they have some blood-brother agreement in there that they're just not going to do that to themselves."

Fort and his colleague James Quirk recently looked at how well leagues did at saturating the top thirty U.S. population centers with teams; baseball, Fort says, was the hands-down winner. "So part of the story then, we think, is [that baseball is] just better at keeping a few cities around to use as this ploy so that they do have some viable alternatives out there to use as leverage against existing franchise hosts. But not so many that an individual owner is going to look around, and the payoff is going to be so large that they'll bolt."

In the end, says Fort, each league's strategy may prove successful. "Major League Baseball chooses to expand, keep the number of cities at a manageable level so that they still have some threat. The NFL chooses not to expand as much, given the pressure for teams, let the teams move around a little more, and then expand and fill in behind them—which is doubtless going to happen in L.A. and Cleveland. Maybe after the fact, in terms of league revenues, either of those strategies works okay." But in either case, one constant remains: Although leagues will allow teams to use cities for leverage all they want, there's no way they'll abandon a lucrative market outright.

Step 3: Leveling the Playing Field

If voters aren't swayed by fears of falling girders or fleeing ballclubs, your next step is to plead fairness: The team simply can't be competitive in the existing stadium. Virtually every owner in every sport has used this appeal, but as Rashid points out, they're seldom clear on exactly what it means—"competitive on the field, or the business is competitive, or what. But it suffices, because nobody asks what they mean by it. There's never a follow-up question."

"The economics of professional sports today is that, without a facility, you really can't compete," Phoenix baseball, basketball, and hockey owner Jerry Colangelo told a reporter in 1997. "And if you can't compete, you can't get support. And if you can't get support, you go out of business." Not literally, of course—in fact, despite recurrent warnings of impending doom by sports owners, no major-league team has folded in more than thirty years. Yet the mere threat of a team's falling into second-class status has been enough to strike fear into the hearts of politicians and fans alike.

This is where the owners' cooked books really come in handy. One favorite gambit of owners is to release an "audit" of team finances that purports to show massive yearly losses. In November 1996, Orioles owner Angelos released a report claiming $6 million in yearly losses, despite the team's league-high attendance and sweetheart lease. Earlier that same year, the stadium-hungry Astros released an audit that claimed the team was losing more than $20 million a year. But since Major League Baseball prohibits teams from opening their books publicly—and privately held corporations have no obligation to make their tax records public—there's no way to verify the numbers. Owners thus have the best of both worlds—they get to parade losses before the media, while claiming that league rules prevent them from providing any hard details.

Baseball, in particular, has been the site of fierce debate over the gap between "have" and "have-not" franchises; with the freest free agency of any major sport (other leagues have salary caps imposed to prevent player contracts from being bid up too high), it is argued, it's far too easy for a rich team like the Yankees ($133 million in yearly revenues in 1996) to buy up all the best players, whereas low-revenue teams like the Pittsburgh Pirates ($40 million in yearly revenues) must rely on younger, cheaper, less talented players. (Baseball owners rejected a plan to share more revenue between rich and poor teams in 1994, helping lead to that year's disastrous player strike.) A new stadium is a way to level the playing field, teams like the Pirates have argued, and indeed, several teams (the Cleveland Indians being the prime example) have seen remarkable on-field improvement coinciding with the opening of a new stadium. In fact, the correlation often seems too coincidental: Several teams have started collecting higher-paid players in the years when stadiums are still under construction, leading to some speculation that small-market owners may keep their teams on a tight budget on purpose to help promote their argument that a new ballpark is necessary for the team to compete for a pennant.

What's more, even when a team in genuinely dire economic straits cries for "competitiveness," there's a problem: What one team has, its rivals immediately want as well. So when a small-market team—say, the Baltimore Orioles—gets a lucrative new stadium, its big-market rivals like the New York Yankees demand an equally lush facility. Because the Yankees' other revenue, primarily TV and radio contracts, dwarfs those of teams like the Orioles—and baseball's relatively weak revenue-sharing plan means the Yankees owner can keep the bulk of this local income—the Orioles can once again cry for "competitiveness" and demand further concessions from their host city, beginning the cycle anew. In fact, those claiming that they need a new stadium to compete have included the owners of the richest franchises (Yankees owner Steinbrenner, whose team rakes in an estimated $24 million in profits per year) and some of the richest men in the world (Twins owner Carl Pohlad, whose family wealth is well over $800 million).

In the NFL, where revenue sharing is much stronger—in particular, TV contract money is shared across the whole league—the tactics used by teams have been somewhat different, notes Fort. "I haven't seen an NFL team go to a local government and say, 'I'm losing money.' They go to the city and say, 'In order to be competitive, I have to get more non-shared revenue sources. So if you want me to go to the Super Bowl, you've got to give me a new stadium, with gobs of luxury suites.'" Ironically, this may make football team owners even hungrier for new facilities, because unlike TV and ticket revenues, income from stadium-based revenue streams like luxury boxes and PSLS doesn't have to be shared with their fellow owners, making a new stadium one of the few sure ways for owners to put money directly in their own pockets.

Step 4: Playing the Numbers

At this point, it's time to pull out those consulting reports documenting the boundless benefits that will befall your city should it grant you a new stadium. If possible, get your friends in government to commission these reports—no point, after all, in paying for anything you don't have to, and local governments have proven eager to fund studies justifying their desires to build new sports facilities.

Baltimore's dual-stadium project alone spawned a mountain of supporting documentation; nearly every year saw another thick tome appear from some governmental study group. After hundreds of pages of minutiae on such items as population growth and sports-magazine circulation by region, each reached the same conclusion: Build something. By the time of the groundbreaking for the football stadium, Maryland governor Parris Glendening could declare confidently that the project would result in fourteen hundred new jobs and $123 million annually to Maryland's economy, and know that somewhere in the amassed paperwork were figures claiming to confirm it.

The numbers themselves here almost don't matter. Predictions of economic benefit, in fact, are all over the map—which should come as no surprise, given that they all amount to little more than guess-work. But even clearly specious numbers can serve an important public relations purpose. In every city in which team owners have won a public vote on a new stadium, a key factor has been the claim that the facility will cost taxpayers little or nothing—or that any cost will be made up for by the resulting boost to the local economy.

The plan to build a new football stadium for the San Francisco 49ers provides a striking example of this. The $100 million in city money that would be required, the team explained, would help create ten thousand jobs in the neighboring community of Bayview–Hunters Point. And best of all, the stadium would come with an attached mall, which, it was claimed, would generate more than enough tax revenue to repay the city's share of the costs.

Two separate economic-impact studies by city officials failed to confirm the team's promises: One projected a near breakeven for the city; the other concluded that expenditure substitution from other shopping areas would cost the city $4.6 million a year in lost taxes. Yet the claims served their purpose: The team was able to promote its stadium as a boon not just for the football team but also for the surrounding neighborhoods and the city as a whole—a strategy that worked to perfection when the stadium referendum squeaked through on the strength of overwhelming support from Bayview–Hunters Point voters.

Step 5: The Two-Minute Warning

No matter how well you've played your cards to this point, there's always the danger that the proceedings may threaten to drag on indefinitely as pesky voters demand referenda or legislative leaders hit gridlock in deciding on a funding plan. At this point you may want to declare a crisis: Proclaim that the window of opportunity on a new stadium will remain open only for so long, leaving unstated what disaster will befall the city if the window should be allowed to slam shut. Rashid calls it the "used car salesman" approach: Buy now because this offer won't be good for long.

Not only can a false crisis jump-start a stalled stadium deal, it can also be repeated as necessary. Astros owner Drayton McLane's stadium negotiations with Houston were a bizarre series of cascading deadlines, each one more "final" than the last. The ploy began with William Collins, a businessman from the Washington DC suburbs who was rumored to be interested in buying the club. "Mr. Collins has made it clear that he hopes to have baseball in the Virginia area by 1996," Astros vice president Bob McClaren said in October 1995. "Common sense would say to us that in the next four to eight weeks, they would have to have something in place." No new construction plans were in place in Houston by then, but neither were they in Virginia, where Collins had run into a wall of opposition for his own demands for a publicly built stadium. McLane bided his time for a while then issued a new deadline: August 1. When D-Day finally came—preceded by increasingly apprehensive media reports—McLane promptly granted another extension. The deadlines didn't stop until mid-September, by which time the local government finally gave in to McLane's demands.

There have even been crises that the participants later admitted to faking to boost public concern. When the Detroit Tigers, in 1991, gave Wayne County executive Michael Duggan an August 1 deadline, no one publicly questioned it. Only later did Duggan reveal that the deadline was his idea—he had, in effect, told the Tigers to blackmail him.

Five years later, Rashid recalls, the Wayne County Board of Commissioners was to decide whether or not to dedicate still more money for a new stadium for the Detroit Lions football team. Rashid and fellow activist Kim Stroud watched as Duggan presented the board with, in Rashid's words, "hundreds of pages of stuff that they had to read in a matter of a few days and then make a judgment on. They were begging for more time. No matter how they felt about the project, they said, basically, we spend more time determining matters that involve tens of thousands of dollars—this is something that's going to involve hundreds of millions of dollars. We don't have time to study this."

The board approved the money, only to watch as the stadium process dragged on for months more as city and teams haggled over the site and the financing. "There was no rush," says Rashid. "The need for the rush was to avoid public scrutiny."

Step 6: Moving the Goalposts

Once you have successfully gotten your stadium on the drawing board, your task is not over—far from it. As any owner knows, the deal struck with your local government on a new sports facility is only the opening gambit. Cost overruns are a certainty, especially if you have plans for technological novelties like a state-of-the-art retractable roof. In any case, since you have the upper hand in renegotiations—you can always change your mind and leave in the middle, after all, but a city can't do much with a half-built stadium—you are free to renegotiate the terms of the deal again and again if you like.

In San Diego, for example, when the $66.6 million expansion of Jack Murphy Stadium went over budget (among other things, the stadium had been built on sandy soil, leading to problems in earthquake proofing), the city quickly agreed to raise the additional cash, selling the stadium's naming rights to computer company Qualcomm for $18 million. "The trick is to get the deal going," says San Diego stadium opponent Richard Rider. "Once it's going, you say, 'We can't quit now!'"

When the city of Toronto first planned the stadium-and-hotel complex known as SkyDome in 1985, estimates were that construction costs would be in the neighborhood of $150 million (Canadian), with the city and the province of Ontario kicking in $30 million apiece. In fact, the stadium, complete with the world's first working retractable roof, would ultimately clock in at a whopping $600 million (roughly $500 million in U.S. dollars), the second-most-expensive sports facility in North American history. (Number one in that category: Montreal's Olympic Stadium, built in a hurry for the 1976 Olympic Games, which cost $1 billion Canadian and features the world's first *non*-working retractable roof.) As a result, SkyDome was a hit with fans and tourists but a disaster for its government owners: In 1990, the new stadium's first full year of operation, the Blue Jays drew a record 3.9 million fans and turned a profit of $13.9 million; SkyDome, meanwhile, saddled with its enormous bonding cost, lost $23 million.

Desperately looking for a way to reduce the $60,000 a day in interest building up on the SkyDome bonds, the province of Ontario had two choices. It could pay off the debt immediately, reducing treasury reserves in order to eliminate the incredible interest payments, or it could sell the stadium for whatever cash it could, in an effort to get rid of this massive money loser. Bizarrely, the province did both, first writing off the debt and then selling SkyDome to private interests for $151 million. By the time the government finally rid itself of the dome, the Ontario public had taken a $262.7 million bath.

The ultimate stadium wheel-and-deal, however, occurred in Milwaukee over several years in the early '90s, as Brewers owner Bud Selig managed to take his own promise to build a privately funded stadium for his ballclub and turn it into one of the biggest public bailouts in urban planning history. A Wisconsin lobbyist would later call the whole process "one of the fanciest pieces of parliamentary maneuvering [he'd] ever seen."

The dance began in 1989, when Selig approached Milwaukee elected officials, asking for permission to build a privately financed park on state land. Only one problem: The land in question had a highway running through it, state highway 41, which would have to be moved at a cost of $6 million. The Greater Milwaukee Committee agreed to move the highway if Selig would pay for the stadium.

Five years later, Selig approached Wisconsin governor Tommy Thompson, already then gaining a national reputation for slashing state welfare benefits, with a new dilemma: He couldn't afford to build the stadium himself. At first Thompson proposed a statewide lottery to raise the money, similar to that which had funded Camden Yards; that plan, however, was rejected nearly two-to-one by Wisconsin voters in 1995. Thompson made sure that his next gambit wouldn't be subject to any messy public votes: He asked the state legislature to hike the sales tax by one-tenth of 1 percent in a five-county area around Milwaukee. When the state senate twice voted down the sales-tax hike by one vote, state senator George Petak entered Governor Thompson's office; at 2 a.m., Petak emerged to announce he was changing his vote. Three hours later, at five in the morning, the state senate approved the tax increase.

Enraged constituents petitioned for a recall election on Petak. (He would be recalled the following June and immediately hired by Thompson as associate director of the Wisconsin Housing and Economic Development Agency.) But the deal was seemingly done: The five-county sales tax would provide $160 million, and the Brewers would chip in $90 million of their own funds. Even this, however, proved too much for Selig to handle. Although $40 million would come from the sale of stadium naming rights to Miller Beer (Thompson obligingly vetoed an antismoking bill to avoid angering Miller's parent company, Philip Morris), the source of the other $50 million remained a mystery for months to come.

Selig was in a bind; even if he wanted to borrow the money himself, he was blocked by Major League Baseball limits on the amount of debt a team can carry. So Selig instead asked the state to borrow the money *for* him, using tax-exempt bonds to lower the costs of interest payments by $2 million a year. "This does not mean taking one cent more from the taxpayers," announced Metropolitan Milwaukee Association of Commerce chair Robert J. O'Toole. This was true enough if he meant only Milwaukee taxpayers, but that $2 million a year would instead come out of the federal treasury, which would be giving up income tax revenue from the federally tax-exempt bonds.

Although the $50 million state loan was ultimately rejected, Selig still was let off the hook—that portion of the money was instead divided up among loans from the city of Milwaukee and from local foundations and business leaders. In the end, Selig would be responsible only for the $3 million in yearly loan payments, plus $1.1 million a year in rent. And because the state also agreed to pay the Brewers $3.85 million a year for "stadium maintenance," the Brewers owner and baseball commissioner, the much-reviled man who, to avoid settling a strike, had cancelled the World Series for the first time ever, will ultimately receive his new ballpark virtually as a gift from the people of Wisconsin, just ten years after promising to build one himself.

Step 7: Review Steps 1 through 6

Follow these rules well, and you can count on receiving a gift-wrapped stadium or arena sitting under your tree within a Christmas or two. The San Francisco 49ers found that out—despite many PR debacles along the way, their combined use of all the tactics in the stadium-seekers' playbook, from economic promises to predictions of on-field doom to the move threat, ultimately won them a $100 million subsidy from a city that had previously denied every request for public sports subsidies.[3]

San Francisco Examiner columnist Stephanie Salter compared the

49ers' pitch for a new stadium to that of a door-to-door salesman: "Good morning, madam. You have five minutes to do what I say. Buy this vacuum cleaner. Never mind how it works. I've explained it to the Chamber of Commerce. It's a great deal. Trust me. And if you don't buy it, I'm going to come back on Sunday while you're in church and bust up your old vacuum cleaner. . . . Furthermore, madam, it may look as if my main purpose is to get you to buy this vacuum cleaner, but, trust me, my needs are inconsequential. Your welfare is why I'm here."

Notes

1. It would ultimately take another nine years and a new mayor before Steinbrenner would get to break ground on his dream home. See chapter 15.

2. Baseball's streak would end at thirty-three years in 2005, when the Montreal Expos moved—or, rather, were moved by the league, which had taken over ownership of the club—to Washington DC. See chapter 14.

3. Thanks to a series of mishaps—including a riverboat-gambling scandal that forced owner Edward DeBartolo Jr. to yield control of the team to his sister—the 49ers had yet to cash in their $100 million taxpayer IOU by 2006. Late that year, with plans for a combined stadium–mall project stalled, team officials announced their intention to seek a stadium near San Jose instead.

5 Deus Ex Pizza

The city has been so desperate for something new. They want
something new that's going to look good from the Goodyear
Blimp. I almost think that if they built a pyramid at the foot of
Woodward Avenue on the riverfront, people would get excited.
—*Bill Dow, Tiger Stadium Fan Club*

I have little patience with people who are paid that well wanting us to spend hundreds of millions of public dollars so that
they have a nicer place to take a shower. —*Frank Rashid, Tiger
Stadium Fan Club*

Of all the citizen groups that formed in response to move threats
by sports teams, the one that garnered the most media attention
may have been the least typical: Save Our Browns, the spontaneous
fan movement that burst forth during Cleveland's battle over its football team. It was everything that sports fanatics are supposed to be:
equally furious at fly-by-night owners and impotent politicians, and
desperate to keep the team in town no matter the cost.

In truth, though, sports fans are a varied bunch, and their lives extend far beyond just following their favorite teams. They are also taxpayers, parents of school-age children, residents of neighborhoods
that would be affected by stadium-siting plans. Despite politicians'

claims that "the public" would crucify them if they allowed a sports team to leave town, public opinion surveys have shown overwhelming opposition to building new sports facilities at public expense, at least until the owners rev up their media campaigns.

In recent years, stadium proposals have brought together numerous citizen activist groups from across the political spectrum to ask why residents should lose either their teams or their wallets. They have included everything from social-justice activists who advocate spending public money on schools instead of stadiums to foes of any government spending whatsoever. All, though, have returned to the same arguments when confronted with the prospect of a new multimillion-dollar sports facility to be built at public expense: It's too expensive, it isn't needed, and above all, don't ask the public to pay for it when the people benefiting will be among the richest in the nation.

Of all these citizen groups, the one that stands out for its longevity, if nothing else, is the Tiger Stadium Fan Club. These were fans, all right—but as two local millionaires would learn over a decade of public battles, they were fans with a vengeance.

Queen of Diamonds

It was a September night in 1987 when five friends gathered at Buddy's Pizza in northeast Detroit to talk over the looming demise of their city's ballpark. Sitting around the table that night were Mike Betzold, a reporter for the *Detroit Free Press*; Jerry Lemenu, an illustrator and courtroom sketch artist whose cartoons often appeared in local newspapers; Bob Buchta, a local photographer; Kevin Rashid, a poet who worked days as a groundskeeper at a local college campus; and Kevin's brother Frank, a professor of English at nearby Marygrove College. As they sat eating pizza and listening to the baseball game on the radio, the five lifelong Tigers fans mulled over how to protest what they saw as the needless destruction of a cherished landmark.

Tiger Stadium was just three years younger than baseball's oldest ballpark, Chicago's Comiskey Park—it had opened for business on

April 20, 1912, tying it with Boston's Fenway Park as the second-oldest baseball stadium in existence—but the site's history went back a good deal further. Pro baseball had first been played at the corner of Michigan and Trumbull, just a few blocks west of Detroit's downtown, in 1896, when the Tigers' owner covered the cobblestones of the city's Woodbridge hay market with sod and erected an L-shaped wooden grandstand. That original wooden park was torn down and built anew in steel in 1912 then enlarged again by the team's owners in 1936. The final result was a fifty-five-thousand-seat structure that would house some of the best teams and most devoted fans in baseball, consistently averaging in the top half of league attendance figures year after year.

But following the Tigers' 1968 championship, local business and political leaders began making noise about joining the first wave of public stadium building, which was then in full swing. They set their sights on a new dual-sport dome on the Detroit waterfront to house both the Tigers and football's Lions, which shared Tiger Stadium at the time. Wayne County, which encompasses Detroit and its western suburbs, actually got as far as issuing $126 million in bonds for the dome before a pair of local activists sued the city and won, arguing successfully that the bond issue had been fraudulently presented— the county had led voters to believe the bonds were backed entirely by stadium revenue, when in fact county taxpayers would be liable for paying any shortfall. The bonds were recalled, and the dome died on the drawing board.

Shortly afterward the Lions football team relocated to the new Silverdome in suburban Pontiac, and the city of Detroit pumped $18 million in renovations into Tiger Stadium, financing the work with a ninety-cent ticket surcharge. The stadium's old dark-green wood seats were replaced with garish orange-and-blue plastic ones, and aluminum siding went up over the gray masonry outer walls. But the thousands of inexpensive bleacher seats were still intact, as were the memories of generations of fans. And the Tigers, unlike the Lions, still played downtown.

But almost before the paint was dry from the stadium's refurbishing, rumblings began in city political circles about tearing the place down. The ballpark was too old, it was said, structurally unsound, insufficient for the needs of a modern sports franchise. As the stadium steamroller geared up once more, Tiger Stadium seemed destined to join the list of historic ballparks that had fallen beneath the wheels of progress.

Act One: Rusty Girders

As Betzold, Lemenu, Buchta, and the Rashids gathered in the fall of 1987 to discuss the fate of their home-away-from-home since childhood, they understood the uphill battle they faced. In addition to being rabid baseball fans, the five were also experienced political activists: Mike Betzold had been a leader in local nuclear-freeze circles; Jerry Lemenu and Frank Rashid had worked for a local civil rights group; and Kevin Rashid had helped spearhead a doomed campaign to stop garbage incinerators from being placed in city neighborhoods. Betzold and Lemenu had also been frequent contributors to *Fifth Estate*, a well-respected anarchist newspaper based in Detroit. Saving Tiger Stadium seemed like a fun way to combine their passions for baseball and social activism.

"We decided to start this thing a little bit on a lark," recalls Frank Rashid, who still lives on a tree-lined block not far from where he grew up on Detroit's inner west side. After moving into his current home, Rashid discovered that Clyde Manion, an obscure Tigers catcher from the 1920s, had lived there after retiring from baseball; photos of Manion and a young Frank Rashid, each in catcher's gear, now face off across a hallway in the house.

He and his friends, Rashid notes, all regular attendees at Tigers games since the early '60s, knew few details apart from the fact that their beloved stadium was facing a date with the wrecking ball. "We didn't want the stadium to go without a fight," he explains. "We didn't know a lot about public financing at the time—we thought it was crooked, we thought it was crazy. But we just didn't know an awful lot about it."

Calling themselves the Tiger Stadium Fan Club, the five set out to drum up support among fellow fans. By pooling their savings, they were able to scrape together enough money for two hundred T-shirts and one thousand bumper stickers reading "Save Tiger Stadium." In the waning days of the 1987 season, as the Tigers drove to the American League East pennant, the small band of diehards could be found each night standing outside Tiger Stadium, handing out blue-and-orange bumper stickers to anyone who would sign their club's mailing list.

The initial response was overwhelming. Hundreds of people sent in a $10 membership fee. At the Fan Club's first public meeting in January 1988, three hundred people packed the small, brick Gaelic League Irish–American Club, a short drive down Michigan Avenue from the stadium, to form committees to fight the demolition. By the time the 1988 season opened, the rapidly growing group had decided to stage a group "hug" of the old ballpark to mark its seventy-sixth birthday; twelve hundred people gathered in a cold rain to encircle the stadium then filed into the ballpark to present the team's grounds crew with a giant birthday card signed by hundreds of supporters. Fan Club member Mike Gruber, a high-school English teacher who had been brought into the group by his college classmate Frank Rashid, had loaned $5,000 of his own money for the publicity campaign for the hug, helping pay for printing a twenty-four-page souvenir program detailing Tiger Stadium's history, and full-page newspaper ads urging fans, "Don't Let Them Make the Biggest Error in Baseball."

It was a popular sentiment at the time. Polls consistently found two thirds of Detroiters favored simple renovation of the old stadium over replacement, and 64 percent of local residents opposed the use of city funds for a new stadium. Even team owner Tom Monaghan, the Domino's Pizza czar who had bought the Tigers in 1983, seemed to like the old ballpark, insisting at every turn that he would love nothing better than to keep the team right where it was. Asked on one occasion if he was angling for a new ballpark, Monaghan replied that he wanted no such thing but would go along with whatever local politicians decided: "I'll let them build a new stadium, then I'll cry."

Behind the scenes, though, Monaghan was telling local politicians that he desperately wanted out of Tiger Stadium, which was, he insisted, out-of-date and decrepit, despite the recent renovations. The politicians dutifully repeated his claims—particularly longtime mayor Coleman Young, the former union activist who as mayor had become a staunch advocate of city subsidies to private developers.

The first major skirmish in the battle over Tiger Stadium came in January 1988, when the Tigers announced the results of the engineering study they had commissioned the year before to "determine the costs of shoring up [Tiger Stadium's] long-neglected foundation and superstructure." This was the study that, the Tigers claimed, had found the existing ballpark in need of $100 million worth of repairs. In particular, the team charged, salt spread in the aisles during snowy Lions football games, in the years before that team moved to the suburbs, had severely corroded the building's steel girders, requiring costly repairs. "Our perspective is that the stadium isn't going to fall down tomorrow, but this grand old lady is getting old," Monaghan stadium aide John McDevitt told reporters. Mayor Young enthusiastically agreed. "Nobody in their wildest dreams expects that stadium to last beyond ten years," the mayor announced. "Most people say it will fall down in five."

The Fan Club asked the team for a copy of the report—at which point Tigers officials demurred, insisting variously that the study was an "informal" one, or even that no written report existed. Finally, a local newspaper reporter, after nearly a year of Freedom of Information Act requests, uncovered the actual study, at which point the reason for the team's reticence became clear: the consultants, it turned out, had actually recommended only $6 million in renovations—much of it for such items as a new sound system. (The $100 million figure, it turned out, was the price for erecting a dome atop the existing ballpark.) They had never even mentioned any salt damage. The Fan Club—which had initially taken the Tigers' claims at face value—began turning a more discerning eye on the public statements of the team and its political supporters.

So the following March, when the city released a consulting report by stadium-builders Hellmuth Obata Kassebaum—who would stand to make millions off a contract to design and build a new stadium—the Fan Club was prepared for the worst. As expected, HOK's report asserted that a new ballpark was the way to go, estimating that it would cost anywhere from $57 million to $245 million to renovate Tiger Stadium to the point where it would meet the team's needs. Instead, HOK proposed a fifty-six-thousand-seat stadium with 150 corporate boxes, a helipad, a Domino's Pizza outlet, and no bleacher seats.

By this time, Fan Club members had come to realize that the battle they were engaged in was over far more than merely saving an old ballpark. By the first summer of its operation, the Fan Club newsletter, *Unobstructed Views*, had moved from talking about members' love of Tiger Stadium to asking, "Should public money be used to increase the profits of one of the wealthiest men in the Midwest? . . . Is the improvement of Mr. Monaghan's profit margin a more pressing need than the education of our children, the safety of our senior citizens, the vitality of our besieged community?" Taking a more political line would cost the Fan Club some of its original support—two local radio stations that had sponsored the initial stadium hug backed off once it was clear the Fan Club meant to take "controversial" stands—but it also enabled them to draw the links between the fate of Tiger Stadium and the future of the city as a whole.

Scrambling to counter the renewed push for a new stadium, the Fan Club struck back in two ways. They launched an immediate boycott of Domino's Pizza—making more enemies in a region where Domino's is one of the largest corporate presences. And they contacted architects John and Judy Davids to prove that the eight-hundred-pound gorilla of the stadium industry was wrong about renovation.

The Davidses, two young architects from suburban Royal Oak who drove downtown for dozens of Tiger games every year, came to the Fan Club late, but they were to become two of its most important and vocal members. The couple was already intimately familiar with Tiger Stadium, having designed a renovated owner's box for Monaghan in the early '80s. They were also frequent visitors to the ballpark, sitting sometimes in the owner's box but more often with their friends in the right-field bleachers. When the Fan Club called to ask if they would design a renovation plan for the ballpark, the Davidses jumped at the chance. Armed with surreptitiously obtained blueprints and the stadium requirements the Tigers had submitted to HOK, the two spent months of evenings and weekends laboring over a detailed proposal to provide everything the Tigers had requested without changing the character of the old ballpark. When completed in January 1990, the Cochrane Plan (named for an extension to the old ballpark that would be constructed over seldom-used Cochrane Street, which ran behind the third-base line) had achieved all its goals, including expanded concession facilities, club offices, handicapped access, and seventy-three new luxury boxes. Best of all, the renovation would cost just $26.1 million, a fraction of the price of a new ballpark.

In developing the Cochrane Plan, Fan Club members discovered something else about Tiger Stadium: Not only was it historic, but it also turned out to be one of the most fan-friendly ballparks in the nation. One day in 1989, Frank Rashid was at the Fan Club office when a phone call came in from John Pastier, an architect and student of ballpark history who was looking for information on Tiger Stadium. "Aw, I love Tiger Stadium. With the catwalks!" Rashid recalls Pastier saying. "Not only are you right that it's a great place to watch a ballgame, by *actual mathematical measurement* the average seat at that ballpark is closer [to the field] than the average seat at any other ballpark."

Pastier, a former architecture critic for the *Los Angeles Times*, had the credentials to back up his opinion: His consulting work included contributions to the design of Camden Yards. But his greater passion was seating distances. As part of a project to study the old steel ballparks built in the same era as Tiger Stadium, Pastier had catalogued the average distance from upper-deck seats—the traditional province of the average fan—to home plate in dozens of ballparks across the country. Tiger Stadium, which to fit the most seats in a tightly confined space had been built with the upper deck set atop pillars right above the lower deck, indeed boasted upper-deck seating that was closer to the field than in any other ballpark—barely half the distance of most of the newer ballparks, including Camden Yards.

The key was in the columns. Anathema to new-stadium designers like HOK because they block the view of some fans in the back rows, these steel support beams are absent in every new park built in the last thirty years, necessitating that upper-level seats be set back from the field to support their weight. It's an argument that both Pastier and John Davids dismiss as missing the forest for the girders. In modern ballparks like the new Comiskey, says Davids, "to lose the three or four thousand obstructed seats that they have, they put twenty thousand seats twice as far away. Which is a bad tradeoff. If you ask people in Chicago to compare Comiskey, which had columns like Tiger Stadium, to the new Comiskey—they've had real trouble selling their upper-deck tickets. People there were used to sitting close to the field, like Tiger Stadium is. I think once they sat in the upper deck a couple of times, they said, 'We're not going to pay fifteen bucks to sit up here.'"

Though Fan Club members blanched a bit at some items in the Cochrane Plan—particularly the luxury boxes that the Davidses planned to install on the stadium's seldom-used third level, which struck some as an affront to Tiger Stadium's egalitarian spirit—by and large, the plan was applauded as a savvy compromise that would fill the Tigers' needs while saving both public money and the character of the old ballpark.

It also helped convince many Detroiters who might previously have dismissed the Fan Club as a bunch of nostalgic kooks. Bill Dow, a local attorney, first saw the Cochrane Plan scale model on exhibit at the Michigan Gallery and was so impressed that he immediately joined the Fan Club, quickly becoming a part of the core group. "When I first heard about the [stadium] hug a couple of years earlier, I just kind of thought, 'Aw, boy, what is this?'" he remembers. "But then when I saw the Cochrane Plan I was just so impressed. After meeting with Frank [Rashid] and John Davids and a couple of people down at the Michigan Gallery, the next day I called up and said, 'What can I do to help?'"

The Davidses, flush with praise, proudly called up Tom Monaghan's office to present their plan to their old boss, certain that he would be elated at their work, which would meet every objection of the stadium opponents while saving millions of dollars. "We were telling people at [the Fan Club] meeting, 'No problem, Monaghan's cool,'" Judy Davids later recalled. "We'll just call him, and we'll tell him who we are." Instead, he refused to meet with them. They called Monaghan's home number and spoke to his daughter; according to John Davids, she replied, "Yeah, I mentioned it to him, and he didn't make any commitment to call you."

The Davidses were stunned that their hard work was to be dismissed without even a hearing from the team ownership. Meanwhile, accolades poured in from other corners of Detroit: the *News* and *Free Press* both ran laudatory editorials about the Davidses' proposal, and the city planning commission recommended seriously investigating the renovation option. Pastier says the Cochrane Plan would have been "comparable to the Wrigley Field remodeling [in Chicago]—an intelligent, pragmatic way of extending the life of a very important structure, something that was very valuable to the sport in terms of its history and character."

As they lobbied for the Cochrane Plan, the Fan Club continued to fight on other fronts. A committee led by Gruber had successfully lobbied the Department of Interior to place Tiger Stadium on the

National Register of Historic Places. The Fan Club mailing list continued to grow, ultimately to eleven thousand, and hundreds would turn out for periodic demonstrations at the ballpark. (One featured a group of kids pulling toy wagons filled with petitions urging the ballpark be saved.) Their twenty core members, all volunteers, took turns staffing their tiny storefront (donated rent-free by the building's owner, a Fan Club supporter) and standing on the corner of Michigan and Trumbull, where they sold bumper stickers and t-shirts and distributed their newsletter. When Tigers president Bo Schembechler threatened that the team would move if a new stadium were not built, the Fan Club immediately gathered to pore over the team's lease, discovering that it solidly bound the team to play in Detroit until the year 2008, a fact they promptly brought to the media.

Tigers management and their allies, meanwhile, fell back on their original party lines. "I'd rather have the old stadium," Monaghan told reporters in the summer of 1990. "But everybody that knows better wants a new one." The following April, Schembechler, an ex-college football coach who had been hired specifically in the hopes that his iconic status among Michiganders would make him a PR asset, made headlines when he declared in an angry speech before the Economic Club of Detroit, "It's unfair for you to think that you can shackle us to a rusted girder in Tiger Stadium and expect us to compete and win."

That May, Mayor Young again predicted that Tiger Stadium was "about to fall down."

The stadium proponents were starting to run into difficulties selling that story, though, according to John Davids: "The Young administration didn't do a very good job of peddling the idea, and Monaghan's organization was a disaster for that kind of stuff." (Monaghan's nadir came when he inexplicably fired Hall-of-Fame broadcaster Ernie Harwell before the 1991 season, leading to a fan boycott that left thousands of seats vacant on opening day.) But starting in late 1990, Wayne County deputy executive Mike Duggan joined the fray, making the stadium issue a personal crusade. Even as he assured Fan Club representatives that he would seriously consider the Cochrane Plan, Duggan was lobbying hard for a new ballpark, paying special attention to members of the media who had been relatively unreceptive to Monaghan.

County officials "spent an awful lot of money and time taking columnists out to lunch and making presentations about how many thousands of jobs the stadium would create and how Tiger Stadium was just too old and couldn't be renovated," says Davids. "They were able to really collar some people and turn some people around who had been supportive of us before."

But though they kept up their rhetoric, the stadium proponents faced a seemingly insurmountable obstacle: There was simply no money to build a new ballpark. The state legislature had rejected repeated attempts to pass stadium-funding bills; Wayne County, meanwhile, was locked in a dispute with the city over where to build a new facility. And when the Detroit city council began mulling putting its own money into the project, the Fan Club led a referendum campaign that resulted, on March 17, 1992, in a resounding 2–1 vote barring any city money from being spent on a new ballpark.

It was, says Rashid, the high-water mark for the Fan Club. Because later that year, two new forces would enter the political mix. Tom Monaghan sold the Tigers for $80 million to Detroit Red Wings owner Mike Ilitch. And Governor John Engler, who had promised on his election in 1990 that no state money would be used to build a new stadium for the Tigers, began searching for a method of doing just that—and a method that would be immune to the desires of the state legislature or the public.

Act Two: Pizza with Everything

When Mike Ilitch bought the Tigers, Bill Dow remembers, "We thought, here's a chance. This guy's a lifelong Detroiter, he had, apparently, fond memories of the ballpark. And we thought, here's a chance that maybe we can convince them to buy into renovation of the stadium." Their hopes were buoyed further when Ilitch agreed to meet with them to look over the Cochrane Plan.

Mike Ilitch, like Tom Monaghan, is a pizza baron, his Little Caesar's running neck and neck with Domino's for fast-food pizza dominance. More important for the fate of the stadium struggle, he is also a downtown developer whose ties to the city-development cabal run deep and strong. A board member of Detroit Renaissance, the corporate-funded redevelopment organization that dominates city planning, Ilitch spent the better part of the early '90s negotiating the rights to redevelop large swathes of downtown real estate, most notably the historic Fox Theater. He now made use of all these connections to pressure city political leaders for a new stadium.

Ilitch, explains Dow, was looked on as "a savior of the city—this businessman who put his headquarters downtown. When we met with Senator Carl Levin, he said, 'You know, my daughter would kill me if I didn't fight for renovating Tiger Stadium.' But then he said, 'How do we say no to a guy like Mike Ilitch?'" To further bolster his cause, the pizza king worked behind the scenes with Detroit city officials to grease the political skids for the new park. Over the course of time, two separate city-development directors would lobby hard for a new stadium then leave public office only to turn up on Ilitch's payroll.

Meanwhile, in Lansing, Governor Engler had fixed his attentions on the Governor's Strategic Fund. This was a pool of money that had been set up as a discretionary fund, under the sole control of the governor, to help environmental groups, small businesses, and minority business startups—"kind of a Democratic-inspired slush fund for worthy projects," explains Rashid. Engler had been a staunch opponent of the fund when it was first set up, deriding it as "corporate welfare." Once elected governor, however, he saw it as the perfect vehicle for funding a new Tigers ballpark—so perfect, he announced, that he would augment its modest $20 million in cash reserves with $35 million more from a new tax on casino gambling on Indian reservations that had just been passed by the state legislature.

The Fan Club immediately filed suit against Engler's plan, calling it a blatant misuse of funds and an unconstitutional end run around the powers of the state legislature to appropriate money. Every lawyer consulted by the Fan Club remarked that their suit looked solid—in fact, says Dow, several told the activists that they had a moral obligation not to allow this theft of funds to become law. But in its first stop, the circuit court in Lansing, the case was thrown out, ruling that the gaming moneys were "not state funds." Stunned, the Fan Club appealed all the way to the state supreme court, which returned a decision that affirmed the stadium opponents' argument but still ruled against them: Engler's move was bad law and would not be allowed to stand as a precedent, but the court would not stand in the way of *this particular* misappropriation of funds.

Meanwhile, Ilitch's lobbying mechanism had kicked into high gear. In March 1996 Ilitch and Mayor Dennis Archer (who was elected to succeed Coleman Young in 1992) went after the ban on city funding that had been the Fan Club's greatest victory, staging a public referendum to reverse the results of the earlier vote. The Fan Club raised about $20,000 to promote the continued ban; the city spent more than $600,000. Archer, remembers Rashid, was on television nearly nonstop during the weeks leading up to the vote, "every half hour on the half hour, with glossy fancy ads telling us basically all the lies, about how the new stadium was going to bring jobs, going to improve schools and police protection."

Archer's allies also raised for the first time something that had not been a major issue in the fight over Tiger Stadium: race. The city politicians behind the stadium push were, like 85 percent of Detroit, overwhelmingly African American; the Fan Club was predominantly white. Organized baseball has long been one of the worst sports at reaching out to people of color, dating back to the days of segregated Negro Leagues and continuing to the present day. (One survey found that just 4.8 percent of fans in attendance at baseball games in 1995 were African American, down from 9.8 percent just six years earlier.) Since the Fan Club had made a conscious decision to recruit its membership from Tiger fans, they were left with a membership that was largely, though by no means entirely, white in a predominantly black city.

Archer and his allies in the black political establishment quickly seized upon race as a wedge to drive between the Fan Club and the black electorate. The *Michigan Chronicle*, a local African American business newspaper, ran a front-page story on Bill Dow headlined "Stadium critic lives in suburbs," the story alluding to "heavy-handed suburban influence" in the upcoming elections. The Fan Club leaders countered that all its founding members and a majority of its executive committee were from the city, and pointed out that neither Ilitch nor his top aides lived in Detroit. But their arguments fell on deaf ears: "They want us to renovate the old Tiger Stadium, yet when those in the suburbs build, they build new," wrote V. Lonnie Peek in a *Chronicle* op-ed. "Detroit deserves a new stadium, not a renovated old one."

The city funding ban fell by a more than 4–1 margin. Soon afterward the Detroit Lions announced that they, too, would be moving back downtown to play in a separate football stadium to be built at public expense. The total cost in public dollars: an estimated $240 million.

Epilogue: Monoculture

"Here is a tremendous theater," Frank Rashid says, pointing to a parking lot. He is driving through downtown Detroit, or what's left of it. "This was the Michigan Theater—wonderful lobby. It's all gone." Down the street a ways sits the Fox Theater, recently renovated by Mike Ilitch after city development director Emmet Moten arranged to have it condemned and sold to Ilitch at a $2 million loss to the city. Across the street from the Fox is the United Artists, which Ilitch similarly arranged to have the city transfer to his control and which the pizza king may now tear down to provide additional parking for the two new stadiums.[1]

Perhaps more than any other modern American city, Detroit has in recent decades pursued a "development" strategy that seems destined to transform its entire downtown into vacant lots. It began in the 1950s with the construction of five major downtown freeways— "they cut through the city, cut it to ribbons," says Rashid, who remembers, as a college student camped out outside Tiger Stadium for World Series tickets in 1968, watching the Fisher Freeway plow through the neighboring Briggs Community. Detroit's old city hall fell soon after, to be replaced by a sterile plaza dubbed Cadillac Square. The city's classic Orchestra Hall was almost replaced by a McDonald's several years ago, before a concerted public campaign brought it back from the brink; meanwhile, the city's oldest brick residential building was bought by entertainer Anita Baker and torn down to make way for an International House of Pancakes.

In their place the remains of failed redevelopment schemes litter downtown Detroit. As Rashid's battered Subaru approaches the city center, a tiny electric train car breezes by atop a concrete track that winds in a tight loop through downtown Detroit. This is the "people-mover," an ill-fated light-rail scheme that cost millions of dollars in federal funds but goes nowhere and is little used.

"What I'm going to do now is take you down Woodward," says Rashid, "so you can see what happened to the city's main street." He pulls the car south onto Woodward Avenue and into a scene of utter devastation. Detroit's downtown shopping district is simply gone. Cavernous department stores and jewelry outlets, blocks and blocks of them, sit vacant and shuttered. In the 1980s, the giant Hudson's department store—the Macy's of Detroit—fled to a suburban mall, and its neighbors along Woodward quickly followed. Now only the buildings remain, and these not for long: The city has announced plans to demolish the Hudson's building, empty since the early '80s, and the others may soon follow.[2]

The car turns off Woodward and bears east along the Detroit River, and suddenly there looms the centerpiece of Detroit's failed hopes: the Renaissance Center, four gleaming steel-and-glass towers isolated from the rest of the city by giant ivy-coated concrete berms. Henry Ford II, grandson of the company's founder, raised the money for the center in the '70s—"maybe he realized that the Ford Motor Company hadn't built a car in Detroit since 1914 and felt guilty about what had happened in Detroit," says Rashid. Ford had offered to build several smaller developments scattered around downtown, but Mayor Young's predecessor, Roman Gribbs, instead chose a megalith that utterly transformed downtown, all right, but not quite in the way that was intended. "All those great buildings downtown that had high office occupancy, [their tenants have] moved to this place and now they're empty," says Rashid. "[The city] basically moved downtown over by a quarter of a mile and contributed to the devastation of Woodward."

Rashid steers past Cobo Arena, the Pistons' waterfront arena until they moved to the suburbs in the '80s, and the adjoining Joe Louis Arena, built with $26 million in city funds for the Red Wings hockey team (now owned by Ilitch) in 1979. "And now Ilitch wants another hockey arena, because he doesn't like Joe Louis [Arena]," says Rashid.

"We say in Detroit that we have a lousy class of rich people," he muses. "They dumped on the city, they abused it, they exploited it, they controlled it, and then they left it." Until the 1920s, Detroit's economy boasted a variety of small manufacturing industries. The rise of the auto industry put an end to that, says Rashid, by creating an economy of booms and busts and continuous plant closings and reopenings and employing a largely Southern-born labor force that erupted in racial antagonism each time the industry took a downturn. The Ford Motor Company, in particular, hopped from Detroit to suburban Highland Park to neighboring River Rouge, leaving crumbling factories and displaced lives in its wake. "Each time," according to Rashid, "[Henry Ford] built up a labor force, a tax base, and then abandoned it, and then foisted off the social costs of his erratic business, his layoffs, and all of that on the cities. It's a fascinating story of abuse of the public coffers."

In the 1980s General Motors, another auto giant that had fled to the suburbs, agreed to return to downtown Detroit—in exchange for the city's agreement to demolish Poletown, a thriving if poor neighborhood of ten thousand, to make way for a sprawling auto plant. Now there is talk that GM regards the Poletown plant as obsolete and is looking to move out of town again.[3]

Rashid drives back through downtown, finally stopping the car in a wasteland of empty lots behind the Fox Theater. This, he explains, is the site projected for parking for Ilitch's new baseball stadium. The city, through its powers of eminent domain, is in the process of seizing this spacious property from its private owners who use it as parking lots and handing it over to Ilitch at cost—to use as parking lots.

Ilitch and his supporters like to boast that the Tigers' owner hasn't demanded the total subsidies that other teams have extorted from their hometowns. The Tigers' 1997 program, for example, after a page of tributes to the old stadium that bears a striking resemblance to Fan Club materials, notes that "it became clear that a new facility was needed to replace the aging and venerable park" and that the new stadium's financing "will include $145 million from the Tigers, the highest team-based financing for a Major League Baseball facility since the Dodgers built Dodger Stadium in 1962." But like Dodger Stadium, which was built with private money on a gift of huge swathes of valuable public land, Ilitch's contribution comes with its own hidden subsidy: The Fan Club projects that *all* this "team-based" money will be covered by revenues from the city-donated parking lots.

It's a pattern that is all too familiar to lifelong Detroiters like Rashid. "One of the things that the auto companies did was make us hungry for the single interest," he says, surveying the wreckage of his city's downtown. "We're so used to being a single-industry town—it's too bad that our single industry is now pizza. Pizza and entertainment—it's now Mike Ilitch. We have ceded over to him one sixth of downtown."

It is the opening of another baseball season, the 86th for Tiger Stadium, the 102nd at the corner of Michigan and Trumbull. But Rashid and the remaining core members of the Fan Club—Kim Stroud, the Davidses, Bill Dow, Catherine Darin—no longer spend their days down in the Tiger Stadium bleachers that they lobbied to save. Press reports had already disclosed that Ilitch had been using the ninety-cent city ticket tax, earmarked for maintenance of Tiger Stadium once the 1970s renovations were complete, for such items as pizza pans at the Little Caesar's concessions stands at the stadium's new food court. Now, in the bitterest irony of all, the city has decreed that Ilitch will be allowed to use the surcharge to pay for the *demolition* of the old ballpark. Frank Rashid, who devoted ten years of his life to saving Tiger Stadium, cannot even go to say goodbye without helping finance its destruction.[4]

What began as a whim by five baseball-loving friends bloomed into a movement that held off the city's political and corporate leadership for almost a decade. And yet, in the end, they lost their war. "We did everything we could do, legally and politically," says Rashid, with more than a touch of sadness. "We used the system. We tried to believe in the system. I don't believe in the system anymore. I mean, I didn't really believe in it before, but I thought, well, give it a chance to work. But it clearly doesn't work. If you don't have money and power, the system will not work for you—that's one thing I've learned."

Notes

1. As of 2007 the United Artists was still standing, stripped of much of its ornamentation, as Ilitch sought a developer for the site who would either rehabilitate the theater or demolish it.

2. The Hudson's building was imploded in a televised ceremony in October 1998. Though officials had promised that it would be a controlled demolition, several chunks of debris landed atop the people-mover tracks, forcing it to be closed for several months. The dust cloud that had engulfed the thousands of onlookers who'd come to see the building fall, meanwhile, was later determined to have been contaminated with lead.

3. In 2004 the Michigan Supreme Court belatedly overturned the two-decade-old court ruling that had allowed the city to use eminent domain to remove Poletown's residents for a private project. As of 2006 the GM Poletown plant employed about three thousand workers, fewer than half what the company had originally promised; it was also ranked on the national Toxic Release Inventory as one of the country's top polluters.

4. In September 1999 Tiger Stadium closed its gates for the last time, following an emotional final game that closed with a post-game ceremony hosted by Ernie Harwell. The next spring, Comerica Park opened and, whether because of lingering affection for the old ballpark or because the Tigers were mired in the basement, was an instant failure, with attendance dipping as low as seventeen thousand per game, next to last in the American League, in 2003, when the Tigers lost a league-record 119 games.

All the while, the old ballpark sat undisturbed at the corner of Michigan and Trumbull while city leaders debated what to do with the site. (Among the suggested uses: a Wal-Mart or a "criminal justice campus featuring jails, courthouses, and law enforcement headquarters.") After a last-ditch effort by a group calling itself the Navin Field Consortium—which included Frank Rashid, Kim Stroud, and other veterans of the Tiger Stadium Fan Club—to reduce the stadium in size and use it for minor-league baseball failed, the city finally announced in 2006 that Tiger Stadium would be demolished by year's end and replaced by condos and retail stores. As of 2007, though, no developer had been found for the project.

No one, meanwhile, has determined what happened to the ticket-surcharge funds, which Ilitch had exhausted by 2005, meaning that Detroit taxpayers will be on the hook for even more money to pay for Tiger Stadium's wrecking ball.

6 Home Field Advantage

For most of us, we feel that supply and demand, the market, capitalism has got us where we are today in the United States, and so there ought to be some sense, some obligation, to allow that to continue. —*Randy Johnson, president, Orlando Area Sports Commission*

This is not about a very rich guy born with a spoon in his mouth that is trying to add to his riches and got the community to build something for him. This is the community saying—in the form of all the major companies—"This is good for the community, let's go forward with this." —*Jerry Colangelo, owner of the Phoenix Suns and Arizona Diamondbacks*

Detroit may offer a dramatic example, but it's hardly alone. In most cities, stadium deals are less an exception to standard urban policy than part of the everyday wheeling and dealing that goes on for public money. The question, then, is if corporate welfare, whether for sports teams or auto plants, is so obviously unprofitable for local governments, why do they keep shelling out the dough?

Frank Rashid spent ten years watching Detroit politicians fight for a new baseball stadium, and the self-interest of elected officials in giant giveaways certainly seems obvious to him. "The local politicians, particularly the mayor and the county executive, know that they get far more mileage out of having a big new project than out of a renovation," he explains. "They have the ability to say who gets the contracts, whose land is used, which developers are employed, which bond attorneys do it—and all of those people are the people who contribute to their campaign war chests." That, he believes, is why expensive projects like new stadiums win out over small-scale ones like the Tiger Stadium Fan Club's Cochrane Plan: "Not because they are intrinsically better for the city or better for the team or anything. There is a political interest in doing it."

This tendency has only worsened as local economies have become more dependent on footloose corporations for their economic well-being, says corporate-welfare researcher Greg LeRoy. "The Fortune 500 is still killing off a thousand to twenty-five hundred fulltime jobs a day, so it's easy for companies to get governors and mayors to compete for the few remaining good projects that are happening," he observes. "And now it's really an expectation of a company, if you're going to relocate or construct a major new facility, you'd probably lose your job as CFO of that company if you didn't go shake a state down for eight figures. It's just part of your job description now."

If there is anyone who resists these deals, interestingly, it's usually state legislatures and city councils, which reap less of the publicity benefits and are left with the task of filling the resulting budget shortfalls. Says LeRoy, "There's a lot of very skeptical state legislatures that have been trying to rein in their governors, and city councils that have been trying to rein in their mayors—it really is an executive–legislative tension. You see that theme over and over again."

As for sports team owners, they can count not only on their lure as economic investors (albeit a rather small one, proportionally) but also on the popularity of their product, which can't be matched by any mere car company. Politicians already predisposed to salivating at the prospect of announcing a new "job-creation" deal can get absolutely fanatical when the deal involves their favorite teams. Minnesota Governor Arne Carlson, a key backer of new sports facilities in his state, declared he wanted to be a college sports booster when he retired from politics. Cleveland Mayor Michael White spent months talking of little but the Browns to local media during the fight over that team. And in an exceptional display of sports exuberance, San Francisco Mayor Willie Brown declared that he would "do a hundred [campaign] appearances in a week if [he] had to" in campaigning for a new stadium for the 49ers and whooped and hollered for several minutes when the favorable referendum results came in. "He wasn't close to hysterical," said a radio reporter who watched as Brown, a 49ers cap on his head, climbed onto a table and swilled champagne from the bottle, screaming at the top of his lungs. "He was hysterical."

The free tickets that are commonly distributed to local political leaders no doubt help grease these political wheels. But the most crucial asset for sports owners is the likelihood of a legislative body for whom a sports star like Jerry Rice, or even a high-powered owner like Edward Bennett Williams, is a celebrity of the first order. As Daniel Finley, county executive of Wisconsin's Waukesha County, told the Sports Facilities Finance conference, "You send Robin Yount or Hank Aaron into the state capital, and they melt."

Add in the generally chummy relationship between politicians and local business leaders, and you have a scenario ripe for exploitation. "It's incredibly incestuous," says Ricky Rask, a child-care activist in Minneapolis who became a leader in that city's fight against public spending on a new ballpark. "Everybody's got a finger in here or a finger in there. They all play golf together." Fears of losing out to other cities, Rask is convinced, are just a smokescreen for politicians whose ties to the old-boys' network are so strong that they are eager to provide for their friends, even at the cost of hundreds of millions of dollars to the public treasury.

Paying to Win

Fortunately for the residents of cities run by these subsidy-happy politicians, local democracy has another means of controlling the public purse: referenda, through which voters can override the will of their elected officials at the ballot box. Not as fortunately, the electoral process has proven to be as susceptible to the power of big money as the politicians themselves.

The stadium-funding opposition has taken many forms in different cities, from established anti-tax or economic-justice groups to ad hoc groups of individual citizens. But in every case, they have one commonality: None of them has even a fraction of the money of the stadium proponents. "It was beyond David versus Goliath," moaned Campaign to Stop the Giveaway organizer Jim Ross to San Francisco reporters, after his campaign against public funding for the 49ers' new stadium was outspent 20–1 by stadium backers. "David at least had a sling. We were throwing rocks with our hands."

A rare glimpse behind the scenes of a pro-stadium campaign was provided at the 1997 Sports Facilities Finance conference, when Jay Cross, president of the Miami Heat basketball team, transfixed listeners with his team's tale of extracting a new sports arena from their county government. By the fall of 1996, the Miami Heat had spent their entire eight-year existence at the Miami Arena, a combined hockey–basketball facility that Dade County had spent $53 million to construct in 1988. Unfortunately for the county, that was the exact moment when the economics of basketball underwent a seismic shift: The National Basketball Association was soaring in popularity, and luxury suites were just taking off as a major moneymaker. Miami Arena, with its paltry sixteen suites and fifteen-thousand-seat capacity, instantly found itself on the small end of league facilities. As stadium consultant Marc Ganis described it, "That facility was obsolete—economically obsolete—before the concrete dried."

The Florida Panthers hockey club, which had shared the Miami Arena with the Heat since the team's founding in 1993, had already whipsawed Dade County and neighboring Broward County into a bidding war for its services, a battle ultimately won by Broward with a bid of $212 million. Heat owner Mickey Arison, the billionaire owner of Carnival Cruise Lines, followed with his own demands, proposing first $60 million in renovations to the still-new arena, then a whole new building of his own. By leveraging the threat to join the Panthers in Broward County, Arison ultimately arrived at an agreement for a $162.5 million arena on the Miami waterfront, of which Dade County would pay three quarters, the team the rest.

The Miami populace, however, was somewhat less obliging. A local lawyer—"an annoying little man," as Cross would describe him to his listeners at the Grand Hyatt—gathered forty-eight thousand signatures to put the arena deal on the November ballot. The election was just eight weeks away. Polls were running 60–40 against the publicly funded arena, and the leading candidate for Dade County mayor was a vocal opponent. Cross, sensing impending disaster, came to a decision. "This is a political campaign," he recalled thinking. "This is no different than if you're running for the Senate, or governor, or mayor. We're talking about winning the hearts and minds of the voters."

To that end, Cross brought in Mike Murphy of Murphy Pintak Gaulter, the firm that had managed the successful gubernatorial campaigns of such GOP standouts as New Jersey's Christine Todd Whitman, Wisconsin's Tommy Thompson, and Michigan's John Engler. The first thing Murphy told the team, according to Cross, was to "get ready to spend some serious coin." A typical mayoral campaign will cost around $2 million over the course of a year; the Coalition for a Greater Miami—the political action committee formed by the team to run the pro-arena campaign—would ultimately spend an astonishing $3.7 million in just eight weeks to convince Dade County voters of the rightness of their cause.

"The next thing we found out from our polls," continued Cross, "was that Pat Riley's one of the most popular guys around." Riley, the longtime NBA coach (and motivational book author) whose contract with the Heat gave him part-ownership of the team, became the centerpiece of the hundreds of TV commercials that all those millions of PAC dollars were buying, with an escalating series of messages (in both English and Spanish) designed to peak in the days right before the election. In the earliest commercials, a smiling, shirt-sleeved Riley, a basketball under his arm, cajoled viewers with promises of "a fantastic waterfront park; a safe, fun place for families to enjoy, with shops, restaurants, and a championship arena" as a computer-generated flyby of the new arena filled the screen.

By the week before the election, the televised images had changed. The message now "went negative," explained Cross. Riley's friendly appeal was gone; in its place were images of vacant lots and a voiceover that intoned, "This is the waterfront the politicians want to save. Broken concrete. A haven for criminals. Dade County deserves better: a safe new waterfront park for all our families. Existing tourist taxes pay the bill, so you don't have to. But some politicians want to kill the new waterfront park and keep the tourist money for their wasteful spending." Although Cross says proudly that the team never directly threatened to leave town if the arena weren't built, the possibility became a less than subtle theme of the ads as well, as residents were depicted reciting the campaign's new slogan: "Vote No, so the Heat won't go."

The arena campaign, befitting the money and expertise brought to it, was slick, subtle, and convincing. By the week before the vote, the Heat had wooed the support of the mayor as well. ("He realized that driving the local millionaire out of town is not exactly smart politics," bragged Cross.)

The final vote was 59 percent to 41 percent, in favor of the Heat. For $3.7 million, the basketball team had bought a 19-percentage-point swing in the polls.[1]

Corporate Cheerleaders

The Heat's successful manipulation of public opinion points up the difficulty of pinning down "public sentiment" on corporate welfare—it all depends on how you ask the question, and those intent on manipulating the process will always ask the question in the way that will most benefit their interests. "The public" doesn't, by and large, see the behind-the-scenes maneuvering that Cross described. For most people, the story consists of what appears on TV and in the print media—and that picture often bears little resemblance to reality.

The media are seldom credited as key boosters of stadium deals, if only because, for the owners and their allies, they can seem like an enemy of their PR attempts, uncovering uncomfortable details of the deal going down. Certainly, much stadium reporting is negative—with all the dirty facts of stadium deals, even a lazy reporter can't help but stumble over a few by accident.

Yet a few incisive articles do little to change the *premises* on which the stadium debate is reported, which often seem lifted straight from the teams' PR manuals. As media critics point out, a few critical articles can easily coexist with a greater editorial push in favor of a project. "There are so many self-deluded reporters in the mainstream media who sneak the truth into one story out of every twenty they write and think they've done their job, because the truth got out," observes Jim Naureckas, editor of the media-watch magazine *Extra!* But the impact of news, he notes, is in its repetition, and occasionally showing glimpses of one side of the story can serve to strengthen the apparent "objectivity" of press coverage that is in fact skewed mightily in one direction.

What's more important than isolated articles, as far as public sentiment is concerned, is how the media frame the issue. Even when critical of some fine point of a deal, they seldom question the need for a new stadium, invariably editorializing against legislators who "hunker down behind the public opinion polls." In this context, public opposition is presented as a mere temporary obstacle to the inevitable course of progress, which will ultimately—*should* ultimately—result in a new sports facility being built.

In Seattle, for example, after voters had narrowly defeated a proposal to build a new stadium for the Mariners baseball team in September 1995, the *Seattle Times*—which had provided free ad space for the pro-stadium campaign—editorialized that this represented "a striking affirmation of the region's commitment to baseball," adding, "half of King County voters would tax themselves to keep the team there." (That slightly more than half had voted *not* to tax themselves wasn't deemed worthy of notice.) The next day, the paper ran a front-page story headlined "Stadium Not Yet Dead," in which it suggested ways that the state government could go ahead with the stadium despite the popular vote. One month later, the state legislature would do just that.

This type of reporting, in which the stadium campaign is itself portrayed almost as a sporting event where the paper roots along with the home team, is endemic to stadium coverage. Two days before the public vote on that team's new football stadium, a *San Francisco Examiner* headline read: "49ers drive toward goal as clock ticks down." In this "pennant-race" coverage, stories become more focused on who's winning or losing than on digging out the truthfulness of the two sides' arguments. The day before the 49ers referendum, a *San Francisco Chronicle* columnist led off his column on a debate between San Francisco Mayor Willie Brown and California state senator Quentin Kopp over the new 49ers stadium by writing that Brown had "won on points," beneath the headline "Brown Wins With His Jabbing." It was left to the readers' imagination whether or not the debate had revealed anything of substance.

"Who Are You Guys?"

As with elected officials, there's no shortage of possible reasons that the media are so owner-friendly.

The most straightforward theory was summarized by Beth Hawkins of the *Minneapolis City Pages* in her analysis of that city's media coverage of stadium deals: "Sports editors and writers freely acknowledge the symbiosis that exists between the news media and pro sports. Newspapers create excitement among fans, who drive up ticket sales. And while pro teams themselves don't create a lot of advertising, a thriving franchise attracts readers to the paper who might not otherwise pick it up." In Seattle, Hawkins reported, press runs of newspapers the day after a game are increased by anywhere from 10 to 20 percent, depending on which team played and whether it won or lost.

But newspapers, especially newspaper *owners*, have a stake in stadiums and other development projects that goes beyond mere sales figures. Modern media enterprises are themselves major corporations, whose publishers often share team owners' interests in promoting public subsidies of business interests and downtown development. In many cities, including Cleveland, Seattle, Milwaukee, and Minneapolis, local newspaper publishers have helped fund pro-stadium lobbying efforts, or even registered as lobbyists themselves to press legislators on their hometown team's behalf.

The most egregious example of media self-interest may be the *Minneapolis Star Tribune*, whose then publisher, John Cowles Jr., raised $10.5 million to help city officials buy land for the Metrodome in the late '70s—in exchange for the right to develop some two hundred acres of land surrounding the site. (*Star Tribune* staffers later took out a full-page ad disassociating themselves from the paper's Metrodome coverage.) Following Cowles's death in 1983, his successors at Cowles Media continued to carry the flame for the Twins' stadium dreams, making unspecified donations to the team's lobbying arm. The donations are well worth the gamble: If a new stadium is built, the paper stands to cash in on the parking lots that would rise on the downtown property that it acquired in the Metrodome deal.

Media owners are quick to deny that these interlocking business deals represent a conflict of interest. They claim that their papers maintain an impenetrable wall between reporters and management and furthermore point to the critical stories they have published on stadium projects (often alongside pro-stadium editorials). The *Seattle Times* went so far as to cite its coverage of its own gift of free ads to the Mariners' pro-stadium campaign as a sign of its impartiality: Executive editor Michael Francher asserted in an editorial that "it was a safe bet" that such a story would never have been published in "a newspaper whose reporting is affected by the publisher of the editorial page."

But the experience of numerous reporters has been that the division between management and editorial, far from being an impenetrable wall, is instead more like a thin screen, across which publishers can subtly influence news coverage while staying technically out of sight. One of the most insightful looks into the inner workings of journalistic self-censorship is *Fear and Favor in the Newsroom*, an hour-long documentary produced by California Newsreel. In it the filmmakers compiled the stories of various reporters who were forced out of their jobs when their zeal for journalism grew stronger than their willingness to toe the corporate line. They cited the example of an award-winning consumer reporter being accused of "bias" for correctly predicting that a nuclear power plant was driving its parent company into bankruptcy, and told how a veteran newsman was fired by NBC for trying to report on Iraqi civilian casualties of U.S. bombing during the Gulf War. In story after story, journalists told how, despite claims of a hands-off policy, on "controversial" issues, management can easily make its wishes known—and carried out.

60 Minutes producer Lowell Bergman, for example, while insisting that he has been able to get unpleasant truths across on his program, told the filmmakers, "It's never been as heavy-handed as someone saying, 'You can't do that story.' But I think it's understood that when you get into that area that you are in a dangerous area."

Sydney Schanberg, the Pulitzer Prize–winning journalist, had his *New York Times* career ended when he stepped on one too many toes. "It happens sort of by osmosis," he explained in the documentary. "There are no notes posted on the bulletin board. Senior editors usually do not tell desk editors like the city editor, 'We don't want you to cover this, we want you to cover that instead.'" Nonetheless, Schanberg found out the hard way that there are lines not to be crossed; when he used his column to criticize the *Times* and other local papers for focusing on soft news like restaurant openings rather than exposing government wrongdoing, he was shoved out the door.

Schanberg's mistake, according to his former colleague John Hess, was in trying to cover New York City in the same way he would Cambodia. "The paper finds it really hard," Hess told the filmmakers, "to tolerate this kind of hard, controversial journalism about the people the publisher is eating with every day." Although the desired slant is seldom phrased in terms of pleasing corporate sponsors, that is still the hidden message, explained Wendell Rawls Jr., an *Atlanta Constitution* staffer who quit when a popular muckraking editor was forced out in favor of a new chief brought in from *USA Today*. "This attitude pervades the entire newspaper, that we are trying to make people feel better about themselves somehow, rather than letting them hold up a mirror to themselves."[2]

Perhaps it's this kind of unstated pressure that produces in journalists what Frank Rashid of the Tiger Stadium Fan Club calls "studied incompetence." New reporters coming onto the stadium beat, he says, seemed ignorant even of their own newspaper's previous coverage of the story. "You'd think at least that person would have the intelligence, especially in this computer age, to go back and check the stories that had been written before. I don't think that *ever* happens. We were having to reorient reporters into the story consistently."

On one occasion, Rashid recalls, he wound up calling the *Detroit Free Press* to complain about an inaccurate story about the Fan Club. He pointed out to a city desk editor that the reporter had printed inaccurate statements by the group's opponents about the Fan Club, statements that the reporter himself had to have known were untrue.

The editor, according to Rashid, replied with indignation, "What do you expect? Monaghan has made money. He's paid his dues. Who are you guys?"

"I really appreciated the honesty," says Rashid. "But, damn! None of us is disreputable. We're all people who are solid citizens, but we don't have money. Solid citizens without money don't count as well as somebody who's got a big corporation. So it doesn't matter that we worked for several years on the issue, or established a track record of being credible, or anything like that.[3]"

The Usual Suspects

Finally, no picture of the urban power structure would be complete without the group that the *Seattle Times* referred to as "The Civic Power Brokers No One Elected." They are the bond lawyers who are called in to give legal authorization for deals between cities and banks when major bond issues are involved, and they are part of the massive network of profit makers that has been making money off urban debt—especially major deals like new stadiums—for decades.

In Seattle the law firm of Preston, Gates & Ellis stands to make a cool $145,000 for its role as legal counsel in the city council's authorization of $336 million in bonds to pay for a new home for the Seattle Mariners. The firm, "the king of bondsmakers in Washington State," according to the *Times*, handled 60 percent of the state's bond work in 1996.

It is up to their attorneys to declare bonds legally enforceable. If they do, and the bond issue is approved, they collect a fee, sometimes topping $1 million. The role that bond lawyers play in encouraging municipalities to go into debt over massive construction projects may be largely behind the scenes, but it's hardly a secret. Jordan Brower, a Seattle activist, told the *Seattle Times*, "These guys take council members and 'educate' them about finances. 'Here's a nice building that you can be remembered by.'"

How influential are bond lawyers and the huge firms they represent? The Sports Facilities Finance conference in New York was officially the Municipal Issuers' & Sports Franchises' Symposium on Sports Facilities Finance—note the "issuers." Hobnobbing among the representatives of professional sports teams and urban governments were lawyers and representatives of some of the country's biggest Wall Street law firms. The convention wouldn't have happened without them.

One Dollar, One Vote

For owners and their political allies, money provides a way around not just the media but the public as well. Having learned from the experiences of franchises like the Heat, teams will seldom go into a public vote without a multimillion-dollar budget for TV commercials and other PR strategies. The biggest spender of all: Microsoft cofounder Paul Allen, who, in a rush to get a football-stadium referendum on the Washington state ballot before his option to buy the Seattle Seahawks expired, simply offered the state $4.2 million to avoid the time-consuming signature-gathering phase usually required to put a proposal on the state ballot. The state legislature happily took him up on the offer, and Allen went on to spend another $5 million (in six weeks) on lobbying the public for a positive vote.

When Minnesota's Metropolitan Sports Facility Commission began hearings on publicly funding a new stadium, says activist Ricky Rask, they were careful to exclude the public in every way possible, shifting meeting dates at the last minute and denying time for public comment. The third or fourth time Rask showed up at a "public hearing" and was denied time to speak, she says, "I stood up and I said, 'Excuse me, but if you're not going to allow public testimony, then you need to retract this statement. Do one or the other, but make it clear about what you're going to do.'" The commissioners tried to silence Rask—"Oh, gee, they were mad!" she recalls—but with TV news cameras on the scene (at Rask's invitation), they had little choice but to open the meetings to public testimony.

Frank Rashid and Kim Stroud had a similar experience at the Wayne County hearings on allocating public money for a new stadium for the Tigers. "It was supposed to be a public hearing," Rashid says. "We heard about it a day before. Kim called up and said what time is the hearing, and they said it begins at noon. We stayed up all night, worked on materials—we knew that they were going to approve it, but we thought we had at least to go down there."

When the Fan Club activists arrived at the county building, they were told that the hearing had in fact started at 9 a.m., though it was continuing through the afternoon. Rashid put his name down to speak, and they settled in to wait for the public comment section. "Finally we got an agenda for the afternoon session, and there was a vote scheduled—and *after* the vote, there was public comment." Only one "member of the public" did get to speak before the vote, he notes wryly: Denise Ilitch Lites, Tigers owner Mike Ilitch's daughter.

The Carrot and the Stick

There are cities, of course, where the coalition doesn't fall neatly together, where a stubborn politician, or a particularly skeptical press, stops a deal for the time being. But mayors and editors come and go, while businessmen such as sports owners stay on—and if the wait is too long for an impatient owner, he can always sell at a profit to someone else who will play the stadium game in his place.

Moreover, for stadiums as for other corporate subsidies, the burden is on the local government once the deal is in place. If local government fails to live up to its end of the bargain, the corporation can simply take its business elsewhere; but a corporation that fails to come through with the jobs or economic development it promised a locality can simply shrug its shoulders and blame the vagaries of the economy—assuming anyone ever even thinks to ask.

Over the past few years, cities and states have begun exploring methods of holding corporations to their end of the bargain, specifically through "clawback" legislation that would force companies to repay their subsidies if job or economic goals are not met within a specified time. But as these depend on enforcement by the same public officials who approve the deals in the first place, corporations are seldom if ever held accountable for their actions.[4]

Arthur Rolnick, a vice-president at the Minneapolis Federal Reserve who has campaigned for years against "the economic war among the states," can't see local politicians ever putting an end to corporate welfare. "In some sense, they come out of it a hero," he says. "The businesses that are involved with this thing, they love this deal, they're getting big benefits, and you can bet that they're going to support this guy's campaign. For the public, they're against it, maybe, but it's one of many issues, and when it comes time to vote, there's a million other issues, and this thing's probably already been done, and so they move on. So it looks like, the way the political aspects of it work, there isn't much downside for these guys."

The downside for the public, though, is another story—often several stories, in fact, as different interests fight to prevent the brunt of the corporate welfare burden from falling on them. Nowhere were these competing interests more evident than in the case of baseball's oldest stadium, which became one of its earliest stadium battlegrounds: Chicago's Comiskey Park.

Notes

1. One tactic, little noticed at the time, that aided the Heat in their arena vote was to make a last-minute switch in their financing plan: Instead of the county putting up the money for construction costs and collecting rent from the team, the team would pay the up-front costs and receive a $6.4 million a year "operating subsidy" from the county. At the end of the day, the team would have the same annual expenses but could claim that the arena was now a "privately financed" project. As for taxpayers, the *Palm Beach Post* reported in 2004 that they were losing more than $15 million a year on the city's three local arenas.

2. Sportswriter John Stebbins noted that reporters don't always have to be told which side their bread is buttered on: "I don't think it was any secret in the *Tampa Tribune* newsroom that if we lose the Bucs, there's going to be a good chunk of advertising revenue out the window." Though as his former editor John Sugg observed, the *Trib* didn't leave anything to chance: The managing editor of the paper in the mid-'90s, when the Buccaneers were seeking a new stadium, directed his staff that "[the paper's] coverage of the stadium [would] be limited to finding solutions for it to be built."

3. Matters didn't improve even after Detroit's new stadium was completed in 2000. When baseball's All-Star Game was held at Comerica Park in 2005, the Associated Press ran a story asserting that "even [Tiger Stadium's] supporters acknowledge it had to be replaced because of its crumbling infrastructure, obstructed views and lack of many luxury suites." Kim Stroud

of the Tiger Stadium Fan Club spotted a prepublication copy of the story on the wire and immediately phoned AP writer Larry Lage to point out that Tiger Stadium supporters had acknowledged no such thing. Lage, according to Stroud, agreed to ask his editor to change the line to "even some supporters," but it ended up published as originally written.

4. On tour for his 2005 book *The Great American Jobs Scam*, corporate subsidy expert Greg LeRoy was fond of showing off the "business assistance form" that had been filed with the state of Minnesota by a Dairy Queen seeking $275,515 in state subsidies. Under "job creation goals" the company had listed "1 new job" with an hourly wage of "$4.50/hr."

7 Local Heroes

If you have to survive, you don't have time to get discouraged.
—*Wentworth Gardens community activist Hallie Amey*

John Aranza has always been somewhat leery of radicals who make a lot of sound and fury for their various causes. His own community activism was centered on electoral politics, his church, and the Boys and Girls Clubs—until the Chicago White Sox demanded a replacement for eighty-year-old Comiskey Park, then threatened to leave town, and his life was changed forever.

The White Sox threatening to leave might not have changed Hallie Amey's life all that much if the team hadn't ended up putting her neighbors' homes in the bulldozer's path. When it became clear that the community she had called home for decades was in jeopardy, the spirited senior citizen decided to do something about it. But then again, Amey has been a community activist for just about her whole life. More than forty years a resident in Wentworth Gardens, a small Chicago housing project on the city's south side, Amey long ago learned that if you wanted to get something done, you have to do it yourself.

It was early spring 1986, and one of baseball's most storied franchises was about to set in motion an unlikely chain of events that would see a historic landmark gutted, dozens of homes and businesses torn to the ground, a new trend in stadium architecture and a newly dominant architectural firm emerge, and, perhaps most unexpectedly, a remarkable convergence occur in the lives of John Aranza, Hallie Amey, and so many more.

Warning Bells

By the mid-1980s, the relatively new owners of the White Sox had escalated their rumblings of dissatisfaction with seventy-five-year-old Comiskey Park and its urban neighborhood. When Jerry Reinsdorf and Edward M. Einhorn purchased the team from Bill Veeck in 1981, it didn't take long for them to decide they wanted more—more television revenues, more attendance at games, more profit from the franchise. Their complaints about the state of the old stadium, the safety of its neighborhood, and their ability to turn a profit grew louder, and their flirtation with St. Petersburg, Florida, to move their team to that region grew more intense.

Local fans began to get alarmed. "We were afraid to speak up then," says Aranza. "I'm no activist, but I'll tell you what I did. It's the first time I ever did this in my life."

Aranza grew up on the South Side of Chicago, home to the city's famous meatpacking industry, century-old Irish neighborhoods, monstrous housing projects, and many of its most infamous politicians. He and his wife make their home in Bridgeport—a white ethnic Chicago neighborhood (one of the city's oldest) known for producing, among other things, future mayors of the city. On Memorial Day 1986, the Aranzas had relatives over for a barbecue on their back patio. From their small bungalow, John could see the light towers of Comiskey Park, and the team's uncertain future was very much on his mind. Aranza remembers the day when, standing there at the family barbecue, he realized he'd had enough. The White Sox were going to move, he told his wife. "You know what?" he remembers saying. "I got a feeling they're gonna move the ballclub. They're going to tear down the ballpark. It's terrible, I don't know what to do."

Aranza asked his wife to get him something he could make a sign with. She returned with an old pillowcase, on which he composed a homemade sign, "Save Our Sox."

With two pieces of bamboo holding up the pillowcase, Aranza made his way the few blocks to Comiskey Park, where he stood on the curb with his homemade sign. When passersby questioned him, Aranza could only reply, "I've got a feeling the ballpark's going to be torn down." Some folks ignored him; others asked what they could do. "'I don't know,' I said. 'Write your congressman. Write the owners. Write state legislators,' I says, 'I don't know who. Write local TV people. Just something.'" After some time the bamboo broke, and Aranza just held his sign in his hands. "I must have looked like somebody on a desert island, waiting for a passing ship to see it, to rescue me, to rescue the ballpark," he says. "I never did this in my life. Never in my life."

His one-man demonstration might have been the end of it but for similar concerns that were plaguing Mary O'Connell, a lifelong White Sox fan despite living on the city's North Side. (Chicago has many historically deep divides between its North and South sides—the North being home largely to the city's elegant tree-lined streets and upper-class white residents, and the South the traditional manufacturing base and the town's black and ethnic white working-class populations. The city's baseball fans are as deeply split, with the National League Cubs making their home and taking their fan base from the North Side, and the White Sox firmly a South Side team.)

"I saw an article in one of the Chicago papers talking about how the White Sox needed a new stadium," O'Connell says. She was surprised at the paper's easy acceptance that Comiskey Park had supposedly outlived its useful life.

Alarmed, O'Connell wrote to the team management and received a cursory response, referring to an enclosed one-paragraph engineering report. She compares the terse justification for tearing down the old stadium to a decision to condemn a house because the roof leaked. "Wouldn't you expect that there would be some kind of analysis or numbers, some kind of detailed description about the state of the girders or the concrete or the wiring or the masonry, or something that would say, 'Well, here's this problem, and in order to repair that it would cost this much money'?" O'Connell found herself wondering. "But it was nothing, it was just this one little one-paragraph thing."

O'Connell responded with an op-ed piece in the *Chicago Sun-Times*. It was after the piece ran that an acquaintance suggested she get in touch with John Aranza.

Saving the Team

"Now when Mary called me," Aranza says, "she said, 'John, we're starting this group and I really want you to be a part of it.' And I didn't want to be. I never did anything, I stayed away from activism and groups, however you want to call it, my entire life, only because none ever appealed to me.

"She would beg me on the phone and I said, 'No, but good luck to you,' and she kept calling me, so I agreed to go to one of the meetings that she had proposed, and it was out of that the Save Our Sox was formed."

The group's initial focus was on keeping the team in the city and preventing the destruction of Comiskey Park. "Our argument was why rip down one of these [old stadiums] and build a brand-new monstrosity that nobody would want to go and see," says O'Connell. "Why not play up the fact that you've got these two great old ball-parks? Use that to attract people and get people to come." If anything, O'Connell and her colleagues argued, public money could be used to preserve and maintain the site's history and appeal. To that end, they campaigned to have the old stadium declared a national monument, to be run by the National Park Service. "If you're going to use tax dollars," says O'Connell, "let's build up the charm and intimacy of the historic ballpark that we have."

Nicknamed the "Baseball Palace of the World" in its heyday, Comiskey Park's fan-friendly construction (both decks of seating stretched to the playing field, putting spectators right up against the action) and colorful history (Shoeless Joe Jackson and the scandalous Black Sox of 1919 played there, along with the 1959 pennant-winning team) made it a proud city landmark, especially for the team's traditionally working-class core of fans. Doug Bukowski, a Chicago writer and member of Save Our Sox, points out that Comiskey's architecture was designed to blend with neighboring Bridgeport's working-class feel. Its arches, which extended around the old ballpark, "suggest the windows of a church or one of the multistory factories that were once so common here," Bukowski writes in *Baseball Palace of the World*, his sometimes humorous, ultimately wrenching look at the old stadium's last season. "[Charles] Comiskey put his ballpark in the middle of a neighborhood filled with people no more than a generation removed from the fields of the old country. They still viewed life the way peasants did and sought connections between work and play and worship. Comiskey provided that with his ballpark."

Members of sos canvassed outside the old stadium, trying to attract sympathetic White Sox fans to their petition campaign and their membership ranks. And many were drawn in that way. Newton Suwe was in graduate school at the time and attended many games at Comiskey. "One day I went to a Sox game," he remembers, "and there were some radicals out there protesting, trying to form an organization called Save Our Sox, and before I knew it I was one of the radicals."

Although he had always been interested in politics and sympathetic to liberal and progressive causes, Suwe had never been involved with a grassroots group like sos before. As was true for many of the group's members, he found this an issue that cut close to home. "You almost feel like, 'Geez, is sports that important to me?' And in a sense yes and no. It sort of struck to close to home."

In his book, Bukowski writes of his first sos meeting, in November 1986. Attendees were asked what had brought them to the organization. "One man stood up in a room full of strangers and said that whenever he got really depressed, he liked to drive by the ballpark; it made him feel good. No skyboxes or playoff tickets or official team products necessary, just a swing by the park."

"I also looked at it as a political and social issue," Bukowski says now, "like, we're going to be using tax dollars to build a new stadium. Corporate welfare. If some other company . . . if I knew they were getting corporate welfare, would I get involved in an organization? Probably not. I'd be upset about it, but I probably wouldn't get involved.

"Baseball and sports no longer mean what they once did," continues Bukowski, with more than a hint of bitterness. "They've transformed themselves into a major entertainment industry, grossly amoral, which I find offensive. What I was doing, in retrospect, was objecting to that, trying to perpetuate sports as I had thought they existed during my childhood and youth."

"I always felt like I was a part of it because it was my soul speaking out," Aranza says. "It was taking away my youth, and I'm sure it was for other people. Taking away their touchstone, taking away their tradition. Like losing somebody—you know that some things maybe are inevitable, but it's wrong the way it happened. Or you grieve, and you know you'll always grieve, and I do."

In their flyers, petitions, and public statements, sos argued that the team could obtain any needed amenities by simply renovating the historic old park. "Should all of Chicago . . . be in the style of the Loop and suburban expressway corridor buildings, with windows that don't open, 24-hour security guards, and steel-and-glass vertical ice cube trays?" read a glossy sos pamphlet distributed in 1987. "Or is there a place for Comiskey Park, with its tubular railings and wooden seats and overhangs like the balconies of the long-lost neighborhoods of our youth?"

To that end they campaigned and petitioned, held public meetings and lobbied their legislators. At its peak the group was able to generate five thousand signatures on its petition to preserve the stadium, and some positive press coverage. But its core membership was never very large.

Bukowski thinks there are several reasons that there never was a massive outpouring of citywide support for the group and its cause. "The fan base for the White Sox tended to be blue-collar. And blue-collar America since the 1970s has taken it on the chin. People with mortgage concerns, job concerns, aren't going to have the psychic capital to expend on stadium issues, no matter how much they love the ballpark. They've got bread and butter to worry about." It also probably helped that the Chicago newspapers waged an all-out campaign to support a new stadium. In 1986 the *Tribune* editorialized: "The ailing mid-South Side needs the economic boost it will get if the rundown Comiskey Park is replaced with an attractive, multi-use stadium." Without economic figures to back up its contention, the *Tribune* turned to more ephemeral claims: "The value of a professional sports team to an urban area is difficult to measure in dollars and cents. The jobs and tax revenue generated may not look impressive in hard figures. But add in what the presence of the team contributes to the overall attraction of living in the area and visiting it, and it becomes immense." That the neighborhood already had a renowned facility, one that with some renovation costing far fewer dollars could provide just that appeal, was ignored.

But, of course, some working-class Chicagoans did get involved with the campaign—united, more than anything, by a feeling that in losing the historic ballpark they were losing part of their collective memory.

Comiskey Park was built on what had been, in the 1880s, a public dump. Legend has it that infielder Luke Appling once tripped over something during a game in the 1930s. Play was stopped, and when the grounds crew went to investigate by raking the infield, they found he had stumbled over an old teapot coming up out of the dirt. Some fifty years later, John Aranza sneaked into the demolition site of his beloved stadium. "I went down in these deep trenches, which were way over my head, and on the sides of these trenches are layers of history, layers of earth. Bricks, wood, bottles. And I was just picking up things to verify what Comiskey was, even before it was built."

There's still a note of wonder in his voice, almost ten years later. "I found an old saucepan, in a more shallow trench where they took out the left field wall."

Though it was rusty, Aranza could see that the saucepan was a blue and white speckled pot—a leftover design from a bygone era. Familiar with the Appling tale, and so many other Comiskey Park legends, Aranza was overwhelmed by the history he had just uncovered. "And I thought to myself, my God, like Aladdin's lamp I'm holding in my hands, just verifying a wonderful piece of baseball lore."

In the Bulldozer's Way

And then there were the residents of South Armour Square, low-income and elderly, whose very homes were threatened because of Reinsdorf and Einhorn's plans. The owners of the White Sox had initially hoped to pull their team out of South Armour Square, the inner-city neighborhood that along with Bridgeport surrounded Comiskey Park, using the need for a new stadium as a chance to get into what was assumed would be a more profitable suburban location. First targeting the southwest suburb of Addison, Reinsdorf and company promised significant benefits if residents voted for the proposed stadium in a local advisory referendum: The state would supposedly receive $100 million in annual economic activity, and twenty-five hundred jobs would be created. But White Sox management ran into strident opposition in Addison. Local residents, worrying about a destructive change in their quiet community, and local environmentalists, fearing a threat to the region's nationally protected wetlands, were organized and vocal in their opposition. After an unfavorable referendum vote, the White Sox owners turned their sights elsewhere.

As location after profitable location proved unworkable, the team had little choice but to return to the same neighborhood it had months earlier rejected as economically unsound and physically unsafe. But rather than choose to renovate the existing ballpark, Reinsdorf and Einhorn went forward with plans for a new Comiskey Park—across the street from the existing stadium. The only problem was that there was already something across the street—dozens of private homes and a good handful of businesses belonging to the overwhelmingly black, overwhelmingly low-income residents of South Armour Square.

Hallie Amey and many other residents first learned of the proposed construction in a newspaper article. Although as part of public housing her apartment wouldn't be subjected to the city's eminent-domain claims against much of the neighborhood, she worried for her private-homeowner neighbors, and for the future of her already isolated community. (With the Dan Ryan Expressway to its east, Comiskey Park on its north, and rail yards at its west side, South Armour Square was particularly cut off from the rest of the South Side.)

Amey was at an advantage when it came to political experience. She and other residents of the Wentworth Gardens housing project were part of Wentworth Residents United for Survival, a neighborhood group that had taken on the government once before. In 1986, concerned about deteriorating conditions in their buildings' physical plant, residents worked with Sheila Radford-Hill, a longtime grassroots activist, to successfully battle the Chicago Housing Authority for more funds to repair their apartment buildings. From that struggle emerged the fledgling residents' coalition, with a victory under its belt providing it with the "vision and strength to organize," according to Radford-Hill. Now, with the threatened demolition of their neighbors' homes, the public-housing activists were determined to organize the community once again.

They formed the South Armour Square Neighborhood Association, Amey explains, "to try to save ourselves, try and save our homes, and try and save the homeowners. Now we were concerned about ourselves, but we were really concerned about them, because these were individual homeowners, and many of them were old and had spent years establishing a home where they would have someplace to live in their old age."

United by their desire to see Comiskey Park remain, the South Armour Square Neighborhood Association reached out to Save Our Sox. Some members from both groups attended one another's meetings to share in their common concerns and brainstorm together.

"We welcomed them and they welcomed us. Made our group a little bigger," Amey recalls with a laugh. "And we all had the same goal. We were not fighting against progress and all of that. We was just fighting for the right to keep homes for people . . . and many of those old folks lost their homes, and many of them did not live very long."

The Good Fight

"We were allied with the neighborhood people," John Aranza says. "Now, the community there was all black. And here's white people, black people united for a common cause. The people I was with I never met before. I didn't know them, they didn't know me, but it was something we all looked at ahead of us, our goal. And we didn't look at each other as our background, religious, job status, color, or anything. We had a goal."

Radford-Hill agreed to work with the residents of South Armour Square to try to save their community from the city's eminent-domain claims—despite the fact that "most people in the city told [her] it was a done deal and forget it." A dispute between the governor and the mayor of Chicago over who would be on the board of the newly created sports facility authority gave community activists some much needed time—a delay of almost a year. At a community meeting, Radford-Hill asked, "[Do] we want to work together over these nine months to try to stop this thing, and if not at least try to get a better deal?" Ultimately, she says, "they were willing to work, basically two years, around getting them a better deal. They got a better deal."

"Our chances were slim to none," Radford-Hill recalls. But the community had also seen how Addison area residents had successfully organized against having a stadium built in their neighborhood. And so the group went forward, Radford-Hill explains, "demonstrating on Reinsdorf's lawn, difficult to do with a bunch of senior citizens," but, she says, "we did disrupt meetings, we had a press strategy. The idea was to make enough noise and be irritating enough that you could eventually blow the deal."

The group held protests at Comiskey Park and at City Hall. At a mock funeral set up by the group at a local school, attendants mourned the death of a community, reminiscing about the good times they'd shared as residents of South Armour Square. In the end the neighborhood coalition wasn't able to stop the destruction of 178 privately owned housing units and twelve community businesses. But it was able to secure payments of market value plus a $25,000 cash bonus and moving expenses for the homeowners being displaced. For those who were being forced to leave, there was some solace in having struggled for a better deal. For those with no choice but to watch their isolated community be further destroyed, it was a harder pill to swallow.

"There was a split at the end of the struggle, which, I think, robbed the residents of a sense of triumph," says Radford-Hill. "When the settlement deal was arrived at between the sports authority and the residents, the sports authority took the position that they were not interested in the community. They were only interested in the homeowners, the people that were actually losing their property. So they effectuated a split, and I think that kind of robbed the residents of a sense of victory."

Those residents who stayed filed a class action suit against the sports authority, state, and city. Forty-nine plaintiffs signed on to the lawsuit, alleging that the new stadium site was selected in violation of their civil rights. If the new stadium had been built north of where it ultimately was, they argued, there would have been fewer businesses and homes displaced. That wasn't done, according to the lawsuit, because the homes that would have been destroyed belonged to white residents.

"Basically the suit lost," explains Radford-Hill. While not denying that individual residents may have suffered, the court entered a summary judgment on behalf of the defendants in the case. The judge also warned he would stick the Armour Square residents with the court costs if they appealed the decision. "So that effectively ended it," according to Radford-Hill.

Amey and her fellow activists were able to ensure that the nearby school, threatened by flying dust from construction of the new stadium, would have air-conditioning installed. And residents of the nearby T. E. Brown apartments had their utility bills paid for by the sports authority for the first year of construction. But "the residents of Wentworth Gardens basically got nothing," says Radford-Hill—they received no monetary compensation, and they were forced to watch their neighboring homes and business destroyed. Still, Radford-Hill points out, Wentworth Residents United for Survival remained an organized, and even more experienced, group. "They became a resident management organization. Now they're in line to manage their own development."

Amey acknowledges the defeat but not any surrender. "But if you have to survive, you don't have time to get discouraged. You don't. You don't have time. . . . Oh gosh," she pauses with a chuckle. "Nothing, nothing, nothing could discourage me. I will just work and fight."[1]

The Plot Thickens

For as long as the debate centered on White Sox demands for a new stadium, sos had a focused fight. But Reinsdorf wasn't about to let the city off easy, so he and other White Sox officials went from hinting at the team's fleeing for greener pastures to actually taking well-publicized trips to Florida to check out the Tampa–St. Petersburg area. (St. Petersburg had, with public money, built a forty-three-thousand-seat baseball stadium in 1988—without having a professional baseball team. Anxious city officials actually flew White Sox executives in, on a Lear jet, so the city could makes its pitch—which included a $10 million loan to Reinsdorf if the White Sox relocated—as the best new home for the Chicago team.) But Reinsdorf, it would turn out, was only courting St. Petersburg at the suggestion of Illinois governor Jim Thompson, who Reinsdorf would later reveal had encouraged him to threaten leaving Chicago if he wanted a new ballpark, saying, "It'll never happen unless people think you are going to leave."[2]

But no amount of renovations was going to be enough for Reinsdorf and Einhorn. They wanted a showpiece of a new stadium, and they wanted the taxpayers of Chicago to build it for them. Reinsdorf had always been fond of Royals Stadium in Kansas City, the fourteen-year-old home of the Kansas City Royals. Designed by the rising architecture firm of HOK, Royals Stadium was considered the first modern ballpark to break the unfortunate streak of perfectly circular stadiums so favored in the 1960s. With its smaller seating capacity and waterfalls overlooking center field, the park was something of a refreshing architectural change, but its artificial turf and symmetry soon lost favor among baseball purists.

Too Little, Too Late

By this time, stadium opponents had garnered enough attention to warrant a meeting with then mayor Harold Washington. When residents of South Armour Square went to meet with Washington in January 1987, Mary O'Connell and Doug Bukowski went along to present sos's plans for renovations to the existing Comiskey Park. "He wasn't going to come out for the renovation of Comiskey Park if the White Sox were insisting they'd leave," Bukowski recalls. "Because then he would be branded as the mayor who didn't care and lost the White Sox. So he just let the whole process continue, which it then did under two other administrations."

It was at that time, when the threat of the team leaving the city seemed very real, that sos shifted its focus—and lost its original core members. Newer recruits suggested that the group take a trip to Springfield, the state capital, to lobby for construction of a new South Side home for the team—at the cost of losing the old Comiskey and the neighborhood homes of South Armour Square. The organization even received a check from one of the minority owners of the team, who intended that it be used to lobby to keep the White Sox in Chicago.

"Because of the whole anxiety that the White Sox would produce with their threats to move, there was this great crisis in the organization as to whether they should get on board and go to Springfield and lobby for the new stadium or not," Bukowski recalls. "I just said, this is wrong. I can't do it. So I left. Maybe this was the only time in my life I could see the future, and it didn't work. I said, this is wrong, corporate welfare. . . . There was no reason to subsidize baseball. In fact it's going to be an inferior replacement. . . . People are not going to be able to see baseball the way they had seen baseball for eighty years. And this has proven true."

"You never win by appeasement," says Aranza, who also left the group at that time. "You never win." What had started as a struggle to save a cherished community landmark ended in bitterness for many involved in their first grassroots struggle. "Go over there and see what the hourly wage actually is, what they're charging for hot dogs," Aranza says in disgust. "It's obscene. They're making obscene profits."

The intensive lobbying of team officials and Major League Baseball higher-ups, combined with high-pressure tactics to prove their threat to yank the team was legitimate, proved too much for the Illinois state legislature. In a midnight session on June 30, 1988, the body approved construction of a new stadium, with $150 million coming from state bonds and the rest from a 2 percent hotel tax. (In fact, it was an after-midnight session; Governor Jim Thompson had the clock turned off at 11:59 to avoid hitting a midnight deadline.) The White Sox would only have to pay rent at their new home if attendance surpassed 1.2 million a year. "It was just an outrageously lavish

lease agreement, and that has become industry standard," says Chicago architect Philip Bess, who drew up blueprints for a compromise
new stadium that would have been less destructive to the neighborhood and cheaper to build.

To add insult to injury, once a new home was approved, team owners were determined to milk nostalgia for the old Comiskey Park for
as long as it still stood. Thus, a ticket brochure before the 1989 season
read: "With the dawn of this new era, we pause to reflect upon the
past glory days of historic Comiskey Park. Nineteen eighty-nine and
1990 are dedicated to remembering the past combined with anticipa-
tion of a bright, exciting future in the new state-of-the-art stadium."
Or, as one ad read in the local papers: "'The last season in historic
Comiskey Park. Years from now, you'll say you were there.'"

Out of the Ashes

By 1991 Reinsdorf, now the principal owner of the team, had his new
home—the new Comiskey Park. The old Comiskey is a parking lot,
and those surviving South Armour Square homeowners have moved
elsewhere. What was once a close-knit working-class African American community—with successful businesses and long-standing
neighborhood ties—has been destroyed. Only the residents of
the two housing projects remain. And what was once one of the
country's most charismatic sports facilities is no more. In the new
stadium, many of the old Comiskey's charms have been virtually
eliminated.[3]

"The last row in the upper deck of the old Comiskey Park, the
very last row, behind the plate, was closer to the field than the first
row of the upper deck in the new Comiskey Park," Doug Bukowski
points out. Even the one idiosyncratic holdover from the park's
Bill Veeck days, the stadium's "exploding" scoreboard, has a new
twist—it abuts the back of the T. E. Brown apartments, whose senior residents must deal, even late at night, with its cacophony. Architecturally, says Bess, the new Comiskey "was the trial run" for the

fledgling HOK architecture firm, which went on to design most of the new stadiums of the 1990s. "And Jerry Reinsdorf bought the trial run." Whether or not he now regrets it is another matter—the new Comiskey has been roundly criticized by baseball purists and fans, and attendance has slipped.[4]

To this day, many of the original members of Save Our Sox refuse to go to games at the new Comiskey Park or will only go if someone gives them a ticket. "I've never paid in the six years it's been open," says Bukowski. "I refuse to."

"If I have a fantasy about all this," Chicago architect Philip Bess confesses, "it's that Comiskey will be economically obsolete, which in a way it already is, and that they'll build another one and do it right."

With the demolition in full swing, Aranza couldn't stay away from the site of so many memories. "As they were tearing down the ballpark, I would sneak in there at night," he explains. "Once I took [friend and fellow SOS member] Hank Trenkle. Him and I went in one night when the park was half down, and we sat in the bleachers. He brought his tape of the '59 World Series. And we're up there with half the park demolished, looking out at 35th Street with all the cars, looking down, and with the sunflowers growing in the middle of the field; some bunches of the sunflowers were bigger than us. And the jangled tubing of the railing, the wreckage out there, and we're just thinking of what was. And I know you can't live on those feelings, but it was just kind of, it was bitter and soothing at the same time."

Every year, at least once, the old core of Save Our Sox gets together to catch up and reminisce at Hickory Pit, an old restaurant near the stadium that had been the site of several SOS meetings. Many in the group have remained friends and have retained a sense that it was a good fight.

Looking back, John Aranza has no regrets about taking that pillowcase sign to Comiskey Park, and the struggle that followed. "So help me God, I knew I did the right thing," he says. "And I overcame something and I achieved something in myself, for a cause and for a purpose and for the team. If anybody has a feeling that something is wrong and they want to change it or correct it or right it, in a decent and proper way, by all means do it. Because you'll go to your death saying, 'I wish I could have done more. I should have done something.' But I learned it that day."

Notes

1. Amey was later appointed to the board of the Chicago Housing Authority, in addition to her role as head of the Wentworth Gardens resident-management group. In 2004 the city of Chicago renamed two blocks of Wentworth Avenue to be "Honorary Mrs. Hallie Amey Avenue."

2. Asked years later by *Cigar Aficionado* magazine about his flirtation with St. Petersburg, Reinsdorf explained bluntly: "A savvy negotiator creates leverage. People had to think we were going to leave Chicago."

3. On the new Comiskey's eighth opening day in 1998, *Chicago Tribune* columnist John McCarron wrote a eulogy for the old park that concluded: "We now know, though certain suits will never admit it, that old Comiskey should have been saved and rehabbed; that the old neighborhood around it should have been renewed, not removed. But it's never too late to use your imagination. Just close your eyes and remember how it used to be."

4. In 2003 the Illinois Sports Facilities Authority granted the White Sox the right to sell the naming rights to the publicly owned building and use the proceeds for additional renovations to the structure. The telecommunications company U.S. Cellular committed $3.4 million a year to rename the building after itself, finally consigning even the Comiskey name to history. The redesigned stadium reopened the following April, with the highest upper-deck seats sliced off, and the addition of a small roof—which was supported, ironically, by view-obstructing columns.

8 Bad Neighbors

To speak logically about the effects of sports facilities on community development should be to speak as much about community as about development. —*Chicago architect Philip Bess*

The pride and the presence of a professional football team is far more important than thirty libraries. —*Baltimore Ravens owner Art Modell*

There were alternatives to new Comiskey. Hellmuth Obata Kassebaum, the architects contracted by the White Sox to build their new ballpark, may dominate new-stadium construction, but they can't stop other would-be sports architects from proposing alternatives to HOK's assembly-line blueprints. Detroit had its John and Judy Davids with their Cochrane Plan, which would have saved both public money and a national landmark. Chicago had Philip Bess.

Bess looked at the planned demolition of Comiskey Park and saw as much a challenge as a potential tragedy. If the White Sox owners were insistent in their demand for a new stadium, he reasoned, why not take the opportunity to see something positive and productive come out of their blackmailing of the city? An architect and teacher in Chicago, Bess set out to design a ballpark that would reverse the trend started in the 1960s of isolating sports facilities from their surrounding neighborhoods and would instead be truly urban—a facility that would provide an anchor for a neighborhood revitalization that served not just visiting sports fans, but local residents as well.

Especially since Baltimore's Camden Yards was built with an eye to the ballparks of yesteryear, new "old-fashioned" ballparks have been in favor. These modern structures are meant to mimic the historic stadiums of baseball's glory days—minus the old-fashioned ticket prices, of course, and equipped with luxury boxes and club seating. Sports commentators and journalists are quick to wax poetic about the new old-fashioned facilities, playing up their contemporary role in the romantic lure of baseball.

And truthfully, for many sports fans—baseball fans in particular—it is difficult to argue with the criticisms of the crop of "modern" circular stadiums that popped up across the country in the 1960s and '70s. Those cement bowls weren't very interesting aesthetically, and they weren't particularly fan-friendly. Three Rivers Stadium in Pittsburgh, Cincinnati's Riverfront Stadium, and Veterans Stadium in Philadelphia, along with their domed counterparts in Houston, Minneapolis, and Seattle, were built to hold as many people for as many sports as possible, with cheaply maintained AstroTurf replacing fresh grass, and bland circular seating charts that placed fans equally distant from football and baseball games.

Unlike football, basketball, or hockey, for which there are precise standards that vary not at all from facility to facility, so much of the baseball viewing experience is about the sights, smells, and sounds of the stadiums in which it is played. In their sterile uniformity, the new generation of baseball stadiums lost the intricately designed angles and crevices of the playing field and spectator seats that used to make no two stadiums alike (and wreak havoc on pitching records and batting averages).

Accepting the destruction of the magnificent Comiskey Park as a foregone conclusion, Bess began work on an alternative to the plan being presented by White Sox owners and the city. His proposed stadium, Armour Field, was designed—in size, cost, and community function—to more faithfully reflect the traditional ballparks of yesterday. Instead of mimicking Royals Stadium, the suburban stadium in Kansas City that White Sox owner Jerry Reinsdorf so desperately wanted to replicate, Armour Field was designed to anchor a revived network of public places and community businesses. Instead of throwing out years of evocative and responsive architecture, Armour Field would be a chance to, at a more modest cost, re-create what was so special about the feel and function of old urban baseball stadiums. "For thirty years," Bess wrote in a description of his plan, "the solution to urban ballpark ills has been urban renewal and the suburban stadium—a dubious practice, analogous to prescribing chemotherapy for a broken leg."

Back to Basics?

"If you've lived in Europe," says Chicagoan Mary O'Connell, "you know that people try to save the best of the old. There's not this endless thing of rip it down and build another, rip it down and build another. Some of the most beautiful and attractive parts of European cities are the older sections, where people have saved them and invested in them over time. And Americans go to Europe to see the buildings, to go drink in the pub that's been there since the sixteenth century, or worship in the places where people have been worshipping for hundreds of years."

In the United States, O'Connell and her fellow members of Save Our Sox soon found, historic landmarks are often torn down for the sake of progress. In the world of stadium architecture, and especially baseball stadiums, the irony goes a bit deeper. In the last ten years, both old and relatively new baseball or multiuse sports stadiums have been razed—in order to make room for more "old-fashioned" replacements. The architectural facades of urban baseball stadiums cherished for their convenient community locations, fan-friendly seating, and low-cost entertainment experience are being copied—

even as the infrastructure of old neighborhoods that used to support them is being eroded or forever altered.

The baseball stadiums built in the first half of the twentieth century were built right in bustling urban neighborhoods—lively communities like Brooklyn's Flatbush, Chicago's South Side, and Boston's Kenmore Square. They were places families could walk to on summer afternoons, places businessmen could get to by taking public transportation, places kids could sneak into on a Sunday afternoon.

"The older ones were not only located in a network of streets and blocks, but they were constrained by the existing network of streets and blocks," Bess points out. "When you go to Fenway Park or Wrigley Field, the parks are literally kind of shoehorned into the block in such a way to maximize seating capacity within a finite site. And one of the consequences of that is that you get these sort of odd, idiosyncratic kinds of playing-field configurations, like the Green Monster in Fenway, and like the wells in left field, the higher center-field bleachers, that you find in Wrigley. And those are a direct consequence of the site constraints."

Those idiosyncratic constraints, combined with individuality in design, gave each old ballpark a unique character and feel. Ebbets Field was located in a bustling Brooklyn community of homes and businesses, with a DeSoto car dealership and a gas station behind its famous right-field wall. Built into an already established neighborhood, it had a center-field wall that was a mere 384 feet from home plate—and that served as a constant advertisement for Schaefer beer (the "h" in the word "Schaefer" lit up for hits, the "e" for errors). The Polo Grounds in Manhattan, with center-field bleachers once called "the cigar boxes" for the Irish immigrant fans who crowded in them, had an outfield wall a staggering 505 feet from home.

Like grand old theater houses or performance halls, these historic stadiums each had a unique character and feel that was as much a part of the baseball experience as the game itself. Seeing Luciano Pavarotti at Carnegie Hall, after all, is not the same as seeing him at Tanglewood. There's a different experience of Bob Dylan at Woodstock than at the Village Vanguard. And certainly seeing Shakespeare performed at the Globe Theater in England has a different feel to it, different sensory and auditory and emotional components, than hearing the same lines performed by the same actors at the local YMCA.

Team owners, meanwhile, latch on to the trend of "old-time" urban ballparks predominantly for the sake of increased profits. Luxury boxes, concessions revenues, and naming rights are their holy grails, after all, and when these revenue producers come into conflict with the requirements of an "old-time" ballpark, modern conveniences win the day.

Can't Tell the Players without a Telescope

Part of the reason, to be sure, has to do with upgraded standards of comfort and the relentless search for new sources of revenue. In the old steel ballparks such as Ebbets Field, the seating capacity was low, often thirty thousand or fewer, and the seats were narrower, with less legroom. Modern ballparks required many more seats and more-spacious accommodations—especially for the high-paying patrons who would be the new stadiums' most lucrative asset. "You put in club seats, those have even more legroom and wider seats than normal for today," architect and stadium historian John Pastier explains. "And they usually have to be in a discrete location, which means a deck of their own, and that starts pushing the upper deck away. Then you have all these suites that nobody ever thought of before, and they take up a bunch of space."

The result: In the typical new ballpark, additional layers—in the case of Jacobs Field in Cleveland, as many as three—of luxury suites and club seats are inserted, raising the upper deck skyward. Because support columns, which allow decks to be stacked more closely at the expense of a few obstructed-view seats, are anathema to modern stadium designers, the upper deck must be set further back from the field—and because a higher deck must be more steeply angled at the same distance from the field, they are moved back still further.

Consequently, as frustrated fans have observed and researchers like Pastier have verified, most fans in the new ballparks are much farther from the action than they were in traditional ballparks. The back row of the upper deck in old Comiskey Park, with columns and no luxury levels, was closer to the field than is the first row of new Comiskey's upper deck, which sits atop a wall of glassed-in suites. Old Comiskey was 75 feet high; new Comiskey soars 146 feet above the streets of the South Side.

The same is true in modern stadiums across North America. In upper-deck seats in SkyDome in Toronto, fans can't even see large portions of the playing field. Even the sterile '60s stadiums score better on Pastier's scale than do popularly praised new "old-time" ballparks like Jacobs Field and The Ballpark at Arlington in Texas; in exchange for steel and brick and quirky angles, fans had unwittingly subjected themselves to some of the worst seats in sports history.[1]

Moving the upper decks up and away from the field has another important side benefit to team owners: It dramatically increases the stadium's volume. "Behind and under the seats, all that space has been growing astronomically," notes Pastier. "There's more space for people to move around; there's much more space for selling them things."

"If I say 'Municipal Stadium,'" says Bess, invoking the name of Cleveland's recently demolished ballpark, "what would be some of the adjectives that come to mind? Cavernous. Well, cavernous Municipal Stadium, which seated seventy-eight thousand, is almost equal in its footprint [the acreage taken up by an architectural project] to Jacobs Field, which seats forty-two thousand. The seats in the upper deck at Municipal, even with that upper deck of seats that goes way back, are closer than they are at Jacobs."

All that extra space has significantly added to the bloated costs of current stadiums—and not just because of the extra land and construction costs inherent in a larger stadium. "In the new Comiskey

Park," Bess explains, "the kinds of things they wanted in the building that are ancillary to the stadium—the dugouts and the lockers and stuff like that—did not fill up all that horizontal space that was created because of the design. In other words, there was a lot of extra space that was created in the new Comiskey Park that was not programmed, and not finished."

When that same design was mimicked in later stadium projects by HOK, the leftover space was filled with such costly extras as enormous and expensive workout rooms for players. Once the land was procured, says Bess, there was little excuse not to fill the space, even though it added still further to construction costs. "All of this is a consequence of literally a lack of physical constraint on where you build ballparks," Bess says, "and on how you build them."

This tremendous increase in sheer bulk—the typical new stadium of today has double the footprint of an older ballpark—is one reason that construction costs have soared in recent years, from as low as $25 million in the late 1960s to $300 million and up today. Even if you were to completely re-create the few remaining old-time stadiums, and even adding luxury boxes as an economically necessary modern amenity, Bess and others believe cities could save a huge amount of money just by following those same historic space constraints. "If you were to build Wrigley from scratch," says Bess, "it would cost between $70 and $80 million."

"Unless you have a client that is passionately committed to building a good ballpark, you're not gonna get a good ballpark," says Pastier. In his estimate, of the first five baseball stadiums opened after 1991, Camden Yards is the clear winner. The Orioles, he explains, were willing to make some tradeoffs. "They combined the suites and the club seats. That helped reduce the height of the thing." At Pastier's suggestion, they cut down on the number of rows in the upper deck—"one way to get the worst seat in the house closer to the field is by removing it"—and made up the seating by extending the grandstand further into left field, which, he says, "was an improvement, anyway. The old parks tended to have one full upper deck in the outfield, if not two. That helps enclose the space and just creates a much better feeling." Camden Yards also features slightly tighter legroom than some other ballparks, further shrinking the depth of the grandstand.

Still, the discrepancy is not that great, and the view from the last row of Camden Yards is more like watching a game from a helicopter than like sitting in an older park like Tiger Stadium, or even Memorial Stadium, which the Orioles abandoned for Camden Yards. "You put kids up there where they can't see," argues Chicago writer Doug Bukowski, "they get bored. And you don't make them baseball fans. Which means when they become adults, they don't want to go. Which means, in the long run, baseball, by pursuing these types of new stadiums, is only eroding its fan base."

Courting Food

Another area where the character and community feel of old-time stadiums is being eroded by today's sanitized monoliths is in food services. Any self-respecting 1990s stadium features a huge food court—oftentimes a "foods of the world" hodgepodge where fans are encouraged to buy German sausages, Tex-Mex tacos, and a wide array of international beers. Modern food facilities can ring up millions of dollars a year in added revenues for a team. Boston's Fenway Park has had its own equivalent for years with its tiny outdoor vendors who crowd together outside the stadium's venerable gates, selling everything from hot meats and drinks to touristy T-shirts. And yet Fenway's homespun marketplace came under fire by team officials, who lamented the state of the antique park for several years as the first part of a drive to tear it down.

Fenway Park, with its renowned Green Monster outfield wall and brick-and-steel single-deck grandstand, has drawn comparisons to cathedrals along with nightly sellout crowds. But, hemmed in by streets on all sides, it had few luxury boxes, little room for increased seating— and no space for expansive concessions areas or lush kitchen facilities.

Entrepreneurship, abhorring a vacuum, has provided where the Red Sox cannot. "Have you been to Fenway?" asks Pastier. "You've seen that thing along Landsdowne [Street, adjacent to the outfield wall] where Mama Mia has her homemade ziti and clam sauce on a little propane heater, right? And somebody else is making funnel cakes right before your eyes, and somebody else has jerk chicken from the Caribbean. I mean, that's the most wonderful thing that you'll find outside of any ballpark, and it makes the Red Sox crazy. That's one reason they want to be out of Fenway Park, because they see dollar signs evaporating before their eyes."

"It gets really comical," Pastier says. "These guys are supposed to be capitalists, and for the free market, but that's the last thing they want! They want to have a monopoly. The free market exists right outside of Fenway Park, and goddamn it, this is one time they're right: The free market is wonderful. Because it's a true free market, it's individual entrepreneurs doing their thing, and therefore providing variety and choice, at not huge cost."[2]

For all the sense of variety, for all the attempts to re-create the spice of life that modern stadiums do in their multiethnic food courts, they are often all run by one snacks provider, usually one of the few big companies that dominate food courts in the entertainment scene. And for the exclusive right to sell in the modern sports palaces, those companies hand over a big share of their profits to team owners. In stadium design, as in every other aspect of professional sports ownership, profit is, and has always been, the bottom line. If artificially re-creating a sense of neighborhood helps in the process, then so be it. Oriole Park at Camden Yards features an outdoor walkway lined with souvenir shops and fast-food outlets—but *within* the stadium gates, for paying fans only and earning revenue for the team with every purchase. Jacobs Field features a private restaurant and an enormous team apparel shop that doubles as a history museum for the team. In the walkway between Jacobs Field and Gund Arena in downtown Cleveland, a lovely mosaic memorial has been installed. It honors, of all things, the once-thriving urban market that was destroyed to make room for the new sports facilities.

When the Seattle Mariners' owners had to pick a location for their new stadium, notes Pastier, they had several sites to choose from, at varying distances from a popular shopping district. The team chose the most isolated location. "They'll certainly get more of the food and the drink and the souvenir sales," he says. "Once you go to the ballpark, you're so far away from those established businesses, you're much more likely to buy those things at the park itself. It's a captive audience situation." This, according to Pastier, is why the White Sox moated the new Comiskey with a hundred acres of parking, and why the Milwaukee Brewers refused to build their new ballpark downtown: Convenient access, it turns out, is less important than a captive audience for four-dollar hot dogs and five-dollar beers.

When more-suburban, sprawling stadiums seemed the better route to go, owners were all for them. But sometime in the design period of the new Comiskey Park, and before plans for Camden Yards were finalized, the trend in architecture, urban planning, and mall construction toward paying superficial homage to the America of yesteryear took center stage.

Nowhere was this more true than for HOK and the other leading stadium architects. "Right now there's a kind of mutually beneficial relationship between baseball owners and the architecture firms out of Kansas City and Seattle that do most of these jobs," Bess says. "The team owners say it has to be this way because the architects say it has to be this way; the architects say it has to be this way because the team owners tell us it has to be this way. That's sort of another major unrecognized scandal of the business. The corporate architects, the stadium architects, market their services to the tenants of these facilities rather than to the clients—that is to say, the people who pay for them."

What owners and architects alike missed along the way, however, was that it wasn't just their old-fashioned use of bricks or steel that made historic ballparks so popular and successful—it was their successful integration with the urban neighborhoods in which they were built. Indeed, though the similarities between the current crop of faux old stadiums and their historic counterparts are often emphasized by team owners and their media cohorts, it is their *differences* that are worth paying attention to. For it is the ways in which a Coors Field is dramatically different from, for example, a Fenway Park that tell us so much about the ways in which the increasing appetite for profits from owners and others shapes decisions about the games we play, the architecture we love, the way we are entertained. And this, finally, has as much to do with the changing face and function of the American city as it does with our favorite summer game.

Bad Neighbor Policy

Although Bess's plan would have also required the displacement of some residents—far fewer than the scores who lost their homes on behalf of the new Comiskey—part of the stadium design included the construction of new residences in previously vacant lots for those individuals who lost their homes. Far from being surrounded by parking lots, as the new Comiskey now is, Bess's proposed stadium would have been directly adjacent to a relocated city park (which would have stood on the grounds of the old stadium and even incorporated its old infield). It may have been this attempt at using the ballpark as a centerpiece of its surrounding neighborhoods that ultimately spelled Armour Park's doom because in racially stratified Chicago, not everyone wanted to bring people together. The proposed stadium and adjacent public park were seen by some as a positive way of linking overwhelmingly white Bridgeport and predominantly black South Armour Square. Because access to the park would have been from South Armour Square, what had been a mostly white recreational area would have become an integrated public space, and the neighborhood of Bridgeport would have lost a buffer between it and its black neighbors.

"My argument has always been that you can generate the kinds of revenues that are needed in today's sports economy with facilities that both are less expensive to build and put fans closer to the action," says Bess. "And so in that sense, with respect to stadium design I'm more of a reformer than I am a revolutionary, because I'm not questioning entirely the premises of the existence of professional baseball. But I do think that where it becomes scandalous is when public moneys are supporting the industry to the extent that they do. And that there could be a lot less public expense involved that could result in better stadiums that still make teams the money that they need. It just wouldn't be squeezing every last little drop out of the lemon."

For Bess, the North Side Chicago neighborhood where Wrigley Field is located is a prime example of how stadiums and urban communities can interact—and an example of an increasingly rare successful *city* neighborhood. "There's eighty-one baseball games a year there, and it certainly is a national draw; people all over the world come to go to Wrigley Field, to that neighborhood," Bess explains. "But the neighborhood functions quite well the other 280 days of the year when there's not a game there. Within a five-minute walk from the pitcher's mound at Wrigley Field, you've got businesses, restaurants, schools, churches, convents, public transportation."

Those details are not unimportant to Bess and others concerned about urban life. He notes, "There's a whole city and the life that goes on there. There's a daily life to the neighborhood that exists independently of the ballpark. The ballpark enhances, and vice versa, but the notion of the city is the notion of a place where people live and work and hang out all the time."

In successful instances like Wrigley Field, the baseball stadium is not the be-all and end-all of a neighborhood's existence. In the new old-time ballparks of the 1990s, such communities do not necessarily exist. And being a part of such urban neighborhoods is not what the new stadiums are about. They are attractions to go to, for people to get in their cars in the suburbs and spend a day at, before returning home. "Stadium construction is part of the same phenomenon as interest in casinos, interest in amusement parks," says Bess. "What's happened is that the 1990s city is implicitly being understood as an entertainment zone. And stadiums are part of this entertainment zone." Thus, says Bess, "to some extent all of the major corporate stadium architects market their services as providing entertainment. The assumption is that the city ought to be an entertainment zone because that's all it can be these days, because nobody really wants to live in the city. Whereas what I'm interested in is making the city better, understood in a traditional kind of way, where people actually live there as well as are entertained there.

"I certainly don't mind suburbanites coming in to go to baseball games," Bess continues. "Some of my best friends live in the suburbs. And I even understand political officials who are fairly desperate to keep revenues in the city. I certainly appreciate that dilemma. But I'm concerned about the way in which professional baseball, and stadium architects, are perpetuating this trend, the consequence of which is to reduce the notion of urban life to entertainment."

For Whom the Ball Wrecks

The problem, of course, is more than just a philosophical treatise on the purpose of cities. Not everyone has fled for the suburbs, and for those left behind—historically, minority, working-class, and poor people—sparkling new sports stadiums and arenas represent both a luxurious form of entertainment and an appalling misuse of increasingly rare public funds. And, adding egregious insult to injury, in city after city, the new sports facilities are often funded by regressive taxes—by flat levies on consumer items that never take into account the consumer's economic status. Those most needing scarce urban funds to be directed toward improved schools, infrastructure, job opportunities, and the like are also footing a disproportionately high percentage of the construction bill. Those taxed the heaviest are the same abandoned urban residents least likely to be able to afford to go to the new stadiums. As Pastier points out, the proportion of cheap seats has steadily dwindled in the newer stadiums, with larger and larger sections reserved for club seats and other high-priced seating.

Bess's notion of the neighborhood ballpark also runs against the grain of urban-development policy, which is increasingly concerned not with holding together communities but with creating high-activity "entertainment zones" that draw suburbanites and tourists back within the city limits. Starting in the 1960s, many cities began devoting an increasing amount of dwindling public resources to construction projects geared toward downtown development and the white-collar market. Instead of putting money into housing or schools, cities looking for economic turnaround cast their eyes on ways to draw pocketbooks downtown: first with hotels, corporate headquarters, and the like; then, as the decades passed, they moved on to malls, museums, casinos, and other kinds of entertainment centers. The trend stretched late into the 1990s, in which the search for financial turnaround via downtown entertainment-based projects became the norm—in everything from hosting the Olympics in Atlanta to building a costly new arts center in Newark, New Jersey. Perhaps most pertinent for boosters of new-stadium projects was the advent of downtown open-air malls (and sometimes fancy indoor ones as well), designed to imitate the historic districts, which they had in many cases wiped out, while bringing in tourists and suburbanites with the promise of familiar shopping experiences.

In packaging urban history as a way of increasing consumer consumption, the faux old-time stadiums have much in common with the waterfront construction projects designed by developer James Rouse in the 1980s. Beginning with the overwhelming success of Faneuil Hall in Boston, Rouse went on to build the immensely popular Harborplace in Baltimore and the reconstructed South Street Seaport in lower Manhattan. Each of these projects re-creates a historic look—from cobblestone paths to historically designed storefronts and antique-looking signs—in order to reinvent the mall as an authentic walk down memory lane. That practically the only thing distinguishing one city's "historic" attraction from another's is the food selection at the chain restaurants within—crab cakes in Baltimore, chowder in Boston—and the city name on the Hard Rock Café T-shirts has not diminished these attractions' popularity.

M. Christine Boyer, a professor of architecture and urbanism at Princeton, points to the faux villages of Disneyland as the first blow for the "historic-marketplace tableau" that has proven so popular in urban centers. No matter where the Disneyland guest travels in the park, she points out, all roads lead back to Main Street USA and its stretch of souvenir stores. Thus, Boyer writes, "Disneyland is quint-essentially a landscape for consumption, not for leisure. In just this manner, South Street Seaport is above all a marketplace, the stage for a particular kind of experience—that of pure desire, where the buyer imagines a fantastical world, which the possession of a certain object seems to promise."

Sites such as Rouse's South Street Seaport are "laden with histori-cal allusions to the traditional vision of the city," writes Boyer, even as they end up contributing to the destruction of the modern Ameri-can city in its most familiar form. "New York is no longer a city con-cerned with such high-Modernist aspirations as providing a broad range of housing, efficient public transportation, or leisure and work spaces for the masses."

These "historic" shopping malls have replaced schools, libraries, and parks as the focus of municipal spending in nearly every Ameri-can city. Now planners and developers use huge quantities of time, public money, and public space—and receive huge amounts of posi-tive publicity—for new historic storefronts and new historic stadiums. The city itself has increasingly become an entertainment–consump-tion zone—one that aggressively milks nostalgic images of what the city should be in order to create an unprecedented consumer-based culture. In order to produce the spaces—physical, social, and eco-nomic—for such nostalgic projects, actual historic buildings and zones are simply destroyed.

The creation of a forced consumer nostalgia for an artificial past may have reached new levels of absurdity in central Florida, where the Walt Disney Company has opened a new town: Celebration,

Florida. Although it has no actual history besides its swampland origins, in the promotional push for the development, Celebration was billed as a "traditional" American town with a not-quite-real grand old history. As Russ Rymer wrote in his compelling look at Celebration in *Harper's* magazine, "What Celebration was promising was the restoration of the aesthetic and communal values of pre–World War II America. The town rising out of the palmetto swamp would be the Experimental Prototype Community of Yesterday."

From the inherent consumerism of Rouse's harbor projects and HOK's new-old stadiums comes the next step in the marketing of history and the blending of community with theme park. The town of Celebration, with its combination of six-figure homes and $600-a-month apartments, white picket fences and spacious walkways, is designed to trigger a nostalgia for an idealized American city that never was. There was even early talk at Disney that the town should have an invented history to provide it with "roots." As Rymer wrote: "What Celebration celebrates, oddly, is an American community that existed precisely in that time before corporations made it their business to build communities—an era before neighborhoods became subdivisions and business districts became malls and culture in all its sources and manifestations became supplanted by the cathode-ray tube and the theme park."

Changing Neighborhoods

It is impossible to watch a broadcast of a game from Camden Yards, or Jacobs Field, or Coors Field in Denver and not hear constant references to those glittering new stadiums as examples of architectural magic. (TV journalists seldom interview fans about the vast distance from their seats to the playing field.) More important, the facilities are repeatedly referred to as major components in their respective downtowns' "renaissance." And certainly, if the number of increased downtown buildings or the pedestrian traffic on game days or at attractive new bars is an indication, those cities have gone through urban renaissances. The problem is, when discussing a downtown revitalization and renaissance, no one ever mentions (or touches base with) the vast majority of working-class and poor residents of those same cities. (A glaring omission but a not uncommon one. Maybe that has always been true of renaissances. It seems unlikely, after all, that fourteenth-century peasants in Florence spent much time admiring art.)

What has happened to these former industrial giants, at the same time that their glittering new stadiums have helped make them official renaissance towns?

Bill Marker wonders just this as he visits one of Camden Yards' less fashionable neighboring areas, an old district known as Pigtown. He is mulling over some other uses to which the state of Maryland could have put its $400 million in lottery money instead of new twin stadiums for the Orioles and Ravens.

"When I worked representing parents and sometimes children in abuse and neglect cases, if you were losing your kids because of your drug use, we could get you into some sort of program," Marker says. "But if you're just generally out on the street and you say, yes, I've got a drug problem and I'm ready to deal with it, you should live long enough until there's a spot for you. And there's nothing more important than that. Not only in terms of the drug treatment, but guess what? If you had enough drug spots available, there'd be a lot of $15,000-a-year jobs for ex-junkies."

The impact on U.S. cities—particularly those unfortunate enough to have been long centered on manufacturing and heavy industry—of decades of corporate pullouts, tax abatements, and redirection of public dollars into enormous consumer centers has been devastating. Expensive new stadiums, waterside malls, and development projects—the cornerstones of many an urban renaissance—have received massive public contributions. They've meant considerable public sacrifice in the form of gobbling up costly land without paying property taxes, taking over what were once true public spaces, and refocusing urban priorities.[3]

Community groups have challenged these spending priorities

in city after city. In testifying against spending public money on a new ballpark for the Minnesota Twins, Minneapolis Federal Reserve vice-president Arthur Rolnick recalls, "I said, let's have a referendum on it, because if you're going to give this money to sports teams, it means you're not giving it to the schools, and you're not giving it to fighting crime or cleaning up your parks and your roads. And I suspect when you rank these things, the public would rank [stadiums] much lower, but I said have a referendum. Now of course they didn't want to do that, because they didn't want to hear what the public had to say. They were pretty sure the public was going to vote against something like the Twins or the Timberwolves—they didn't have much support." In fact, a poll by the *Minneapolis Star Tribune* in January 1997 found that if given a choice of how to divide their tax money, citizens would spend it quite differently than would stadium boosters: 44 percent for education, 29 percent for crime prevention, 13 percent for transportation, and 8 percent for the arts; a stadium ranked dead last, at 6 percent.

Crumbling schools, staggering African American infant mortality, and lingering unemployment are the undiscussed realities behind Cleveland's stadium-enhanced renaissance. "The result is what has been termed the *dual city*," writes Cleveland State University professor Dennis Keating, "in which downtown areas can thrive, and the white-collar sector mostly employing white suburban commuters can grow, whereas poor neighborhoods and their working-class and poor residents, especially blacks and Hispanics, do not share in this growth and must cope with high rates of poverty, unemployment, and other social problems." Jacobs Field and Gund Arena were built with public money and their tenants given significant tax abatements on the property they were built on. In the state of Ohio, property tax goes to public education, so the progress for wealthy owners is linked to further education cuts. Using numbers from the Cuyahoga County Auditor, the Cleveland Teachers Union charges that city schools lost more than $3.5 million in 1995 alone on tax abatements granted to Jacobs Field and Gund Arena.

When it comes to the $450 million Gateway complex, Cleveland teacher Michael Charney was more outraged by the choice of funding recipient than by the tax-abatement loss of dollars that the Cleveland schools so desperately needed. "The political corporate forces went for an increase in taxes on beer and wine and cigarettes," Charney points out, "and decided that the most appropriate use of those taxes was for a stadium complex—rather than for either dealing with social service problems or dealing directly with the capital problem of the Cleveland public schools falling apart physically."

The business community in Cleveland, and its political cronies, had a chance to "fix up those broken buildings, or hire social workers to deal with the kids' problems, or open up the schools at night," according to Charney, "so they [could] become stabilized institutions in a totally destabilized community." Instead, those same civic committees backed the funding of Gateway.

The problem extends far beyond former rust-belt headliners. In 1997 in Austin, Texas, a state senator proposed legislation that would end abatements on property taxes that fund schools. A study conducted by the senate's Economic Development Committee found that Texas schools had lost almost $480 million in local property-tax revenue from 1985 to 1995 because of tax abatements.

For Charney and other longtime activists who've watched the shift in urban planning and emphasis over the past thirty years, the symbolic impact of costly new stadiums is enormous. "I think that's more of a metaphor for a society's priorities than it is the actual drain on the actual cash," Charney says.

The same can be said for other entertainment-zone specialties in cities such as Cleveland. After all, it's hard to persuasively argue that the public school children of Cleveland somehow benefit—besides by having an increased appreciation of Little Richard—from the placement of the Rock and Roll Hall of Fame on the shores of Lake Erie. In fact, because the museum was built on valuable property with tax abatements, the opposite could be argued—and has been, for decades, by local activists.

Charney, who's been a public school teacher for more than two decades and has been active with the teachers union for the last ten years, wishes that "there were as much effort [put] into making sure that every child in Cleveland had a home library by the time they were in first grade, where they had ten or fifteen or twenty books that they owned, rather than just fixing up the stadium." He'd take it a step further and declare that "admission to a Browns, Cavaliers, or Indians game would be the price of a ticket plus a children's book. At least [for] the people in the loges." It certainly might be one way, in the current construction-crazy climate, to force a reexamination of urban values. "Just as there is a somewhat moral obligation that people don't starve," Charney argues. "I think there may have to be created a moral obligation that children have the right to be literate by the time they're seven or eight. And that's not only the problem of the narrowly defined public school system, but society at large."

The underfunding of Cleveland's school system is a daunting problem—one directly related to a shift in the city's priorities. "The legacy of that lack of capital investment shows up in the massive illiteracy of the adult population," Charney says. "The same people pushing these stadia are the same people who live in the suburbs, moved their businesses to the suburbs, and now say, 'Fix it, the schools are lousy.'"

Likewise, in Detroit, Bill Dow and other members of the Tiger Stadium Fan Club faced an uphill battle in trying to force politicians to look at the opportunities lost by putting so much emphasis on building a new stadium. "We kept saying, if you ask any urban-planning expert, if you had that kind of public money to spend toward urban renewal, one of the last things they would say would be a baseball stadium that's used eighty-one days out of the year," Dow says. "But they just fell for it."

"There's a real desperation in Detroit," Frank Rashid points out. "I understand it—we all had that feeling when the Renaissance Center came, that one big thing is going to make the difference. It's the politics of desperation, and it's self-defeating. Finally, what we have to do is what you've got to do to rebuild a city, block by block, making sure that the business climate is right, planning carefully, and making sure that you're investing in things that are going to improve the quality of life for your people, to make your city an attractive place to live and work. It's not pretty, and it takes time. The problem with these big projects is when you invest everything in them you can't *do* the other stuff; there's nothing left. The lost opportunity is what's so frustrating, and so awful."

Structural Adjustment

Public money spent on private construction projects instead of social services, severe cuts in social welfare even as corporate welfare continues unchecked, growing inequities between the haves and have-nots, deteriorating quality-of-life indicators in so-called renaissance towns—if these were part of urban planning in the Third World, they'd have a name: "structural adjustment."

In some ways, the public funding of huge stadium projects, outdoor malls, and casino halls, coupled with enormous cuts in local spending on social services, can be viewed almost as the domestic version of the structural-adjustment plans pushed on developing nations (and increasingly on Western Europe as well) by the World Bank and the International Monetary Fund. The formula is simple: Devote ever-decreasing amounts of public wealth to support the services needed by the poor and helpless and invest more and more in ways that will return increasing profits to the small numbers of rich and privileged. Oftentimes in the Third World that has meant an emphasis on the tourist and export economy over more indigenous industrial or agricultural solutions. A similar emphasis on tourists over residents is happening in city after city across the United States. The new Comiskey Park was built with an eye for the outside baseball fan coming to the South Side to check out an exciting new attraction—not for locals, whose homes and businesses were destroyed as a necessary part of the process.

Seeing once-proud downtowns reduced to clamoring for tourist dollars is oddly reminiscent of witnessing Third World countries continually redefining themselves and their priorities, or being redefined, by their relationship to the almighty U.S. dollar. For years, development investment in Latin America and elsewhere has been linked to large-scale cutbacks in social services. Indeed, that link has been the cornerstone of World Bank and International Monetary Fund policies in much of the Third World. In U.S. cities, meanwhile, money becomes available for large-scale private projects like sports arenas or privately owned prisons at the same time that it's reduced for education, low-income housing, or public health services. Increasingly, the two are intricately connected—they don't just happen to occur coincidentally.

Indeed, if adjustment policies are forcing activists in the developing world into new strategies, their urban U.S. equivalent has inspired local activists to do the same. The Cleveland teachers' union organized a successful petition drive to place a referendum on the ballot in August 1997 calling for limits on tax abatement. Confronted by the links between downtown development and their deteriorating schools, a local union was stepping far past a traditional workplace issue to combat the current powers that be. "Gateway does not represent something new that 'we have'—it's rather treating Cleveland the way the rich nations treat the Third World," said one Cleveland radio commentator in the aftermath of the successful drive for a new football stadium. "Only instead of being dominated by foreign powers, we're dominated by a small group of powerful local people who manage to convince us that we are the beneficiaries when they are robbing us."

The way in which local stadium projects are reported—the discussion of those ever-popular urban renaissances—also mimics in many ways U.S. press reports on the complicated economics and politics of Third World countries. When the *New York Times* writes that a Latin American country is doing well economically, it usually means that its exports are up, that profits to a small group of corporate or industrial elites are up as well, and that thus by the paper's own definition of success the country's adjustment has been a success. Economic success is simply not connected to the actual well-being of a majority of the population. Instead, a substantial percentage of the population simply becomes irrelevant when the discussion focuses on economic success. And the same can be said for cities such as Detroit, Cleveland, and Baltimore.

Baltimore has built its reputation as a renaissance city on one glorious project: the Inner Harbor. Ringed by numerous malls featuring the trendiest in retail shops and boutiques, and served by the numerous hotels constructed adjacent to it over the past decade and by "water taxis" that take you to historic Fort McHenry (site of the "rockets' red glare" that inspired Francis Scott Key to pen "The Star-Spangled Banner"), Harborplace was among the first Rouse-designed architectural "triumphs." Just to the west of the harbor you'll find Baltimore's Otterbein neighborhood, one of the first experiments in state-sponsored gentrification, where the city filled houses vacated for an aborted '70s highway project by selling homes to "urban homesteaders" for $1 a pop. And just west of *that* is the culmination of Baltimore's redevelopment: Camden Yards, complete with its own self-contained mall in the ground floor of the old B&O warehouse, now redeveloped as a symbol of urban revival through tourism.

Keep going west a few blocks past Camden Yards, and you're in Pigtown, where, as in many other Baltimore neighborhoods, among the most notable landmarks are the numerous pawnshops. From here you can just see Oriole Park at Camden Yards and its new football neighbor. One of the best vantage points is Copper's Lot, a huge plot of vacant land cleared for urban renewal. It remains vacant years later because of toxic wastes left by the factory that formerly occupied the site, which the city shows no great desire to clean up.

As others have argued before, the United States is increasingly a country whose economic system does not require that the vast majority of people be employed. In the modern American city with its modern old-time stadium, people who go from suburbs to the ballparks, tourists who stay in area hotels and take in a game for an afternoon, and even some successful downtown residential fans can pass by the people whose needs are simply not counted. Urban planners can draw up entire downtown developments while ignoring big chunks of the population as if the local needy didn't exist.

And even when communities organize to stop new-stadium deals, they still face tremendous odds. That's certainly been the case in three high-profile towns in the 1990s, where spirited opposition by local activists, a determinedly resistant public, and outrageous demands by team owners weren't enough to stop the stadium juggernaut from rolling on.

Notes

1. When the New England Patriots began construction on their new stadium in 2000, team coo Andy Wasynczuk actually bragged about the distant nosebleed seats, telling the *Boston Herald*: "Even though the base of the new building is significantly lower—probably 60 feet lower—than Foxboro Stadium's, by the time it's finished the new stadium will vertically be higher than the current stadium. It's going to be a pretty impressive structure."

2. In 2006 the owners of the Sacramento Kings walked away from a tentative deal to build a new downtown arena, in part because city officials had refused to agree to a clause prohibiting "competing" restaurants from opening nearby.

3. A 2005 study by the budget-watch group City Project revealed that fully 60 percent of the total assessed value of New York City real estate was exempt from paying property taxes.

9 Repeat Offenders

Sports is a way of life, like eating. People say, "You should pay to feed the homeless." But the world doesn't work that way.
—*Minnesota Twins owner Carl Pohlad*

redit Seattle's team owners and local politicians with audacity, if nothing else. In five years the city's two professional sports franchises went up for sale, threatened to leave town, and wrangled huge public deals for new stadiums from a concerned populace. Twice they were met by a spirited, never-say-die opposition that maintained its multi-pronged attack long after deals were signed and funds committed. When the dust cleared and the bonds were issued, the lawsuits thrown out of court and the public referenda ignored, King County taxpayers would be left with one of the most enormous sports debts in recent history—close to $1 billion and counting for new homes for baseball's Mariners and football's Seahawks.

The first fight began in the early 1990s, over the fate of the Mariners. Saddled with what he claimed were insurmountable debts and a dwindling fan base, team owner Jeff Smulyan put the club up for sale in the winter of 1991. Early fears that the team would leave Seattle for greener pastures—presumably one of the southern cities then making overtures to Major League Baseball—were assuaged when the Baseball Club of Seattle bought the Mariners for more than $100 million in early 1992. The club, a consortium of local businessmen headed up by Nintendo officers, would need official league support—and some controversy did arise over partial foreign ownership of the "American pastime." But their bid was successful, and almost a year after buying the team, its owners began pushing for a new baseball-only stadium to replace the not yet twenty-year-old Kingdome.

A September 1995 referendum to institute a sales-tax increase to fund a new Mariners stadium was narrowly defeated, but team owners were undeterred. They declared that by October 30 the state would have to come up with a commitment to build a new stadium or else they'd put the team up for sale. Just in the nick of time, an emergency session of the state legislature approved a plan for a $320 million stadium to be paid for with new taxes on restaurants and car rentals. It was a move that outraged those who'd already questioned the priority of funding a new public facility—and who thought they'd had a victory with the September referendum's defeat. "If the Mariners need a new stadium—if any private business needs to build a new factory—then find the money on the private market," says attorney Shawn Newman, who, on behalf of his citizen group CLEAN, sued the state, and ultimately lost.

Citizens for More Important Things was another grassroots group formed to oppose the public funding of a new stadium. With only three people at its founding in 1995, the group at its peak had eight hundred donors and approximately four thousand volunteers, according to Chris Van Dyk, one of the organization's founding members. An investment broker and adviser, Van Dyk had an apparently boundless supply of energy when it came to taking on the stadium barons. "Every time they put up a dike to stop the flow of opinion," he once told the Seattle Times, "we know exactly where to dig a hole."[1]

By June 1996 the architectural plans had revealed yet another old-time stadium—this one with a retractable roof to shield players and fans from the notorious Seattle rain. But in large part because of the cost of that high-tech roof, within months the Public Facilities

District created to oversee the stadium project had declared that the new stadium was going to cost some $45 million more than initially projected. Additionally, the retractable roof would not be ready for the venue's planned April 1999 opening.

Reaction was swift and concerted. Despite their push to see a new stadium built for the '99 season, the Mariners hadn't yet signed a lease for the new facility. Local politicians, no doubt wary because of public outcry over the highly publicized cost overruns in such cases as Cleveland, wanted assurances that forking over an additional $45 million was really worth it. By December 1996 four city council members wrote a letter to the PFD urging a delay of the stadium opening until these issues could be better examined.

The reaction from the Mariners was harsh and unequivocal. Within two days, team owners announced that they were selling the team and pulling out of the stadium project. In a statement read live on local radio, team owners declared, "Recently, after more than three years of work toward fulfilling the dream of thousands of fans, the Baseball Club of Seattle has concluded that there is insufficient political leadership in King County to complete the ballpark project in 1999. [The] owners of the Mariners take great pride in having fulfilled all commitments and obligations to those who looked to us to preserve Major League Baseball for Seattle. To them, and to everyone, we cannot explain why those who represent the people have chosen to let baseball go."

The team owners declared they weren't interested in any more talks with King County officials, but like any good hostage takers, they were bluffing. There wasn't much point in holding a gun to taxpayers' heads if team management didn't think they could ultimately get their way. Sure enough, within two weeks of the Mariners' declaration, Republican senator Slade Gorton had stepped in to broker yet another deal with team owners—this one handing the petulant bosses more profits and fewer expenses. Based on media coverage of the ensuing events, local officials might as well have been dealing with armed guerrillas at the governor's mansion as with supposedly respectable local business owners. "Gorton helped persuade the owners to reconsider," the *Seattle Times* reported in one Christmas Day story. "He has urged governments to accede to the Mariners' demands and has criticized the city for its dealings with the team."

Under the terms of the new deal, the city of Seattle would pay for police traffic control, cleanup, and extra transit, and would compensate the local neighborhood for the stadium's impact—all of which was originally supposed to be covered by the Mariners. What had once seemed outrageous was about to become reality. The Mariners had their conditions met; ground was broken at the new stadium site in March 1997.[2]

Give Them an Inch . . .

Meanwhile, with the Seattle Seahawks' ownership in California businessman Ken Behring's hands for nine years, rumors surfaced that the team's position in northern Washington State was less than secure. "In Washington State," explains attorney Shawn Newman, "the worst thing you can be is a California developer." A local owner was needed, supposedly, to keep the team in town. But once such a prospective homegrown buyer was found, he followed the pattern of local owners across the country.

When Microsoft cofounder and local billionaire Paul Allen expressed interest in buying the Seahawks in early 1996, he made one thing perfectly clear: A new stadium to replace the twenty-year-old Kingdome was a necessary condition of his purchase. His interest was greeted with joy by many in the Northwest community, despite the warning bells that hundreds of millions in public money was about to be requested once again. The hero worship was appalling to Newman. "They paint the local guy as the savior on the white horse," the Olympia resident says in disgust, "where we're picking up the droppings."

At hearings to determine the viability of another massive publicly supported project, Allen and other new-stadium proponents rallied busloads of supporters to the state capital to express their enthusiasm. Shawn Newman, whose law offices are just down the street, took a stroll to the hearing to check out the scene and get his own two cents in. "They've got all these people drooling on themselves, testifying what a great deal it is," Newman recalls. "They never even read the damn bill, they don't know what they're talking about."

This was an emotional issue, pure and simple, and new-stadium proponents had brought in the heavy artillery. "And I don't mean to criticize these people," Newman explains, his frustration evident. "They talk about how their sons or daughters are so enamored, that the Seahawks mean so much to them, that my little boy [has] leukemia and [is on] life support and that it was because the Seahawks had done something that had got him out of death's grip, or some bullshit."

Of course, Allen's call wasn't just for a facility to make the sick children of Seattle happy. Instead, the team's massive PR campaign emphasized the many uses of the new stadium. They brought in representatives from the U.S. Olympic Committee to argue that such a venue would be ideal for hosting future Olympic soccer matches, quoting the commissioner of Major League Soccer to the same end.

When it was Newman's turn to speak, he told those gathered that "the real question you have to ask yourself is one of priorities, and whether or not the voters are going to respect you in the morning after you get done with another stadium shuffle. Because you want priorities." A bigger concern is that "forty thousand legal residents of Washington State are going to lose their food stamps this summer. About eight thousand are going to lose social security benefits. Legal residents. That's an emergency, not building a new stadium for a billionaire."

By February 1997 Washington governor Gary Locke had called for a statewide vote on the creation of a 10 percent tax on licensed sports apparel and memorabilia in order to fund the public's share of the proposed $402 million new stadium. When that proved controversial (as well it might, with apparel giant Nike based in neighboring Oregon) politicians agreed that the funding would instead come from an extension on the state's hotel–motel tax and a tax on Seahawks tickets and parking.

Allen himself had pledged at least $100 million toward stadium construction, and he now took the unheard-of step of single-handedly financing the statewide referendum—which ran him $4.2 million. Allen's supporters said that he did so only because state politicians had insisted that if there was to be another statewide vote, taxpayers would not be made to pay for it. But the step was an alarming one for many. "I just don't recall ever seeing someone pick up a total tab for an election," North Carolina political science professor Thad Beyle told the *New York Times.* "It bumps up against questions about just how far you can let democracy go."

Paying for the election was a bold step for the billionaire in another way as well. "Paul Allen never voted in an election," claims Van Dyk. "The first election there's any public record of him having voted in is the election he purchased."

That vote, and those dollars, would be key in what would be the most expensive initiative campaign in state history. In June 1997, voters narrowly approved the new stadium for the Seahawks. For kicking in some $3 million, Allen got his $300 million-plus public contribution, and years of luxury-box revenue from this new stadium. It apparently was money well spent. Seattle is getting its two new facilities, and its taxpayers are going to be paying for them for a long time to come.

Minneapolis: Win a Few . . .

In the early '90s, Minnesota would have seemed an unlikely target for teams seeking new facilities, if only because it had two of the newest buildings around. The Target Center, built in 1990 with minimal public money, was home to the new Timberwolves basketball team. Just blocks away in downtown Minneapolis sat the Hubert Humphrey Metrodome, a fabric-roofed sixty-four-thousand-seat stadium that housed both baseball's Twins and football's Vikings.

The Metrodome itself was built mostly at public expense—$55 million of it, financed largely by hotel, motel, food, alcohol, and beverage taxes. The pitched battle between community activists and local business interests that surrounded its construction presaged some of the public-stadium fights of the late '80s and '90s. Particularly at issue, remembers neighborhood activist Carla Bruenig, were the questions of housing because many buildings were torn down to make way for parking for the new stadium, and traffic, which suddenly flooded into the local streets on game days.

The Metrodome was never a thing of beauty. During daytime baseball games the translucent Teflon roof made every fly ball an adventure, and the Twins never did seem able to find the right artificial turf to prevent balls from bouncing twenty feet over outfielders' heads. But it quickly felt like home to the Twins and Vikings, especially during the Twins' two world championship seasons of 1987 and 1991, when fan noise inside the dome out-decibeled a jet taking off. With a new stadium firmly in place, Minnesotans could at least consider sports-subsidy battles a thing of the past—doubly so when NBA expansion team owners Marv Wolfenson and Harvey Ratner spent $81 million of their own money (along with $23 million in public funds) to build the Target Center in 1990 for their new Timberwolves basketball team. Minneapolis–St. Paul was sitting pretty: one of only six metropolitan areas with franchises in all four pro sports leagues, and the only one with state-of-the-art facilities for each to play in. Throw in a generally strong, diversified state economy, and Minnesota's largest urban center had reason to brag.

Until the North Stars packed up and left town.

Minneapolis's hockey team had been playing in the Met Center in nearby Bloomington, and that suburban arena was suffering in both attendance and revenue because of competition from the new Target Center. The team's owners considered relocating to share the newer building with the Timberwolves but instead opted to find an arena where they would collect a greater share of the revenue streams. They found one in Dallas, becoming the Dallas Stars in 1993, and leaving the publicly owned Met Center empty.

Meanwhile, the Target Center was facing a sudden cash crisis. Wolfenson and Ratner had counted on paying off the $35 million in construction costs with revenue from ticket and suite sales, but the building ultimately came in at $104 million, leaving "Harv and Marv," as they were universally known, with $10 million in debt payments and property taxes due each year on the arena and no way to pay it off. After the failed attempt to get the North Stars to relocate to the Target Center, the pair took a hard look at the sea of red ink and turned to the city government for a bailout.

To get the city's attention, Harv and Marv announced in the spring of 1994 that they were moving the Timberwolves to New Orleans for the upcoming season. The NBA rejected the move but only on the condition that Minneapolis agree to spend $74 million to purchase the arena, financed largely by sales and property taxes at the building—money that previously went directly into general city revenues. Wolfenson and Ratner, as part of the deal, sold the team to a local millionaire for $88.5 million, turning a 172 percent five-year profit on their original $32.5 million investment. And despite promises by proponents that the buyout would help lure a new hockey team to Minneapolis, when the NHL announced its intent to expand to the Twin Cities in 1997, it was to a proposed new arena across the river in St. Paul, which would replace the twenty-five-year-old Civic Center Arena. The seven-year-old Target Center, Minnesota Sports Facilities commissioner Henry Savelkoul explained, no longer had the "provisions," in the form of revenue from luxury suites, advertising, and concessions, to support pro hockey.

The Target Center bailout left the Minnesota populace wary of "economic development" subsidies—all the more so because it came on the heels of another notorious corporate giveaway involving Northwest Airlines: In 1992 the state legislature had granted Northwest Airlines an astounding $761 million in loans, tax breaks, and cash in exchange for a promise to build two maintenance bases in the northern part of the state. But as the legislators soon discovered, Northwest was in no position to build anything. Its new owners had severely overextended their finances in their leveraged buyout of the company, and Northwest had already lost $1 billion in the two years since. The company—which was "very close to bankruptcy," according to the Minneapolis Federal Reserve's Art Rolnick—promptly canceled the planned bases but kept the no-strings-attached state loans to help pay off their debts. "The [bases were] bogus," says Rolnick. "It was just a ploy to say, I'm going to give you jobs up north, an economically depressed area, if you loan me this money." Only after years of public outcry did Northwest finally agree to a scaled-back version of the plan that would create just 954 jobs, less than a quarter the number originally promised.

For a state with a long liberal and union tradition—Minnesota's state Democratic Party is known as the Democratic-Farmer-Labor Party—the Northwest deal was an expensive lesson in the costs of corporate welfare. The state responded by passing the Minnesota Corporate Welfare Reform Law in 1995, requiring that businesses that receive state or local economic aid must show net job growth for the state within two years, or else refund the money.

Deals like these may have soured the public on subsidizing local business leaders with nine-figure expenditures, but it only whetted the appetite of Twins owner Carl Pohlad for the riches available via corporate welfare. Pohlad, despite a team that broke attendance records at the new dome, had often complained of feeling like a second-class citizen there. Seating in the multipurpose stadium was arranged more for football than for baseball, and, perhaps more important, the Vikings controlled all the luxury-suite revenue, leaving the Twins to survive on ticket sales and concessions revenue alone.

In September 1996 Pohlad went public with his request for a new ballpark, hinting that he would activate an escape clause in his Metrodome lease if a new stadium were not in the works by 1998. Pohlad, the billionaire head of a banking empire, had a checkered business history in the Twin Cities, including experience with profiting from the public till: After he was tapped by the state in 1959 to head up a bus company that had been brought to the brink of bankruptcy under the control of local mobsters, Pohlad wound up cutting bus maintenance and pension-fund payments, demanding a fare increase despite turning profits—and siphoning off at least $4 million in interest-free loans to help buy the Tropicana Casino in Las Vegas. Pohlad was later part of Frank Lorenzo's scandal-plagued management of Eastern and Continental Airlines in the 1980s. Through all this, his family fortune, which began when he took control of a local bank in the 1940s, soared to more than $1 billion.

The opposition to a new Twins ballpark was unusually well organized from the start. Jon Commers, a former state legislative aide, launched Fans Advocating Intelligent Spending out of the offices of a local progressive activist group. Along with Ricky Rask's Fund Kids First, Commers set out to muster public opposition to Pohlad's demands, focusing particular attention on the eighteen state legislators who had sworn during the 1996 election campaign not to spend public money on a new stadium.

On the Twins' side, meanwhile, was only one prominent politician: Governor Arne Carlson.

Proclaiming himself the state's "number one fan," Carlson was an unabashed rooter for all of Minnesota's sports teams and expressed an interest in becoming a sports booster when he retired from public office; he once called a press conference to criticize the officiating at a college basketball game. So when the Twins came looking for an ally, the state's highest public official was more than happy to jump on board. Once asked why Pohlad couldn't spend his own money on a stadium, Carlson snapped, "That's irrelevant," and accused people opposed to subsidizing billionaires of promulgating "class warfare."

In January, Pohlad and Henry Savelkoul of the Metropolitan Sports Facilities Commission proudly announced that they had a plan that would satisfy everyone. The state would spend $277.5 million toward a $360 million stadium with a retractable dome; in exchange, Pohlad would give the people of Minnesota ownership of 49 percent of the team. At the time, Major League Baseball had a stated policy against public ownership of any portion of a franchise, which would mean opening their secret bookkeeping to public scrutiny, but this didn't stop the plan from being hailed by *Star Tribune* sports columnist Sid Hartman as a marvel of generosity: "Never has the owner of a football or baseball team offered a package such as the $158 million gift and 49 percent interest in the team that Twins owner Carl Pohlad has offered the state."

On January 26 the first polls came in—and they gave Carlson's plan a resounding thumbs-down. Fully 69 percent of Minnesotans said they opposed the deal; even self-identified Twins fans were slightly inclined toward opposition. When asked to list public spending priorities in order of importance, those polled ranked pro sports dead last. Worse yet for the Twins, the *St. Paul Pioneer-Press* reported that Pohlad's $82.5 million "contribution" to the stadium—not $158 million, as Hartman had erroneously reported—would in fact be a loan, not a gift, one that he expected to be paid back should he sell the team. The Twins quickly backpedaled, claiming that calling it a gift had been a "miscommunication," but the damage was done.

From there, the Twins quickly stepped up their campaign. The consulting firm Arthur Anderson was hired to produce a glowing report on the economic benefits of a new ballpark. Pohlad began to make more-overt threats to move the team elsewhere if his demands weren't met, though skeptics wondered if the cities rumored as destinations for the ballclub—which included such metropolises as Charlotte, North Carolina, and Portland, Oregon, the home of the Twins' top minor-league team—would bring him any more revenue than he was already getting in Minnesota.

The team also tried to leverage the star power of its players, parading Kirby Puckett, a local hero whose Hall of Fame career was cut short by glaucoma, around the state to stump for a new ballpark. Although some Minnesotans resented what they considered Puckett's prostituting himself for a new baseball stadium, one state senator who Puckett and other Twins stars had lobbied defended the visits, asserting that "it's not unlike when you want to pass the victim's rights bill; you bring in the victim."

He paused, then added, "That's not a good analogy."

...Lose a Few

Meanwhile, the Twins and state couldn't even agree on a price tag. The cost of the new ballpark—with retractable roof, of course—fluctuated wildly between $300 million and $500 million over the course of the winter.

Public opinion remained unenthusiastic—a citizen's panel brought together by the *Star Tribune* and a local TV station unanimously panned the deal. "If I invest two thirds of the money, I want more than 49 percent," said retired lab technician Bob Koebele. And Deb McNeill, a store manager who supported the stadium before the forum, announced that she had changed her mind: "I grew up thinking of the Twins not as a business, but more as a public entity. But the team isn't. They are a business. I'm not able to defend public funding. I have nothing to defend it with."

With the public ownership option going nowhere—one sports commission member declared it "dead as a smelt"—Carlson turned to more likely prospects for revenue. First, the governor suggested a ten-cents-a-pack cigarette tax, earmarking nine cents for stadium construction and one cent for antismoking programs; that bombed with public health advocates, who asked why all ten cents shouldn't be devoted to public health. Finally, a bill was introduced to place slot machines at a local racetrack, which its legislative sponsor optimistically predicted would generate $50 million a year for the state—raising an outcry from the state Indian reservations that relied on casino revenue to fund their own budgets. "If ever someone gets around to writing a brochure on 'How a Bill *Doesn't* Become Law,'" the *Star Tribune* concluded, "the author might use the proposed Twins stadium as a case study."

The clock finally ran out on May 19, as the state legislature closed its session without voting on a stadium bill. Six months later, it reconvened in special session to once again consider stadium options. This time, there was an immediate threat on the table: In October, Pohlad had signed a deal to sell the Twins to North Carolina businessman Don Beaver, who would move it to that state's Triad region (Greensboro, High Point, and Winston-Salem). The deal would be called off only if the legislature approved a stadium-funding bill by November 30.

The bill that was finally submitted for legislative approval was a bizarre hodgepodge of different proposals. Under this plan, Pohlad would give the team to a nonprofit foundation, which would pay off his $86 million in accrued debts by selling it to another local owner within five years; Pohlad would also earn a substantial tax break on the "charitable contribution" of his team, valued at $140 million, to the foundation. The state, meanwhile, would pay the entire cost of building a $404 million stadium, this time via an all-new funding scheme: redirecting income taxes and sales taxes from the stadium to pay off the construction bonds. (A similar mechanism, known as "tax-increment financing," is commonly granted by cities to private developers in other industries.) Proponents argued that this was no different from other fees, such as hunting licenses, that were earmarked for specific purposes; critics pointed out that as these funds would otherwise go into the state's general fund, this was as direct a subsidy as there could be. "The financing of the thing is too screwy," one *Star Tribune* reader wrote to the paper's Web site, noting that if players' income taxes could be used to pay for a stadium, "I think my income tax should go towards improving the place I work."

Legislators, by and large, agreed; the tax-increment scheme garnered little support. At the last minute, stadium proponents frantically tried to fashion a different bill that would pay for the new stadium entirely with "user fees"—profits on the future sale of the Twins by the foundation, higher parking and sales taxes at the ballpark, and surcharges on player salaries and sports broadcasts. But even as the baseball players union and local broadcasters screamed bloody murder, that plan ran into a still more imposing obstacle: the money raised wouldn't be nearly enough to pay construction costs. A new stadium, just as Robert Baade and his fellow economists had predicted, couldn't pay its own way.

The calls that poured in to the capitol switchboard were running 3–2 against stadium funding; Minneapolis voters, meanwhile, over-whelmingly approved a $10 million cap on city funding of any new ballpark. Finally, on November 13, the legislature threw in the towel, with the House voting 87–47 to reject the last-ditch proposal, then adjourning the special session for good. "On November 13, profes-sional baseball died in Minnesota," proclaimed House stadium-bill sponsor Loren Jennings.

Yet Pohlad, who had earlier insisted that his sale of the team would kick in if the legislature adjourned without passing a stadium bill, still hesitated. "Everybody says it's dead," he said after the House vote. "I don't know if it is or not." The November 30 deadline passed with the future of the Twins, and the stadium, still undecided.

San Francisco: If at First You Don't Succeed . . .

San Francisco's history with sports owner demands has been par-ticularly epic—involving "ten years, five mayors, four referenda, four cities, and one earthquake," as one observer put it. It began in 1984, when then San Francisco Giants owner Bob Lurie, who had bought the team eight years earlier to prevent it from being moved to To-ronto, declared that he would sell the team to out-of-town interests if he didn't get a new stadium. Candlestick Park, the team's home since moving west from New York in 1958, was best known as the coldest and windiest place in the Bay Area (Giants pitcher Stu Miller was once blown off the mound by a gust of wind), and Lurie was determined to get a replacement at public expense.

San Francisco, however, has a very different means of approving public expenditures than do most U.S. cities. Virtually all city bond issues are subject to approval by the electorate (this was true even before Proposition 218 passed new statewide restrictions on issuing bonds in 1996), meaning the Giants would have to subject their stadium demands to a public referendum.

The first such referendum was Proposition W, in 1987, which called for an $85 million stadium in the South of Market warehouse district. Held during a mayoral election in which three of the four candidates opposed the initiative, it went down to a 53 percent to 47 percent defeat. Two years later, having swayed new mayor Art Agnos to climb aboard the stadium bandwagon, the Giants tried again with Proposition P. By this time, the price tag had risen to $115 million, the site had shifted several blocks to the San Francisco waterfront—and the margin of defeat was 1 percent, helped along by an electorate more concerned with rebuilding from the previous month's earthquake than with upgrading a ballpark that had remained standing throughout the temblor, beneath the feet of sixty thousand fans waiting for a World Series game to begin.

The following year Lurie tried a new strategy: Sick of San Francisco voters, he pitched a multi-city funding effort to build a new stadium south of San Francisco, near San Jose. This time the Giants managed to win one vote—but lost three others, sending the complicated funding scheme down to defeat. In 1992 yet another referendum, this one limited to San Jose, crashed and burned when 55 percent of city voters declined to hand over $185 million in utility taxes for a new ballpark.

Every time Lurie had come back to the public asking for money—more and more money each time, in fact—he had presented the upcoming vote as the "last hope" of keeping the Giants in the Bay Area, and it was understandable if the citizenry was beginning to suspect he was crying wolf. But then Bob Lurie did what no baseball owner had done in twenty years: He sold his team to a group of investors from the Tampa Bay area. The team, it was announced, would begin play in Florida in 1993. Finally, it seemed, an owner had been pushed too far; without public subsidies you really couldn't guarantee that a sports team would stay put, even in a populous area like San Francisco.

The National League owners voted to reject the sale.

The reasons were complex. A Giants move might help spread fear in other cities faced with pending stadium legislation, but it would also take Tampa Bay out of the running as a locale for other teams to move to—as several teams were then threatening to do. The San Francisco Bay Area was the nation's fifth-largest TV market; Tampa Bay ranked fourteenth, meaning a potential loss of network TV revenue for the whole league when the national broadcast contract came up for renegotiation. And finally, there was a local ownership group, led by Safeway supermarket magnate Peter Magowan, ready to buy the team and keep it in San Francisco, albeit at a slightly lower price than what the Tampa Bay group was offering. The league told Lurie to take the Magowan bid; Lurie took it. All those referenda, it turned out, hadn't been the last hope of retaining the Giants but merely the last hope of retaining Bob Lurie.

Magowan immediately set out to secure the new ballpark that Lurie had failed to get, with one major difference: This time, the Giants were prepared to foot the bill themselves. The Giants would build and own the planned $255 million waterfront ballpark, with almost the entire cost paid for out of a private bond issue and the sale of naming rights and luxury boxes. Proposition B passed in May 1996 by a two-to-one margin, and the Giants at last had their ballpark.

The San Francisco story to this point has become near-legendary among anti-stadium activists: the little electorate that could, calling the bluff of the leagues and getting to keep their team and their money, too. Even the $1.2 million a year in hidden subsidies later approved for Magowan's privately funded ballpark (for relocating a Port of San Francisco maintenance yard on the same China Basin site rejected in the 1989 referendum), and the $15 million in public tax-increment financing (in which the city would divert property taxes on the land into the construction fund) didn't dim enthusiasm: The Giants were still building the first privately funded baseball stadium in three decades, largely because voters had indicated loud and clear that they had no intention of footing the bill.

The Giants controversy would pale, though, in comparison to the next demand placed before the San Francisco electorate. The Giants had a cotenant at Candlestick Park: the immensely popular 49ers football team. And 49ers owner Eddie DeBartolo had decided it was time to cash in on the sports-welfare gold rush.

Mall in the Family

The 49ers management set out to prove that, done right, even the most anti-subsidy city in the United States could be forced to cough up money for a new stadium. Then they proceeded to do almost everything wrong.

The first rumblings came in late 1996, as the aftershocks of the previous year's move of the Cleveland Browns to Baltimore and the announced shift of the Houston Oilers to Tennessee were still reverberating in the ears of football fans. Team owner Edward DeBartolo, a multimillionaire real-estate developer, warned that the team, which had turned a $19 million profit in 1995—tops among NFL teams—and was fresh from its fifth Super Bowl victory in fourteen years, could no longer field a "competitive" team without the help of a new stadium. "Given the fact that there are many cities that would build them a new stadium at no cost, it's a real tribute that the 49ers have moved from asking the city for money to looking for some kind of alternative," said Jack Davis, who the 49ers hired to lead their campaign for a new stadium.

Davis and the 49ers didn't look very hard. By February 1997 the team was asking for $100 million in public subsidies for a new stadium on the Candlestick Park site. The referendum—actually two referenda, Propositions D and F, one to approve the funding and the other to ease zoning restrictions—would go before the voters in June.

The first thing DeBartolo and club president Carmen Policy did was to insist (as the Miami Heat had in their campaign for a "waterfront park" the previous year) that they weren't really asking for a stadium at all. The new 49ers stadium, they announced, would be but a mere portion of a planned mall development to be built by Mills Corp. If eight days of football a year—plus the three Super Bowls over the next thirty years that NFL commissioner Paul Tagliabue was dangling as an incentive for the city to build a new stadium—wouldn't generate enough economic activity to make the public investment worthwhile, what of a giant shopping mall, drawing consumers from all over the region? And where $100 million might look like a lot to invest in a $325 million stadium, it would be a mere fraction of the cost of a $525 million "entertainment complex."

"For every $4.25 that the 49ers put on the table," Davis told the press, "the city puts $1, and the dollar is not a dollar that comes out of the budget for police and fire. When the public takes a look at the deal, it's clearly and convincingly about jobs and economic opportunity."

The first member of the public to take a close look at the numbers disagreed. On February 7, San Francisco Board of Supervisors budget analyst Harvey Rose released a study claiming to show that the city would lose $4.6 million a year on the new stadium, and possibly more if the mega-mall drew off shoppers from other retail outlets in the city. City controller Ed Harrington promptly issued a competing report claiming that the new mall "should generate new revenues sufficient to pay all, or a substantial portion of" the construction costs—and Harrington's report, unlike Rose's, would be included in the official city voter guide for the referendum.

The next obstacle for the team came from the stadium's opponents. The anti-49ers campaign was being led by Joel Ventresca, a veteran of the successful fights against subsidizing the Giants, but it was a pair of local individuals who would cause the biggest uproar. Taking advantage of a San Francisco law allowing residents to buy space in the city voter guide to argue for or against ballot measures, the pair paid $269 for a satirical ad *in favor* of the stadium project. "Opponents call it 'Candlestick Pork' and 'corporate wel-fare,'" wrote local attorney Dan Larkosh and self-proclaimed "aspir-ing millionaire" John Hlinko. "Perhaps. But when you're from Ohio, making money in San Francisco means expensive flights, paying for dual housekeeping staffs, limo drivers, etc. This adds up!" Larkosh signed the missive, "Multimillionaires for Corporate Welfare." Crit-ics charged the pair with making a "laughingstock" of the election; Larkosh responded, "If the truth is funny, so be it." The ad wound up being kicked into the "con" section of the voter guide but not before the ensuing public uproar had introduced millions of area newspa-per readers to the arguments within.

The biggest fiasco of all, though, was brought on by the 49ers' campaign director himself. DeBartolo was determined to keep him-self and his $600 million net worth out of the limelight, and Policy was less than silver-tongued with the public. (In first announcing the team's desire for a city-funded stadium the previous fall, Policy had declaimed, "Once the mayor gets into the posture where he believes and sees you're not trying to milk the cow dry, but only enough to fill the glass so you don't choke on the cookies, can we proceed.") So the team hired Jack Davis, a well-known local political operative who had managed the Giants' referendum campaign the year before, to make their case before the voters.

Davis looked like the perfect choice for the job. A former cam-paign director for Mayor Brown and other prominent area politi-cians, he kept a low personal profile while pushing the 49ers' stadium project at every opportunity. Until, that is, May 3, when Davis threw himself a fiftieth birthday party to which he invited Mayor Brown, 49ers president Policy, and other local luminaries. That wasn't the story; the entertainment was: a performance artist who, dressed in a Native American headdress, had a colleague carve a satanic star into his back, urinate on him, and sodomize him with a whiskey bottle.

It was hardly the sort of thing the team wanted associated with its PR specialist. "The Party" dominated headlines for days, with reac-tion ranging from ridicule to outrage. Denni Woodward, director of

Stanford University's American Indian and Alaska Native Program, summed up the performance as "combining [an indigenous culture] with some kind of cheap horror movie. I think he's probably offended everybody from the Apache Mescalero to the Satanists."

The 49ers responded with a flurry of new promises in an attempt to drive the Davis party uproar from the front pages. One day the team was announcing that it would provide health benefits to domestic partners of gay employees; another it was taking out an insurance policy (a legally toothless one, it turned out) against the city's having to pay any money out of general funds. The new stadium, it was promised, would provide jobs for the impoverished residents of nearby Hunters Point. By the end, DeBartolo himself had entered the fray, defending the stadium deal with every argument he could muster.

"Candlestick is almost to the point where it'll be condemned," he told a group of undecided women at a "For Women Only" pro-stadium event in May. To renovate it, he insisted, "would cost too much—$180 million."

"Is that your estimate or someone else's?" asked one woman.

"Look, you'd be throwing good money after bad," DeBartolo replied. "The key thing is the economic benefit to the city. People don't understand why the mall is there, but it's the engine that runs the train."

Going into the June 3 vote, public expectation was that the two propositions would go down in defeat, just like the four attempts by the Giants at public funding. The team's threats to take the team to hated rival Los Angeles had been met more with derision than concern: "Threatening to go to Los Angeles is like holding a gun to your own head and threatening to kill the hostage," quipped one newspaper columnist. The last poll, taken two weeks before the election, had shown the stadium initiative trailing by nine percentage points, with little sign of change during the months of lobbying by the team and the mayor.

Instead, it squeaked to victory by a little more than a thousand votes. Huge margins of victory in Hunters Point led to allegations of voter fraud, especially after it was reported that polls had been opened at city-run housing projects in that neighborhood several days before election day. City employees, it was further revealed, had been pressured ("encouraged," insisted the mayor's press secretary) into taking off the day of the election to do pro-stadium campaigning.

The deal, however, was done. After spending more than $2 million on the pro-stadium campaign—$33 per yes vote—including $1.25 million of DeBartolo's family fortune, the 49ers had their stadium funds. "The guy upstairs must really have wanted for this to happen," exclaimed Policy at a jubilant post-election party for the 49ers and their backers.

Presumably, he wasn't talking about DeBartolo.

The Stadium Merry-Go-Round

In June 1997 *Your Money* magazine ran a list of all the major-league baseball, football, and basketball franchises and their stadiums and arenas; an asterisk marked each team that was seeking a new building. Out of seventy-four teams, there were twenty-nine asterisks: from the Boston Red Sox to the San Diego Padres, the Sacramento Kings to the Charlotte Hornets. And that didn't include the twenty-one teams already playing in new or newly renovated facilities, or the fourteen that had new buildings under construction. It also left out an entire country (Canada) and major sport (hockey), which would have accounted for perhaps a dozen more stadiums and arenas, in progress or under negotiation.

Despite all the concrete that has already been poured, the new stadium craze shows no signs of abating—in fact, it has spread to such places as England and Australia, where publicly funded soccer stadiums increasingly dot the landscape. In North America there are more stadiums and arenas going up each year than at any time in history. The sports industry seems to be settling into an equilibrium where at any given time one quarter of major-league teams is playing in a new building, one quarter is awaiting the construction of one, another quarter is lobbying to get one built—and a final quarter is waiting in the wings for its turn at the plate. And once those teams have gotten their new toys, it will be time for the last round of stadium-beggars to line up again for another handout, for their stadiums will be slipping into "economic obsolescence."

"If you go into building a new stadium now and aren't prepared for major changes by that second decade," Mark Rosentraub told the *Minneapolis Star Tribune* in the midst of the Twins fight, "you're being Pollyannaish about it." As San Franciscans can attest, if you *don't* build a new stadium now, just wait a couple of years—someone will doubtless make a new pitch for one then.

Notes

1. Van Dyk and Citizens for More Important Things reemerged in 2006, during debates over a new arena for the Sonics basketball team, when the group sponsored a referendum to block city money from being spent on private sports facilities unless the public was guaranteed a return on its investment. The measure passed overwhelmingly—at which point Sonics owner Clayton Bennett declared that while he still hoped to remain in King County, "Seattle will now be relegated to a second-tier status."

2. By the time Safeco Field, named for an insurance company, opened in July 1999, the total cost had soared to $517 million. Though the Mariners' owners had promised to pay for all cost overruns, team execs now declared that the added expenses were actually "unanticipated capital costs," not cost overruns, and should be paid by the public. After a threatened lawsuit went nowhere, the team finally agreed to pay the additional $100 million out of its own pocket—in exchange for promises that the county would be on the hook for all future upgrades to the stadium.

10 The Bucks Stop Here

The loyal rooters never doubted for a moment that their beloved Bums were as much a part of their heritage as Prospect Park. They discovered they were wrong. The Dodgers were only a piece of merchandise that passed from hand to hand.
—*Baseball owner Bill Veeck*

When Cleveland Indians outfielder Albert Belle left the team, and the city, for a huge contract with the rival Chicago White Sox in the spring of 1997, Cleveland fans were outraged. (They showed it by greeting him with a chorus of boos and obscene gestures when he returned to Jacobs Field to play as a member of the visiting team.) It was as if, in leaving the Indians, Belle had betrayed his citywide extended family—a family that had been extorted by its own parents to fork over hard-earned dollars to keep the team in town by paying for a new stadium.

If They Don't Win, It's a Shame

For generations, the special emotional presence of the local team has been played up—by sports promoters, by the local media, by fans themselves. These are home teams: unique, regional representations of a city's heart and soul. The intensity of the connection between local fan and hometown team has divided family loyalties, driven real-estate decisions, and dominated debate at countless dinner tables.

Decades later, there are still New Yorkers who have never recovered from the awful day in 1957 when Walter O'Malley abruptly yanked the Brooklyn Dodgers out of Ebbets Field and moved them three thousand miles to Los Angeles. There are grown men and women who walked away from baseball fandom that day and never looked back, others who switched allegiance to the crosstown Yankees or Giants, still others who raised their children on Brooklyn lore—reminiscing about a long-gone franchise. The Dodgers were a neighborhood team, they represented a proud if increasingly struggling urban community, and they were as much a part of daily life as the local churches or recreation centers. The bond was a real one—at least from the point of view of the fans.

How important is that relationship? When major league baseball was hit by financial disputes and labor unrest in the early and mid-1990s, one of the great fears heard among sports marketers and commentators alike was about the alienation of fans. What would happen to the sport's popularity, it was wondered, when fans thought of the ballclubs as collections of free-agent millionaire athletes looking out for their own financial best interests before the good of their team—thus willing to leave Americans without their beloved baseball in the interest of higher salaries? And what would happen when fans thought of professional owners as similarly self-interested billionaires—willing to shut down America's pastime before agreeing to player demands, willing to search for more-hospitable climes when local municipalities couldn't produce sparkling new diamonds? It's a concern that pops up periodically, among sports journalists and bottom-line network presidents, among professional sports leagues and hot-stove league fans. What would happen, in other words, when the myth of home teams' belonging, emotionally, morally even, to home cities was exploded in the face of faithful fans?

What happened, apparently, was a great deal of sound and fury without any clear significance. Major league baseball attendance dropped, but it had already been on a downward trend. For years, league officials have bemoaned the difficulties of bringing America's youth back to the game. Of course, that occasional disinterest on the part of the country's future consumers may have just as much to do with overpriced seats and concession items, fancy new stadiums with distant views, and the increasing popularity of other sports as with a realization that there isn't any guaranteed "home" in your hometown baseball club. But still, the warning was out—beware the alienation of the fan, beware the cynicism of the consumer. The myth of public participation in local professional sports needed to be as strong as ever, in order to prevent further declines in fan interest and avoid threats to franchise profits.

Out of the Mouths of Legislators

But what *are* concerned citizens supposed to do if their sports team is threatening to leave town unless it gets a publicly funded new stadium? Sympathetic to the plight of sports fans who don't want to lose their team or shell out large amounts of tax dollars, some legislators have tried to find a solution through the law. Unfortunately, these approaches do not offer a readily apparent way out of the problem.

The main focus of legislative efforts to put the brakes on stadium subsidies thus far has been a bill sponsored by New York senator Daniel Patrick Moynihan. Nearly all activists spoke of it with some hope, and perhaps not surprisingly, nearly everyone at the Sports Facilities Finance Conference spoke with some apprehension about the Moynihan bill.

Picking up from where the 1986 Tax Reform Act fell short, the Moynihan-sponsored Stop Tax-exempt Arena Debt Issuance Act (STADIA) would essentially rule out altogether the use of federally tax-exempt bonds for any pro sports facilities.

However, by late 1997 the bill had few sponsors. And even if it were to somehow pass, it was likely to have exemptions tacked on by members of Congress seeking special projects in their districts.

Furthermore, the Moynihan bill wouldn't stop stadium construction, just raise the cost of capital. Cities would be under pressure to sell taxable, rather than tax-exempt, bonds. Since they carry higher interest rates, these bonds end up costing much more. An extra 2 percent a year—the standard difference in rates—on $400 million in bonds would amount to $8 million per year in extra costs to the local government issuing the bonds. The problem is that that 2 percent extra interest is a lot of money because these bonds usually have a long maturity. If they mature in twenty years, the extra interest would amount to $160 million. The Moynihan bill could easily end up just shifting this part of the subsidy from the federal government to local governments.

There have been other attempts at federal legislation. Oregon representative Earl Blumenauer has proposed a bill saying that in order to keep congressionally granted monopoly privileges, leagues would have to allow municipal ownership and would have to give current cities first dibs on buying teams before the owners can move them. Ohio representative Martin Hoke introduced a similar bill in 1996, only to have it "lobbied to death by the NFL's hired guns," a Hoke staffer told *U.S. News and World Report.*

Other activists have tried devising various means of stopping corporate welfare in general. Corporate welfare activists like Greg LeRoy have proposed various "clawback" provisions (where states get money back if the promised jobs aren't created), and multi-state commissions to develop regional no-competition pacts among states. They sound promising enough, but some other corporate-welfare opponents (notably Arthur Rolnick of the Minneapolis Federal Reserve) don't see them going anywhere—clawbacks are only as good as the will to enforce them. (For example, a clawback law was in place with Northwest Airlines, but the state of Minnesota later renegotiated it to avoid alienating the airline company.) Additionally, every attempt at a regional commission so far has fallen apart when one of the parties gets the opportunity to steal a plum business from another locality.

Rolnick instead has a proposal that, he insists, would stop corporate welfare in its tracks: Have the IRS tax corporate welfare as imputed income. In other words, if your state builds you a $400-million stadium, you have to declare $400 million income on your taxes. Needless to say, this would greatly reduce the incentive for companies to seek corporate welfare.

Rolnick says he's had numerous legal experts look into the possibility of such a law, and he is certain it's constitutional. He thinks it compares favorably with interstate agreements to stop corporate welfare, since, as he says, the Compact Clause of the Constitution "really doesn't allow states to make contracts like this—that's what you've got Congress for."

Whether this is politically feasible is another story. One would think that Congress would have no interest in maintaining local corporations—why should the federal government care where in the United States a company is located—but, of course, Congress itself is made up of locally elected politicians, who have the same ties to corporations and dependence on their campaign contributions and the like as local politicians do. In 1997 Minnesota representative David Minge introduced a federal bill to levy a 35 percent excise tax on local-government subsidies, but it likely faces an uphill battle in Congress.[1]

Bringing 'em Home

There is one other solution that has been suggested for stadium subsidies. It's one that would tap into the very mythology that pro owners use when trying to persuade local populaces to build them new stadiums. It's always about "our" team, after all, at least according to the owners' public relations flacks—about our town and our pride. In the spring of 1985, when the Cleveland Indians were facing yet another ignominious season on the playing field and the city itself was being asked to build a new stadium to keep the team in town, someone in the club's public relations office came up with an appropriate catchphrase to drum up support for the new baseball season. "Tribe '85," went the saying, printed on bumper stickers and pins, home game giveaway items and local advertising, "This Is My Team!"

But what if it really *were* our team?

When the world champion Chicago Bulls basketball team takes the court before each sold-out game at the United Center, they are often presented by the dramatic public address announcer as "your Chicago Bulls." But what if they really were?

When Clevelanders heard Art Modell was pulling the Browns out of town, they were stunned. These were the Cleveland Browns; they weren't Art Modell's to pick up and scatter whichever way the financial windfalls blew. They belonged to the town as much as Lake Erie and pierogis, battles over school desegregation and deindustrialization, didn't they?

Amid the demands for petition drives and rallies were few calls for one obvious solution. They were the Cleveland Browns, after all. Why not have the city buy the team? One group, at least, saw it as an easy choice: "The state, county, or city of Berea, where the Browns Corp. is located, can legally take over the team. Modell can be paid off later but the team will stay," read an Ohio Communist Party flyer handed out at local rallies. "You, the greatest fans in the world, can make this happen. . . . Get your union, church, or community group to speak out in favor of public takeover of the Browns through eminent domain."

And really, the demand seemed fairly straightforward. If they belonged to the city, the Browns would still be packing 'em in at Municipal Stadium. Winter Sunday afternoons would still mean big crowds at corner taverns, paper dog bones pasted into store windows, "Go Browns" spelled out across corporate vistas. Why *shouldn't* the team belong to the city?

After all, hasn't it worked for the Green Bay Packers for nearly fifty years?

Well, yes and no. The Packers, though often cited as a "publicly owned" team by the media, are not actually owned by the municipality of Green Bay, but neither are they run by a single private owner. In 1950, when the Green Bay Packers football team was on the verge of bankruptcy, the team went public as a non-profit corporation, with about five thousand shares of stock at $25 apiece. The team now has 1,915 stockholders (mostly Wisconsin residents, but also citizens from every state and three foreign countries)—none of whom have ever received dividends. Instead, profits are directed back into the franchise. Ownership bylaws prohibit any individual from holding more than two hundred shares; if stockholders want to sell, they must first go to the board of directors' executive committee. That committee decides if it will buy the shares back or reissue them. And so for decades the team and its unique ownership group have wrestled with the big issues in modern sports—the executive committee spurned the chance to build a dome over hallowed Lambeau Field but authorized the addition of luxury boxes. The wait for season tickets is in the tens of thousands, and the city has long been renowned for its enthusiastic embrace of the team.[2]

Public Is as Public Does

Like corporate heads recognizing the public relations value in striking "partnerships" with employees who would otherwise unionize, team owners have risen to the challenge in recent years and talked about putting teams more in "public" hands. Their recent method of choice? Team owners have mimicked the situation in Green Bay, but only in the most superficial sense, by making public offerings of millions of shares of stock in the ballclubs—but only as much as 49 percent of the club, leaving the team firmly in private control. Given that *public* is so often a dirty word in the contemporary U.S. corporate lexicon, and that its authentic meaning would challenge the fundamental interests of the very private owners of sports teams, the only acceptable role for the public is as Wall Street traders.

Both the Boston Celtics, the historic basketball team, and the Florida Panthers, an expansion hockey franchise, sold stock to the public.

Panthers owner Wayne Huizenga apparently decided to make the public offering, in November 1996, to bring in even more money for his billion-dollar coffers. Huizenga, the former Blockbuster Video owner whose holdings also included the Florida Marlins baseball team, maintains control of the team, making the public offering a purely symbolic—and potentially fruitful—gesture. (He sold 49 percent of the common stock but retains other, non-trading, stock for himself.) "I don't think the institutionals will touch this," David Menlow, the president of IPO Financial Network, told the *Fort Lauderdale Sun-Sentinel* at the time. "This is a nostalgia buy rather than an investment." But with a minimum $1,000 investment, Huizenga stands to profit off that nostalgic gesture. And the fans themselves, those who think they're buying a true stake in their hometown team's fortunes, are in for a rude surprise. "If the pattern of previous publicly traded teams holds," according to the *Wall Street Journal*, "most Panthers certificates will end up hanging on barroom walls, given as birthday presents or the like."

The Celtics, which became the first team to go public when they did so in 1986, have seen below-average stock performance since that move. But that initial offering also gave the team's owners a windfall profit of some $48 million. "On the one hand, you can say [the Celtics are] the exception," says sports economist Rodney Fort. "On the other hand, you can say, so what if they're publicly traded? Nothing is really different about the Celtics than any other team. Because, after all, if you issue lots of stock in little bitty bunches, and you maintain the majority of the stock, then who cares?"

The most recent attempt to ease public concerns by offering publicly traded shares came from the Minnesota Twins. And though Twins owner Carl Pohlad's offer of 49 percent stock in the team caused the local press to declare it would be "essentially creating a partnership between the Pohlad family, who owns the Twins, and the state of Minnesota," apparently nobody else in the state was fooled enough to drum up support. When it became clear that the locals weren't going to be taken in, Pohlad withdrew the offer.

But what about actual municipal ownership? Some cities, when confronted with jittery owners threatening to skip town, have attempted to utilize their right to eminent domain—the governmental right to take over private property (including land) for public use. They tried it in Oakland, when the Raiders football team announced it was fleeing to Los Angeles in 1980. The California Supreme Court rejected the case on the grounds that the seizure would "impermissibly burden interstate commerce." Public officials had even less luck in Baltimore when the city tried to prevent the Colts from leaving town; that team's middle-of-the-night flight to Indianapolis occurred before the city could make its case in court.

But what if a city had a chance to buy or own a professional sports team, without having to claim it through eminent domain? It's been done at the minor-league level with baseball teams in New York and Ohio, and in the Canadian Football League. And it almost happened in major league baseball with the San Diego Padres.

When Joan Kroc inherited ownership of the San Diego Padres baseball team in 1984 from her husband, the late McDonald's founder Ray Kroc, she had little interest in baseball as a sport or in the team as a franchise. But the multimillionaire's mind was changed when she saw how the Southern California community supported its local ball club, and she became convinced that the Padres should truly belong to their hometown.

So the philanthropic heiress, who would in 1997 make headlines by giving out thousands of dollars apiece to flood victims in the Midwest, made the city of San Diego an offer it truly couldn't refuse: She wanted to give the team to the city, and include a $100-million trust fund for the city to operate it. San Diego Mayor Maureen O'Connor greeted the offer with delight and enthusiasm, as did other city officials. It would have kept the team in San Diego, rid it forever of ugly ownership battles, and provided the capital to attempt a management structure.

It seemed too good to be true, and it was. Because when Kroc took her suggestion to the owners committee of Major League Baseball, they refused to even consider it. A truly publicly owned team apparently would have meant a huge headache—if nothing else, by opening up the heavily guarded major league financial books to public scrutiny.

"If the city owned it, we would have it in perpetuity, and that is obviously the best of all worlds," O'Connor told the *San Diego Union-Tribune.* "I was sick, personally, when it didn't come off, because with a $100 million trust fund, . . . it would have been great. . . . I can tell you I was very sad when they turned her down."

The events in San Diego—and in Montreal, where the Expos ownership had wanted to sell the team to a public–private interest that included the province of Quebec—were a harsh reminder that professional sports teams do not exist to foster the public good. They might have the names of cities on them (at least for now, although a more honest approach might follow the lead of Japanese baseball teams and call them the Steinbrenner Yankees, the Turner Braves, and so on) but, despite owners' claims to the contrary, they are profit-making machines like few others—and no right-thinking for-profit owner would want anything to tamper with his or her setup. "Think about the way owners deal with cities now, with an artificial maintenance of scarcity of teams," says Rodney Fort. "You can't lose in that situation: 'Give me what I want, or I'll split.' Well now, if the city decided to keep a marginally valuable franchise hanging around, to keep a minority of potential voters happy, then the value of your league goes down. They'll never do it in ten thousand years."

There was briefly, in the early 1990s, an attempt by economist Andrew Zimbalist, sports agent Richard Moss, and others to create a competing professional baseball league, the United Baseball League (UBL), that would have teams owned by consortia of players, municipalities, and private investors. Mike Stone, the former president of the Texas Rangers, was to be the proposed league's first CEO. Citing the league's unique philosophy as what drew him in, he said in a 1995 interview that "baseball should be a partnership among owners, then between owners and players, between franchises and communities, and between franchises and their fans."

In the UBL, cities would actually have received some revenue. And teams would have pooled half their television and radio revenues, and 30 percent of their gate receipts. Initial hopes were to have teams in Florida, Puerto Rico, New York, and Washington, DC, in its Eastern Division, and Los Angeles, Portland, Vancouver, and New Orleans in its Western Division. The hope was to have play begin in 1997, but when an all-important promised TV contract fell through in 1996, the league officially suspended operation.

If Only

If sports teams were municipally owned, sports stadiums would not be nearly as expensive to build. Existing structures wouldn't have to be razed to satisfy an eager owner's desire to see team profits or his own net worth rapidly increase. Instead, cooler heads might prevail when changes in architecture or money making cause some to cast a longing eye toward sparkling new facilities. For if they aren't inherently cooler-headed, local politicians at least have some democratic accountability to local taxpayers—something corporate owners are sorely lacking.

"It's a logical thing to happen," says Zimbalist. "Sports teams are just perfect vehicles for public ownership for all sorts of reasons—the most important being the large investment the public is expected to make in these teams, but also because it's really a public good, and it has a cultural dominance that's unlike anything else in our society."

True municipal ownership might have to mean a radical rearranging of our society, and a significant challenge to powerful interests who will not stand passively by and let this happen. To bring this public good—that is, the ball clubs that are invested not only with public money but with public spirit as well—under public control raises broad issues about how other resources are to be managed in our society.

When Seattle attorney Shawn Newman went to testify in the spring of 1997 before state senate hearings on publicly funding a new stadium for the Seahawks, he had one crucial point to make. "I said the bottom line is that a lot of people out in the audience have T-shirts on which say, 'It's our team. It's our team.' And I said, 'It's not our team. It is Paul Allen's team, or it's this Ken Barron, the bad developer's, team. It's not our team.

"State law, believe it or not, would allow us to buy the damn team. Counties or cities can buy the team. I talked to the governor's lobbyists over here, and he said we can't do that, we can't buy the team, because the NFL has changed the rules. No more Green Bay Packers—you can't do that anymore. So it's not our team. What it is, it's our debt."

Notes

1. Representative Minge's Distorting Subsidies Limitation Act never made it out of committee in several tries. Minge himself was voted out of office in 2000.

2. Sadly, even public ownership didn't make Green Bay immune from stadium shakedowns. In 2000, Packers execs lobbied for a public vote on a 0.5 percent sales tax hike to raise $169 million toward an expansion of historic Lambeau Field. "There's well over $100 million worth of work that has to be done on the stadium," declared team president Robert Harlan. "If the referendum would fail, it doesn't mean that the stadium would stand for thirty years on its own." But Harlan didn't leave it at the image of the forty-three-year-old edifice suddenly tumbling into Lake Michigan; he also publicly speculated that, without a new stadium, the team could go bankrupt in a few years, at which point the NFL could rescind the franchise and grant it to another city, such as Los Angeles. Sports-industry reaction was largely a hearty guffaw—L.A. had resolutely shown no interest in shelling out public money to lure a new NFL franchise—but local media reports were full of Harlan's non-threat threat. Six months later, the referendum passed, with 53 percent of voters supporting it, so neither of Harlan's claims was put to the test.

11 Winning Isn't Everything

Seattle activist Chris Van Dyk has noticed a new term emerge in civic debates in his town. When it's time to discuss budget issues or policy decisions, a relatively new expression is thrown around. When the merit of supporting a new project arises, concerned taxpayers or city council members now ask, "Is it a More Important Thing?"

A little more than two years of furious lobbying and petitioning, granting media interviews, and suing as part of opposition to two stadium deals did not produce victory for Citizens for More Important Things. But their impact on the political vocabulary in Seattle suggests that they had a real, if modest, impact on consciousness there.

So did the Cleveland Teachers Union (CTU) and other opponents of out-of-control tax abatements in Cleveland. In a town that had seen three new publicly funded stadiums authorized in six years, they succeeded, in the summer of 1997, in getting a public vote on the future of tax abatements. It was one of the only times in memory that a community group had brought the way corporate construction projects are typically financed nationwide onto the table for discussion. That measure ultimately lost but not before receiving national media attention—including a glowing endorsement in *USA Today*—and having an impact on the way people in that city talk about stadiums and schools. Indeed, in the midst of their collective-bargaining battle a year earlier, the CTU threatened to march from each major symbol of tax abatement and opportunities lost for the Cleveland schools—Jacobs Field and the downtown Tower City shopping mall—to City Hall. And, in a significant departure from most economic struggles, which tend to be defined in very narrow terms, in that 1996 campaign the CTU successfully projected the connection between public spending on sports boondoggles, tax abatements, low teacher salaries, and poor service to their pupils. When the administration learned through polling that the teachers had won widespread public support, their once-resolute opposition collapsed and they yielded, allowing the CTU to win a historic agreement.

The lessons to be learned from all the stadium battles past and present are complex. The money, media, and resources behind team owners and local politicians make them formidable opponents, and their winning streak in getting new stadiums is impressive. But the terms of debate are changing, even if so far the teams have consistently won the arguments. Politicians must be increasingly careful to appear to stand up to owner greed—witness Cleveland mayor Michael White's attempt to lead the opposition to Art Modell's pulling the Browns out of Cleveland at the same time he was speaking out on holding down costs in the construction of the new football stadium. The fact that White's rhetoric seems to many observers both insincere and misplaced does not change the fact that, as an astute politician, he felt he had to take an anti-owner stance in response to changes in popular thinking.

Team owners must devise increasingly devious and manipulative ways of gaining access to the public's wealth to finance their new sports facilities. The popularity of personal seat licenses, naming-rights deals, and roundabout tax-financing schemes are no coincidence—they've come about because owners and their political allies have learned that many city residents don't want publicly funded new stadiums. More newspaper and magazine articles are written exposing the stadium swindle, and fewer people now take seriously the argument that funding sports stadiums is good business for city governments.

There's a tendency, particularly in the sports world, to frame success in terms of winners and losers. Yet the "losses" for the grassroots anti-stadium campaigns—and for the schools, the public housing, all the public amenities that are forced to go without when corporate welfare is made a priority of public spending—point only to how necessary these types of campaigns are. When a multimillionaire sports team owner can sway politicians, buy elections, and con the public all through the power of the purse, what better sign that something drastic needs to happen to change the balance of power in our society?

For the activists fighting block by block and referendum by referendum to put an end to sports subsidies, seeking small victories in the larger defeats has become a familiar pursuit. "Moral victories are wonderful, but I'd still rather win the election," says Seattle's Van Dyk with a laugh.

In *Captain Newman, M.D.*, his classic novel of American GIS during World War II, Leo Rosten writes of the importance of people's ability to hold onto important values while resisting seemingly overwhelming forces. He addresses both the dignity of undertaking apparently quixotic struggles and the necessity of working for meaningful and winnable change.

What if Destiny came down to an island community, Rosten asks, and told the inhabitants they'd be inundated by a tidal wave tomorrow? Rosten's wise man responds that he'd study how to live underwater. "I too never forgot that story," his Captain Newman says. "When our cause seems doomed and the future lost, when despair becomes unbearable, and the heart is on the edge of breaking, let men summon hope and honor and high resolve in yet one more stubborn affirmation: Come let us assemble our wisest men and begin at once to think, to study, to try to learn—even to learn, if we must, how to live underwater."

The effective blackmail that professional teams wield over cities is not good, it is not correct, and it is not eternal. It is the consequence of a particular state of affairs in which public agencies have become beholden to private power. It can be changed, and it's worth changing.

12 One Year

Buying the team, instead of building a stadium, could save New York City $35 million to $530 million. The cost of buying the Yankees could be paid off using profit from the yearly Yankee Stadium and media revenue of $130 million. Yearly profits after the investment is paid off could be designated to go to support New York City schools or economic development projects in low-income neighborhoods. *—New York state assemblyman Scott Stringer*

Scott Stringer's proposal is a concept that could conceivably work in two places: Communist China and Cuba. *—Colleen Roche, press secretary to New York mayor Rudolph Giuliani*

The year 1998 began quietly enough, with only a few new teams entering the stadium derby. The Minnesota Twins' threatened move to North Carolina, declared a certainty the previous fall, remained on the back burner as team owner Carl Pohlad bargained with residents of his intended home. The New England Patriots began negotiations with the Massachusetts legislature for a new stadium in Foxboro, while Montreal Expos manager Felipe Alou opened the team's winter promotional caravan by declaring, "If we don't have a downtown ballpark, the team will leave." But by and large, it was an uneventful winter for stadium demands, and as April dawned more eyes were fixed on the new baseball season than on luxury-suite prices and tax-abatement schemes.

Then the roof fell in. Literally.

Crumble in the Bronx

At 2 p.m. on April 13, Anaheim Angels team muscle therapist Bill LeSuer was walking in the outfield at Yankee Stadium when, he later told *Newsday*, he "heard a tremendous bang." He recalled, "I saw a big puff of smoke and chunks of concrete coming down. I said, 'Did anyone else see that?' Then I realized I was alone, talking to myself. I thought the stadium was falling down."

What had fallen was an "expansion joint," a quarter-ton chunk of steel wedged between two beams to allow them to adapt to changing temperatures. The foot-square joint had somehow worked its way loose that afternoon and crashed through the roof of the stadium's loge level, leaving New Yorkers to wonder aloud whether the House that Ruth Built was falling apart.

The timing of the "crumble in the Bronx," as the *New York Post* headlined it, made it all the more momentous. Three days earlier, as the Yankees opened their season before a record 56,717 fans, team PR guru Howard Rubinstein had declared, "The traffic and the parking are horrendous on a packed house like today. The skyboxes are inadequate. Things like the bathrooms and the seating are sort of uncomfortable and inadequate. And all of the other teams with new stadiums outdraw [the Yankees]." It was a common complaint for Yankee management, which had been angling for either a new stadium or renovations to the old one for more than a decade, and when the rogue joint seemed determined to prove the stadium's inadequacy, there was much speculation on the convenient timing: *Daily Show* host Craig Kilborn quipped that owner George Steinbrenner was "unavailable for comment because he was at Sears returning a blowtorch and a hacksaw."

The morning after the beam incident, New York mayor Rudy Giuliani, a longtime booster of a new stadium over Manhattan's West Side rail yards, stood outside the shuttered stadium and reiterated his contention that "both the Yankees and the Mets are entitled to new baseball fields." From there the mayor ran through the stadium playbook in record time. First up was the obsolescence claim. Alluding to the stadium's approaching seventy-fifth birthday, Giuliani argued, "You couldn't have a more dramatic argument that the Yankees need a new stadium."

Dramatic, certainly. Yet as with Tiger Stadium and Comiskey Park before it, Yankee Stadium was actually in fine shape for its advanced age. A weeklong city inspection confirmed this, finding only superficial damage to the stadium's concrete facade. (Upkeep had been left to the Yankees, who had somehow neglected to schedule an inspection in the last nineteen years.) "From a structural perspective, there's no reason why Yankee Stadium can't be around for another seventy-five years if it's maintained properly," declared city buildings commissioner Gaston Silva.

By then, however, the mayor had already moved on to economic arguments. On April 19, as Silva was granting the stadium a clean bill of health, Giuliani announced that a Manhattan ballpark would cost the taxpayers less than a new stadium in the Bronx—conveniently overlooking the option of retaining the old stadium. A new West Side stadium, the mayor added, would create $1 billion in economic impact and generate $45 million a year in taxes and "thousands and thousands and thousands of jobs."

The next morning, the *New York Times* revealed that a 1996 study, issued by consultants KPMG-Peat Marwick in the mayor's first push for a Manhattan stadium, had projected an economic impact of only $102.5 million, a mere tenth what the mayor was claiming. Shortly thereafter, the city's Independent Budget Office (IBO) issued its own report on the stadium plans, finding that new stadiums for both the Yankees and Mets (who were turning up the heat on their own stadium demands) would generate a mere 570 jobs and $5 million in new city taxes—nowhere near enough to pay the estimated $75 million-plus in yearly bond payments. Giuliani's projections, it turned out, had assumed the construction of two new luxury hotels as the result of the new ballpark, an assessment that baffled the IBO's Stephen Mark. "I guess they thought that somehow the stadium would transform the neighborhood," says Mark. "And they're assuming that there's no reduction in activity elsewhere in the city."

The next week, local tabloids cited unnamed sources (presumably in the Yankee hierarchy) as saying that "secret talks" were under way to hustle the team across the Hudson River. When New Jersey governor Christine Todd Whitman denied any interest in luring New York teams to her state with ballpark subsidies, Giuliani declared that he had successfully scared her off by threatening to steal New Jersey's teams (a proclamation that would not stop him from continuing to raise the specter of a New Jersey move throughout the upcoming months). A week after that, it was the need for "competitiveness" that was paramount, said the mayor. "I would like New York to have competitive baseball teams," announced Giuliani on May 6, as the Yankees surged to the best start in their history, en route to breaking the league mark for most wins in a season. "Whether you like it or not, that means they have to spend a lot of money. Otherwise, you're going to be in the cellar."

In making a pitch for a new stadium, however, Giuliani was going up against more than resistance to public funding. Even as George Steinbrenner disparaged its Bronx location at every turn, Yankee Stadium was incredibly popular among fans. For years, polls had shown overwhelming support among city residents for keeping the Yankees in the Bronx; perhaps more significantly, even New Jersey residents wanted the team to stay put, with a mere 27 percent voicing support for a Yankee move to the Garden State.

At Yankee Stadium's reopening on April 24, some of the thirty-nine thousand fans in attendance jokingly wore hardhats and carried signs reading "Good For 75 More." "If you build a new stadium for more luxury boxes, what that means is you would leave the ordinary fans out. It will be a stadium for corporations, not a stadium for you and me," one fan told a reporter. Another simply remarked, "This is the center of the universe. You can't move the center of the universe."

The mayor's response? "I bet if we were playing in Baltimore, we would have more than forty-five thousand people."

Baltimore became a particular fixation of Giuliani's throughout the spring, and when the Yankees made their first road trip to that city, the mayor took full advantage of the moment. Ostensibly in town for a fundraising event (for a Republican gubernatorial candidate who, it so happened, opposed stadium subsidies), Giuliani took the opportunity to tour Camden Yards and loudly proclaim how wonderful such an edifice would look on the West Side of Manhattan. He also made an appearance on the Yankees' radio broadcast, chatting up announcers Michael Kay and John Sterling for the first of many times that summer on the benefits of a new stadium.

But for all his friends in high places, the mayor still lacked the money to build his dream ballpark. Giuliani announced that he would raise $600 million by extending the city's commercial rent tax—a staggering sum of money, especially in a city whose schools were literally falling down. City council president Peter Vallone, planning his own race for the governor's office that fall and spotting a popular issue on which to take on the mayor, declared that no stadium money would be spent without a public referendum. With the mayor and council deadlocked, the council wrote its own budget—without the stadium funding—and passed it over the mayor's veto for the first time in history. For at least one more year, George Steinbrenner would have to wait to escape the Bronx.

Meanwhile, across town in Queens, the New York Mets announced plans for their own new facility. Featuring a retractable roof, seventy-five luxury boxes, forty-five hundred club seats, and a facade vaguely reminiscent of the Brooklyn Dodgers' old Ebbets Field (if twice the size), the new park would be "one of the most fantastic stadiums that's ever been planned," according to Mets co-owner Fred Wilpon.

Possibly its most fantastic element: a retractable *field* in a "bathtub" of dirt and sod, which would roll out into the parking lot to leave a hard floor for basketball games or boxing events. Estimated cost: $500 million.

Wilpon, the *Daily News* reassured its readers, "definitely would contribute an unspecified amount" toward construction.

The Tide Turns?

Two hundred miles to the northeast, another historic ballpark was quietly fighting its own battle against the wrecking ball. Fenway Park had long been considered not just a baseball stadium but a baseball shrine: the home to Babe Ruth and Ted Williams, Carl Yastrzemski and Wade Boggs, its "Green Monster" outfield wall and jury-rigged dimensions had been copied by many nouveau "old-time" parks like Jacobs Field and The Ballpark at Arlington. Despite the presence of view-blocking pillars and seating that could only charitably be de-scribed as "cramped," fans had proven their loyalty to the eighty-six-year-old ballpark: attendance was near capacity even in years the Red Sox were cellar-dwellers, making Fenway the number-one tourist at-traction in the entire state.

For the Red Sox, however, Fenway's charms paled in comparison to the luxury seating and expanded food courts afforded by new ball-parks. (Though ranked among the top ten baseball teams in terms of overall revenue—thanks to both their generous television con-tract and the highest ticket prices in the nation—the Red Sox placed only thirteenth in "venue revenue" in 1997.) And so in April the team let slip to the media that they were pursuing plans to build a new stadium across the street—forcing the relocation of dozens of busi-nesses—while demolishing most of the existing ballpark, leaving only the Green Monster and a small slice of grandstand as museum pieces.

The *Boston Globe* quickly jumped on board, editorializing that Fen-way was "too cramped and unprofitable to allow the team to thrive in the high-priced baseball environment of the 1990s." Sox fans were less enthusiastic, with one turning up at an early May game at Fenway with a placard reading, "If you build it, we won't come."

"The Red Sox have done a pretty good job of managing the issues," says Steven Rubin of Save Fenway Park!, which had been founded in the fall of 1997 to explore ways to renovate and expand the existing ballpark. "If you're a preservationist, it bothers you terribly; why tear down the real thing and then build it across the street and go through all that aggravation for a replica? But if you're an average fan, and you like the experience, except the seats are bigger, it sells pretty well. The average fan totally misses that they're going to get screwed, because they're not going to get seats in the new place."

While Bostonians argued that their existing ballpark was more than adequate for the Red Sox, residents of Birmingham, Alabama, pondered funding a facility for a nonexistent team. In 1998 Birmingham faced a $703.2 million proposal called MAPS (Metropolitan Area Projects Strategy), a laundry list of development projects whose centerpiece would be a seventy-thousand-seat domed football stadium. The brainchild of one Rick Horrow, a sometime Harvard sports law professor and NFL stadium consultant, MAPS was to be funded with a countywide one-cent sales tax hike, raising the rate to 10 percent in some parts of the county.

Birmingham's MAPS was a near-replica of a similarly named project that Horrow had successfully sold to Oklahoma City in 1993, declaring it "a defining moment in Oklahoma City's quest to become a major league region." That city's $238 million collection of museums, downtown canal and "riverwalk," renovated convention center and state fairgrounds, minor-league baseball stadium, and hockey arena had a bumpy ride from the beginning—among other things, the new ballpark's architects underestimated the amount of steel necessary by 50 percent—and city officials were soon debating whether to extend the sales tax hike into a sixth year or instead trim some of the projects. Worse yet, when the NHL issued its choices for four new expansion teams in 1996, Oklahoma City didn't make the cut; city leaders conceded that the town's meager population (forty-third among all TV markets in the country) had doomed their bid, new arena or no.

Horrow, though, had by then collected his $67,500 consultant's fee and had moved on to pitch MAPS plans to Hampton Roads and Norfolk, Virginia—and Birmingham. Birmingham residents were polled the fall before Horrow's arrival, and just 35 percent backed spending public money on a domed football stadium, ranking it next to last among thirteen suggested projects; only a new library system, improved transportation, and zoo expansion were supported by a majority of respondents. Horrow's solution—lumping together popular and unpopular projects—had worked in Oklahoma City; in fact, Oklahoma City mayor Ron Norick had later bragged that "if we would have voted on that piece by piece, we would have gotten [a new library and new dams on the North Canadian River] and that would have been it."

To counter Birmingham's $1 million MAPS campaign, headed by such local movers and shakers as the CEOs of HealthSouth and Alabama Power, a hastily organized group called "RAPS" (Real Accountability, Progress, and Solutions) presented a three-pronged argument: the regressivity of the sales tax hike; the unprecedented powers of the MAPS authority that would be created, including exemption from many competitive-bidding rules; and the lack of evidence for any positive economic impact from stadium projects. "It sprang full-blown from a group of men who obviously could afford this themselves, and they made horrible missteps with all the money they had—it was kind of like shooting fish in a barrel," says RAPS activist Alice Durkee. Among the missteps: underestimating the amount per person that the project would cost (the MAPS proponents said $44 a year; the actual number was closer to $250), and hiring as a political consultant Hank Sheinkopf, a former aide to Dick Morris on Bill Clinton's presidential campaign. "That doesn't play in Alabama," observes Durkee.

When the August 5 vote was tallied, the results showed 57 percent opposed, 43 percent in favor. Mayor Richard Arrington, who had spearheaded the campaign for MAPS, conceded defeat, saying there was no plan B to revive the project. "It's the voters who make the decisions," he said, "and we've done that tonight, and that's all we can ask for."

Plans for a publicly funded new facility were also put on hold in San Antonio, Texas, where popular sentiment had long run against subsidizing an arena for the Spurs basketball team. San Antonio built its Alamodome in 1993 for an NFL team that never materialized. The dome had since been pressed into duty as a home for the basketball team, but team owner Peter Holt had consistently argued that a new profit-friendly venue was necessary to make money in small-market San Antonio—and to keep high-profile players like young superstar Tim Duncan.

The city sales tax used to fund the Alamodome remained unpopular in San Antonio, and earlier rumblings about using a similar tax to fund a new arena had met with quick and loud public opposition. "I do not believe the city should build an arena," then-mayor Bill Thornton told the *San Antonio Express-News* in 1996, when the team was voicing threats to move up the road to Austin. "That's a short sentence, with small words that are clear."

So Holt and company presented the city with a new plan: Build an 18,500-seat arena in an abandoned rock quarry in the northeast part of the city, using tax-increment financing. (TIFs, the same mechanism used to help fund the San Francisco Giants' new park, are intended to avoid the controversy of raising new taxes by instead diverting existing property taxes to pay for the cost of a construction project.) The Spurs would kick in a mere $20 million for a project estimated at $157 million, and San Antonians, it was promised, would have a basketball team for years to come.

There would be no need for a citizen campaign against the TIF plan, as it turned out. The Spurs' proposal needed approval not only from the city and county but also from the East School District that faced losing up to $18.5 million in revenue to TIFs. When the district board's meeting ended in the wee hours of December 15, it voted 5–2 to withdraw from discussions of the plan, effectively killing it.[1]

"I'll go out and tell people how important the Spurs are to San Antonio," Bruce Bennett, the school board president, said at the time. "I just don't think education dollars should be spent for an arena."

Twins or Triplets

In every city where there is backlash against stadium subsidies, the same warning can be heard: Vote it down, and you risk losing your team. In 1998 that threat was put to the test in Minnesota. The previous November, the Minnesota Twins had been declared all but gone from Minneapolis following the state's decision not to replace the fifteen-year-old Metrodome. All eyes then turned to a field in tiny Kernersville, North Carolina, where local businessman Don Beaver hoped to build a forty-thousand-seat ballpark to bring about the first Major League Baseball franchise shift in twenty-five years, luring the Twins south to be reborn as the Carolina Triplets.

But Carl Pohlad's supposedly ironclad deal to sell the team to Beaver was starting to run into choppy water. Pohlad's fellow owners, who had enthusiastically backed his demands for a new stadium, began to get cold feet when faced with abandoning the nation's fourteenth-largest TV market for an ill-defined region around Greensboro, Winston-Salem, and High Point known as the "Triad"—one often confused by out-of-towners with the seventy-five-mile-distant "Triangle" of Raleigh-Durham-Chapel Hill. One member of baseball's Ownership Committee, which must approve all franchise relocations, told the *Minneapolis Star Tribune*, "If you're going to move a team, it should be Pittsburgh or Montreal, who continue to fail to draw, even when they have winning teams. The Twins drew 3 million people in 1992."

Down in North Carolina's Guilford and Forsyth counties, meanwhile, voters were preparing to go to the polls May 5 for the ballpark vote—and they didn't look too happy about it. As the vote neared, polls were running more than two to one against a 1 percent tax on restaurant meals and a 50-cent ticket tax to fund two thirds of a $210 million stadium. (The sale of naming rights would take care of most of the "private" portion.)

Vote Yes for Major League Baseball, the pro-stadium campaign bankrolled by such local corporate heavy hitters as R. J. Reynolds and Wachovia Bank, had hit snags from the start. An initial plan for restaurant chains Wendy's, Subway, and Pizza Hut to provide information on the stadium campaign to customers collapsed after managers were deluged by angry phone calls from customers, who pointed out that they would be endorsing a tax on their own products. Plans for a "bottle hanger" promotion on bottles of Pepsi were canceled when local supermarket chains complained. The Guilford County Board of Commissioners voted 6–5 to oppose the plan, calling the food tax "repulsive." Said commissioner Chuck Winfree, following the vote, "The economics of baseball have gotten to the point where they simply need taxpayer support to make it feasible. That doesn't justify that taxpayers actually have to do it."

Still, the stadium campaign forged ahead, running a slew of radio and TV ads, including several featuring popular racecar drivers touting the benefits of a baseball stadium. Behind the leadership of Walt Klein, whose resume included stints managing a U.S. Senate campaign and the successful push for Coors Field in Denver, the Vote Yes for Major League Baseball campaign quickly locked up the endorsements of the mayors of all three Triad towns, and Governor Jim Hunt.

In the end, Vote Yes won the spending battle but lost the war: Despite outspending stadium opponents $716,000 to $26,000, the stadium backers were defeated soundly at the polls. In voting more than twice as heavy as at a typical primary election, Forsyth County rejected the stadium bid, with 59 percent opposed; in Guilford, 67 percent opposed it. As local newspaper columnist Lenox Rawlings quipped, "The [Winston-Salem] Warthogs would have done better against the Yankees."

Minnesota state senator John Marty, who had helped block the Twins' stadium push the previous year in Minnesota, declared the referendum's defeat "a victory not only for taxpayers in North Carolina but for taxpayers up here and elsewhere." Marty noted that while the landslide vote should serve as a "wake-up call" to baseball owners, "the problem is, it's like the snooze button on the alarm—they keep hitting it over and over."

Thirteen days later, the city of Charlotte, North Carolina, released a feasibility study on building a baseball stadium to lure the Twins, even as polls showed 63.6 percent of residents opposed to using public money on a new ballpark.

It's stories like these that have led many observers to wonder if the free ride for sports teams may be nearing an end, as both the public and elected officials tire of throwing money at increasingly wealthy owners for increasingly elusive benefits. But the danger, as always, is that it's hard to keep a bad stadium idea down. In Pittsburgh, where voters had banned using new tax dollars for sports stadiums in November 1997, local elected officials quickly arranged to circumvent the public vote by dedicating *existing* tax dollars to new stadiums for the Pirates and Steelers. With the Philadelphia Phillies and Eagles also in search of new stadiums, the controversy soon spread statewide. It would end in early 1999 with a vote by the Pennsylvania legislature to provide the state's four baseball and football teams with a $320 million "loan" to help with construction costs—a "loan" that the teams would be allowed to repay out of state taxes collected at and around the new stadiums.

Quipped Pittsburgh representative Thomas Petrone following the vote: "It's not a grant. It's not a loan. It's a groan."

More Than a Ballpark

The 1998 World Series will be remembered as the exclamation point on an unforgettable year in baseball—the year of Mark McGwire and Sammy Sosa's home-run race, the year that the New York Yankees won 114 regular-season games and coasted to a world championship. But the '98 Series was also a historic pairing of two teams that were aggressively pursuing new facilities in their hometowns. And while the Yankees may have easily won the Series, it was the San Diego Padres who scored first in the new-stadium sweepstakes.

The fate of San Diego's Jack Murphy Stadium—renamed Qualcomm Stadium in 1997 in exchange for an $18 million naming-rights fee—was first challenged by the San Diego Chargers in the early 1990s. As a condition of renegotiating his long-term lease with the city, team owner Alex Spanos insisted that the stadium be expanded and renovated. In May 1995 the Chargers signed a new lease with the city, which, mindful of its bid to host the 1998 Super Bowl, agreed to $60 million in renovations. It was as part of that deal that the Chargers received their controversial ten-year seat guarantee from the city of San Diego, which agreed to reimburse the team for the face value of every unsold general admission ticket in any game in which fewer than sixty thousand such tickets were sold. The difference would affect the team's annual rent payment to the city, sometimes dramatically so—after a miserable 1998 season that saw few fans go to games, the city faced extending some $3.8 million in rent credits to the Chargers.

With more than ten thousand new seats, dozens of new luxury boxes, and an upgraded scoreboard added to Qualcomm Stadium— all for the benefit of the Chargers—the Padres were next in line to cry foul. Houston software tycoon John Moores had purchased a majority share of the Padres in 1994, alongside new team president and minority owner Larry Lucchino, who as CEO of the Baltimore Orioles had led that team's push for Camden Yards. Lucchino and Moores' complaints were familiar ones: Qualcomm was ill suited for baseball, the team was in financial trouble, and the need to remain competitive on the field and in the boardroom necessitated a new ballpark. But Moores and company had a new weapon on their side: This wasn't to be any old new ballpark. This was to be a new ballpark *district.*

The $411 million project, Mayor Susan Golding announced, would include a new stadium and new offices, hotels, and stores in the immediate area—twenty-six square blocks of the city's East Village. The deal promised $225 million in public bond money, to be paid back by yet-to-be-generated funds from the local hotel occupancy tax, plus $50 million from the city's redevelopment organization and $21 million from the San Diego Unified Port District. Stadium boosters pointed to the team's $115 million commitment to the project, plus its reported $300 million commitment to developing 850 new hotel rooms, 600,000 square feet of office space, and 150,000 square feet of retail space, as proof that this was no swindle.

Critics were quick to point out, however, that the team's promises had little cold cash behind them. Included in the $115 million, for example, was money from naming rights; another piece would come from credits given them for the value of concessions fixtures and utilities put into the new stadium. And as for Moores' private-development plans, wrote Don Bauder, a business columnist for the *San Diego Union-Tribune*, "Why should San Diego give $275 million for a ballpark we don't need in return for $300 million-plus of development that is largely unrelated?"

The November referendum campaign officially kicked off with a pep rally in the East Village neighborhood where the new stadium was to be built. Padres outfielders Tony Gwynn and Steve Finley spoke at the event, as they and other players would continue to do throughout the vote drive. So did third-base coach Tim Flannery, who warned of dire consequences if the referendum wasn't approved: "You don't want to be, five years from now, watching players that were once Padres playing in a different city and you say, 'Golly, I didn't know that was going to happen.'"

It was to be a constant refrain in the summer and fall of 1998. "If we don't build it, Padres will be gone," a *San Diego Union-Tribune* headline stated. "Time running out," read another. But the emphasis was on more than just the team. Emphasizing the ballpark "district," the referendum campaign's official slogan was "Yes on C—redevelopment works for all of us." Proposition C, campaign literature promised, was the "final jewel in the crown of downtown redevelopment."

Such claims may have defied common economic wisdom. By the end of August, Standard & Poor's, the Wall Street rating agency, had lowered the city's fiscal outlook from "stable" to "negative," citing the potential impact of the ballpark project on the city's general fund.

Area residents also began raising concerns about the fiscal wisdom of a publicly funded stadium. Chris Michaels, a photographer, had moved into the East Village area in 1997 as part of the city's drive to bring residents to a former industrial neighborhood. When he and other locals realized their homes and livelihoods were in the bulldozers' path, they formed Strike Three on Proposition C (STOP-C) to try to combat the stadium referendum.

The city's approach infuriated Michaels. "They went out of their way to rename this area East Village in 1996 to make it more residential-friendly," he says. "So, where's the village in a forty-six-thousand-person stadium, high-rise hotels, office towers, and parking lots? I feel betrayed. They invited me here."

Outspent nearly a hundred to one, STOP-C waged a grassroots effort to educate San Diegans about the risks involved in the massive public expenditure—and about the tremendous profit the Padres stood to make from a new facility. (One popular bumper sticker: "Stadium? Thanks, got one. A *library* I could use.") But their uphill battle was made more difficult as the Padres found themselves in pennant contention for the first time in years.

"As much as I wanted to see the Padres do well in the Series," says Michaels, "I really feared what it would do to our campaign. . . . Especially during the Series, we were considered practically anti-American," he continues, recalling bumper stickers ripped off the cars of those daring to proclaim their opposition to the new ballpark. "I'd say the Series was probably good for 5 percent of the vote. The feeling I got was that people here had difficulty distinguishing between the stadium and the performance of the Padres."

Said Mayor Golding after the stadium passed with nearly 60 percent of the vote on November 3: "We're getting a chance to make this the best downtown in the country." And there's no doubt that the new district will be a good one for John Moores and friends. By committing to aid in downtown redevelopment, Moores effectively gave himself and his colleagues first dibs on prime land. A Moores-controlled company, the *San Diego Reader* noted, had purchased a half-block piece of property near the stadium site the day after the successful referendum vote—property expected to appreciate in price by millions of dollars once the ballpark is constructed. "Not only did John Moores get a huge subsidy for his team," says Chris Michaels, "but if the redevelopment works he'll also be able to cash in on significant control of a third of downtown."

It didn't take long for the city's baseball euphoria to lose some of its post-election glow. Despite profits and values likely to soar with a new facility, the Padres weren't able—or willing—to match the highest bidder on new contracts for their popular players. By early 1999 the Padres had lost stars Ken Caminiti and Kevin Brown to free agency. Steve Finley, who'd wondered aloud about the Padres playing in a different city if Proposition C was defeated, instead signed with the Arizona Diamondbacks as a free agent. Fans were outraged, even more so when the team traded popular slugger Greg Vaughn to Cincinnati. "How do you think the players in the [Padres] locker room feel?" asked a stunned Vaughn, speaking for many when he found out about the trade. "They're told how competitive we'll be as a team when we get the stadium, and then when we get the stadium, we're gone."

The Path of Lease Resistance

The Padres weren't the only team whose drive for a new stadium was aided by on-the-field heroics. After years of frustration and near misses, the Denver Broncos took home a Super Bowl victory in 1997—and promptly told local residents the team might be forced to leave town if it didn't get a publicly funded replacement for fifty-year-old Mile High Stadium.

The Broncos have consistently sold out the seventy-six-thousand-seat structure. But in 1987, reportedly in need of quick cash, team owner Pat Bowlen sold control of Mile High's luxury boxes to Penthouse Suites Ltd. for $18 million. He also agreed to a lease that gave the city all concession and parking revenues, in addition to the revenues from scoreboard advertising. The thirty-year lease was considered particularly strong by many in the business. It also left the flamboyant millionaire out in the cold compared to many of his fellow NFL owners.

Now, years later, Bowlen was loudly comparing his team's facility to Coors Field, the new, publicly funded home of the Colorado Rockies baseball club. Bemoaning his inability to remain "competitive" in the NFL without a new stadium, Bowlen pushed hard for an extension of the sales tax that funded Coors Field. "What I say is, the tax is minimal," he said in 1995. "It's an insignificant amount of money, in my mind. If you're against that, what you're saying is you don't give a shit about the Broncos."

The Broncos stadium campaign was particularly surreal: In order to build a new stadium, the city had to figure out a way to break its solid lease with the team. With no apparent irony, the *Denver Post* reported on August 7: "City officials announced a deal Thursday that will keep the Broncos in Denver for 25 years if a new stadium is built. As part of the deal, the city would release the Broncos from the franchise's lease at Mile High Stadium, which does not expire until 2018." Among the provisions of the new lease: the new stadium was not to cost more than $360 million, with a $270 million cap on public funds ($395 million with interest), to be paid for from an extension of the sales tax used to pay for Coors Field; the Broncos would receive almost all stadium revenues; and the new facility would feature a twenty-seat luxury box for the Metropolitan Football Stadium District Board—the entity ostensibly created to represent taxpayers in negotiations with the Broncos. Board member Joy

Burns defended the perk, saying, "Someone has to take care of our visiting dignitaries."

"Incredibly, while our negotiators gave away the farm to Pat Bowlen on our behalf, they managed to salvage something for themselves and their friends," responded Ray Hutchins, the spokesperson for the newly formed Citizens Opposing the Stadium Tax (COST). COST was a vocal presence in the months leading up to the November referendum—holding spirited rallies, loudly demonstrating at local meetings, and filing a federal complaint against Jacor Broadcasting, the radio home of the Broncos, which COST members charged had prevented them from stating their case on the air.

After a triumphant 1997 season, the Broncos continued their winning ways in '98. This proved to be bad news for stadium opponents in Denver, much as the Series had in San Diego. On November 3 the referendum passed by a full 14 percentage points. Pollsters estimated that the team's undefeated record as the November election approached could possibly sway as much as a third of the electorate.

Big dollars had to help too. Bowlen contributed $1.98 million of his own money to the pro-stadium lobbying group Citizens for a New Stadium. It was the biggest single donation to an issue campaign in the city's history.

Domed to Failure

The Toronto Blue Jays didn't win anything in 1998. (Their ace starter, Roger Clemens, did win the Cy Young Award but then immediately demanded a trade to a better team.) But as recently as 1994, the Jays had been two-time defending World Champs, with a ballpark, Sky-Dome, that was the envy of all of baseball.

The "world's greatest entertainment centre" (as its builders dubbed it) opened to a packed house on June 3, 1989, and saw its tickets sold out for years thereafter. In 1990 the Blue Jays became the first team in baseball history to sell four million tickets in a year; they would top this mark in both of the next two years. And even as team owner Labatt Breweries funneled a portion of the resulting windfall into player salaries—the Jays' two championships in 1992 and 1993 came largely on the backs of high-priced acquisitions like Jack Morris and David Cone—the team's value soared to an estimated $180 million, trailing only the New York Yankees and Dallas Cowboys in all of pro sports.

For this, Labatt could thank the province of Ontario, which had agreed to finance a $150 million stadium in 1985—and kept on writing checks as the cost ballooned to $600 million. A large chunk of the inflated price tag was traceable to a hotel and health club that were tacked on during construction—not to mention the dome's retractable roof, which at least actually worked, unlike its equally expensive predecessor in Montreal. But the true reason for the staggering cost overruns was an official mystery. Bruce Kidd, the University of Toronto athletics director who was appointed to help investigate the mess, recalls that although there was talk of a public inquiry, "we thought it was more productive to just get out of the damn thing. And the people we had been negotiating with may well have been embarrassed by a public inquiry, and we needed their cooperation."

As a result SkyDome opened with a $300 million mortgage, payable entirely by the people of Ontario. In its first year, the dome brought in $17 million in revenues—and had $40 million in debt service. (To fully pay off its debts, it was estimated, the dome would have to be in use six hundred days a year.) The dome's revenues weren't enough even to pay interest on the debt—meaning the debt was actually *growing* every year. Realizing it had been stuck with a fiscal lemon, the province sold off SkyDome to private investors in 1994 for a bargain-basement price of $151 million, writing off some $262 million in remaining debt as a loss to taxpayers.

But the dome's woes were far from over. In 1994 the Blue Jays sank into the cellar for the first time in a decade. The dome, meanwhile, celebrated its fifth birthday, the traditional end of a new ballpark's "honeymoon period" with fans and tourists, just as a strike wiped out the final third of the baseball season, creating tremendous anger and resentment among fans. The combined effect was enough to drive yearly attendance below three million for the first time in Sky-Dome history, and there it remained, the once-jammed stadium now half-empty much of the time.

And so, in late October 1998, as the city of Toronto was overseeing the removal of seats from Exhibition Stadium, in preparation for the building's planned December demolition, a $50,000 check arrived from the Toronto Blue Jays. The ownership of the Jays, who had spent twelve and a half chilly years at the Ex before SkyDome was built, delivered the check along with a startling request: Don't tear it down; we might want to move back in.

The pundits had a field day—Jays coach Nick Leyva compared returning to the Ex to "riding a bicycle after driving a Mercedes"—but the gambit worked: By the end of November, SkyDome management had agreed to a new lease that would divert an estimated $72 million in dome revenues into the team's coffers. As this would leave SkyDome itself without enough money to pay its costs, the dome's management promptly declared bankruptcy.

Even as the dome was readied for sale yet again, this time by the bankruptcy court, the groundwork was being laid for still one more raid on the public treasury. Asked how the dome's fiscal problems could possibly be remedied, SkyDome CEO Patrick McDougal replied, "We pay in excess of $12 million in [property] taxes a year. . . . There's a tremendous amount that would have to change. But one of the major things is the tax situation."

"Touchdown!"

In the end 1998's biggest stadium story took place not under the bright lights of the Big Apple or Southern California but in a small-ish northeastern city without a big-time professional team to its name. The Hartford Whalers, Connecticut's only big-league team, had relocated to Raleigh, North Carolina, in April 1997 in exchange for a new publicly funded arena. (While waiting for their new home to be readied, the new Carolina Hurricanes played two seasons in distant Greensboro's arena, to some of the most abysmal crowds in recent NHL history.) Tiny Hartford (ranked twenty-seventh among U.S. TV markets) was left with only the women's pro basketball New England Blizzard and the minor-league hockey WolfPack to fill the twenty-two-year-old Hartford Civic Center. Connecticut's capital was shut out of the ranks of "big-league" cities—from all indications, for good.

Up in Massachusetts, meanwhile, Robert Kraft, the owner of the New England Patriots football team, was getting nowhere in attempts to persuade the state to help finance a replacement for his team's stadium in suburban Foxboro. House Speaker Thomas Finneran insisted throughout the summer that the state would spend no money on construction or land acquisition (he did offer $52 million for highway and infrastructure costs), and when the state house and senate failed to agree on a joint proposal, the stadium bill died. Finneran bragged that his firm line against subsidies would be "the second shot heard round the world."

On November 19, Connecticut governor John Rowland dropped his own bombshell: The Patriots were coming to Hartford. As part of Adriaen's Landing, a $1 billion convention-and-entertainment complex that had been bandied about in the state legislature for years, the state would construct a $350 million football stadium. The team's only contribution: a 10 percent tax on ticket sales for the course of the thirty-year lease.

The announcement of the Patriots move came as a particular shock because Rowland had never once mentioned the possibility during his just-completed reelection campaign. "It would have been the key issue in the race, I think, if we had known prior to the election that John Rowland was already negotiating with Bob Kraft," says local Reform Party activist Donna Donovan, who became one of the key members of the grassroots activist group Stop the Stadium. According to Donovan, these negotiations had been going on for months or even years, brokered by Jay Malcynsky, a lobbyist with Gaffney Bennett, the state's largest lobbying firm.

The reaction of the local media was appropriately restrained. "Touchdown!" blared the front-page headline on a special edition of the *Hartford Courant* printed specially for the occasion. (The paper would later offer framed copies of the front page for sale to its readers.)

"The Connecticut media, especially the *Courant* and major TV stations, were pretty awful," says Tom Sevigny of the Connecticut Green Party, who helped found Stop the Stadium. At one point in January 1999, Sevigny recalls, Hartford radio station WTIC ran a commentary attacking the Stop the Stadium leadership, claiming their figures were outdated, their arguments weak. "Half an hour after that commentary, WTIC makes a grand announcement that they will be the home of the New England Patriots in the coming football season."

The stadium project, meanwhile, was rapidly growing beyond its initial $350 million estimate. An investigation by the *New Haven Advocate*'s Carole Bass revealed that although the stadium construction cost was capped at $280 million, the additional $70 million in site cleanup was only an estimate—and one that could soar if the former industrial site turned out to be more polluted than expected. The initial estimate also missed $100 million in highways and parking spaces to be provided by the state; the undetermined cost of relocating a steam-generation plant that was still operating on the proposed stadium site; and the Capital Improvement Fund of $115 million (plus an inflation allowance) that the governor had agreed to provide for stadium improvements over the course of the thirty-year lease. It also omitted perhaps the most controversial piece of the stadium agreement: a guarantee by the state that the new stadium's 125 skyboxes and six thousand club seats would sell out for the next ten years. If they failed to do so, the state would reimburse the team up to $17.5 million a year for the lost revenue.

Rowland promptly commissioned frequent stadium consultants KPMG-Peat Marwick to conduct an economic study of the project, one that reported that the state would break even on the deal. The report became a staple of stadium boosters' public pronouncements—until the consultants turned out to have been under a mandate to design not an economic projection, but a scenario under which the stadium would break even. A Connecticut Office of Fiscal Analysis study reported that the state's losses could amount to as much as $257 million over the course of the deal.

Meanwhile, as the state legislature had already shut down for the year, Rowland called an emergency session to vote on the stadium package. The day of "public hearings" quickly turned into a fiasco, with stadium advocates (including both Rowland and Kraft) filling the afternoon invitation-only session, and $8-an-hour paid "line waiters" ensuring that much of the evening open-mike session was taken up by speakers handpicked by Gaffney Bennett's lobbyists. Smith College economics professor Andrew Zimbalist, who had been invited by one state representative to testify on the lack of economic benefits of stadiums, sat cooling his heels throughout the entire hearing and was never allowed to take the floor.

The following weekend, the governor and top legislators huddled to hammer out a compromise deal: The state's suite guarantee would be limited to half the cost of all boxes after the first fifty, and the price of club seats would be lowered from $5,000 to $4,000—which would still be far above the league average. "For the first time today, I can say I'm confident the plan will pass in the Senate," declared Senate president Kevin Sullivan. "We can tell our colleagues we listened to their concerns."

Two days later, the stadium bill easily passed both houses of the legislature. The revised lease, Rowland announced, would cut the state's annual guarantee from $17.5 million to $13 million. In cutting the price on club seats, Rowland and Kraft had also reduced how much money the ticket tax would generate to pay off the stadium bonds—but if anyone noticed, they never brought it up on the floor of the legislature.

The Peat Marwick studies and the revised seat guarantee had provided valuable political cover for legislators who wanted to switch their votes—but from all accounts, it was good old-fashioned arm-twisting that got the job done. A state representative from Mansfield, according to Sevigny, later told a public meeting that "the day of the vote, at around noon, they had enough votes to defeat it. And by three o'clock that afternoon, things totally turned around. She said there was just so much arm-twisting and threatening going on—people saw their political careers going down the toilet, so they held their noses and voted for it."

But if the backroom deals were effective in ramrodding a stadium bill through, they also awakened public outrage at the inability to have a say on the proposal. As 1999 dawned, the newly formed Stop the Stadium's phones were ringing off the hook with people offering to help collect a hundred thousand signatures calling for repeal of the stadium bill.

"I think the opposition will just get louder and louder," said Sevigny in early March. "The low-income housing assistance is being cut again for the third year in a row. A report just came out that thirty to thirty-five schools in Hartford alone are not up to safety codes. They have leaky roofs, no heat; kids are wearing coats all day in school. Where's the priorities here?"

The stadium debate rumbled on into the spring of 1999, until April 29, when Rowland and Kraft huddled in the governor's office in Hartford amid reports that environmental problems could delay the stadium's opening until the year 2003. Emerging from the meeting to meet the press, a grim-faced Kraft would say only, "Our goal has always been to play in a new stadium in downtown Hartford in the year 2002." Rowland reiterated: "My goal and the Patriots' goal is to open the 2002 season here in Hartford. As I've said so many times before, it will happen. Failure is not an option."

The next afternoon, even as the *Hartford Courant*'s front-page headline declared "Kraft, Rowland Reassure State Deal Is Still Alive," the word came down: The deal was officially dead. In place of the $374 million-plus promised by the state of Connecticut, Rowland was set to return to Massachusetts, where political leaders were finalizing a plan to provide $70 million in roads and sewers for a new stadium to be built by Kraft in Foxboro with his own money. "That's bankable money the team could count on for the next thirty years," sports consultant Marc Ganis said of the Connecticut package. "The idea of walking away from that without having another deal firmly in hand is unbelievable."

The reasons for Kraft's stunning turnaround were many. Difficulties with relocating the steam plant, concerns about pollution, and a miscalculation that might have forced one corner of the stadium to be suspended over a major highway all helped convince the Patriots' owner to take a lesser deal in Massachusetts. Possibly more important: In March NFL owners began putting their own pressure on the Patriots to reconsider their move to Hartford, which would have left the league without teams in three of the largest TV markets in the country. To help ease the pain of staying in Massachusetts, the league offered Resolution G-3, a new incentive plan for teams in the nation's top six media markets (Boston is sixth): guaranteed loans from the NFL itself to pay up to half the cost of any new stadium. Kraft himself chaired the league finance committee that introduced the G-3 plan.

Still, the Stop the Stadium activists take some credit for helping derail Hartford's stadium push. "I really believe that if we hadn't forced disclosures about all the loose ends in this deal, it might not have fallen apart the way it did," says Donovan. "I think everyone who carried our petition or signed a petition can take some credit for getting Connecticut back on track."

What the Future Holds

In all, public financing proposals for sports facilities won five and lost four in 1998, with several more contests headed into overtime as the year drew to a close. Along the way, several new economic studies had confirmed the findings of earlier researchers, uncovering no indication of any economic boost to cities that had built new stadiums. When the city of Phoenix attempted to counter these studies with its own report on increased sales tax revenues around the new downtown Bank One Ballpark, it was discovered that at current rates these would fully pay off the stadium's $253 million public cost in a mere 358 years.

Yet if the tide had turned, sports team owners had apparently not gotten the message, for their demands were only growing larger: Hartford's failed offer to the Patriots would have been among the most lucrative deals in history but still paled in comparison to the billion dollars-plus being proposed for stadium projects in New York, Boston, and Mesa, Arizona. And by early 1999 the list of stadium suitors had grown to include the St. Louis Cardinals (stadium built 1966, renovated 1996), the Tampa Bay Devil Rays (stadium built 1990, renovated 1998)—and the Chicago White Sox, whose owner, Jerry Reinsdorf, began lobbying for a new ballpark just eight years after his new Comiskey Park uprooted a neighborhood at $150 million in public expense.

"I used to be a lot more idealistic," says San Diego's Chris Michaels while awaiting word from the city about what he hopes will be a fair offer for his home and studio. "The way the world really works is that cities do break the law, when given the opportunity to do so. They're not always working in the interests of the people that voted them there. I really see how when you get people with money and power together, each on their own they're nothing, but together they can really do terrific things or scary things."

"I think people have been kicked around so much," says Connecticut's Donna Donovan. "I think we have like a battered-citizens syndrome going on in this country, where people sort of lay back and say, 'Well, he promised not to do it again.' They feel like they are powerless to change things. But once you get to a certain point where 'I'm mad as hell and I'm not gonna take it anymore,' if you give them the information, and you give them the vehicle for change, and you give them hope that they can effect change, they are inspired and they pack their bags and they walk out the door and they don't turn back."

Notes

1. The Spurs ultimately got their new arena in 2002, when the $175 million SBC Center opened, funded primarily by county hotel and car rental taxes.

13 The Art of the Steal Revisited

We don't want a new building just to have a new building. We would just stay where we are. If we're using the revenue to build the building, then we're not getting the revenue, and we're right back where we started, and why do we have a new building? —*Orlando Magic vice-president Cari Coats*

If I set you up in a business, and give you the key to the door, and you don't have to pay rent, and you get to keep 100 percent of everything that gets in the door, it's much more lucrative. Excuse me for being a cynic, but that's what this game is all about. —*Former Orlando Arena director John Christison*

The million-plus readers of the *Beijing Evening News* must have gotten quite a shock one May day in 2002 when they opened up the paper to read that the U.S. Congress was threatening to move out of Washington if it didn't get a new Capitol building. "If we want to stay competitive, we need to upgrade," the article quoted House Minority Leader Richard Gephardt as saying. "Look at the British Parliament. Look at the Vatican. . . . Without modern facilities, they've been having big problems attracting top talent." If a new building with more bathrooms and better parking wasn't erected, the article said, then U.S. lawmakers were prepared to pack up and move to Memphis or Charlotte.

The story, of course, was a joke: An inattentive *Beijing Evening News* editor had lifted it verbatim from a U.S. newspaper, without noticing that the paper he was plagiarizing was the satirical weekly the *Onion*. That his bosses utterly failed to get the joke—the *Evening News* editors later ran a brief correction bemoaning how "some small American newspapers frequently fabricate offbeat news to trick people into noticing them, with the aim of making money"—is a sign of just how prevalent these sorts of "if you build it, we won't go" threats had become by the dawn of the twenty-first century.

Since the previous edition of *Field of Schemes* was published in 1999, the case against putting public funds into private sports facilities has only grown stronger. The piles of economic studies showing that sports facilities are a net drain on public coffers have now grown into towering stacks. With the end of the economic boom of the 1990s, and once-flush city and state coffers drained, legislators can no longer blithely write checks for $300 million without having to worry about fiscal impact. Popular opposition to stadium deals has mounted, forcing teams to step up campaign spending to secure passage of stadium referenda. And after a decade-plus of breakneck construction, the list of teams left without new homes has grown shorter and shorter.

Yet the stadium juggernaut has rolled on. In Minnesota, where the Twins and Vikings were still making do with the more-than-two-decade-old Metrodome (and complaining about it every step of the way), the two teams kept up their pressure on the state legislature, even as the combined price tag rose to $800 million. New York City, long a holdout in the stadium chase, was making up for lost time with a staggering $3.6 billion in proposed stadium projects, about $2 billion of which would be paid for by taxpayers. And even some beneficiaries of the current stadium boom simply went back to the head of the line for more subsidies, with the owners of the Chicago White Sox and Seattle Sonics leading the way in demanding additional money to rehab or replace facilities that were built or renovated barely a decade earlier.

Meanwhile, new cities rushed in to fill the stadium vacuum: Las Vegas, Memphis, and other smaller metropolises eager to attain "major-league" status at whatever the cost. When the New Orleans Hornets, only recently arrived in Louisiana after bolting Charlotte for a new-arena deal in 2002, were displaced by Hurricane Katrina, Oklahoma City jumped in with an offer of free rent; prepaid arena operations; housing, office, and training-camp costs; and a promise to reimburse the team up to $10 million if it fell short of the previous year's profits—all just to be the temporary home of a team that had finished dead last in its conference the year before.

Every year, it seems, there are predictions that the stadium boom has run its course—either because local officials have gotten tougher about resisting team demands, or because the pool of franchises seeking new homes is destined to soon dry up. And every year, they're proven wrong as another crop of new buildings breaks ground. In part, it's because teams have been able to keep finding virgin territory, or at least newly elected political leaders with short institutional memories. And nearly two decades into the stadium boom, they've learned that the most important ingredient is patience: Unlike on the field of play, it takes only one win to bring home the grand prize, with a payday big enough to make up for an awful lot of past losses.

Take Minnesota. In 2006, after eleven years of beating his head against public opposition, Twins owner Carl Pohlad finally succeeded in winning nearly $400 million in public stadium funds, after portraying the team's requested 0.15 percent sales tax hike as merely "three cents on a $20 purchase." (It might just as fairly be called $320 per man, woman, and child in Hennepin County, but stadium boosters were careful not to frame it that way.) "In '97 we shut down the capitol switchboard, there was so much opposition," recalled state senator John Marty. But since then, "stadium fatigue" had built up, both among residents tired of the fight and among legislators who just wanted the issue to go away. "We're all sick of the issue, so one of the lobbying efforts that's very effective is 'the only way this issue will ever go away is if we pass it,'" said Marty. At the same time,

Ricky Rask, the reverend who had spearheaded the opposition that had flooded the state capitol switchboard in 1997, was ill with a brain tumor when the final Twins stadium debates began, and never got involved.

The Twins executives, meanwhile, with the lure of a multimillion-dollar payday, didn't get fatigued—nor did the $15 million worth of lobbyists they hired over the years to talk up their stadium plan. "Minnesota rightly has a reputation of being a cleaner state than most, and I've never suggested that the problem with the legislature is vote-buying," said Marty. "The problem is they don't buy votes, they buy access and goodwill. If I give you a thousand bucks, you don't have to know anything about me—you're probably going to like me a little better, even if it's subconsciously."

In the waning days of the Twins' stadium campaign, Marty noted, two polls of Minnesotans found more than 2–1 opposition to spending public money on a baseball stadium. "Because of lobbying, most legislators don't believe that," he said. "'This may be true statewide, but not in *my* district.' Because they spend all day talking to the lobbyists, the Twins executives; the teams are constantly running ads on television, at the games, telling people 'contact your legislator.' So they are convinced the public opinion is split, and angry on both sides, but basically favors this." The incessant lobbying, he said, "warps our perspective of what's going on in the world."

Marty noted grimly that Timberwolves owner Glen Taylor, asked if once the Twins and Vikings got new homes he'd be next in line, would say only that it wasn't politically prudent to mention that yet. "As soon as we pass these stadiums, give them two years. They'll be here," Marty predicted.

The Twins' ultimate success, after years of Minneapolis's being the textbook example of a city holding firm against stadium-subsidy demands, is a sign that team owners have become expert at rotating through the playbook that we laid out back in chapter 4—if the carrot of an "economic renaissance" doesn't sway the populace, perhaps the fear of losing their team to a more free-spending municipality will do it. On the rare occasion that some team exec does dream up a new twist on an old tactic, you can practically hear the pen scratches as the rest of the sports industry rushes to take notes.

Home-Field Disadvantage

The first weapon in the stadium arsenal remains "obsolescence": The old place has been around for years, and who would begrudge us a new one? What has changed markedly is that "old" doesn't mean what it used to.

When the new-stadium boom first began in the 1980s, the shelf life of a sports facility was generally considered to be thirty to forty years. Now, that seems positively ancient, as buildings barely out of their teens are routinely marked for the wrecking ball. In 2004, Toronto Blue Jays general manager J. P. Ricciardi declared the then fifteen-year-old SkyDome to be "obsolete," saying the artificial turf field "may have been state of the art fifteen years ago, but it's old now" and the fifty-thousand-seat capacity was "too big for baseball now." Added Ricciardi of the building that cost Ontario taxpayers a then record $600 million in 1989: "If the dome's open and it's a nice night, it's doable, but that's about it."

For basketball and hockey arenas, the life cycle has become even shorter. Of the new arenas opened for NBA expansion teams in 1988 and 1989, the Miami Arena was abandoned in 1999, and the Charlotte Coliseum in 2005; Orlando Magic owner (and Amway billionaire) Rich DeVos has bitterly complained for years that the Orlando Arena's twenty-six skyboxes and built-in TV studio are inadequate, and demanded that taxpayers pony up for a $250 million replacement. By the early years of the twenty-first century, both the Sacramento Kings' Arco Arena and the Milwaukee Bucks' Bradley Center (each opened in 1988) had been declared hopelessly antiquated as home courts. And when the Vancouver Grizzlies moved to Memphis in 2001, it was contingent on that city's constructing a replacement for the Pyramid—built way back in 1991.

The problem isn't that modern-day engineers are somehow unable to construct buildings to last. Rather, sports stadiums and arenas are undergoing a sort of planned obsolescence. The breakneck pace of new sports facilities, each with more revenue-generating luxury suites and ever-vaster concessions concourses, has left owners scrambling faster and faster to keep up with the Joneses.

"Some of it is just ego: The guy down the street's got a bigger, better, faster, flashier arena than I do, which may be one or two generations ahead, and therefore I want one too," former Orlando Arena director John Christison observed in 2001 of the arena class of 1988-89. "When those buildings all came off the construction pallet, they were pretty much state of the art. And they're still damn fine buildings. The question is, do they generate enough income for the teams?"

Washington State University sports economist Rod Fort was more blunt. "I don't see anything wrong, from an owner's perspective, with the idea of a new stadium every year. It's an expensive way for him to get out of a lease—but not expensive to *him*."

Faking a Move

Between 2000 and 2006 the list of teams that dropped hints they'd hightail it out of town unless their demands for a new home were met grew to include the Buffalo Sabres, Florida Marlins, Vancouver Grizzlies, Minnesota Vikings and Twins, New Orleans Saints, Sacramento Kings, Pittsburgh Penguins, Montreal Expos, Oakland A's, Kansas City Chiefs, Seattle Sonics, Charlotte Hornets, San Diego Chargers, Indianapolis Colts, Jacksonville Jaguars, and innumerable soccer teams and minor-league baseball and hockey franchises. Of those, the only teams that actually moved were the Expos, Grizzlies, and Hornets—but several of the others had positioned themselves to get new or upgraded facilities at home.

Occasionally, it's still team owners themselves levying the warnings, usually in the form of the non-threat threat. "We're not a threatening type of ownership," Bob Vander Weide, president of the Orlando Magic (and son-in-law of Rich DeVos), said when a new arena was on the legislative agenda. "But if another opportunity came along, we've got to look." Seattle Sonics (and Starbucks Coffee) owner Howard Schultz insisted, "We want to stay in Seattle. We would think it would be tragic if we had to leave," mere weeks after he said he'd seek "other alternatives" if the state legislature didn't come through with $200 million to renovate KeyArena. "If there's no renovation of the sports complex, one or both of these franchises will be gone," Kansas City Chiefs team chairman Clark Hunt told local officials in 2005; county sports authority chief Mike Smith promptly told reporters, "It's got me real nervous. I would not take it as a threat but as a message."

When it comes to delivering messages, team owners are increasingly likely to call on a local politician like Smith—or even more commonly, a friendly newspaper sports columnist. After all, getting stadium funds out of a wary public requires leveraging the goodwill that's been built toward "their" team, and it's hard to convince people to open their wallets when they're busy hanging you in effigy. As Minnesota Vikings stadium lobbyist Lester Bagley explained to a group of local sports editors: "We try to get our ownership not to talk about other markets. It's not helpful in a public-relations sense."

For billionaire oil baron Jerry Jones, owner of the Dallas Cowboys, the most valuable franchise in football, it was *Fort Worth Star-Telegram* columnist O. K. Carter who rode to the aid of their demand for tax dollars to pay for half the cost of a new $650 million stadium. Carter wrote that although Jones "should pay totally for any stadium," he "doesn't have to. Any of a half-dozen franchise-hungry cities in the country will happily cough up a big chunk of the tab for the Cowboys."

Carter's words might have been more convincing if not for another column he'd written just three months earlier. In that one he'd insisted that the Cowboys "simply can't use the old 'give us a new stadium or we'll leave' threat. They've become one of the most valuable sports franchises on the planet because of that 'Dallas' in front of their name. Even if they left, the thunder we'd hear would be the sound of air crashing into the empty space left by a half-dozen other franchises trying to be the first to fill the Cowboys' vacuum. No, the Cowboys are stuck here, no matter what."

The undisputed prize for service to his team, though, has to go to *Minneapolis Star Tribune* columnist Sid Hartman, a self-proclaimed "close personal friend" of Bud Selig who spent more than a decade insisting that without a new stadium, and pronto, the Twins had one foot out the door. A review of the past decade's Hartmanisms by the *Minneapolis City Pages* in 2005 revealed a time line of doom-filled prognostications that made up in melodrama what they lacked in accuracy. In January 1997, as the team geared up for its first big stadium push, Hartman predicted that "the Twins will be in Charlotte, North Carolina, by the year 2000 if a new stadium is not built." That April, Hartman wrote: "You can write this in stone: The Twins will not be here after 1998, when Pohlad can escape his Metrodome lease, if a new stadium isn't approved during this legislative session." In May: "My prediction: This franchise will wind up in Mexico City in 2000 if a new stadium isn't built." A new stadium wasn't built, and the Twins didn't leave, but Hartman was undeterred, predicting that 2002 would be "the last season of Major League Baseball in Minnesota."

By May 2005 the Twins were still in place and still seeking stadium funds. Wrote Hartman, "Believe me, if this stadium plan falls through, the Twins are done fighting for a stadium and the owners will either cut the payroll to $25 million from the present $56 million or sell the team to somebody who might move it." The next year, the Twins payroll had risen to $63 million—and the team was back in the state legislature, stumping for the exact same plan.

Even once the Twins had won, old habits died hard. On the day that the legislature approved the stadium, Hartman ran a column citing Selig as saying the team had been about to move: "We were coming close to the end. And if anybody thinks that was an idle threat, they were kidding themselves."

Leveling the Playing Field

In October 2004, as the city of Washington DC considered spending more than $400 million dollars on a new stadium to lure the Montreal Expos down from Canada, *Washington Post* columnist Steven Pearlstein wrote: "The economics of baseball are such that there simply is no way to have a viable team without some form of public subsidy. The amount of subsidy already in the system has generated player salaries and franchise prices so high that there's not enough money left over to pay market rent for a stadium."

It's certainly a familiar claim: that old, unsubsidized facilities may have been fine in your grandfather's day, but they simply don't allow teams to compete in the modern era. But is it true?

There's certainly plenty of circumstantial evidence to the contrary. The Boston Red Sox, playing in ninety-two-year-old Fenway Park, won the World Series in 2004; the year before, the Florida Marlins took the crown, despite being then in their sixth year of insisting that a new stadium was necessary for their team to compete. In the NBA, the Houston Rockets, San Antonio Spurs, and Chicago Bulls all won championships in buildings they were looking to leave, as did the NHL's New Jersey Devils. Clearly, a taxpayer-funded new home isn't a requirement for on-field (or on-court or on-ice) success.

It's undeniable, though, that new stadiums do bring in more revenue for their tenants—especially when it's the public paying the construction bills—and some of this trickles down to spending on players. (Because of the pricey premium seats that typify new sports facilities, owners have a greater incentive to sign high-priced players, knowing that the fannies they put in the seats will be that much more valuable.) An examination of the link between new baseball stadiums and winning percentage for the Baseball Prospectus book *Baseball between the Numbers* revealed that new stadiums were worth about 5.5 wins a year to their teams. That's about as much as they could gain by adding one ace starting pitcher—bringing to mind the Minnesota legislator who, a few years back, suggested that instead of spending hundreds of millions of dollars on a new stadium so the

Twins could afford to re-sign Brad Radke, it would be cheaper for taxpayers just to pay for his contract.

If anything, though, new stadiums and the riches they've brought to the teams that play in them are driving payroll costs through the roof, making it still harder for low-revenue teams to compete—and making it difficult even for some teams with new homes, since all their competitors have them, too. (The concrete was barely dry on Pittsburgh's new PNC Park before Pirates owner Kevin McClatchy declared that he still had no intention of raising his payroll above the league average.) As it became clear that plenty of teams were going to finish at the bottom of the standings even with new homes, league officials changed their tune—slightly. "People say, well, new stadiums are not the panacea," said Selig in June 2004. "They are not the panacea. But there are some cities, for example, take Detroit; they couldn't continue in Tiger Stadium. At least [the new stadium] gives them a lot more revenue to be competitive." At the time, the Tigers had spent four years in their new park and were coming off a season in which they lost a league-record 119 games.

Then there's Oakland, where A's owner Steve Schott, often joined by Selig, made "we can't compete" an annual spring-training refrain—even as his team stubbornly won division titles year after year. Immediately after making the playoffs for the fourth year in a row in 2003, Schott griped, "It's very frustrating to have to go through this every year and not have a realistic chance of signing guys like [Jason] Giambi and [Miguel] Tejada. I don't think I have to make my case anymore. It's pretty clear why I can't. I look at other teams rolling back their payrolls and they have new stadiums."

In the land of sports-owner logic, even when teams have new stadiums built for them and fail, it's a reason to build more stadiums.

Playing the Numbers

In 2004 the city of Arlington, Texas, hired the consulting firm Economic Research Associates (ERA) to measure the likely impact of the

$650 million football stadium the Dallas Cowboys were looking to build there—with $325 million in sales, hotel, and car-rental taxes. Their findings: a new stadium would create $238 million a year in "economic impact," more than repaying Arlington for its investment.

"Economic impact" is a favored statistic of consultants, because it dramatically inflates a project's effect by including all money spent at or around a facility, whether or not it benefits the public. If a team doubles its ticket prices, for example, that counts as double the economic activity, even if the resulting revenue goes directly into the owner's pocket.

A more accurate way of looking at the costs and benefits of a project is to examine how much actual new tax revenue it would bring into a city's coffers: "fiscal impact," in public-policy lingo. ERA included those numbers as well, predicting $2.9 million a year in increased tax revenues—while Arlington would be handing out more than $20 million a year in subsidies. And if that wasn't bad enough, ERA touted the creation of 807 long-term jobs—which would come to more than $400,000 in expense per job created, one of the worst ratios in economic-development history.

Nonetheless, the ERA report enabled Arlington mayor Robert Cluck to declare the project an economic boon, saying, "You have to spend money in order to make money." Shortly thereafter, following a $5 million ad blitz by Jones, Arlington voters approved the stadium project.

Lukas Herbert, a city planner in New York's Westchester County who, as a member of the community board in his Bronx neighborhood, voted against a Yankees stadium project backed by a similar ERA report, said these studies are typical of the sort of rosy economic projections that come across his desk to justify dubious projects. If you're a developer, said Herbert, "you hire a firm like ERA and say, 'Here, put in some numbers and make us look good.' They can make any project seem like an economic-development dream come true."

That was certainly the finding of the *New Orleans Times-Picayune* when it investigated economic-impact projections in Louisiana. The numbers provided, the paper found, were seldom reliable, especially when the beneficiaries of the development deals were the ones conducting the studies. In one case, when organizers of a festival in Texas were unhappy with an economist's projection of $16.1 million in economic impact, they sent him back to the drawing board. His new calculation: $321.6 million. "I've had people tell me that: 'I want the biggest number I can get,'" University of New Orleans economist Timothy Ryan told the newspaper.

One problem, says economist Rod Fort, is that economic-impact consultants rely on computer models that are only as good as the assumptions you feed into them. "It's the worst kind of analytical dodgeball," says Fort. He recalls asking a Washington State University colleague with expertise in these models, "If you want to answer the question, should we spend $200 million more to upgrade KeyArena here in Seattle, how do you find out how much *new* stuff is coming out of the existence of the team?' And he said: 'Oh, you tell it.'"

The studies also tend to overlook or downplay the two major pitfalls of economic-development claims. The first is the *substitution effect*, which measures how much spending is just cannibalized from somewhere else in town, as when fans spend their disposable income on stadium hot dogs instead of at the local pizzeria. The second, *leakage*, is a measure of the degree to which stadium spending is taken out of the local economy before it can be recirculated—whereas that pizzeria owner would likely have spent much of his income at local stores, the same isn't true for the team owners and players who reap the bulk of the proceeds from sports spending.

For example, after its successful report for the Dallas Cowboys, ERA was hired by New York City to study its plans to build a new stadium for the Yankees. Its findings: the new stadium would bring in enough new fans to generate $225 million in new tax revenues for the city and state. Yet its analysis overestimated economic impact in several obvious ways: It accounted for leakage in ticket sales but not substitution, even though every dollar spent on baseball tickets is one less dollar that fans have to spend elsewhere. For concessions, meanwhile, it accounted for substitution but not leakage, even though much of the new revenues would go directly to the Tampa-residing George Steinbrenner through increased fees from concessionaires.

"The things that make for good economic growth are not very sexy to write about," explained University of Chicago economist Allen Sanderson. "It's easy to go to Yankee Stadium and take pictures of the fifty thousand who are there, but it's harder to go to a mall or a restaurant and interview some guy who says, 'Yeah, my business was off by 3 percent tonight.' And yet in dollar amounts, the winners and losers are just the same."

The Two-Minute Warning

Setting arbitrary "deadlines" remains a popular sports-owner pastime, in part because neither elected officials nor local journalists ever seem to notice when drop-dead dates pass and the sky doesn't fall. In late 2000, after a year in which the St. Louis Cardinals drew 3.34 million fans, the second-best turnout in baseball, the team's owners declared that if no stadium plan was in place by the following May, they would start to look out of state for a new home. The date came and went without incident, and it would take until December 2002 before a stadium plan would be agreed upon. The Dallas Cowboys—another team immensely popular in its current location, and unlikely to move—were even more bald-faced in their public statements. Team spokesman Brett Daniels told reporters: "June 30—that's our target goal. Part of it is to create a sense of urgency."

The undisputed reigning king of the phony deadline, though, has to be Florida Marlins president David Samson. Samson came to Florida when his stepdad Jeffrey Loria got the team in a three-way swap that ended up with former Marlins owner John Henry landing the Boston Red Sox, and Major League Baseball itself taking over Loria's Montreal Expos. Loria and Samson's first move—after removing all the computers from the Expos offices and lugging them south to Florida, leaving the league-owned franchise with no scouting data on opposing teams—was to set out in search of the stadium subsidies that had eluded two previous owners, Henry and Wayne Huizenga.

Samson's first line in the sand was March 15, 2004, a date by which he said the Florida legislature needed to approve an additional $30 million worth of stadium subsidies, on top of $198 million plus free land already approved by the city and county, or else. "It's my experience that without a deadline, nothing ever gets done," Samson told the Associated Press. "The deadline is firm. It's not flaccid." When March 15 came and went and the legislature was no closer to approving stadium funds, Samson promptly moved the drop-dead date to May 1: "We're confident that forty-five days from now, we'll stand before you celebrating the Florida Marlins staying in South Florida." A month later, as state legislators declared the stadium bill "certainly dead for this year," he pushed back his deadline by another five days, to give Miami commissioners time to vote on it. "This is it," Samson told ESPN.com columnist Jayson Stark. "It has to happen in the next week. And if not, we'll move on."

It didn't happen. But far from moving on, as of 2007 the Marlins owners were still pushing for that extra $30 million, while jetting around the country to such locales as Las Vegas and San Antonio to strike fear in the hearts of local legislators.

Moving the Goalposts

In May 1999, with the Seattle Mariners' Safeco Field nearing completion, the team had already gotten $336 million in public subsidies, thanks to Senator Slade Gorton's last-minute move to squeeze an extra $45 million out of the city of Seattle. Yet following that, thanks to the Mariners' numerous design-change requests even after concrete had started being poured, the stadium's cost had soared still higher, standing at a staggering $514 million—$100 million more than had been budgeted.

Although the Mariners had agreed as part of the Gorton deal to pay for any additional cost overruns, team execs now came back with a novel argument. The added costs, the team explained, were not "cost overruns" but rather "unanticipated capital costs"—and it asked the state to refinance the ballpark bonds and use the proceeds to bail out the Mariners. If it did not, the team threatened, it would have to cut loose star players Alex Rodriguez and Ken Griffey Jr. to pay for its extra cost. (Griffey, annoyed at being dragged into the dispute, promptly griped, "Every time money comes up with ownership, it's Junior and Alex's fault?")

A judge ultimately disagreed with the Mariners' argument, and the team ponied up the extra $100 million out of its own pocket. (Griffey and A-Rod both ultimately departed—and the Mariners promptly won a record 116 games in the 2001 season.) More successful were the San Diego Padres, who took a November 1998 public vote for $225 million in stadium subsidies and leveraged it into $299 million by the time Petco Park finally opened in 2004, while eliminating a promised park where fans could watch games for free (an admission fee is now charged on game days) and demanding to build taller residential towers than had been approved by voters. If their demands weren't met, Padres president Larry Lucchino had warned, "the question of relocation [would] have to be addressed." He'd added, "I think that's a viable prospect."

Increasingly, teams were using a new gambit to claim further subsidies down the road, even as they locked themselves into thirty-year leases. A typical stadium lease these days contains "state-of-the-art" clauses guaranteeing that the building will remain one of the most modern facilities in its sport.

As a result, when the Cincinnati Bengals demanded artificial turf at their four-year-old Paul Brown Stadium in 2004, taxpayers were forced to pay the tab because a lease clause put Hamilton County on the hook for installing any and all new technologies that had been adopted by fourteen NFL teams, or by seven using public money. Among the "Level I enhancements" specifically listed in the lease were such items as "smart seats," "stadium self-cleaning machines," and a "holographic replay system."

"The lease is like the Energizer bunny," county commissioner Phil Heimlich told the *Cincinnati Enquirer*. "You know how it keeps going and going? Well, we keep paying and paying."

Of Carrots and Kitchen Sinks

State-of-the-art clauses are just one of the new twists that sports-team owners have added to the tried-and-true tactics in the stadium playbook. Others have ranged from the desperate—as when the Florida Marlins signed star third baseman Mike Lowell to a contract extension that would make him a free agent if the team didn't get a new stadium, hoping fans would back their funding plan to keep their favorite player in town—to the bizarre, as when Marlins president David Samson sent a letter to Florida's house speaker claiming that Wayne Huizenga, the former Marlins owner who was now the team's landlord, "has informed us that it will not, under any circumstances, extend or renew the current lease; thereby, giving the Marlins no place to play in South Florida after that time." (This gambit backfired when state senate president Tom Lee promptly declared, "I don't negotiate with terrorists," and collapsed when Huizenga himself publicly insisted that he had no intention of evicting the team: "Let's say for some reason or another they didn't get their thing done and they wanted to stay. Okay, fine. That's not the end of the world.")

For those without Samson's creativity, there were still a few new cards to be played. One popular carrot to dangle in front of cities has been the promise that they will be eligible to play host to a Super Bowl if they build new NFL stadiums. (For baseball stadiums, the All-Star Game is typically the lure.) In recent years, NFL commissioner Paul Tagliabue made the same promise to San Diego, Minneapolis, Indianapolis, Kansas City, and New York, in each case portraying the NFL's big game as the source of a flood of new tourists and a multi-million-dollar boon to local economies.

Yet the numbers tell a different story. When University of South Florida economist Philip Porter studied tourism figures for cities that had held the Super Bowl, he found no discernible uptick during the week of the game. Especially in warm-weather cities, it seems, Super Bowl tourists merely displace visitors who would ordinarily be taking up hotel space, because anyone not interested in football steers clear during game week. In fact, explained Porter, Super Bowl tourists can ultimately be less beneficial to a local economy than the regular kind because hotels often require booking weeklong hotel stays even if fans are flying in only for the weekend. The result is windfalls for the national hotel chains that jack up prices for the event, but not much for local merchants who miss out on lost sales during much of the week.

While it's increasingly tough to convince voters of the need to subsidize sports-only projects, if it's a "ballpark village" with housing and retail space, well, that's a fuzzier issue. Attach a bunch of other development to your stadium plans, and you can hope to muddy the waters enough that no one can understand the finances, even if you're asking for dozens of acres of free land.

Rod Fort traces the origins of these everything-but-the-kitchen-sink plans to what he calls "Huizengaland," a massive development project that then-Marlins owner Wayne Huizenga proposed to build in the late 1990s, with baseball and football stadiums as its centerpiece. While Florida officials rejected Huizenga's plan—along with what Fort recalls would have been a "staggering" public subsidy—the idea soon spread to other cities. The San Diego Chargers promised to build their own football stadium if they were granted sixty acres of free downtown land for an accompanying residential development; the St. Louis Cardinals accompanied their new stadium with a "Ballpark Village." Oakland A's owner Lew Wolff, a real estate developer who was part of a group of partners who'd bought the team from Steve Schott in 2005, presented an even more audacious offer: He'd build a baseball stadium with his own money, and a new neighborhood of condos and restaurants, too—all he wanted was free land and lucrative development rights.

While these deals are often just as costly to the public as standard stadium-subsidy projects, they have a big advantage for team owners: If anyone tries the counterargument that stadiums are bad economic deals, they can respond truthfully that "this isn't just a stadium"—and point to the economic benefits of the attached project as an excuse for demanding public aid for the sports facility. "If folks don't go for the stadium part of it, they have a hard time rejecting the other development aspect," says Fort. "And I think politicians know that as well as team owners."

TIFs: The "But-For" Problem

If kitchen-sink plans are hard for the general public to understand, what could be the most significant addition to the stadium playbook takes the cake for the most obfuscatory gambit of recent years—and one of the most popular, as well.

This latest trick debuted in the stadium world in 1999, when the state of Pennsylvania was wrangling over demands by four of its major sports teams—the Pittsburgh Pirates and Steelers, and the Philadelphia Phillies and Eagles—for government aid in building new stadiums. State officials had agreed to a formula where the cities, the state, and the teams would each pay for one third of stadium costs but not on how to fund it.

The solution, which was approved by more than two-thirds votes in both the state house and senate, was described in the newspapers as an "interest-free loan," but it was nothing of the sort. Under the plan, the state would determine how much sales tax revenue the state was currently getting from the four sports teams; if sales tax receipts at the new stadiums exceeded this, any increase would be kicked back to the teams to repay their stadium costs. It was this self-proclaimed "hybrid" of a loan and a grant that led Pittsburgh state representative Thomas Petrone to quip, "It's not a grant. It's not a loan. It's a groan."

What it was, in economic development terms, was a TIF, short for "tax-increment financing." (The "increment" being the slice of additional tax revenues that gets funneled back into the project.) Though new to sports stadium deals, this mechanism had been growing more popular among state development officials—too popular, according to its many critics. First developed in California in the 1950s, tifs took off in the '80s as local governments sought ways to find money to entice developers. By the mid-1990s, Minnesota was handing out $750 million a year in tifs. (The Mall of America, built atop the ruins of the Twins' old Bloomington Stadium, got $105 million.) Since Proposition 13 curtailed property-tax hikes in California, tif has become "an industry unto itself," reports Howard Greenwich of California's East Bay Alliance for a Sustainable Economy, with tif projects soaking up 8 percent of all property taxes in the state.

It wasn't long before tifs caught on in sports as well—the Phoenix Coyotes, Dallas Cowboys, Minnesota Twins, New Jersey Nets, and backers of Louisville and Kansas City basketball arenas and a Norfolk baseball stadium, among others, would all subsequently issue tif plans after seeing Pennsylvania's plan in place. By using only "new" revenues, the argument went, tifs answered a prime criticism of stadium subsidies: This wasn't money that could be spent on other services because it wouldn't exist without the sports project.

But there's a pitfall to tifs, and it's a doozy. It's what development experts call the "but-for" problem. While tif subsidies are provided under the assumption that no new development would happen "but for" the tifs, developers often strain the limits of that concept. In Minnesota, subsidy expert Greg LeRoy notes, city officials were recently found to be handing out tif money for projects that otherwise would still occur, just on a different block.

In recent years, Chicago has become the poster child for a city whose tax base has been reduced to Swiss cheese by runaway tifs. Concerned that the city's 121 separate tif districts were draining off tax dollars to subsidize projects in pricey neighborhoods that would have been built anyway, the grassroots Neighborhood Capital Budget Group (ncbg) in Chicago studied thirty-six districts' property-tax growth rates before and after TIF. Their findings: Of the $1.6 billion in "incremental taxes" redirected to TIF projects, $1.3 billion would have gone into city coffers even without the special tax districts. As a result of this, the NCBG calculated, Chicago public schools had lost more than $600 million. "They sell it as 'cost free,'" complained the NCBG's Patricia Nolan. "But there's always a tradeoff."

"TIFS are among the most problematic kinds of subsidies in America today," in part because of their speculative nature, says LeRoy. "Real estate markets are cyclical. During the crash in real estate values in the early '90s, some places got caught in the downdraft, and the increment evaporated. And you've got a situation where a liability that was supposed to be taken care of by the TIF is now eating the lunch of the general fund." In Washington DC when $73.6 million in TIF financing for the Gallery Place mall ran into a brick wall after bond buyers balked at the revenue projections, the district was forced to expand the TIF to cover nearly half of its downtown core. A California study of thirty-eight TIF districts found that only four had generated enough property-value growth to justify their tax subsidies. Then there's the doomsday scenario: St. Petersburg, Florida, according to a report by the New York City Independent Budget Office, saw property-tax revenues actually fall in one TIF district, leaving the city to bail out the project with existing taxes.

As *St. Paul Pioneer Press* columnist Edward Lotterman wrote on the absurdities of TIFS: "My wife and I have often talked about a small addition that would extend the back porch the full width of the house. . . . It would be nice if the government would give us the money to do this. The value of the house would increase and so would our taxes. The higher taxes would pay the government back eventually, so it wouldn't cost taxpayers anything. . . . It seems like a great idea, but for some reason the government is not willing to step up to our plate. We threatened to move to Portland or Charlotte if we don't get help, but officials just laughed."

How Much Is That Stadium in the Window?

TIFS are just one example of the types of hidden subsidies that are becoming more popular as citizen resistance grows to direct outlays from the public treasury on stadiums. Instead of cash, the thinking goes, you ask for operating subsidies, free rent, or tax breaks—all lease items that can help subsidize stadium costs on the back end.

The prevalence of hidden subsidies was revealed by Princeton urban planner Judith Grant Long, when she set out to study whether or not cities were learning from past mistakes in cutting lease deals with their pro sports franchises. Long quickly realized that she'd need to compile accurate data to make the comparison—and so she spent years poring over team leases and stadium-finance documents, trying to discover who was ultimately paying for what.

What she found was that large amounts of public subsidy were obscured because they were contained not in the stadium-construction deal but in the accompanying lease terms. Modern leases, explains Long, are "very different animals" than were their predecessors from previous decades: "The leases that were in effect in the '60s and '70s were very favorable to the public sector because they were traditional leases where the teams had very little control over any of their revenues. They paid a substantial amount of rent, they paid a substantial amount of the share of concessions, they didn't get revenue from non-major-league events, there were no luxury suites, there were no naming rights." These days, by contrast, public stadium owners get little to no rent, as "the major-league franchise is often siphoning off revenues from other events in the facility, even if the facility is publicly owned. They're also taking the ice-show revenue, they're taking the monster-truck-show revenue." On average, Long discovered, sports stadiums were costing their host cities 40 percent more than was being publicly reported—and that figure was on the rise.

Perhaps the most notable of all the new stadium gambits, though, was the one concocted in Major League Baseball offices in preparation for the league's showdown with its players union in 2002. This was "contraction," the threat to wipe two teams off the baseball map unless cities and the union agreed to concessions—and as to which teams, those wouldn't be identified until all the stadium cards were on the table. It was a logical extension of the move threat: If you could only get cities to literally bid against each other for a scarce resource, like in an eBay auction writ large, you could potentially see your price skyrocket as local officials feared being outbid.

Of course, you can't really sell a sports team on eBay. But as Bud Selig was to prove, you can do the next best thing.

14 Youppi! Come Home

Nobody is better equipped to show people how to fleece the taxpayers into building them a new stadium than Allan H. [Bud] Selig. He could write a textbook on how he committed the taxpayers of Wisconsin to build a stadium at no cost whatsoever to the Seligs. —*Wisconsin state senator Michael Ellis*

On August 12, 1994, according to Quebecois legend, baseball was put to death in Montreal. That was the day that major league baseball players went on strike for the third time in fourteen years, in a stalemate over owner demands to impose a salary cap. Two months later, MLB commissioner Bud Selig would cancel the World Series, and fans of the Montreal Expos, who were sitting in first place in the National League East with baseball's best record at the time of the strike, had their dreams of a championship crushed. By the next spring, when baseball resumed play, the Expos had sold off two thirds of its starting outfield, and its top reliever, and fans began deserting the team in droves, never to return.

That's the legend, anyway. And who's going to nitpick that some of the details aren't exactly true? The Expos made another run at a pennant in 1996, for example, behind a kid named Pedro Martinez that they'd picked up in an earlier salary-dump deal. And the fans stuck around for a while, as well: While Montreal was never a hotbed of baseball diehards, attendance hovered around the 1.5 million mark through 1997, with the Expos managing to outdraw the big-market New York Mets in two of the three years following the strike.

Eventually, though, Martinez was dealt as well—one week after being awarded the 1997 Cy Young Award as the league's best pitcher—along with most of the team's other talent, and attendance suffered. New team ownership arrived in 2001 and promptly demanded a more lucrative TV deal; when their cable carrier balked, the Expos played the entire season with no English-language TV broadcasts. It didn't escape attention that the new revenue-sharing plan that baseball had put in place in 2002 increased the incentive for teams to cut payroll to the bone then turn a profit by receiving checks from their more successful competitors; it also didn't hurt that an unsuccessful team could help ownership make the case for needing a new stadium.

Montreal's Olympic Stadium, admittedly, wasn't anybody's idea of a baseball jewel. A stark concrete doughnut resting uncomfortably across the street from the city's botanic gardens, the building became known locally as "The Big Owe" for the $1 billion price tag it racked up when rush-built for the 1976 Olympics. From the start, the stadium was plagued by a balky retractable roof; when this was finally replaced by a $37 million permanent Teflon roof in 1998, the new lid promptly collapsed under the weight of snow during an auto show and had to be replaced yet again. Quebec cabinet minister Louise Harel went so far as to submit that the dome was afflicted by a "divine curse."

In what was to become an annual ritual, *Montreal Gazette* columnist Jack Todd—the Sid Hartman of Quebec—grumbled in March 1999 that "it is all but inevitable now: the Expos will be sold and moved. This will be their final season in Montreal." Jeffrey Loria, the New York art dealer who'd wrested control of the Expos in 2000, announced that he'd break ground soon on a privately funded stadium in downtown Montreal, to be called Labatt Park (the beer company had pre-purchased naming rights), but then demanded that either the government or his minority partners pitch in to help pay for it.

When the partners balked, Loria seized control of their shares of the team instead, leading to a lawsuit that would drag on for half a decade. But when it came to government help, Loria soon found that Canada was not the United States. "We're not in the business of helping sports teams," Canadian prime minister Jean Chrétien had declared in 1999, a sentiment that was echoed by municipal and provincial elected officials. The Expos owner hinted at the usual move threats, but nothing came of it.

At this point, a new word entered the baseball lexicon. In the summer of 1999, Colorado Rockies owner Jerry McMorris first leaked word to *Sports Illustrated* that baseball owners were considering something called "contraction." In a reverse of the usual expansion cycle, in which leagues open their doors to new cities in exchange for hefty entry fees, under contraction the league would buy out the owners of between two and four underperforming franchises and reallocate their players—and their share of national TV revenues—to the remaining teams. It was a gambit that had been tried just once before, when the National League reduced itself from twelve teams to eight—following the 1899 season.

The Expos, by then the lowest-revenue team in baseball, were assumed to be one of the targets. But baseball czar Bud Selig refused to name names, leading to speculation that contraction was just a ploy to put pressure on every rumored target city in hopes of shaking loose public stadium money. It also served as a threat against the players union: Give in to a salary cap, or we'll wipe out fifty big-league jobs.

As threats go, it was one that baseball owners were extremely unlikely to pull the trigger on. Tulane sports-law professor Gary Roberts called the proposal "a legal nightmare," "a public-relations disaster," and "economically stupid," while economist Rod Fort insisted that the recouped TV and other revenues would pale in comparison to the estimated $500 million cost of buying out two owners. And that was just for starters. "Whatever long-term leases these two have, even just with popcorn vendors, those are all going to have to be bought out," explained Fort. "So the cost mounts, and the cost mounts." Florida's attorney general declared that he'd file an antitrust suit against MLB to stop any attempted liquidation of the Marlins or Devil Rays, and a Minnesota county judge issued a temporary restraining order against baseball eliminating the Twins; Minnesota governor Jesse Ventura, a staunch stadium-subsidy opponent, proclaimed: "If they eliminate the Twins, I say we eliminate their antitrust status."

The contraction gambit was all the talk of baseball throughout 2002 but fizzled when a new labor agreement that fall prohibited baseball owners from so much as talking about eliminating teams until after the 2006 season. This left Selig with a dilemma. As part of the contraction talks, the league had executed a complicated three-way dance with the owners of the Expos, Marlins, and Red Sox in late 2001 that had resulted in former Marlins owner John Henry taking over in Boston, ex-Expos chief Loria getting Florida (bringing along his stepson, David Samson, as team president), and the Montreal team itself ending up a ward of the state, co-owned by its twenty-nine big-league rivals. With contraction off the table, Selig now found himself stuck with the booby prize. He was determined to turn that to an advantage.

The Extortion across America Tour

In December 2002 Selig issued his plans for disposing of the Expos: a multiple-city auction to determine the team's new home. Unlike previous team sales, though, this one would not be pitched to prospective owners. Rather, delegations from cities hoping to land the Expos for 2004 would be invited to meet with a "relocation committee" that would decide where to award the franchise. "MLB wants to know, 'What evidence do you have your market can support a franchise?' and 'Where are you going to play and how is that stadium going to be paid for?'" an MLB source told the *Washington Post*. "In a perfect world, jurisdictions should have all approvals in place and money set aside."

And thus began what baseball business writer Doug Pappas would dub Bud Selig's Stadium Extortion across North America Tour. By any measure, Selig had a rough road ahead of him. By 2002 not many major markets remained untapped by MLB. Denver, the perennial relocation bridesmaid of the '70s and '80s, had received its own expansion team in 1993. And Tampa Bay, which at one time or another had seen seven different baseball teams play footsie with it in order to extract stadium concessions from their hometowns, had landed the expansion Devil Rays in 1998, after MLB blocked the San Francisco Giants' move to St. Petersburg, and Florida officials threatened an antitrust lawsuit if a new team wasn't promptly supplied.

The Expos' suitors instead included a mixed bag of cities, each with its own liabilities when it came to hosting a major-league baseball team. Portland, Oregon, had been a rumored relocation site before but was relatively small, had a minor-league team plagued by poor attendance, and boasted a local political culture that abhorred sports subsidies. (In the early 1970s, Portland had turned down an offer of an NFL team if it built a domed stadium; it never looked back, by 2000 landing the top spot in *Money* magazine's rankings of most-livable U.S. cities.) Las Vegas had a thriving tourist trade but little in the way of local fan base, and the added taint of being a den of gambling, baseball's official bête noire ever since the Chicago Black Sox scandal in 1919. San Juan, Puerto Rico—where Selig had arranged for the Expos to play twenty-two "home" games in 2003—and Monterrey, Mexico, were on baseball's official short list but mostly as a nod to building baseball's international market; hardly anyone took seriously the thought of trying to pay big-league salaries with pesos.

That left what was by far the largest remaining market: Washington DC. The nation's capital had gotten the short end of the stick in baseball's last relocation, when the Washington Senators bolted for Arlington, Texas, way back in 1972. Ever since, DC had been widely considered baseball's best vacant market. The Houston Astros had threatened to move to DC's Virginia suburbs during their own 1990s campaign for a new stadium, and Selig himself had called the nation's capital the "prime candidate" for relocation as early as January 2002.

But even as Washington left owners salivating over its eighth-ranked media market, it had two major drawbacks. One was the presence of the Baltimore Orioles just up the road; while DC technically wasn't Orioles territory according to MLB bylaws, there was no guarantee that team owner Peter Angelos would see things that way. Angelos—a superlawyer best known for extracting $4.4 billion for the state of Maryland in a tobacco class-action suit and demanding a quarter of the proceeds for himself—had already proven his willingness to buck the tight owners' fraternity during the players' strike of 1994–95, when he alone among the owners refused to field a team of "replacement players" during spring training.

The other problem with DC was the same as for other cities: stadium money. Washington had a big-league-ready stadium in place—RFK Stadium had been the home of the Senators from 1961 until they departed for Texas eleven years later—but MLB's condition of granting the franchise was a new building, ideally paid for entirely with public dollars. Mayor Anthony Williams, a former city finance chief who had assumed the top job in 1998, was offering $275 million toward a $425 million stadium—nice enough, but not the free ride that Selig was seeking; if the Expos' new owner were expected to put up $150 million in private funds, after all, that would be $150 million that MLB couldn't extract in sale price. And Williams had not identified a source for the money, a major concern, given that the city council still hadn't approved a new stadium. A *Washington Post* poll in the summer of 2002, meanwhile, had found that whereas 84 percent of DC residents favored the return of major-league baseball, only half would support public funding of a new stadium.

The final alternative was to site a stadium in the Virginia suburbs across the Potomac, thus tapping the DC metro population without competing as directly with the Orioles. But although this might have pleased Angelos, it would have reduced the team's value to MLB: A Virginia team would only reach half the market, and half of DC was little better than Portland.

Searching for Suitors

Selig's would-be bidding war got off to an inauspicious start, with city officials all proclaiming their love of baseball but not exactly throwing open their checkbooks. Northern Virginia pitched a stadium plan paid for one third by the team and one third by ticket taxes and stadium-related sales and income taxes; the remaining $100–150 million, according to the AP, had "not been accounted for." Portland pinned its hopes on a special tax on baseball players' salaries, which was supposed to generate $150 million in stadium financing; the other half of the construction costs would come from, well, no one seemed sure. Las Vegas mayor Oscar Goodman proposed to "fully fund a magnificent new retractable stadium" [sic], then backtracked and mumbled something about unspecified casinos paying the tab.

Meanwhile, the Expos free-for-all was bringing out of the woodwork anyone and everyone who had a pet scheme to bring a baseball team to their backyard. In San Antonio, Bexar County judge Nelson Wolff—a former mayor of San Antonio and author of the book *Baseball for Real Men*—suggested that the Expos split time between San Antonio and either Monterrey or Austin, playing in a converted minor-league stadium (coincidentally enough named Nelson Wolff Stadium) while waiting for the city to grow to major-league size: "Ten years from now, things may be completely different around here." A Connecticut newspaper columnist suggested that the state buy the team and move it to the University of Connecticut's new football stadium in Hartford. And a Florida movie mogul named Craig Marquardo offered to buy the Expos and move them to a new stadium in Portland that he'd build entirely with private money; he faded from the headlines once it turned out that he'd apparently invented several items on his résumé, including having played minor-league baseball, been wounded in the Gulf War, and sung backup for Sting.

Perhaps the most unlikely bid, though, came from Norfolk, Virginia, a longtime minor-league baseball town that suddenly found itself entered in the Expos sweepstakes by a pair of young entrepreneurs named William Somerindyke Jr. and Jason Osborne, invariably described in the press as "a pair of twenty-six-year-old former stockbrokers." (As Doug Pappas pointed out, this was "a phrase not likely to inspire confidence.") The Norfolk duo promised a Navy-themed stadium with twin gun turrets on the roof that would shoot fireworks, and launched a season-ticket sales drive to drum up public support; Somerindyke confidently declared, "We think we'll have enough support to go to New York, and we can put the numbers on Bud Selig's and Bob DuPuy's desk and say, 'Here, now just give us the franchise.'"

Several months later, the *Virginian-Pilot* newspaper finally thought to dig into how two twenty-somethings had managed to find themselves in the chase for a major-league baseball team. Somerindyke and Osborne had claimed to be officers of an investment-banking firm; in reality, the paper discovered, they'd each worked briefly as brokers at Merrill Lynch, but there was no evidence they ever worked in investment banking. The companies they claimed to run, Summit Broadcasting and Efirms.com, turned out to have been shut down, if they'd ever existed to begin with. "Some of their accomplishments," concluded the *Virginian-Pilot* dryly, "have been embellished."

DC and Virginia remained the frontrunners, but neither was quite laying out the red carpet that Selig had sought. In Virginia demonstrators picketed a Virginia Baseball Stadium Authority news conference, while supporters of the DC library system rallied carrying signs reading "Books Not Baseball." Arlington, the preferred site from among the Virginia suburbs, withdrew its bid, saying residents were hopelessly split on the merits of the project. Worst of all for MLB, both DC and Virginia officials were levying demands of their own: Give us the team *first*, they said, and then we'll talk stadium. MLB officials, not wanting to give up their only leverage, refused. A stalemate was born.

It would drag on for almost two full years. In January 2003, asked if the Expos would definitely have a new home the following year, Selig replied: "Ask me that later this year." On July 10, five days before a relocation-committee deadline to decide the team's fate, MLB spokesman Rich Levin demurred, "I know [July 15] was the goal when the committee first set out, but I don't know how serious and absolute it was." By September, Selig was talking gamely of finding a temporary home for the Expos just for 2004, or perhaps forcing the team to split time among several cities: "Obviously the options are the various cities that have expressed interest, as well as the cities that have expressed interest in a series of games or all the games. The relocation committee is hard at work in finding a home for the Expos. We'll make that determination in the coming weeks, or how long it takes."

The year 2004 dawned with the Expos still on their Montreal-to-San Juan treadmill, and with Selig's right-hand man, MLB COO Bob DuPuy, taking the reins of the relocation effort. One day after declaring that he "would rather get [the relocation of the Montreal Expos] done sooner rather than later," DuPuy clarified the league's stance: "It is an objective to have a facility committed for and understand how the facility is going to come together before a decision is made. We don't want to do something in the blind." DuPuy added a few weeks later: "We'll get it done this year, I promise you." The following month, Selig said he hoped to have a new home selected for the Expos "by the All-Star Game this year." He added: "The relocation committee is hard at work and we all agree by the middle of the season we ought to have a buyer and a site."

Asked by *Sports Illustrated*'s Tom Verducci if the ongoing Expos' saga had become an embarrassment to baseball, Selig could only reply: "I don't know if 'embarrassment' is the right word."

Au Revoir, Montreal

By late 2004 "laughingstock" seemed the right word. The previous year, the Expos had unexpectedly found themselves in pennant contention, only to have MLB refuse to allow them permission to bolster their roster with youngsters after the end of the minor-league season, as every other team does, to save $50,000 in salaries. In 2004 first baseman Nick Johnson complained that he'd been stuck in a season-long slump thanks to ownership's refusal to pay for game film of opposing pitchers. And yet despite the penny-pinching, the lame-duck team was still mired in red ink: Baseball Prospectus' Derek Zumsteg estimated that the other twenty-nine MLB teams had lost at least $130 million in three years of owning the Expos. "That probably wouldn't build a stadium anywhere near a metro market that could support a team well," wrote Zumsteg. "It almost certainly would have allowed them to complete the financing to fill the gap in Portland, though, and probably in Northern Virginia as well. If baseball had gone to DC with that kind of money, they could almost certainly have gotten that deal done, too. It might even have been able to revive baseball in Quebec, for that matter." The Expos bidding war was turning into an expensive game of chicken.

Then, just as baseball officials issued 2005 schedules with the team listed merely as "Expos," with no city named, the stalemate abruptly broke. The catalyst arrived via what should have been bad news for baseball: In DC's Democratic primaries, three pro-stadium city council members went down to defeat at the hands of stadium opponents. Once the three new members took office in January—in DC, there's essentially no chance that a Democrat will lose in the general election—any hope of a council majority would evaporate, and with it baseball's hopes of wringing stadium funding from the DC treasury. "We need to get this done sooner rather than later, and we should get it done in this [electoral] cycle," DC mayor Anthony Williams pointedly told reporters shortly before the primary vote. "We can't take for granted the political support that is now in place for this."

With the clock ticking, Selig and DuPuy decided to roll the dice with what was on the table; Angelos and the DC council could be dealt with when the time came. And so, on September 29, 2004, Selig called DC officials to let them know: The Expos were theirs. At a celebratory press conference, Mayor Williams donned a red cap with the white "W" of the long-gone Washington Senators, and joined seven council members in singing "Take Me Out to the Ballgame." "I'm beyond thrilled," he declared. "The American game is rounding third and at last heading back home to the nation's capital."

The announcement came just hours before the Expos' final home game of the season—and, it now appeared, for all eternity. Disgruntled fans tossed a few golf balls onto the field in the early innings, briefly holding up play. But, mostly, the crowd of 31,000, including thousands of walk-up ticket buyers who'd rushed out to Olympic Stadium when it was clear this might finally be the end, was more in the mood for sad goodbyes than for recriminations. After the Expos had gone down in defeat, 9–1 to the Florida Marlins, fans wandered the artificial turf and mingled with members of the 1994 Expos squad who were on hand for the occasion.

"Major League Baseball didn't want a team here," said lifelong Expos fan Bob Hall as he walked the field with his eleven-year-old son. "That was pretty obvious. It's kind of like your wife saying, 'I want a divorce,' and she says it for ten years, and you say, 'Do it and go away.'"

In DC, meanwhile, Mayor Williams produced in a matter of days a bona fide stadium plan, complete with one of those waterfront sites—with a view, it was promised, of the U.S. Capitol, though about a mile distant—that gets the sports pundits drooling. It was the financial plan, however, that got MLB excited. Mayor Williams's office declared that "there is no money that will come from the general fund" for the stadium, while the baseball booster group DC Baseball echoed that it "will not be paid for by DC residents' tax dollars." But the truth was something very different.

Williams's estimated price tag for a new stadium stood at $440 million, to be paid off from three sources: about $22.5 million a year from a tax surcharge on large DC businesses; $12.5 million a year from in-stadium taxes on tickets, concessions, and merchandise; and $5.5 million a year in rent payments by the team. Each of these would largely siphon off money that could otherwise go into the city's general fund. Although the business tax was sold as a special "baseball tax," local business leaders made clear that they'd bitterly oppose any further hikes, meaning the stadium would tap out this source of city revenues for good. The "in-stadium taxes" would include a mix of existing sales taxes and special tax surcharges—much of which would be subject to the substitution effect and so merely end up cannibalizing sales taxes on, say, movie tickets elsewhere in DC. And even the rent payments would be offset by naming-rights fees: Though the city would build and own the stadium, the team would get all proceeds from slapping a corporate name on it, cutting baseball's rent costs by anywhere from $2.5 million to $4 million a year. All revenue from events at the stadium, meanwhile, whether baseball games or rock concerts, would go to the team.

In the end, DC taxpayers would be on the hook for about $320 million of the stadium costs, MLB for $70 million. (The remainder would end up largely diverted from the treasuries of Virginia and Maryland as commuters chose to spend more of their entertainment dollars inside the Beltway.) And because Williams had agreed to pay all cost overruns, whether for stadium construction, land, or infrastructure, the city's share could only go up. It was to prove to be a momentous detail.

Overall, it was an extraordinarily generous deal, given the going rate. The most recent baseball stadium to be approved, St. Louis's new Busch Stadium (the third in forty years to bear that moniker), was being funded about one third by taxpayers, two thirds by the team; the Minnesota and Florida legislatures were mulling proposals for about a 50–50 split. Yet DC, with the Expos' owners up against a wall, had agreed to cover at least 73 percent of the stadium costs. Even baseball officials were stunned at the generosity: The *Post* quoted an executive at baseball's executive council meetings as noting, "People were amazed that the District had done the deal that they did."

The following week, *Post* baseball columnist and longtime baseball-for-DC booster Thomas Boswell would write approvingly that one prospective ownership group, led by former Nixon aide Fred Malek, had "helped convince the mayor that his only chance to get the Expos, and use them as part of his urban development initiatives, was to demand of baseball, 'What are your exact terms?' And then stun baseball by meeting them."

Schools versus Stadiums

The response to the pending arrival of the Nationals was not all red-and-white caps and hosannas. In 2003 a group of city nonprofits and local residents, noting the mayor's escalating stadium-subsidy offers, had banded together as the No DC Taxes for Baseball Coalition. This group would now do battle with the combined forces of Major League Baseball and their allies in the mayor's office.

The group's Web site laid out its credo: "The DC area is the largest metro area without a team and one of the wealthiest in the nation. Major League Baseball should be begging to come here rather than making outrageous demands. The District is struggling to meet basic needs—in environmental protection, education, libraries, health care, and other areas. It should not put in a baseball stadium before other investments that could do a lot more to improve the quality of life for DC residents and businesses." A poster was plastered along the streets around City Hall featuring the familiar bowtied figure of Mayor Williams handing over a baseball marked "$440 million" to a top-hatted plutocrat, flanked by rundown schools and shuttered hospitals.

Unlike in some other cities, where the overriding concern of local activists was saving a landmark ballpark or fighting tax hikes, in DC the primary concern was how the city was spending its scarce resources. One of No DC Taxes' founders was Ed Lazere of the DC Fiscal Policy Institute, a good-government group focused on spending priorities; another, Chris Weiss, was head of DC Friends of the Earth, not normally a group expected to be at the forefront of a stadium battle. "One of the reasons an environmental group got involved in this," explains Weiss, "was because our biggest problem is funding environmental initiatives. Like any group, it comes down to 'where's the money going?'"

As the mayor and other baseball boosters staged support rallies—one was sponsored by the Department of Health and Human Services, run by Tommy Thompson, who was Wisconsin governor when Selig ran the Milwaukee Brewers—No DC Taxes for Baseball countered with rallies of their own. "We did a million of them, it felt like," says Lazere. "What I mainly did was walk through the flyer we did: DC pays for all the costs of construction, all the future capital costs—we essentially paid for everything, including the risk of cost overruns. Meanwhile, MLB got all the benefits—all the revenue from tickets, from naming rights, from parking, from advertising, from TV." Lazere recalls giving his presentation to his own organization's board, which included a local labor leader who sat on the pro-stadium metro labor council: "He just turned ashen—he couldn't believe how bad it sounded."

Ninety economists from across the country signed on to an open letter to the DC council, stating that the "vast body of economic research on the impact of baseball stadiums suggests that the proposed $440 million baseball stadium in the District of Columbia will not generate notable economic or fiscal benefits for the city." No DC Taxes for Baseball conducted a poll of DC voters, finding that two thirds were now opposed to using any public funds for a baseball stadium. (A *Washington Post* poll a few weeks later confirmed this figure and further found that 60 percent of district residents thought the mayor's plan in particular was "a bad deal.") Meanwhile, Marion Barry, the former mayor who was one of the three new council members waiting to take office in January, declared, "I'm going to stop this baseball stadium and take the money and spend it on housing and schools"; Barry would later call the deal "the biggest stick-up since Jesse James and the great train robbery."

"We say to this mayor and some members of the city council that you will not get this stadium when people are sleeping on the streets and schools are crumbling," declared veteran civil rights activist Damu Smith of Black Voices for Peace at a No DC Taxes rally outside City Hall. "You are not going to have an easy way to get this stadium through."

Still, the stadium deal looked like a fait accompli, largely because of the document that Mayor Williams's staff and MLB negotiators had hammered out and signed in a matter of days back in September. The Ballpark Agreement, as it came to be known, was a direct challenge to the council's power of the purse; at every turn, Mayor Williams insisted that that the city had a "contract" with MLB and couldn't back out now. DC council member Adrian Fenty told the *Post*, "Where else are they going to go? They've already left Montreal. And no one else has a stadium ready," and called for the city auditor to review the mayor's financing plan. In response, his pro-stadium colleague Jack Evans, who'd helped broker the Expos deal, snapped: "Are you willing to kill baseball? . . . We do not play at RFK. It's not on the table. That's been negotiated away. It would break the contract."

Meanwhile, Williams was heavily lobbying fence-sitting council members to back his plan. How heavily was revealed when the *Post* got ahold of the list of tens of millions of dollars worth of quid pro quos that the mayor had promised to various council members in order to secure their votes for his original stadium proposal. Among them: $45 million in library funding in council member Jim Graham's district, $40 million for commercial development in Sandy Allen's district, and $2 million in laptops for high school students and $10 million for a hospital feasibility study in Vincent Orange's. "Everybody understands that this occurs," opposition council member David Catania said disgustedly. "What makes it incredible is that they would put it in writing. Everyone realizes votes are bought off, but this takes it to a new level."

"Our chances, if we had a vote today, are pretty slim," conceded Lazere in October. Added Fenty: "At this point, I don't think that there's going to be enough to stop it. The mayor and some council members are so far out on a limb on this one, almost nothing could stop it."

A Million Here, A Million There

And then, the bills started arriving. On October 28, as the council prepared for its only scheduled public hearing on the stadium plan, DC chief financial officer Natwar Gandhi unearthed an extra $91 million in road and infrastructure expenses, pushing the total cost to more than $530 million. Council chair Linda Cropp, already a lukewarm backer of the stadium plan, began wavering, suggesting that it might be cheaper to build near the existing RFK Stadium, instead of the site near the Navy Yard that Williams (and MLB) preferred. Meanwhile, angry e-mails continued to pour into city council in-boxes, and raucous stadium hearings dragged on long into the night. At one, an angry resident waved his checkbook at Evans, demanding to know, "How much money does it take to buy back this city council?"

Eight days later, Cropp dropped a bombshell: She would propose a bill to instead build a new baseball facility on land near the existing RFK Stadium, a move that, so she claimed, could save the city an estimated $83 million. The mayor, predictably, was furious. "This is going to blow the thing up," fumed Williams, adding: "The dream of having baseball back in Washington is at risk. . . . We have waited 10, 20, 30 years for this and now it is in jeopardy." *Post* sports columnist Michael Wilbon called Cropp "a complete fraud" guilty of "bait-and-switch idiocy," with a detour to lash out at "the stupid junk I read from academics who spin their silly obstructionist excuses on what stadiums don't bring."

The following week, unable to secure council support for her plan, yet unwilling to support the mayor's proposal, Cropp abruptly cancelled a scheduled stadium vote. It looked like the wheels were coming off of the sure thing.

The impetus that turned the council chair from one of those singing with Williams at the September press conference into an opponent of the stadium deal, it turned out, was the swiftly escalating cost of construction. According to Cropp, even the DC CFO's new estimates were too low; the true cost, she believed, would be closer to

$600 million. A *Post* investigation soon confirmed these fears: Items like expansion of the Navy Yard Metro station, which could handle only a fraction of the tens of thousands of baseball fans expected to pour into it on game nights, would raise the total bill to $614 million, putting it in the running for most expensive baseball stadium ever built. (DC baseball aide Stephen Green promptly suggested—presumably with a straight face—that overcrowding would actually be a good thing, as it would force fans to walk from the next station and possibly patronize nearby stores and restaurants.)

Cropp seemed determined to propose a counter-plan that she could claim had gained concessions for the District; what that plan was, though, changed almost daily. She soon gave up on the RFK site, instead suggesting a deal that would use $350 million in "private financing" to help pay the stadium's soaring price tag. This, it soon turned out, was mostly a shell game: It would not be private *funding*—no developer in their right mind would invest in a project where all the proceeds were already guaranteed to the team owners—but rather that a private developer would pay for construction, and get repaid by the city with tax money from tickets, concessions, and parking. Meanwhile, thanks to a convoluted leasing scheme whereby DC would effectively sell its depreciation rights to the developer (governments can't take advantage of depreciation because they don't pay taxes), about $10 million a year in expenses would be deflected from DC area businesses to federal taxpayers. The combined benefits would magically generate about $250 million in tax savings for the developers, without significantly affecting the cost to the District.

When that plan went nowhere, Cropp changed sides again, announcing that she planned to vote for the stadium—and then promptly sent a last-minute letter to her council colleagues offering still more changes to the bill. An initial vote—in DC, council legislation must be approved in two separate votes, two weeks apart—squeaked through by a narrow 6–4 vote, but stadium boosters worried at the three members, including Cropp, who'd ominously voted "present" and asked Williams to go back to MLB to seek more concessions.

The day of the deciding stadium vote finally arrived on December 13, 2004. Cropp had promised the mayor she would vote to approve the deal without major changes, but somewhere during thirteen hours of council debate, she changed her mind yet again. When the vote came, she insisted on inserting a provision to add a last-second clause that at least $140 million in stadium costs would have to be privately financed: "My basic belief is that there are too many public dollars going into this. This will make the mayor seek private dollars more than anything else."

Cropp Blinks

What had happened soon became clear. A letter from MLB responding to Cropp's request for modifications to the original stadium deal had made it into the council chair's hands in the middle of the hearing. When she determined that MLB had essentially refused to make significant concessions, Cropp spent time madly scribbling at the dais—at one point turning over the hearing to council member Jack Evans to run while she consulted with her staff—and finally emerged with the private-financing requirement, stunning Williams, who thought Cropp was an assured "yes" vote.

MLB flew into a carefully stage-managed rage. DuPuy issued a harshly worded press release that declared the council vote to be "inconsistent with [the] carefully negotiated agreement and . . . wholly unacceptable to Major League Baseball"; in a new twist on the move non-threat, DuPuy wrote: "Because our stadium agreement provides for a December 31, 2004, deadline, we will not entertain offers for permanent relocation of the club until that deadline passes." A scheduled press conference to introduce the team's new uniforms was hastily called off; the team store, which had opened just days before, was shuttered; fans who'd bought tickets were encouraged to request refunds. Friendly sportswriters, meanwhile, took aim at the council chair with both barrels: *Post* baseball columnist Tom Boswell moaned, "The bits of charred ash and shattered fragments that you see falling from the sky are the remnants of the destruction that Cropp wrought," while at the *Washington Times*, sports columnist Tom Knott dubbed Cropp "the Grinch who stole baseball" and asked, "Does the W in your middle initial stand for Weasel?"

Cropp blinked. The following week, the council reconvened for its final scheduled meeting of the year—and this time, under Cropp's direction, approved the stadium by a vote of 7 to 6. The "private-financing" provision was now a suggestion, not a requirement. The only concession achieved by Cropp's last-minute grandstand play: The city's costs would be capped at $535 million, plus an additional $50 million for cost overruns. Anything above that, and it was back to the drawing board.

Stadium boosters at the council hearing, many wearing brand-new red baseball caps—the same as those they'd donned three months earlier, but now representing the brand-new Washington Nationals instead of the Senators—broke into another round of "Take Me out to the Ballgame." On December 29, Mayor Williams signed the stadium bill into law. Four months later, the Nats would take the field at RFK Stadium for the first time. The price had been steep—"Of course it's not the world's greatest deal, but that's what it takes to bring baseball here," admitted Williams—but Washington DC had its baseball team.

It had all been a bizarre bit of gamesmanship, given that Cropp's "private-financing" scheme would hardly have been a hardship for baseball; in fact, the option ended up being quietly dropped the following spring after the council belatedly realized it wouldn't really save the public any money. MLB, meanwhile, had seemingly risked everything: Without DC, it would have been back to the drawing board, and with Virginia not an immediate option either—the state's stadium authority was set to go out of business on December 31, the same day that the DC baseball agreement would lapse—Selig and DuPuy would have been forced to turn to their motley crew of Portlands and Norfolks. This, most dispassionate observers agreed, was never going to happen; as baseball business writer Maury Brown later observed, noting the $450 million sale price MLB was expecting to fetch for the Expos in the nation's capital: "If it had been a smaller market, maybe they would have talked about pulling out of there, but there were 450 million reasons that they would never have left DC."

If it was MLB that had been backed into a corner, though, city officials never realized it. The city council "definitely didn't think they had any leverage," says Lazere. Local elected officials, he says, "would say on the one hand that we are the best place for baseball to be—look at our demographics, our population, our income." Yet— aside from council members Catania and Fenty, who had written in the *Post* that DC's frontrunner status should have put it "in a strong bargaining position, a position that should allow it to compete for a team without offering substantial stadium subsidies"—they never thought of this as a hammer for extracting concessions from baseball. "Even the people who voted against the stadium were pretty confident that that could kill the deal, and that's why it was so contentious," says Lazere. "The message we tried to get out, that rejecting this deal wasn't saying no to baseball, it was saying no to this deal, is not a message that ever really connected."

The Fat Lady Sings

And yet, unbelievably, this still wasn't the end. In March 2005 city finance chief Natwar Gandhi sent up a warning flag, revealing $46 million more in land costs, bringing the total to within $4 million of the $585 million cap. To many, it was a suspiciously convenient number. Choosing his words carefully, Lazere says: "He clearly was under a lot of pressure, and if he had gone $1 million over the $165 million and killed the deal, it would have been a very hard life for the CFO."

Then, in December, as the council prepared to debate the Nationals' lease on their new stadium, the other shoe dropped: Gandhi issued a report that the true stadium cost would be a whopping $667 million, thanks in part to the cost of upgrading the Metro station, rising land values, and especially the soaring price of steel in the wake of Hurricane Katrina. A DC government source admitted to the *Post* that the mayor's office had intentionally low-balled contingency costs in its initial estimates, to make the deal more palatable to the council.

With council support flagging—the No Ballpark Three were in place by now—Williams pulled the stadium lease from the council's agenda to make what he called "small technical changes," and never put it back on. DuPuy threatened to take the dispute to binding arbitration, though only the Baseball Agreement, not the as-yet-unsigned lease, contained an arbitration clause—and as the council hadn't signed the Baseball Agreement, it was unclear if it was even subject to its provisions. Rumors of the Nationals moving yet again started back up, and even talk of contraction, once owners were allowed to bring it up following the 2006 season—though as one unnamed baseball official told the *Post*, "They're not going to contract. We're not talking about the Expos anymore—losing $40 million a year in Montreal. We're talking about a team worth $450 million, that made $10 million last year."

The denouement at last came on February 7, 2006, sixteen months and countless council hearings after Mayor Williams had first declared his pursuit of the Expos a success. The council voted 8 to 5 to reject the lease, with the three new members, Marion Barry, Vincent Gray, and Kwame Brown, joining holdover dissidents Jim Graham, Phil Mendelson, Carol Schwartz, David Catania, and Adrian Fenty.

And then, as newspaper reporters filed their stories declaring the stadium dead—Tom Boswell posted a story on the *Post* Web site that declared that "the interaction between Major League Baseball officials and District politicians was a marriage made in hell" and now "the future of baseball in DC is on the verge of going to the devil"—a knot of legislators huddled in the council chambers with city administrator Robert Bobb. A short while later, they emerged with a stunning announcement: Four council members were switching their votes to endorse the stadium lease, so long as the city's bond costs were guaranteed not to exceed a final number of $611 million. The vote switchers included all three of the newly elected "anti-stadium" members, plus Carol Schwartz, who the previous winter had said that the then $535 million stadium deal would "give the store away."

Reported the Associated Press: "The members who switched their votes said they wanted to send a message to baseball officials that the city would build a stadium, but not at any cost." One "key player" in the negotiations between baseball and the city told the *Post*'s Marc Fisher, "It was time to declare victory and move on."

It was a stunning finish, and one that left the stadium critics dismayed at the actions of their former council allies—who had, after all, been elected back in September 2004 in part because they'd explicitly promised their constituents they would oppose any stadium giveaways. Weiss, a former council staffer, concluded that Brown, Gray, and Barry were each merely "trying to be perceived as a team player, assuming that it'll affect committee assignments down the road."

In the end, after all the haggling back and forth, DC officials had agreed to a deal that cost taxpayers $171 million more than the one the mayor had at first promised. They could only console themselves that they'd fashioned a compromise that was equally disliked all around. "People feel betrayed on both sides," declared Williams. "There's bad faith on both sides. And I think the only thing everybody agrees on is they don't like me."

Tallying the Bill

When Bud Selig and Bob DuPuy decided to move the Montreal Expos to Washington, they were facing a hugely uphill battle. They needed to negotiate a stadium deal and get it passed by the city council, all in a tight three-month window before the new council members took office. And yet, despite seemingly everything going wrong that could go wrong—spiraling costs, Cropp's wavering, the need for vote after vote after vote—they still emerged victorious.

To some degree MLB lucked out by picking the right adversary. "The accounts from inside the room were that the mayor's negotiators were not very good," says Lazere. "They either weren't skilled at it, or they were so desperate to get the team that they ignored any leverage that they had." For Selig and DuPuy, on the other hand, using hardball negotiating tactics was their one undeniable forte. "Brinkmanship is something that baseball is intrinsically aware of," says Maury Brown. "They deal with it every four years with the union. If they can do brinkmanship with the state of the game that way, they certainly can do it with municipalities that quite honestly are ill-equipped in most cases to deal with baseball's workings."

Early in the negotiations for the Expos, for instance, Williams had suggested that the city would be willing to build a ballpark with two thirds of the money coming from the public and one third coming from the team. That reportedly drew this response from MLB negotiator Jerry Reinsdorf: "Two thirds / one third is fine. But three thirds / no thirds is more of what we had in mind."

"The mayor," says Lazere, "I think because of his desperation, and his lack of negotiating skills, didn't say 'fuck you' back to Reinsdorf to that, which is what he should have said. Something to show that he was not just going to take anything. Rather than pushing back, he apparently said, 'We'll see what we can do.'"

For baseball, meanwhile, what at several points had looked like a fruitless game of chicken had left them looking at a windfall. In May 2006 the ex-Expos were finally sold, to developer Ted Lerner and former Atlanta Braves exec Stan Kasten for $450 million. Even after accounting for Zumsteg's estimated $40 million a year in losses, the other twenty-nine teams had still more than doubled their initial $120 million investment.

More important, though, Selig and DuPuy had successfully ended a long, slow slide in the value of stadium subsidies—and simultaneously pumped new life into the threat to relocate teams if they didn't get their way in stadium talks. The Expos-go-round, says Brown, "was a derby to leverage the markets they were actually trying to place the team in—because to be honest about this whole thing, they were looking to place the team in Northern Virginia first, and Washington DC second." The Portlands and Norfolks, then, were "to help that leveraging process."

Beyond that, though, says Brown, Selig's strategy served a more long-term goal. It went back to 1983, when Reinsdorf, who had just become co-owner of the Chicago White Sox, jetted down to St. Petersburg, Florida, to meet with local officials there who were seeking a team. While he had no intention of really moving, Reinsdorf later explained: "A savvy negotiator creates leverage. People had to think we were going to leave Chicago."

Reinsdorf would be just one of several big-league baseball owners to use Tampa–St. Petersburg as leverage to extract a new stadium from their hometowns. In 1998, though, the expansion Tampa Bay Devil Rays were brought into existence, leaving baseball owners without a leading threat to hold over the heads of their cities. And once DC was filled, the void would grow even worse.

In this light, Selig's Expos gamble hit the jackpot: Not only did he get a new stadium to pour more money into MLB's shared pot, but he jump-started baseball fever in other cities like Portland and Vegas that had previously been dismissed as too "bush league" to be seriously considered for membership in the MLB club. "There was some method to the madness," agrees Brown. "They wanted to have these other markets do their due diligence and come up with funding, to see if they were options in the future. Markets investigating whether there is the ability to come up with public funding—you can't do that without a team being available."

Within days of the announcement that the Expos were headed to DC, baseball boosters in San Jose began gearing up their own plans to lure a team, while Marlins president David Samson announced: "Everyone realizes as soon as the Expos [were] announced, the likelihood of the Marlins relocating without a stadium significantly increases." Editorial writers for the *Minneapolis Star Tribune* would later raise the specter of the Expos' fate to throw a scare into the local populace, noting: "Even after covering operating losses in Montreal and paying other expenses, MLB's owners stand to make a windfall of $150 million. The lesson is clear. Moving a struggling team makes money for all owners. Reinvesting the windfall in the next movable team—the Twins—may be irresistible. As early as next year, look for MLB to make Pohlad an offer he'll have trouble refusing."

As for what the city got, that wouldn't be clear until 2008 at the earliest, when the new Nationals' stadium would open its doors. The early previews, though, were not promising. In a long analysis of the stadium designs, the *Washington City Paper*'s Josh Levin revealed that MLB had arm-twisted the DC sports commission into agreeing to a double-decked layer of luxury suites that would both increase construction costs and raise the top deck twenty-one feet higher than it was at the RFK Stadium—but would boost team revenues and so the league's potential sale price for the team. Adding insult to injury, upper-deck seat widths would be reduced from the twenty-inch standard at RFK to a mere nineteen inches, while high-priced seats in the field-level section would be an ample twenty-two inches wide.

Yet in addition to shelling out $600 million that could otherwise have gone to schools or hospitals, and squeezing fans' butts into tinier seats, the costs to DC, says Weiss, go beyond mere dollars and cents. "This mayor put the whole administration onto working to get the baseball stadium here—people's hours and time were used," he says. "And that doesn't show up in the budget analysis. In the years the mayor has been here, I've never seen so much energy going into doing anything as much as I saw him trying to bring baseball here."

In the end, DC residents were left with the feeling that MLB didn't have to hoodwink DC—Mayor Williams did it for them. By the time the stadium opens, says Weiss, "he'll be gone, and we'll have this commitment we have to take care of. And we'll be screwed. We're going to continue to be screwed for many years."

15 The Perfect Storm

There are only two things you do not want on a valuable piece of real estate. One is a cemetery, and the other is a football stadium. —*University of Chicago sports economist Allen Sanderson*

We make "investments." We don't do subsidies. We get our money back, and we make money. —*New York mayor Michael Bloomberg on his administration's stadium deals*

All told, it hadn't been a great couple of years for New York mayor Rudy Giuliani. He'd had an extramarital affair and his subsequent estrangement from his wife exposed in the press, and he'd received treatment for prostate cancer and been forced to drop out of the race against Hillary Clinton for a U.S. Senate seat. His popularity had rebounded after his calm performance on 9/11, but even then, a last-minute proposal (by Giuliani himself) to extend the mayor's term by three months failed, leaving "America's Mayor" out of a job.

Perhaps most gallingly to the ex-mayor, Giuliani left office with one dream denied, that of cutting the ribbon at a new major-league sports stadium. At one point, the mayor's desk bulged with plans for eight city-subsidized sports facilities: new homes for the Yankees and Mets, a football stadium for the Jets, a replacement for Madison Square Garden, new pro soccer and cricket fields, and two new minor-league baseball stadiums, one in Coney Island and one on Staten Island. In the end, the only ones to be built were the last two, for a pair of low-level affiliates of the Mets and Yankees—though at a cost of $110 million to taxpayers, at least Giuliani could justifiably brag that he'd built the most-expensive minor-league baseball stadiums in history.

And so, with one week left to go in his term, the mayor made one last-ditch effort to ensure that his sports legacy would go on without him. On Christmas Day 2001, Yankees president (and former Giuliani deputy mayor) Randy Levine leaked to the press that the mayor was set to announce agreements with the Mets and Yankees for new retractable-roofed stadiums. The cost: a record $800 million apiece, with half the cost to be covered by the city.

It was a masterstroke of timing: With any likely critics unreachable on the holiday, the news coverage of the stadium plan was unsullied by opposition. Still, the mayor made sure to launch a preemptive strike against any naysayers. "I know there's a knee-jerk misunderstanding of it," declared the lame-duck mayor, "but somehow leadership is about getting beyond knee-jerk misunderstandings."

But just weeks later, Giuliani's successor, a business media mogul named Michael Bloomberg, who'd financed his mayoral campaign with $73 million of his own money, declared the stadium plans dead. "Given the lack of housing, given the lack of school space, given the deficit in the operating budget, it is just not practical this year to go and build stadiums," said Bloomberg. The fifteen-year-long battle over new homes for New York's sports teams, it seemed, was finally over.

Yogi Berra, needless to say, would have begged to differ.

Deputy Dan

When Bloomberg took over after eight years of Giuliani, the new mayor promptly cleaned house, bringing in mostly people new to City Hall. For the key role of deputy mayor for economic development, Bloomberg selected a forty-three-year-old investment banker named Dan Doctoroff.

Doctoroff, who had ties to some of the city's biggest real estate developers (and more than a passing resemblance to a young Albert Brooks, down to the obsequious grin), came fresh from the top job at NYC2012, a business-funded group dedicated to landing the 2012 Summer Olympics for New York. As Doctoroff himself liked to tell the story, he had had an epiphany one hot July afternoon in 1994, while watching Italy and Belgium face off at Giants Stadium in the World Cup soccer semifinal. "The passion and intensity absolutely floored me," he would later recall. "When you injected national fervor into the event, it totally changed its character."

Giuliani had initially targeted a plot of land on Manhattan's West Side for a stadium for the Yankees but abandoned it in 1999 after the city council, in an unprecedented show of independence, wrote its own budget rather than approve the mayor's stadium-funding plans. (It was no coincidence that the council speaker, Peter Vallone, was then running for governor.) At the time, the mayor had thrown out an alternative—a domed football stadium and "new Madison Square Garden" to be built on the same West Side rail yards site—adding, almost as an aside, that the complex could even be used to host the Olympics.

On arriving in City Call, the Olympics booster Doctoroff picked up the ball and ran with it. Asked if his new boss was on board with plans for an Olympic stadium despite his statements that the city had more important priorities, Doctoroff replied: "He wouldn't have picked me, and I would not have accepted, if we were not in sync."

On November 3, 2002, the first part of Doctoroff's Olympics prayers were answered when the U.S. Olympic Committee announced that New York would be its next candidate for the Summer Games, duking it out in an international competition with the likes of London, Paris, and Istanbul to be the 2012 host city. New York's Olympic backers, who'd gathered in a hotel ballroom to await the decision, erupted in glee; Mayor Bloomberg promptly hugged the nearest person to him at the time, who happened to be Billy Crystal. For the city's official coronation the following week, a squadron of former Olympic athletes lined up in City Hall's Blue Room, where USOC CEO Lloyd Ward awkwardly praised New Yorkers' trial under fire after 9/11: "If there's any place that's demonstrated the power of hope, New Yorkans have done that."

The next morning, New Yorkers awoke to wonder how exactly the Olympics would be paid for. For the cornucopia of beach volleyball stadiums, equestrian centers, and velodromes that would be needed for the two-week event, organizers promised that $2.7 billion would be financed by Olympic revenues. That left the Games' proposed centerpiece, an Olympic stadium to be built over rail yards west of Penn Station, which could run close to $1 billion. Add in a concrete platform to support the structure while commuter trains rumbled underneath, and a new subway line to bring spectators to the far western edge of Manhattan, and the overall price tag would soar to $3 billion. And that was before any of the cost overruns that were proving a given for Olympic host cities: Atlanta, according to one accounting, had lost an estimated $1 billion on the 1996 Games, and, according to an audit by the state of New South Wales, Sydney's "best Olympics ever" in 2000 ended up costing the Australian public more than $1.2 billion.

As for the site targeted for a makeover by the Doctoroff plan, Manhattan's Far West Side had a long history of both tempting and frustrating would-be developers. Once the site of a thriving seaport, during the mid-twentieth century the area in the West Thirties and Forties along the Hudson River had been sliced up by access roads for the Lincoln Tunnel and Port Authority Bus Terminal. What was left had remained a world apart from the office towers of nearby midtown, with a patchwork of light industry and small apartment buildings where about twenty thousand residents enjoyed the low rents and easy access to the adjacent theater district.

The proximity to midtown Manhattan attracted the eyes of more than just starving actors. John Fisher, a theatrical stage manager who moved to the area in 1981 and quickly became a leading tenant advocate, notes that the neighborhoods known as Hell's Kitchen and Clinton made an alluring target for developers and real-estate speculators. This interest intensified after the 1980s, when city zoning incentives helped advance the edge of the business district two blocks west, from Sixth Avenue to Broadway; the following decade, Fisher launched the Clinton Special District Coalition to fight off a push by developers to allow Broadway theaters to sell their air rights to developers west of Eighth Avenue, who would have used them to demolish low-rise apartments in favor of high-rent skyscrapers. "The area from Thirtieth to Forty-second Street, they felt, didn't have a huge residential population, although it was growing," he says of real-estate interests' view of his neighborhood. "In their eyes, it was this big wasteland."

A wasteland, however, represented both opportunity and dilemma: No one would want to build there without something more than auto repair shops and cheap tenement apartments to jump-start interest. A stadium would serve a twofold purpose: Not only would it be an "anchor" for new development (much as the Javits Convention Center, built along the river's edge, was supposed to be twenty years earlier), but it would provide the impetus to extend subway service one mile west and south from its current western terminus at Times Square. In the same way that the original subways had helped seed such virgin locales as Harlem and the South Bronx with row houses after train lines were run through what had been open fields, West Side landowners could hope that a stadium and accompanying subway line would at last bring skyscrapers to midtown Manhattan's last frontier.

First, though, somebody had to pay for it. The finance plan for what was being called Hudson Yards, first floated by Doctoroff when he was still at the helm of NYC2012, was incredibly complex, requiring a brain-numbing flowchart just to detail all the city and state agencies that would lease and sublease various pieces of the project to and from each other. The New York Jets, who under the plan would relocate from New Jersey to the West Side, were set to supply an unspecified share of the stadium's construction costs. As for all the rest, it would be paid off by the public—though Doctoroff tended to steer clear of any specifics as he carted his PowerPoint presentation around to show to business and political leaders. When James Sanders, chair of the city council's economic development committee, asked Doctoroff at a hearing: "And the city won't have to put any money in the plan?" Doctoroff simply replied: "No existing tax money will be used."

The key word: "existing." To raise the necessary $3 billion, it turned out, Doctoroff was proposing to use tax-increment financing: The property taxes for a huge swath of the West Side, running from Twenty-eighth Street to Forty-first Street and from Ninth Avenue to the Hudson River, would be frozen at their current rate. Any new taxes from the office buildings that were to sprout like mushrooms across Hudson Yards would go not to the city treasury but to pay off the construction bonds for the subway extension and the city's share of the stadium. "That is not city tax money," explained NYC2012 CEO Jay Kriegel, "because that is not money that's available unless you do the plan."

Others, though, pointed out that the proposed stadium site had a monster of a problem passing the "but-for" test that haunted TIF projects in other cities. "If it's the most underutilized area in Manhattan, then why wouldn't it develop anyway?" wondered California TIF expert Howard Greenwich when told of Doctoroff's plan. (In fact, apartment towers were already rising on the site, to take advantage of the easy walk to midtown.) By slicing off fifty-nine square blocks of prime Manhattan real estate—"the grandmother of all TIF districts"—Greenwich noted, "you're tying the hands of future governments twenty years from now, because these property taxes will be off-line, and there's nothing you can do about it." There were also questions whether bond buyers would even purchase the Hudson Yards debt without costly bond insurance. "Someone's going to have to guarantee those bonds," insisted Dallas TIF guru Ryan Evans, noting that for projects in his city, bond buyers demanded costly bond insurance even after construction was already under way. He observed, "It sounds like a rough row to hoe, because someone has to take the risk, and then hope there's enough taxes generated to pay it back."

Publicly, at least, Doctoroff seemed unworried about the naysayers. To those who wondered if dropping a huge swath of skyscrapers across the West Side might cannibalize office-space development that was already being counted on to revitalize lower Manhattan following 9/11, he replied, "We don't have that concern." But the criticisms—or the worries of the bond market—were clearly weighing on his mind. On January 30, 2003, Doctoroff was scheduled to make a presentation of his Olympic finance plan to the city council. Instead, he requested a two-month delay. It would be more than a year before he returned with a revamped plan.

It eventually became clear that the deputy mayor was making a last-minute lineup substitution: Out were TIFs, and in was a concept called payments in lieu of taxes (PILOTs), whereby developers would be entirely exempted from property taxes, then pay special fees to a newly created Hudson Yards Infrastructure Corporation. As Doctoroff himself explained, "The precise structure may be different than a classic TIF but the concept of using incremental revenues generated in the area is still exactly what we're planning to do. The name will be different."

Something else that would be different: Unlike a TIF, PILOTs would not require a vote of the state legislature. It was the first sign that though Doctoroff was plotting one of the biggest planned developments in the city's history, he had no intention of asking either New Yorkers or their elected representatives for permission.

Hoops and Cheesecake

While Doctoroff shuffled acronyms in Manhattan, another sports-facility controversy was brewing across the East River in Brooklyn. Like the Jets plan, this one proposed to bring a team from New Jersey to a New York rail yard. The way it played out, though, would be very different.

The New Jersey Nets already had history on both sides of the Hudson River. Born in 1967 as the New Jersey Americans of the fledgling American Basketball Association, the team had bounced back and forth between the Garden State and Long Island over the years, ultimately landing in 1981 at the then new Brendan Byrne Arena, built on a plot of land wedged between Giants Stadium and the New Jersey Turnpike.

By the turn of the millennium, the Nets had played in their first NBA finals and had at last begun to compete with the Knicks for the attention of city sports fans. But success on the court hadn't translated into success at the ticket window: The Nets' arena, isolated in the New Jersey swamps, was difficult to get to by public transit, and the legendary traffic jams after Nets games helped lead USA Today to rate the arena as the worst facility in the NBA. In the late 1990s the team's owners began working on a deal to move to a new arena in downtown Newark, where two commuter rail lines could have been used to draw fans from New York City. But talks quickly broke down in 2003 when the team's owners began insisting that the city of Newark would have to front the entire construction cost, with the team repaying just one third of the debt payments.

It was at this point that Bruce Ratner entered the picture. The heir to a family-owned real-estate empire—named Forest City Ratner, for its roots in Cleveland—Ratner had been a major player on the city real-estate scene for the better part of two decades. Starting in the late 1980s, when he partnered with the city to build the massive MetroTech office complex that demolished several blocks of downtown Brooklyn, he'd been steadily remaking the Brooklyn skyline, most recently with a pair of suburban-style malls near the busy intersection of Flatbush and Atlantic avenues.

The first word of Ratner's interest in basketball came in July 2003, when the Newark Star-Ledger broke the news that the developer was looking to build a $500 million basketball arena atop the rail yards just south of his Atlantic Center mall. Brooklyn borough president Marty Markowitz—a longtime Brooklyn politician who had recently ascended to the borough's top spot, and who would become best known for standing astride the Brooklyn Bridge with a megaphone during the summer's blackout and shouting, "Welcome home to Brooklyn!"—gushed with joy to the press: "As a boy, I cried when the Dodgers left in 1957. I'm looking forward to shedding tears of joy when the NBA comes to Brooklyn."

The site that Ratner had identified for a new arena was prime Brooklyn real estate: Sitting at the nexus of the booming neighborhoods of Prospect Heights, Fort Greene, Park Slope, and Boerum Hill, it was served by ten subway lines and a Long Island Rail Road commuter terminal, making for easy access for both city and suburban fans. Nonetheless, it had some problems. For one thing, although the open-cut rail yards stretched for three blocks along Atlantic Avenue, they were only one block wide—less than two hundred feet—and any self-respecting NBA arena would need a footprint at least twice that size. With Atlantic Avenue, a major thoroughfare, to the north, the only way to expand would be south, requiring the closure of another street and demolition of an entire block of apartment buildings and row houses.

As it turned out, this was exactly what Ratner intended, though at first he didn't let any of the block's residents in on his plans. Dan Goldstein, a thirty-three-year-old Web designer, was just moving into a newly renovated seventh-floor condo on Pacific Street when news began to spread of the arena project. "When I was looking to buy this place, they had some newspaper articles saying how great the area was, and there was a mention of maybe a new basketball arena in the area," he says. "I thought, 'Oh, that's cool.'" It wasn't until he spotted local community activist Patti Hagan putting up flyers warning "This Neighborhood Is Condemned" outside his front door that he realized his apartment was targeted for the wrecking ball.

That December, at a packed press conference at Brooklyn Borough Hall hosted by Markowitz ("Those tears of joy are swelling up in me," burbled the borough president. "I just can't wait!"), Ratner was joined by rapper Jay-Z (who'd joined his team as an investor) and celebrity architect Frank Gehry to introduce the project he'd dubbed "Atlantic Yards." It was far more than an arena: Across five blocks of Brooklyn real estate, two of them currently occupied by buildings, Ratner proposed to build a series of high-rise apartment and office towers, all represented in Gehry's models by a few blocks of balsa wood hastily glued together. ("Don't worry about these funny shapes at this point," the architect, whose credits included such modernist icons as the Guggenheim Bilbao and Seattle's Experience Music Project, reassured the assembled crowd. "These are just blocks. We'll make something out of it as we go.") The tallest of the funny shapes, an office building dubbed "Miss Brooklyn," would tower sixty stories over the low-rise brownstones that surrounded it, dwarfing even the nearby Williamsburgh Bank building, a clock-faced landmark that was the tallest building in the borough.

Concerned locals, including Goldstein, immediately began gearing up to fight what they saw as both a publicly sponsored land grab on behalf of a big developer and an incursion of Manhattan-style development into their low-rise neighborhood, and launched the group Develop Don't Destroy to oppose Ratner's plan. As for the invited guests at Ratner's coming-out party, as they exited Brooklyn Borough Hall clutching "BBall" tote bags and free samples of Junior's cheesecake, only a very few had likely noticed that as Ratner presented his dream, he had carefully avoided mentioning who would pay for it.

In the Footprint

Bruce Ratner may have been small in stature—at one press event, he donned the fedora of former NBA great World B Free and almost disappeared into it—but he was a giant when it came to connections. A law school chum of New York governor George Pataki, Ratner had begun his career as New York City's consumer affairs commissioner and had long been a major donor to local politicians of both parties. Perhaps because of this political clout, he soon came to specialize in construction projects that required public land, money, or both.

For MetroTech, which replaced several square blocks of Brooklyn's old downtown with a collection of corporate towers segregated from the streetscape on their own self-enclosed campus, Ratner had received not only the use of city eminent-domain powers to evict existing residents but also an extra $300 million in city rent subsidies to lure Chase Manhattan and Bear Stearns to rent space in his office towers. Across the street from his planned Nets arena site, Ratner's Atlantic Terminal tower—derided as "the Ugly Building" by locals peeved that its brick-and-glass bulk blocked views of the Williamsburgh Bank building—had somehow garnered $114 million in tax-exempt Liberty Bonds earmarked for rebuilding lower Manhattan. And in perhaps his most audacious project, Ratner used the state's eminent-domain powers to obtain land at below-market prices for a new headquarters for the *New York Times* off Times Square—then requested an additional $400 million in federal Liberty Bonds when he couldn't find sufficient tenants to fill it.

To hear Ratner tell it, though, his mission was less to produce profits than to remake the face of the city, and in particular Brooklyn. "I was never interested in traditional real estate—you know, luxury high-rises in Manhattan," he told one reporter. "I mean, there are lots of ways to make money. I found my niche, creating buildings that keep jobs in this city."

While "jobs" would be Ratner's watchword, some Brooklynites wondered about his record in that area. Velmanette Montgomery, the state assembly member whose district included the proposed Atlantic Yards site, noted that in addition to getting the city to subsidize rents for MetroTech, Ratner had filled out one of his malls by renting out $1.6 million a year worth of office space to the state's Department of Motor Vehicles and the Empire State Development Corporation—the latter the same agency that was to take the lead in building Atlantic Yards. "We are essentially bailing out this white elephant," said Montgomery. Ratner's own figures would show that the malls had created only a little more than half as many jobs as had been projected.

Nonetheless, Ratner continued to sell Atlantic Yards as a boon to city taxpayers. To pay for his planned Nets arena, Ratner first floated the notion of "incremental tax revenues," implying a TIF- or PILOT-style plan on the model of the Jets deal. But he soon replaced this with a more nuanced argument: Any public money or tax breaks he required for the project would be more than repaid by the surge of resulting new tax revenues.

To that end, Ratner enlisted an unlikely ally, hiring Andrew Zimbalist, the renowned sports economist who had made a name for himself debunking the alleged benefits of publicly financed sports facilities, to conduct an economic-impact analysis of Atlantic Yards. Even before beginning his study, Zimbalist had declared that he considered the Nets plan an exception, in part because it would relocate a team across state lines—"if they came to Brooklyn, [players] would pay $5.5 million or 11 percent of their income to New York State and New York City," he told *Newsday*. In his report for Ratner, Zimbalist estimated that by generating around $1.5 billion in new revenues and just under $700 million in new costs, "the fiscal impact of the Atlantic Yards project" would be "a significant plus for the New York City and New York State treasuries."

Zimbalist's figures, though, showed very different results for the basketball piece and for the rest of the development. The arena, he estimated, would bring in $257 million in new city and state revenues—largely from the Nets fans who he expected would travel to Brooklyn instead of New Jersey, bringing their spending money with them—but could cost the public even more, if one included the cost of such items as decking over the rail yards to create space for the arena. Ratner's planned forty-five hundred new units of housing, meanwhile, accounted for nearly 60 percent of Zimbalist's projected benefits, leading some to wonder why, if housing was the real cash cow for the public, the state wasn't looking into finding a developer who would just build apartment buildings, which would require neither eminent domain (since, unlike an arena, housing could be fit atop the narrow rail yards site) nor special subsidies (though it would be eligible for the same "as-of-right" tax breaks that other developers—including Ratner—habitually received for building in New York's outer boroughs).

Brooklyn activist Gustav Peebles and economist Jung Kim issued a rebuttal to Zimbalist's report, charging, among other things, that it had overestimated the incomes of both tenants and workers in the project, underestimated the degree by which Brooklyn office space vacancies were largely filled by government agencies, low-balled the value of the Long Island Rail Road yards where the arena would be built, and failed to account for the cost of educating the estimated 931 public school students who would live in the complex. Their conclusion: Zimbalist's $800 million profit for the city would turn into a loss of between $100 million and $500 million.

When the city Independent Budget Office was asked to investigate the costs and benefits of Ratner's project, it largely supported Zimbalist's findings that the arena itself would generate a "modest" fiscal benefit for the city—but threw up its hands on the larger project, thanks in part to the "methodological limitations in estimating the fiscal impacts of mixed-use developments." Arenas attached to commercial skyscrapers and office towers, it seemed, were beyond the understanding of even trained economists.

If this wasn't confusing enough, neither Ratner nor his government allies could explain exactly where the money for the project would come from. When the city's economic development director was asked by city council members how the $2.5 billion project would be paid for, he replied, "We don't know." Council member Letitia James, whose district included the planned arena site, summed things up: "We don't know how much subsidies are involved. We don't know how much the MTA rail yards are being sold for. We don't know how this project is going to be financed. We don't know how much subsidies will be involved with respect to the affordable housing units, and how many units are actually going to be affordable, and for what income bracket. There's a lot of unanswered questions."

Ratner was pursuing the everything-but-the-kitchen-sink strategy to a T. Even local activists who were immersed in the minutiae of Atlantic Yards were hard-pressed to wrap their brains around how the financing was to work. "It took me six months of living with the people at Develop Don't Destroy, basically, to not be intimidated to open my mouth about the project, because there was so much that I didn't know," recalls Candace Carponter, a lawyer who joined the group in early 2004. "And that works to Ratner's advantage. It is so complicated on so many levels—the financing and the political support and how he accumulated this land and what really constitutes a public subsidy, and the whole issue surrounding whether or not you want a stadium in this neighborhood. All that stuff is so complicated that people just run the other way."

Before anyone could begin untangling the finances, though, the Atlantic Yards debate would take on a different tone entirely.

Whose Community?

Even as the public debate raged, Ratner moved swiftly behind the scenes to dispel as much local opposition as possible, offering lucrative buyouts to homeowners in the path of the arena, so long as they agreed to a gag order prohibiting them from speaking out against the project or giving money to groups that did. The board of Goldstein's condo building, which was set to be demolished to make way for the arena, was told that as a condition of Ratner's purchase of their apartments they would need to designate two homeowners to "testify in favor of the project at hearings" and to the press. Mailings promising "jobs, hoops, and housing" clogged mailboxes across the borough, while a new tabloid newspaper, the *Brooklyn Standard*, began appearing on the streets of adjacent neighborhoods, the headline boasting "BROOKLYN'S BOOMING: Atlantic Yards Will Bring Jobs, Housing and Hoops." The newspaper's publisher: Forest City Ratner.

As far as building public credibility was concerned, though, Ratner had his eye on a bigger prize. Word soon spread that Ratner was looking to implement a "community benefits agreement" that would guarantee specific benefits for the project's neighbors in exchange for their endorsement.

CBAS, as they're known, were a relatively recent addition to the lexicon of urban redevelopment. The original model, in fact, was named for a sports facility, though one that was already in place before its namesake agreement was struck. After the Staples Center in Los Angeles opened in 1999, its developers sought permission to build an adjacent development that would include housing, entertainment outlets, a forty-five-story hotel, and an expansion of the nearby convention center—with as much as $150 million of the cost being underwritten by the public. Thinking back to how the arena had landed in their midst with little community input, a coalition of labor and community groups, under the banner of the Figueroa Corridor Coalition for Economic Justice, negotiated a binding contract assuring that the developers would supply $1 million for parks and a recreation center, would offer seed loans to create affordable housing, would guarantee that at least 70 percent of the jobs created would pay a living wage, and would provide job training for local residents. "It's a huge step forward," said Madeline Janis-Aparicio, executive director of the Los Angeles Alliance for a New Economy, and one of the lead community negotiators. "Bringing all these groups together showed how housing relates to jobs relates to environment. These are holistic people with holistic needs, and to have a developer take that into account . . . is just amazing."

Ratner's CBA was a somewhat different animal. According to Carponter, who headed the Develop Don't Destroy legal team, Ratner's agreement was, "as legal documents go, a completely non-binding agreement." Unlike the Staples Center CBA, the Atlantic Yards agreement included no government signatories—meaning the only groups with the standing to enforce Ratner's promises were the community groups that negotiated each specific provision.

As for those groups, many that cut deals with Ratner shared a singular distinction: They hadn't existed beforehand. Existing neighborhood groups complained that they'd never even been allowed to approach the negotiating table. The project's most prominent backer, meanwhile, was Brooklyn United for Innovative Local Development, or BUILD, a community-development group that was formed in early 2004 and immediately began turning up at public meetings to testify in favor of the project. (BUILD's director, James Caldwell, declared on one occasion, "If this thing doesn't come out in favor of Ratner, it would be a conspiracy against blacks," and described the developer as "like an angel sent from God" for agreeing to negotiate with local black leaders.) Only after a neighborhood resident uncovered BUILD's tax statement was it revealed that the organization's sole funder was Forest City Ratner. Even BUILD's office space came courtesy of the developer: a floor in a Ratner-owned building right next door to Goldstein's apartment.

The real coup for Ratner, though, was securing the backing of the Association of Community Organizations for Reform Now. Known universally by its acronym ACORN, this was a national group founded in the 1970s to fight for affordable housing, against substandard wages, and on other issues affecting low-income families; its Brooklyn chapter had previously demonstrated outside Ratner's malls, with director Bertha Lewis decrying "dead-end, low-wage, non-union, no-benefit jobs" and demanding that "if you are feeding at the public trough, then you must at least pay your workers a living wage."

It was a bit of a surprise, then, when in May 2005, Lewis joined Ratner and Mayor Bloomberg at Brooklyn Borough Hall to announce what the mayor called a "50–50" affordable housing plan for Atlantic Yards: 50 percent of the new housing would be offered at below-market rent. "This agreement represents the first time that this concept of 50–50 has been implemented in a private agreement by a private developer in a project of this scale," Lewis said—after which she planted wet kisses on the two men as news cameras flashed.

Critics later charged that the "50–50" claim was mere hype: It only applied to the forty-five hundred rental units, not the more than two thousand condos that Ratner planned to build; many of the "affordable" apartments would cost $2,000 a month or more; and even most of these would not appear until the promised Phase II of the project, years after the arena was completed. It was also noted that ACORN, which would be responsible for enforcing the guarantee of affordable apartments, was also to be in charge of running the housing program itself. "We're concerned about traffic, hell, yeah," Lewis subsequently explained, after critics charged her with selling out the concerns of other local residents. "We're concerned about density, hell, yeah. . . . But we decided if we could make one nudge, one impact, what we could do, what we could kick ass on, it would be housing."

None of this, though, assuaged the fears of residents that Ratner was using the CBA to divide and conquer neighborhood groups by offering carrots on specific issues rather than discussing the overall scope of the project. (Some also recalled Lewis's previous foray into sports projects, a battle over a temporary minor-league stadium proposed for Brooklyn's Parade Grounds, which had ended with ACORN holding a press conference to announce that it was cutting a deal to endorse the ballpark before its allies in the opposition had even learned about the offer.) The more than $200 million in city and state money going to the project, meanwhile, had no strings attached—as Carponter explained, "All this stuff is being given to Ratner on the basis of his promises that are contained in the CBA, but there's absolutely nothing that can be done if he chooses not to follow the CBA." Ratner nonetheless slapped a printed seal reading "Guaranteed by a Legally Binding Community Benefits Agreement" on his subsequent borough-wide mailings.

In any case, the public battle lines had been drawn: From then on, public meetings would be a battle of neighborhood residents who'd signed on to the Ratner plan in exchange for promises of jobs and housing, and those who opposed it as an oversized land grab. And because most of the leaders of the opposition, like Goldstein and Carponter, were white, and Lewis and Caldwell were African American, it was easy to cast the debate in a racial light—even though a poll of Brooklynites conducted by *Crain's New York Business* found that a smaller percentage of African Americans than whites supported the project.

"I think race was used from Day 1 to window-dress the project," Reverend Clinton Miller, pastor of Brown Memorial Baptist Church in Brooklyn's Fort Greene, told the *New York Times* in late 2006. The problem, suggested city council member Charles Barron, was that Brooklyn's poor communities were in such dire straits that many leaders were willing to grab at any project that seemed to offer escape, no matter what the cost: "The devil could bring in a project and say it's jobs and affordable housing, and some of us will go for it, because we're on a survival level."

The race card, concluded *Daily News* sportswriter Michael O'Keeffe, made people "forget the most important mantra when it comes to sports, arenas and developer promises: Follow the money. This fight is more about green than black and white."

When Elephants Fight

As the Brooklyn battle raged, the Jets stadium lurched fitfully ahead. In late 2003 the *New York Times* reported that the Jets were soon to announce a "nonbinding agreement" with both the city and the state of New York, with the team paying $800 million for the stadium, and the public spending about $600 million for the rail yards platform and a retractable roof; this would be on top of the $2 billion or so in PILOTs that would go to build the new subway line and other infrastructure, plus another $1.5 billion to expand the adjacent convention center. "This is an incredibly complicated jigsaw puzzle," Deputy Mayor Dan Doctoroff explained when asked when a deal might be consummated. "We want to make sure that we have all the right pieces in all the right places."

Up to this point, one piece in the West Side jigsaw puzzle had been Cablevision, the multi-billion-dollar cable company that owned, among other things, the New York Knicks and Rangers, and their home building, Madison Square Garden. Early renderings of the Jets stadium included a diagram in which the structure could be reconfigured to host a basketball court, and at a June 2003 hearing on the Hudson Yards plan, a Cablevision exec had praised the plan for "providing needed flexibility to our efforts to plan for the future of Madison Square Garden."

By early the next year, though, the cable company's ardor for the project had begun to cool. First, the *New York Times* reported that the Jets were working on redesigning their stadium to *not* be usable for arena-sized events; Cablevision, apparently, was no longer interested in being a tenant and now feared that the Jets stadium would compete with Madison Square Garden for sporting events and concerts. If this redesign was meant to placate the Garden's owners, it didn't work. By the spring of 2004 Cablevision had officially joined with local residents and elected officials to form the New York Association for Better Choices, which would take the lead in fighting the stadium.

Thus began what was surely the most well-funded anti-stadium campaign in history. Slickly produced ads started appearing on local television, asking, "What could New York City do with $600 million?" and listing such items as schools and firehouses as better public investments than a football stadium. Mayor Bloomberg, who until this point had remained fairly quiet on the Jets plan, preferring to let his deputy Doctoroff take the lead, went ballistic: "There is an allegation that one company in order to protect their own commercial interest is trying to stop jobs coming to this city. That's an outrage," he declared at one news conference. "The biggest guys that are making a fuss here, are plain and simple, Cablevision—the Dolans," he said on another occasion. "It is an outrage that you let your own personal economics, or economic interests, stop a major project in this city." The mayor even suggested he might strip the Garden of its twenty-two-year-old property-tax exemption—a $12 million-a-year gratuity that city budget watchdogs had long criticized as a waste of public funds but which none of a series of mayors, including Bloomberg, had moved to cut off.

The public debate, which had previously centered around Doctoroff on one side and neighborhood figures like John Fisher on the other, soon became a battle of billionaires. The Jets hired two former aides to Republican governor George Pataki and one former Democratic deputy mayor to lobby for the stadium; Cablevision countered with a former aide to State Assembly Leader Sheldon Silver, and the son of State Senate Majority Leader Joseph Bruno. Public hearings on the plan became dueling rallies where Jets minions handed out caps proclaiming "Jobs!" in team colors, while opponents dressed in black "No West Side Stadium" t-shirts. In total, according to figures compiled by Common Cause New York, the two sides would rack up more than $50 million in lobbying fees alone, with Cablevision outspending the Jets by a three-to-one margin.

Doctoroff, meanwhile, personally pressured city business and good-government groups to back the stadium plan. "It didn't change my mind," one board member of the Regional Plan Association told the *New York Times* after receiving a phone call from the deputy mayor shortly before the group's board voted to put off taking a position against the project. "But whenever somebody like that calls, you have to pay attention because there are serious potential consequences. He makes important business decisions for the city." The *New York Observer* further noted that six of the seven corporations to get multi-million-dollar corporate-subsidy packages from Mayor Michael Bloomberg had donated to the city's Olympic committee; one city lobbyist told the paper: "If a client came to me and said, 'Look, I want to get in with this administration,' I'd say, 'Hey, give to the Olympics.'"

The End Run

There's little sign that all this big spending had any significant effect on public opinion. From the start, polls had shown that while a sizable minority of New Yorkers wanted nothing to do with the Olympics—"I haven't rooted this hard for England, France and Russia since World War II," quipped one *New York Post* reader—a majority did support bringing the Summer Games to town. Just as consistently, though, residents opposed using public money to do the job. In numerous polls conducted over the years on the West Side plan, large majorities reiterated that they were opposed to spending money on a stadium unless it paid for itself. "The stadium argument comes down to tax dollars," said Quinnipiac University Polling Institute director Maurice Carroll. "If the claim is correct that the stadium will generate enough income, New Yorkers say, 'Build it!' If taxpayers have to pick up the tab, 'No way,' they say."

Under the plan that Doctoroff had crafted, though, the public—and its elected representatives—would have minimal input on the stadium decision. Under the new PILOT plan, the mayor would be able to single-handedly grant property-tax exemptions to developers; in return, they would pay fees to the newly created Hudson Yards Infrastructure Corporation, which would use them to pay off bonds for the new subway line, plus new streets and other infrastructure. As a result of this fancy footwork, the entire $2.8 billion project could be set in motion with no more than a single rezoning vote in the city council.

On January 18, 2005, the council voted 46–1 to approve the rezoning bill and, along with it, nearly $3 billion in city-backed bonds. Council speaker Gifford Miller, asked why he was voting for the rezoning even though he opposed the stadium, replied, "We're not going to cut off our nose to spite our own face."

And yet, several major hurdles still remained. Even with the PILOT gambit, the city and state still needed to come up with their planned $600 million share of the stadium itself. When the state legislature showed little enthusiasm for appropriating $300 million, Empire State Development Corporation chief Charles Gargano suggested that New York's City Council could take on the entire nut, with Governor Pataki finding a way to compensate the city under the table, perhaps by having a state agency pick up a larger share of a joint city–state project. Legislators fumed—assembly member Richard Gottfried snapping, "Silly me, I thought the state constitution required legislative approval for the spending of the state's money"—but several predicted such a scheme was all too possible. "The State of New York's budget operates like a slush fund, because that's how it's been set out by Governor Pataki, and the legislature hasn't stopped it," admitted state senator Liz Krueger. "When Chairman Gargano seems to imply '$300 million there, $300 million there, I can find that in the petty cash drawer,' it disturbs me immensely, but he may be right."

On the city level, though, Doctoroff was having just as much difficulty finding a source of stadium funds. In late 2004 the deputy mayor had let slip that he was considering dipping into the tens of millions of dollars a year in PILOT payments made by developers to the city's Industrial Development Agency, part of the net of quasi-governmental agencies and sub-agencies that control much of the city's development spending; though this was money that normally ended up in the city treasury, Doctoroff suggested that the mayor could redirect it to the stadium without council approval. Miller immediately introduced a bill to block the PILOT slush-fund plan, declaring that "we'll take every legislative and other remedy available to stop the mayor from making an end run around the city legislature."

Meanwhile, the state-run Metropolitan Transportation Authority was balking at Doctoroff's proposal that it hand over valuable development rights to the rail yards for free to the city, which would then turn the land over to the Jets. (The deputy mayor had argued that the city would be building the MTA a $2 billion train line in exchange, overlooking the fact that the transportation agency didn't particularly want a West Side extension.) As the two sides bickered, even bringing in former U.S. Senator George Mitchell to arbitrate the dispute, Cablevision leaped in with its own $350 million offer to buy the rail yards and build housing on them, spend $250 million to relieve the city of the cost of decking over the rail yards and, unlike the Jets, pay property taxes as well—a bid that Bloomberg promptly called "a joke," while Doctoroff and fellow deputy mayor Marc Shaw called MTA chair Peter Kalikow and urged him to reject it as "an act of sabotage." Other developers said privately that they would have bid on the rail yards land as well but were afraid to get on City Hall's bad side. "There is a reign of terror in this town," said Regional Plan Association director Robert Yaro, recalling his own group's battles with the mayor's office over its stadium stance. "The litmus test is 'Do you support the Olympics?' If so, then you can do business with the city."

At this point, attention started to shift to an obscure state board that had been set up in the 1970s to oversee the growing debt load of state authorities. Because the MTA fell under its purview, the Public Authorities Control Board (PACB) would need to give its unanimous approval before the Jets stadium deal could move forward.

New York's state government had been criticized as "three men in a room," for the process whereby the governor and the leaders of the state assembly and state senate would meet and hash out important decisions then present them to the rest of the legislature as a fait accompli. (In 2004 New York University's Brennan Center for Justice awarded New York's legislature the title of "most dysfunctional" in the nation.) The PACB was a creature of this world, with five members, only three of whom could vote: Governor Pataki, Senate Majority Leader Bruno, and Assembly Speaker Silver. Any one of the three could veto a measure by voting no, or simply by abstaining.

While Pataki was a backer of Hudson Yards—at least since it had been broadened to include expansion of the Javits Convention Center, a pet project of his—and Bruno had indicated he wouldn't stand in its way, Silver had consistently hedged on his stance, saying repeatedly that he was "not convinced" that a stadium was right for the property. Silver's district included lower Manhattan, which, the speaker stressed, was having its own problems: "We are going to create 20 million square feet of commercial space in midtown Manhattan to compete with the business looking for space downtown. That's the real question." The *New York Times'* Charles Bagli noted that Silver's "ambivalence [was] driving other politicians slightly batty."

This ambivalence showed its first signs of turning to opposition in February 2005, when Silver declared that "the MTA is under a public and moral obligation to get as much money as possible for that site. If that land is worth $900 million by their own appraisal, it seems to me they should be under an obligation to get nine-hundred-some-odd million dollars." A few days later, the PACB hearing that was supposed to rule on the Jets deal was abruptly canceled. This began what would be three months of delays and stall tactics; by May, Pataki was scheduling meetings every few days, and Silver and Bruno were canceling them just as fast.

Finally, after what one state legislator described as "a very bad meeting" among representatives of the governor, mayor, Jets, and legislative leaders, Silver and Bruno dropped the bomb: When the PACB finally met on June 6, both voted not to approve the Jets stadium deal, effectively killing it. The stadium, declared Silver, had been "used as a shield" to "shift the financial and business capital of the world" from his downtown Manhattan district to midtown. Mayor Bloomberg immediately charged Silver with having "let America down" by torpedoing the city's Olympic bid, but the deed was done. When, following Silver's prepared speech, a reporter asked if the stadium was dead at last, the speaker smiled and said: "It was never alive."

Hudson Yards, though, would survive without its anchor stadium, with the city and state moving ahead to spend billions on the subway extension and convention center expansion, despite fears that the expected commercial development would never materialize. And shortly after the death of the Jets plan, Silver would introduce a bill containing tens of millions of dollars a year in tax breaks and rent subsidies for businesses relocating to his lower Manhattan district. Within an hour of landing on legislators' desks—before many had even had time to read it—the bill had passed unanimously.

King George and the Stadium Dragon

The stadium calm lasted barely one week. Then, after a whirlwind set of negotiations with Olympic organizers over the course of a weekend, the mayor announced his fallback plan to save the Olympic bid. A stadium would be built in Queens, in the parking lot of Shea Stadium, to be the new home of the Mets; if New York landed the Olympics, it would be expanded to eighty thousand seats for a summer, and the Mets would move in with the Yankees for a season. As for George Steinbrenner's squad, they would get a new home of their own across the street from Yankee Stadium—right where Rudy Giuliani had wanted to put it four years earlier.

Three days later, the news media packed into the Stadium Club inside Yankee Stadium for the team's official announcement. The Yanks' iconic home, declared team president Randy Levine, was "becoming nonfunctional" but would be replaced by a newer, better stadium with all the modern amenities: "Today's announcement is not the end of a legacy, but the continuation of one." And better yet, added Steve Swindal, George Steinbrenner's son-in-law and heir apparent to the Yankee throne, "There will be no public subsidies."

Mayor Bloomberg, after joking that he was already practicing his curveball to throw out the first pitch in the new stadium, echoed Swindal: "The state helping the way, but George footing the bill—it doesn't get any better than this."

What had changed in the four years since Rudy Giuliani had offered a 50–50 public–private split as the best the city could hope for? For one thing, baseball's internal finances had made it more palatable for teams to pick up a greater share of stadium construction costs. Under the revenue-sharing plan put in place in baseball's 2002 labor agreement, teams had to pay an average of forty cents on each new dollar of revenue into a pool to aid lower-revenue teams. The tax was levied on gross revenue, not net—no deductions were allowed on expenses, with one exception: "stadium operations" costs, which were defined to include payments on stadium construction bonds.

For a team looking to build a new stadium, this was a huge windfall: For every $100 million you spent, about $40 million could be recouped by reducing the revenue-sharing checks you sent to the league offices—effectively passing along 40 percent of construction costs to your competitors. It was no coincidence that the first stadium to be approved following the new labor deal, a new home for the St. Louis Cardinals, featured one of the highest team contributions in decades, with the Cards picking up about two thirds of the price tag. The Mets and Yanks would continue that trend, by picking up an unprecedented 100 percent of construction costs.

But not *all* costs. Although the teams would be responsible for all the costs of building the stadiums themselves—enabling them to reap the maximum revenue-sharing deduction—the city and state were set to provide a long list of goodies that belied Swindal's "no subsidies" line.

First and foremost was land. The Yankees planned to erect their stadium in what was currently a public park, and state law required that the city replace the parkland with equal acreage elsewhere. That cost was initially estimated at $135 million (later raised to $195 million), though only about $100 million was for actual replacement parkland; the rest was to go for such things as demolishing the existing stadium and relocating a water main that stood in the way of the new facility. All of this expense would be covered by city taxpayers.

Secondly, Steinbrenner's long-standing yen for more parking for his suburban fan base was to be met with four new parking garages, also to go up in what was currently parkland. The state government would kick in $70 million toward the garage construction, with the rest coming from an as-yet-to-be-determined private developer. Though the state initially claimed that taxpayers would recoup their investment, it later admitted that all parking revenues would go to the private operator—the $70 million was a "capital subsidy" that would not be repaid. Meanwhile, the Mets, who had no need for garages, would get a similar state subsidy in the form of "infrastructure" money to sink pilings for the foundation of their new stadium.

The publicly reported subsidies, though, were only the tip of the iceberg. At their old ballparks, both teams paid an annual rent—though only after deducting maintenance expenses. (A clause required annual audits by the city comptroller to weed out excessive deductions. On one occasion, Steinbrenner had tried to bill the city for an engineer who had somehow managed to work 168 hours per week.) In exchange for the teams' taking on all maintenance and operations costs of the new stadiums, the city had agreed that they would henceforth play rent-free—a tradeoff that Bloomberg claimed would save the city "hundreds of millions of dollars" on the upkeep of Shea and Yankee stadiums.

The city, though, had previously been earning money off the team leases. In particular, the Yankees, whose attendance and ticket prices were both soaring, had in recent years paid enough annual rent to easily cover both maintenance costs and any additional capital expenses the city might incur. The "hundreds of millions" figure, a city spokesperson later explained, was the cost of meeting the Yanks' demand for a stadium "on par with other first-class major league baseball facilities located around the country."

And there was more. Though the stadiums would be paid for by the teams, they would be owned by the city, so that both teams could be exempt from paying property tax. (In the bizarro world of sports facilities, it's often more lucrative for team owners *not* to own their stadiums, so long as they control all the associated revenues.) Likewise, they would receive special exemptions from paying both mortgage recording tax and sales tax on construction materials. The MTA would build a new commuter rail station for the Yankees, at a public cost of at least $45 million. And under the terms of the Mets deal, owners Fred and Jeff Wilpon would get the first $7 million a year in parking fees at their new stadium, money that currently had to be shared with the city—even though fans would be parking their cars in the exact same lots as before.

Finally, as part of his going-away present to the two teams, Mayor Giuliani had approved $5 million a year per team in "stadium planning" credits for the years 2001 to 2005. Bloomberg extended the rent credits another three years, costing taxpayers another $30 million. And, whereas under Giuliani's plan the city would have recouped the rent credits by deducting them from its own stadium construction expenses, under the Bloomberg plan the city had no stadium construction costs to deduct from—meaning the mayor was effectively tearing up nearly $50 million in IOUs from the two teams.

When all was said and done, the Yankees' new stadium would cost city and state taxpayers about $551 million dollars; the Mets park would add $353 million more. Even the city's own economic consultants, notes corporate-subsidy analyst Dan Steinberg of Good Jobs New York, who conducted an in-depth study of the Yankees project, projected that the city and state would gain just $225 million in new tax revenues, not nearly enough to pay back the public's costs. Yet the city still insisted the public would make money on the deal. "They did some very sneaky things with the numbers," says Steinberg, including counting as a $25 million city "benefit" the savings from not having to renovate the old park. "They hadn't spent that much money on those parks in the past twenty years. But then they used that to say, 'That's $25 million we saved by doing this project.'" The city also excluded the cost of tax breaks from its analysis, he discovered, even though "by their own protocol, it's almost unheard of for them not to quantify the value of sales and property-tax breaks— these are numbers that are routinely included."

As for the Yankees and the Mets, after all the tax and revenue-sharing benefits, they would be on the hook for just $350 million and $306 million, respectively. (Counting the federal subsidy of the tax-exempt bonds, the two teams would actually end up spending less on their new stadium than taxpayers would.) But the teams would have an important advantage over the public: They would get to defray their costs with lucrative naming-rights and concessions revenues, none of which would have to be shared with taxpayers.

Bloomberg's stadium plan, admits Steinberg, "is better than the Giuliani plan"—though he notes that under the old agreement, the teams would have shared 4 percent of home-game receipts with their city landlords, a clause that would have brought in enough money from the Yankees alone to pay off $175 million in stadium costs. However, given that neither team was likely to leave, and that their current stadiums were already cash cows, the city had hardly driven a hard bargain. "Because of the Yankees' success in recent years, because of the economy, because of the strength of the real-estate markets, the city was in a privileged negotiating position," he says. Yet the teams were handed all the revenues from the new buildings, and, after all the tax breaks and other public subsidies, were paying a smaller share of the costs than the public was.

Concludes Steinberg: "The taxpayers were fleeced."

Hallowed Ground

As for the stadiums that would fall to the wrecking ball to make way for the new ones, they evoked very different emotional reactions from New Yorkers. Shea Stadium was a 1960s-era concrete doughnut, best known for bitter winds off Flushing Bay and the roar of airplanes landing at nearby LaGuardia Airport; arguably, its biggest claim to historical fame was as the place where Beatlemania first touched down in the United States, with the Red Sox's epic collapse in the 1986 World Series a distant second.

Yankee Stadium was something else entirely. In 1923 the New York Giants, jealous at the Yankees' newfound success behind box-office superstar Babe Ruth, had booted the team from Manhattan's Polo Grounds, at which point the team simply hopped across the river to the Bronx, where it would win an incredible twenty of the next forty world championships. (In that same time span, the Giants won two.) Following the mass demolitions that hit baseball in the 1990s, the House That Ruth Built was left as baseball's third-oldest stadium, with the Boston Red Sox's Fenway Park and the Chicago Cubs' Wrigley Field the only other survivors from the days of the original steel-framed ballparks.

By 2005, though, Yankee Stadium was also no longer the ballpark of DiMaggio and Mantle. In the mid-'70s, after the team's then-owners threatened to take the Yankees to New Jersey, the city of New York had agreed to fund a $25 million renovation of the stadium that added luxury boxes and removed view-obstructing columns. (It also stripped much of the architectural detail, including the renowned copper-friezed roof, making the stadium ineligible for city landmarking.) As stadium historians Bill Shannon and George Kalinsky wrote at the time, the renovation "will leave us with a great sports landmark structurally mauled somewhat beyond need, in our view. But some Yankee Stadium is better than none, and that seemed to be the alternative choice."

The price tag for the renovation would ultimately soar to $119 million, even as promised improvements to the surrounding Bronx neighborhood were hastily scrapped. But George Steinbrenner, the Cleveland-born shipping magnate who purchased the Yankees from CBS for a cut-rate $10 million in 1973, never seemed happy with the rebuilt stadium, griping that its Bronx environs were too shabby, and parking and highway access insufficient. In the mid-'80s, Steinbrenner had begun alluding to the possibility of moving the team to New Jersey if his demands weren't met. Even the emergence of a new Yankee dynasty in the 1990s and subsequent boom years at the turnstiles—the Yankees set a new American League record in 2005 with nearly 4.1 million tickets sold—weren't enough to convince him that the old ballpark had economic life in it.

Mayor Bloomberg seemed to agree, telling the Stadium Club crowd that Yankee Stadium was "antiquated" and "fails to reflect the glamour of the club." The old stadium, team officials promised, would be retained as a "Heritage Field"—though a glance at the hastily assembled architectural model on display made clear that the stadium itself would be razed, with only the field and perhaps a few thousand seats remaining as a Little League and softball field. (Even this remnant would later be eliminated from the plan.) Across the street, a new fifty-two thousand-seat stadium would rise, with a facade reminiscent of the original Yankee Stadium; hiding behind its concrete skirts would be a hundred-foot-wide shopping concourse, an entire deck of club seats, and sixty luxury suites. To make room for the new high-priced seating, the entire upper deck would be shifted about thirty feet farther back from the field, putting the last row in the new smaller building just as far from the action as the last row in the old fifty-seven-thousand-seat stadium. Meanwhile, all that luxury seating would come at a high price to fans: The estimated average ticket price for a game at the new stadium in 2009, according to city projections, would leap from $27 to $57.

Then there was the matter of what currently stood where the new stadium would go. Macombs Dam Park was first dedicated as parkland in the early years of the twentieth century, when Babe Ruth was still building his House on the other side of 161st Street. By the 1990s it was not much to look at: a running track with a soccer field perpetually pounded into bare dirt at its center, plus a couple of baseball diamonds, ringed by a line of old oak trees that provided the park's only greenery. Across a street to the north, Mullaly Park featured tennis and handball courts and one of the neighborhood's few playgrounds.

If the parks looked perpetually worn, though, it was because they were so heavily used. Macombs Dam Park played host to soccer, baseball, and track meets for both pickup teams and the local schools; numerous local residents, many of them elderly, would walk the running track for daily exercise. "As far as I can remember, there were always people in that park, from early morning to late at night," says Anita Antonetty, who moved to the Highbridge neighborhood overlooking the park in 1968. "It was a wonderful large space to go and take your kids. Or just to just sit and look at the trees—it was really a nice place to be, because the trees were big old trees, so they gave a lot of shade."

Under the Yankees' plan, all of Macombs Dam Park and the southern section of Mullaly Park would be eliminated; the team's new outfield would stand where the running track had been. There would be a scattering of replacement ball fields, some on the old stadium site to the south, some on the far side of the Major Deegan Expressway. For the residents of the densely populated art deco apartment buildings along Jerome Avenue, though, their view would no longer be of greenery, but of the outside wall of a baseball stadium and multistory parking garage. "It was just a very convenient place, that park, in the middle of a residential area," says Antonetty. "Now you're going to have this giant stadium in between to get around. It's poor planning, that's what it is."

Bronx Jeers

For those who lived in the Bronx neighborhoods around Yankee Stadium—Highbridge, Morrisania, Melrose—the news that the Yankees planned to build a baseball stadium on top of their local park came as a shock. Lukas Herbert, a city planner in suburban Westchester County who'd recently moved to the area, recalls walking by a newsstand and spotting a headline about the new stadium plans. "At first I thought this would be really great for the neighborhood," he recalls. But as more details emerged, Herbert, who was a member of the local Community Board 4, began to wonder.

Antonetty, the community board's recording secretary, recalls that Bronx borough president Adolfo Carrion had presented the board's executive committee with a similar stadium plan the previous summer. (Carrion, who in his inaugural speech as borough president in 2002 had declared that "New Yorkers need schools and not stadiums, and I will never abandon that fight," was hoping to include a conference center and high school in the stadium development, though neither the Yankees nor the mayor seemed very interested.) Antonetty recalls that one board member, land-use committee chair Mary Blassingame, raised concerns about having the stadium in the park and how it would affect residents of the Jerome Avenue apartment buildings facing the site. "The borough president said, 'This is not the final plan, this is just an idea, and we'll work on it later.'" The next the board heard about the plan, she says, was when the Yankees held their Stadium Club press conference: "That's when we saw that this was really going to happen."

Slowly, by word of mouth and the occasional flyer taped to a lamppost, news of the stadium plan filtered out to the neighborhood. Herbert was at his job in the suburbs when he learned that the city was holding its first public hearing on the Yankees project. "I was reading the Tri-State Transportation Campaign's e-newsletter, and it said, 'Yankee Stadium draft scope release, public hearing will be held.'" After phoning the community board's district manager, who was likewise in the dark, Herbert tracked down the agency in charge of the public-hearing process—in this case the Parks Department, which not only controlled the parkland but owned Yankee Stadium as well—to find a copy of the stadium plan.

Herbert remains aghast that, if not for this chance discovery, the public comment period might have begun without anyone from the public being alerted. "You can't possibly tell me anybody in that neighborhood knows to look on the environmental notices bulletin for the state Department of Environmental Conservation to find the lead agency contact name," he says. "Most people around here don't even have computers." At the scoping hearing—designed to get feedback on what issues the city environmental impact statement should evaluate—Herbert estimates he was one of only three or four people in the room who had actually read the documents that testimony was being solicited about.

Not that that stopped those present from providing plenty of feedback. The overflow crowd in attendance complained that it would be five years before new parkland could be built on the old stadium site ("I'm concerned with our youngsters not having to wait until the Yankee stadium is up before they can play in these parks"), about increased traffic from new parking garages ("It's absurd to bring more cars to this neighborhood when all the kids are sick with asthma"), about how construction would affect residents of apartment buildings on Jerome Avenue across from the proposed stadium site ("I feel like I'm being forced out of this neighborhood, and I've lived here thirty-five years. . . . I don't know what the plan is, but I don't think the plan is for a lot of us to remain"). The final speaker, a Jerome Avenue resident named Daniel Tavares, pointed to his tank top as evidence of his frequent use of the Macombs Dam running track. "This is not a stadium that's for the Bronx," he thundered, noting that most local residents can't afford high-priced tickets. "If this is not a done deal, we have to march around that stadium fifty thousand times"; the rest of his remarks were drowned out by thunderous applause.

Soon, local residents, including Antonetty, Herbert, and several other Community Board 4 members, had banded together to tell the city and the Yankees that if they needed to build a new stadium, it shouldn't be in their park. Joyce Hogi, a longtime resident of the neighborhood who would become an integral member of the group, had attended several meetings of a local nonprofit concerned about the approaching stadium but had been turned off by the group's focus on "what the community could get out of this." (It didn't help that the group held its meetings during the day, when she, like most other neighborhood residents, was at work.) "One day I was walking the dog," she recalls, "and I saw a flyer on a car windshield, and I picked it up. And it was about a meeting about the Yankee Stadium project. It was that evening, so I thought, oh, I think I'll go. It sounded a little different."

Calling themselves Save Our Parks, the group set out to build community awareness, slipping flyers under doors and gathering thousands of signatures calling for changing the stadium plan to preserve the parks. Mostly, though, the nascent organization turned out residents to pepper Yankee and city officials with questions about the need for the project. At a rally on the steps of the Bronx County Courthouse, with the Yankee Stadium light towers visible two blocks away, neighborhood resident Dilsa David wondered to reporters: "If they're not allowed to build a stadium in Central Park, why should they be allowed to build in our park?"

At one community board meeting, New York City Economic Development Corporation vice-president Hardy Adasko seemed surprised at the intensity of the audience questions, sputtering when asked for economic-impact figures that "the city considers the whole deal a major net benefit—I don't have the numbers." Asked why the Yankees couldn't stay put at a refurbished Yankee Stadium, Adasko insisted it would be impossible to provide "an adequate number of ladies' rooms," drawing a burst of incredulous laughter from the mostly female crowd.

The inadequacies of Yankee Stadium were a constant theme in presentations by Yankee execs. At one "town hall" meeting, facing a crowd of more than two hundred Bronx residents who had greeted Borough President Carrion with angry chants of "You work for us!" Yankees president Levine insisted, "We love the present Yankee Stadium [but] it's not going to last ten years"—conveniently ignoring the findings of the city's own buildings commissioner in 1998 that Yankee Stadium could last another seventy-five years if maintained properly. "As much as we love our present home, it's becoming nonfunctional," Levine declared at another public hearing. "We need a new one." On still another occasion, Levine insisted that the team would have to knock down the elevated subway line that ran behind the right-field bleachers in order to have room to renovate.

In fact, Carrion's predecessor as borough president, Fernando Ferrer, had commissioned a study in 1998 on renovating Yankee Stadium that determined the old ballpark could be upgraded and restored to its pre-renovation look for just $189 million. (The architects, Beyer Blinder Belle, had just completed overseeing the restoration of Grand Central Terminal.) Members of the community board, meanwhile, suggested that any new stadium should be put south and west, near the planned Bronx Terminal Market mall—another project that had been pushed through with little community input just a few months earlier.

Under the city's Uniform Land Use Review Process—the public process that the Jets' stadium had evaded by being run by a quasi-public state authority—the community board for the affected district was required to cast a vote on all city planning projects. Community Board 4 debated the Yankees plan for three and a half hours, during which just one out of thirty-six speakers spoke in favor of the project. Though there had been reports beforehand that the borough president was heavily pressuring the board to back the plan, the final vote was sixteen to eight, with five abstentions, to oppose the proposed new stadium.

As the count was announced, the meeting room at the Bronx Museum, packed with more than two hundred local residents, broke into a sustained whoop of applause. Afterward, community organizers gathered in a local diner, where one was heard to exult: "We beat the Bronx machine!"

No one knew it at the time, but it was to be the Bronx opposition's high-water mark.

Eight Days in June

The first sign that the Yankee Stadium debate wouldn't follow the same leisurely pace as the Jets project had come just eight days after the press conference announcing the new stadium plans. On June 23, the next-to-last day of the state legislative session, the legislature passed a bill "alienating" twenty-two acres of Macombs Dam and Mullaly parks. From the perspective of the state government, they were no longer parks at all, just plots of land ripe for development.

Steinberg, a former state senate staffer, was dumbfounded that the legislature didn't hold off on alienating the parkland to strike a better deal for the community, as was common practice. "In eight days, the state legislature proposed the bill, debated it, got a home-rule message from the city council, and passed it. And just like that, twenty-two acres of parkland in the South Bronx no longer belonged to the people."

During those eight days in June, Steinberg later discovered, the state legislature had sent a request for the city council to issue a "home-rule message" approving the alienation bill. This request arrived in the council "preconsidered"—which meant that no public hearings were required. Meanwhile, the council's finance division provided members with a fiscal-impact statement indicating "no impact on [city] expenditures resulting from the enactment of this legislation"—though by the city's own admission, it was to be on the hook for more than $135 million in land and infrastructure costs. According to council minutes, council members barely discussed the issue before unanimously approving decommissioning the parks. (Brooklyn arena opponent Letitia James abstained.) Three days later, the state legislature passed its alienation bill, and the Yankees had their land.

"No alienation has moved as fast as the Yankees'," Christian Di-Palermo, executive director of New Yorkers for Parks, later recalled. The requirement that the state formally alienate land, he noted, was put in place to prevent land-scarce cities from turning parkland over to developers whenever they needed a large plot of land. He observed, "Obviously the taking of parkland is going to be the cheapest option, because it's public land. It's not like eminent domain where you're taking private land, and you have to pay somebody. We think it should be the last choice. It's fast becoming the first choice, and that gives us a lot of concern."

Back at Community Board 4, no one had heard a word of these machinations. "All of that was done behind closed doors," says Antonetty. "We didn't even know that was going on. There were no public hearings at all before the parks alienation, so we found out about that after the fact."

While the city land-use process required public hearings, residents soon found out that public input was another matter entirely. The community board's vote was only advisory. Next the plan went before the City Planning Commission, which swiftly approved the city's draft environmental-impact statement—a seven-hundred-plus-page tome that, residents complained, was unreadable to the Bronx's many Spanish speakers. While by law the EIS was required to include citizen comments, these were mostly dismissed with a perfunctory wave of bureaucratese. (Sample text: "The commenter's assertion that the proposed project is 'laden with hidden public subsidies' is outside the scope of [this] analysis. . . . Neither the City nor the State will have any obligation to pay for construction of the new stadium. Thus, there are no hidden public subsidies.") The final report also dismissed rebuilding on the current site as a proposal that "would not meet several key project objectives"—first among them, bizarrely, that "the House that Ruth Built, the 1923 stadium, would be entirely obliterated."

The Mets stadium, the city had decided, was covered by a Giuliani-era environmental study, and so was exempt from further public hearings. Therefore, with the Yankees' EIS complete, the final stop for the twin stadiums was the city council, which was scheduled to take up the matter at a single public hearing in March. The day before, taking a page from Bruce Ratner's playbook, the Yankees announced a "community benefits" package that would donate $800,000 a year to Bronx nonprofits—and that had been negotiated solely with the Bronx legislators who already supported the plan. (Yankees officials claimed that the agreement would also provide $8 million to improve Bronx parks, though it was later revealed that this would actually come out of the city budget.) In addition, the team sent canvassers door to door in the neighborhood with a "Stadium Plan Frequently Asked Questions" sheet asserting that "the taxpayers of the City of New York are NOT paying the approximate $800 million cost" and "it would cost more to renovate the old stadium and make it handicapped accessible than it would be [sic] to build a spectacular, new, state-of-the-art Yankee Stadium."

At the council hearing, after the public had waited more than three hours to speak, Save Our Parks member Hogi testified, "We're not opposed to economic development, but this project is not about economic development—it's about a land grab from a disenfranchised community. There is no amount of community benefit agreement that can mitigate the giving up of public parkland to a private enterprise." Shortly thereafter, the committee chair in charge of the hearing announced that everyone would have to walk across the street to a tiny meeting room in another council building—another committee needed the room. The next day's press coverage would be dominated by the appearance of Yankees great Reggie Jackson, who had admitted that "the Yankees have not always been a good partner with the Bronx" but promised that from now on, things would change.

It would be the sole opportunity for council members to hear from the public before voting on the stadium projects. The morning of April 6 began with unseasonable snow flurries swirling outside the City Hall windows. Inside, news reporters, Bronx neighborhood activists, and pro-stadium construction workers cooled their heels for over an hour waiting for the deciding council meeting to begin. Word quickly spread: Christine Quinn, who'd succeeded the term-limited Gifford Miller as council speaker, was downstairs whipping the Democratic caucus into toeing the line on the stadium deal.

The vote itself was anticlimactic. One by one, council members insisted straight-faced that they'd given "extensive deliberation" to the matter of handing over city cash and parkland to the world's most lucrative sports franchise, before voting in lockstep to approve the plan. The project "will bring eighteen acres of parkland to the Bronx," raved Quinn, carefully not mentioning the twenty-two acres of parkland that would be displaced; Manhattan council member Gale Brewer, a frequent critic of corporate-subsidy deals, gave an eloquent speech detailing the "many questions" that remained about the plan, before voting yes. Bronx council member Helen Diane Foster, whose district included the apartment dwellers along Jerome Avenue whose windows would look out directly on the new stadium, cast one of only two no votes, but not before publicly apologizing for listening to her constituents and not her party leaders. "I tried to find a way to say yes, [but] I don't believe this is the best deal for the community," she said. "I believe it's the best deal for the Yankees." One council member's entire speech consisted of "I have always liked the Yankees, and I will like them even more now."

The final vote was forty-five to two, with two abstentions. In thanking her committee for the one hour of work that it put into discussing the Yankees' plan that morning before the vote, land-use chair Melinda Katz declared, "The one thing this project has shown is that folks are listened to."

It Ain't Over Till It's Over

There were still two more hurdles facing New York's baseball stadium plans. In the 1980s, the city had received federal money for renovations to Macombs Dam Park—and federal regulations required that the National Park Service sign off on any demolition of federally funded parks, to ensure that replacement parkland of equal "value and utility" was being provided. To Bronx residents, this was a no-brainer. "The replacement parkland that they're building is almost a mile away on the waterfront—you've got to take this scary pedestrian bridge to go over there, across some railroad tracks, underneath an elevated expressway," argued Herbert. "It's going to be really difficult for senior citizens and kids to get there. It's not equivalent. Right now, you walk out your front door, and the park is right there."

The other remaining obstacle affected both teams and involved the $1.56 billion in tax-exempt bonds that would be used to raise money for construction. Ever since the 1986 Tax Reform Act, it had been considered illegal to use federally subsidized bonds for projects where more than 10 percent of the cost would be repaid by a private entity. The Mets and Yankees stadiums were to use 100 percent private money to repay the bonds—but, the city claimed, these payments were technically not private but rather "in lieu of" the property taxes that the teams were not going to have to pay.

It was a distinction fine enough to raise more than a few eyebrows among development experts. One national bond expert, speaking on condition of anonymity, called the city's argument "a transparent end run around the 1986 provision saying stadiums cannot be financed with private-activity bonds. We have simply interposed an empty box into which the Yankees' stadium-related revenue would be placed, labeled that box 'PILOT,' and transformed black into white. If only solving the problems of real life were that simple."

Dan Steinberg recalls a meeting of the city council's finance committee where members split unprecedented semantic hairs over the difference between "public" and "private" money. "The entire point of the hearing was to determine whether or not the council was comfortable using money that the city would normally collect," he says. "But meanwhile, throughout this very hearing, you had council members defending the project by arguing that it was privately financed. I remember thinking, if the IRS were in this room, and heard the arguments that the council members were making, it would be very difficult to justify the use of payments in lieu of taxes."

Tax experts questioned the legality of the bond plan (the city Independent Budget Office called it "a very, very aggressive interpretation of the IRS code"), and Park Service officials promised, "There are no shortcuts—we have a responsibility to follow the law." Nonetheless, in the course of one week in July, both federal agencies approved the project without comment. Four weeks later, the official groundbreaking ceremony was televised on the Yankees' own cable network, while a few dozen protesters were herded into police pens a block away from the televised groundbreaking ceremonies. Within a week, the park had been bulldozed, trees chainsawed, and an enormous rock hill at one end pulverized into gravel. The residents of Jerome Avenue began keeping their windows shut tight, even in the heat of summer, to keep out the dust.

And there was still one final indignity to be visited upon the Bronx residents. The $5 million a year in "stadium-planning" rent credits that Mayor Giuliani had handed out back in 2001, it turned out, had gone to pay for more than just architects and engineers. Included on the expense reports the Yankees submitted to the city were portions of the salaries of top executives, including Randy Levine and several members of Steinbrenner's family, plus such high-priced lobbyists as former Republican state chair Bill Powers, who'd handpicked George

Pataki for his successful 1994 gubernatorial race and raised $1 million for Rudy Giuliani's 1993 mayoral campaign, and Stephen Lefkowitz, who'd also worked on the Jets' and Nets' campaigns. Even the lawyers who drew up the sweetheart lease in the first place, it turned out, had been billed to city taxpayers.

It was an "alarming" revelation, noted Dick Dadey, director of the good-government group Citizens Union, calling it "like padding the expense account, but the people who pay are the taxpayers." Common Cause's Megan Quattlebaum agreed: "You've created this weird circular situation where the city is, effectively, paying with taxpayer money to have itself lobbied for potentially more taxpayer money. Taxpayers would not be pleased at all to hear that the city is subsidizing someone to come back and hold their hand out to lobby for more."

One taxpayer in particular was especially displeased. "Whoa, that's disgusting," said Lukas Herbert upon learning the news. "So basically the city has allowed the Yankees to hire lobbyists for free on the city's dime?" He considered this, then added: "I should be able to deduct the hours that I spent working to save the parks in my neighborhood from my city income tax."

The Two New Yorks

In December 2000 the *New York Post*'s Richard Wilner penned a column on New York's "$3 billion sports stadium crisis." The city, wrote Wilner, was "facing the possibility of having to build five sports palaces in the next five years," counting new buildings for the Yankees, Mets, Jets, Knicks, and Rangers. It was, he concluded, a daunting task, especially given New York's history of allowing the new-stadium craze to pass it by: "Will fans ever get to experience a home game at a state-of-the-art stadium?"

Within Wilner's five-year time span, though, New York would find itself in the midst of the greatest—and most expensive—sports-facility frenzy the world had ever seen. Barely four years after Bloomberg's "it's not practical" speech, the city had considered three new stadiums and two arenas (Cablevision was proposing a new Madison Square Garden inside the landmark post office building across the street from the current one), not to mention a NASCAR track on Staten Island. The Jets stadium may have died an ignoble death, but the Yankees and Mets received their new parks in record time; and the Nets' move to a new Brooklyn arena, as 2007 dawned, remained on track. The total cost: close to $3 billion, with well over $1 billion of that to be borne by taxpayers.

What broke New York's stadium logjam, and why were the Jets left out? It certainly wasn't about need—New York's teams were all unfathomably rich, even by the standards of sports franchises: The Yankees and Mets ranked first and third, respectively, in *Forbes*'s rankings of most valuable baseball teams, and the Yankees had brought in an incredible $277 million in revenues the year before, $70 million ahead of the second-place team, and more than the Toronto Blue Jays and Tampa Bay Devil Rays combined. None of the ballclubs could legitimately threaten to leave town: The baseball teams' values, in particular, were tied to the immense cable television revenues that flowed from their presence in the nation's largest urban area. And public opinion was likewise unmoved: Both the Jets and Nets projects were unpopular in polls, especially when New Yorkers were asked if they'd support using public money for construction; the Yankees' and Mets' projects sped to approval before anyone had run a citywide poll. One *New York Times* poll in the summer of 2005 revealed that when residents were asked to name "the worst thing [Bloomberg] has done since he became mayor," the top-ranked item was "new stadiums."

Why, then, were the Yankees' and Mets' owners looking ahead to new stadiums, while the Jets were left to work on sharing a new building in New Jersey with the Giants, a building to be paid for mostly with team and league funds, and why had Ratner's Nets' project languished for years in limbo? One difference, certainly, was Cablevision, whose ready cash turned the issue of public spending on sports stadiums into a front-page debate—and a bone of contention in the halls of power. "We would never have had the access in Albany that this campaign got without the Garden's lobbyists, and that's the reality of politics in New York," Hudson Yards/Hell's Kitchen Alliance spokesperson Anna Levin admitted after the Jets' stadium was finally defeated. Moreover, because the Jets' plan targeted Manhattan, it was both primed to receive more-prominent media coverage—the *Daily News* had its editorial headquarters in a building slated for demolition to make way for Hudson Yards—and opposed by better-connected politicians. (West Side assembly member Richard Gottfried, in particular, was a vocal opponent with strong ties to assembly speaker Silver.) As for the Brooklyn opposition, although it may have lacked a corporate sponsor, it did boast elected officials critical of the plan, and a well-connected populace: Actors Steve Buscemi and Rosie Perez would become frequent speakers at anti-Ratner rallies, and novelist Jonathan Lethem brought national attention to the Brooklyn arena battle with an open letter to architect Gehry in the Web magazine *Slate*.

The Bronx, by contrast, was run by a tightly controlled Democratic political machine that threw its weight behind the Yankees' project—even Helen Diane Foster, who ultimately came out against the deal, had initially co-sponsored the initial home-rule message to endorse decommissioning the parkland. Led by powerful state assembly member José Rivera, whose son Joel chaired the city council committee that authored the home-rule legislation, the Bronx machine swiftly closed ranks and gave the cold shoulder to local concerns; when community board member Antonetty asked to have a Save Our Parks delegation meet with José Rivera, she says he quickly brushed her off. Unlike in the other boroughs, the only organized political opposition in the Bronx came from Community Board 4, and it paid a high price: After the stadium deals were done, borough president Carrion moved to purge several longtime board members who had been vocal in their opposition to the Yankees' project.

"The discussion will always come back to the fact that this project was in the South Bronx," says Steinberg. "That matters in terms of the resources that they had, it matters in the extent to which public officials weren't overly concerned with the project, it mattered that so many people who participated were single mothers or had obligations and could show up to a hearing, but couldn't dedicate the type of time that you see from community board members in other areas." It also mattered in terms of media attention, which was hard to come by for a borough that few middle-class white reporters frequently visited, let alone lived in. "Several times there were meetings that drew over two hundred people, where you'd have two or three reporters," recalls Steinberg.

"There's clearly a double standard here," says Herbert, noting that council member Christine Quinn, who was at the forefront of the campaign to stop the Jets' stadium in her Manhattan district, pushed for quick approval of the Yankees' and Mets' plans once she was elected council speaker. Herbert concludes: "Stadiums are bad in middle-class or upper-middle-class white neighborhoods, but they're wonderful economic development opportunities in black or Hispanic neighborhoods where everybody is poor. There are a lot of middle-class people that live in this neighborhood. But there's also a lot of poor people here. And we were just told to shut up and take the project because it's good for us."

"In no other community would they accept a stadium across the street from where people live, and accept parking garages to replace parkland," says Antonetty. She, like other Bronx residents, had not forgotten the Yankees' official who, a decade earlier, had explained the team's reluctance to contribute to neighborhood improvements by complaining about the "monkeys" playing in the local playgrounds. "That disdain has always been there," she says. "And that's the reason that they could look across the street and not see a park; they could see an empty lot where they could build a stadium."

As 2007 dawned, Brooklynites were still fighting over Atlantic Yards. The project had received its final approval from the PACB, the same three-men-in-a-room board that had eighty-sixed the Jets' stadium but faced several lawsuits from Develop Don't Destroy's legal team. In the Bronx, meanwhile, residents watched as construction crews excavated what had been Macombs Dam Park, a pile driver pounding beams into the ground with a steady beat that shook the surrounding buildings. "When you walk out of the building, you get hit with the dust," said Donna Johnson, a resident of an ornate art deco apartment building that sits across from the stadium construction site. "There was one point, I felt like I had a shard from the rocks in my eyes—it didn't come out for a couple of days." Other Jerome Avenue residents complained of noise from trucks rumbling in day and night, and giant rats attracted by the garbage blowing around the former park site.

Hogi, at least, consoles herself with the fact that she and her neighbors fought back. "This thing was going down if we had walked around naked," she says with good-natured resignation. "My peace with all of this is that we fought it, and hopefully raised the awareness of people. I would be really upset with myself had I done nothing, and just buried my head in the sand."

16 Saving Fenway

If there isn't a new ballpark by 2006, there more than likely won't be any Boston Red Sox. —*Boston Globe columnist Bob Ryan, April 11, 2000*

On a Sunday in May 1999, the *Boston Globe* ran a special section titled "Fenway: A New Pitch." Inside, the *Globe* detailed the Boston Red Sox's plans to tear down Fenway Park, the team's home of eighty-seven years, and build a half-billion-dollar replacement across the street. This, the *Globe* coverage made clear, was all for the best. "Proposed $545m ballpark to retain cherished details," read the lead headline; the accompanying story, by reporters Gregg Krupa and Meg Vaillancourt, raved that the new stadium "mimics so many characteristic details of the beloved current stadium that the team even plans to dig up some of the old turf and play on it in the new facility." Another story described neighborhood response to the new ballpark proposal as "quiet admiration for the proposal's aesthetic dimension," despite some "fresh questions over how ordinary life in the area would be affected." Those who argued in favor of keeping the old ballpark were described as expressing "nostalgic melancholy that a legendary institution would be irreparably altered."

Baseball columnist Dan Shaughnessy, coauthor of a Fenway Park "biography," wrote: "Leaving Fenway isn't going to be easy for a lot of us, but if the Sox can do what they say they'll do, it'll be their best move since they brought Babe Ruth to the old ballpark when the old ballpark was the new ballpark in 1914." So certain was the *Globe* that a new ballpark was a fait accompli that it ran a special "Thanks for the memories" section featuring staffers' reminiscences of Fenway.

This public showcasing of the Red Sox's new stadium plans was no accident. John Sasso, a former ad exec and chief of staff to Governor Michael Dukakis, had been hired by the team to stage a series of "informational meetings" with local business, political, and media leaders around the stadium proposal. Among those met by Sasso's "small army of consultants, architects and image-buffers," as *Boston Globe* business columnist Joan Vennocchi would later describe them, were the editorial board and staffers of the city's largest newspaper.

"That first week was remarkable, really, in its favorable press coverage," Vennocchi later recalled. "It was a very coordinated effort, in the newspapers, television—they got a great sendoff. Then they came in here immediately afterward to answer questions and make us feel that we were part of the process."

For anyone reading the *Globe's* coverage, the overall effect was of a stadium that was on the way, no matter what the hopelessly nostalgic—the "zealots," as they would soon became known on the *Globe* sports pages—might think. Veteran sportswriter Bob Ryan summed up the mood of the day by writing that "there is nothing contradictory about loving Fenway and pining for something new and efficient. Put me down with the progressives. I'm looking forward to sitting in Son of Fenway, and sooner, rather than later."

Those picking up the *Globe* that day might have easily missed the news that, three days earlier, a small group of historic preservationists, neighborhood residents, and baseball nuts had issued their own call for the Red Sox to improve Fenway Park, not replace it. And certainly no one could have predicted that in the end, the zealots would win.

The Fenway Factor

When Fenway Park opened on April 20, 1912—the day, as genera-tions of Sox fans were later to memorize, that word of the Titanic sinking first reached the mainland—it was just another of the many steel-framed ballparks that were then springing up across the coun-try to meet baseball's rising popularity. Red Sox owner John Taylor had chosen to wedge his team's new home into an irregularly oblong block in the Fenway section of town, necessitating some odd conces-sions to geometry: Both the field and the bleachers bulged out into the ample space available in right field, while down the third-base line, Lansdowne Street cut so close to the action that a thirty-seven-foot-high wall had to be erected to keep every line drive from becom-ing a cheap home run. In 1933 new owner Tom Yawkey had the park expanded and its remaining wooden bleachers replaced with brick and steel, but aside from a handful of "roof seats" added following World War II, Fenway remained an old-fashioned single-deck ball-park into the modern era.

The first rumblings that the Red Sox might seek to replace Fen-way came in the mid-1960s, when there was talk of a then-fashion-able domed stadium to boost attendance, but nothing came of it. By the 1990s, though, as the first wave of new "retro" stadiums like Camden Yards and Jacobs Field came on line, there was again talk that Fenway's time could be running out. "Fenway is a wonderful ballpark," said John Harrington, the Red Sox's chief executive officer. "But the sad truth is it's economically and operationally obsolete. It just doesn't allow us to compete like teams with modern ballparks do." As Fenway prepared to host the 1999 All-Star Game, the *Globe* quoted one Boston business leader with ties to the team as saying: "The All-Star Game is a great opportunity for everyone to celebrate Fenway—and say a gracious goodbye."

Red Sox and city officials first discussed a new "megaplex" along the waterfront near South Station to host baseball, football, and con-ventions, but that idea died quickly amid opposition from local landowners and South Boston's famously insular political establishment. Instead, the team began to focus on a fifteen-acre plot of land immediately south of Fenway that was occupied by a mix of low-rise commercial buildings, including auto repair shops, fast-food restaurants, and souvenir stands. There, the team made plans for a new stadium with Fenway's field dimensions but a modern, double-decked grandstand seating forty-four thousand; the famed Green Monster left-field wall and old infield grass would remain as tourist attractions outside the gates, while the rest of the ballpark would be demolished and redeveloped. Announced Harrington: "What we want to do is to preserve the old site, and move the sod and the spirits of Ted Williams and Carl Yastrzemski a hundred yards down the street."

This notion of "preservation" didn't win many fans among actual historical preservationists. In 1997 the Boston Preservation Alliance (BPA) began running public service announcements insisting that saving the stadium made sense not only for the city but for the Red Sox: What the group dubbed the "Fenway factor" had helped the team sell out games even in years when the team was out of the pennant race, and the Sox themselves had touted the ballpark as the state's most popular tourist attraction. The Boston franchise, meanwhile, according to *Financial World* magazine's annual calculations, ranked a respectable sixth in baseball in revenues ($88.4 million) in 1996.

By the summer of 1998, recalls Dan Wilson, then a volunteer working with BPA on its Fenway preservation efforts, "it became clear that this was going to be too hot to handle" for the BPA, which wasn't in a position to challenge the city's power brokers head-on. And so, one night in September 1998, as Mark McGwire chased Roger Maris's single-season home-run record on TV, nine people met at the Fenway apartment of Kim Konrad, a former staffer with the Boston Landmarks Commission who was also a volunteer on BPA's Fenway campaign. The group included a mix of preservationists and Sox diehards who didn't want to see their team's home park meet the wrecking ball; its first president would be Konrad, who was a baseball novice but an expert in historic-preservation issues. The group filed for nonprofit status and, with the help of a $5,000 loan from the BPA, placed an order for white-on-green bumper stickers bearing the new group's name: "Save Fenway Park!"

The experienced political campaigners in the group knew that they needed to move fast, before the Sox could present the stadium as a done deal. "They were moving slowly, but we could see it coming," says Wilson. "If we had waited until they had a concrete proposal, we would have been dead in the water."

The activists' first break came in January 1999, when they were approached by Charles Hagenah, an architecture professor at Roger Williams University who wanted to do a project with his students on the possibility of renovating Fenway. Did Save Fenway Park! have any such plans? No, the group admitted; perhaps Hagenah and his students would like to design one? The Save Fenway activists put together a list of the team's stated demands for seats, luxury seating, restrooms, and so on, and passed them along to the architect with instructions to find a way to fit them into the existing site.

"The whole point was to create alternatives," says Erika Tarlin, a lifelong Sox fan who was on her way into the last home game of the 1998 season when she was handed a bumper sticker, and soon after found herself a Save Fenway regular. "You can't just stand there and say, 'No, don't do it.' So you had to take what their alleged needs were and show how you could satisfy them."

The Hagenah plan was presented to the public on May 13, 1999. It was a double-decked model with the same number of club seats and luxury suites as the Sox plan, but built atop the base of the existing ballpark, with the field and Green Monster intact. A new upper deck, seating ten thousand, would be cantilevered over adjacent streets, while buildings alongside Fenway would be pressed into service for such uses as team office space and food preparation.

Even as the press conference was under way, recalls Wilson, the Red Sox issued their own press release announcing that they would present stadium plans two days later. "But we had beat them to the punch," he says. "And from that point on, this was an issue of you are either for renovation or for the new stadium. There were two alternatives."

"It's Just Unrealistic"

According to the Red Sox proposal, a new stadium would come with an initial price tag of $545 million, including $350 million for the building itself, plus additional expenses for new garages, land acquisition, and other infrastructure. (The city would also need to use its power of eminent domain to seize a bit more than ten acres of private property—another five acres would come from closing existing streets—to make way for the new structure, which would take up 50 percent more ground than the old ballpark.) Beyond indicating that they would roughly split the costs with the city and state, team officials were unspecific about how the project, which would be the most expensive sports facility in U.S. history, would be paid for.

As for the option of renovating the old ballpark, Sox execs insisted that it would be far too expensive, if even possible at all. "It would be easier to straighten the Leaning Tower of Pisa," Harrington declared; HOK architect Earl Santee added, "You can't renovate Fenway because the footprint is too small to fix what needs to be fixed." Mayor Tom Menino, who had recently jumped on the Sox stadium bandwagon, added: "I love Fenway Park and I was an advocate of renovating it right where it is, too. But I was educated and I now realize it's just unrealistic."

When word got out that Mayor Menino was questioning the Hagenah plan because it didn't include a cost estimate, Save Fenway convinced a local firm to do one pro bono, on the grounds that Menino wanted it. The resulting figure came to $395 million, less than three quarters the cost of the Red Sox's new-stadium plan. "The mayor was absolutely furious," says Wilson. "The last thing he wanted was for us to go out and get a cost estimator." The mayor later announced that a draft study by PricewaterhouseCoopers found that renovation costs "would exceed $500 million," but Save Fenway later got the consultants to admit that they had likely overstated costs. And in any case, even a $500 million price tag would be less than the Sox were budgeting for a new stadium.

The team's main public argument for a new stadium, though, was not cost but comfort. A four-page paid "advertorial" insert that ran in both the *Globe* and the *Boston Herald* the Sunday before the Sox home opener in 2000 not only touted the economic benefits of a new stadium but also promised "10,000 additional affordable seats without a single obstructed view." Sox fans may have loved their "little lyrical bandbox," as Sox fan John Updike had famously called it, but they also griped about cramped seating and high ticket prices, and the team was determined to capitalize on this angle. "If we could get a 45,000-seat ballpark in the city," Red Sox vice-president John Buckley told business leaders on one occasion, "I could assure you that ticket prices . . . would fall back into the middle of the pack." Starting in the summer of 1999, Red Sox game telecasts broadcast ads that featured computer-generated flybys of the new stadium and made the spatially dubious promise of "seats that are closer to the field, not to the fan next to you."

Of course, expensive tickets and tight legroom could also be seen as a reflection of Fenway's popularity and intimacy, but that wasn't how team officials saw it. "Somebody who had been working for the Red Sox for years said he thought it was just that Mr. Harrington was just tired of fixing the leaky pipes," says Wilson. "He wanted something new that was easier to maintain—you didn't have to put a coat of paint on it every year."

There was another theory as to why the man running the Red Sox was so eager to leave Fenway behind. Though Harrington was in charge of the team, he didn't actually own it. He was, rather, the head of the nonprofit Yawkey Trust that had inherited the team after former owners Tom and Jean Yawkey died, and as such, he had an obligation to maximize the value of the team. It was an incentive, notes Wilson, for short-term thinking: "All you had to do was get a new stadium deal through the legislature, as had been done in other places, and the value of the franchise went through the roof."

To the State House

On May 19, 2000, the Red Sox owners finally proposed a detailed financing plan for their new stadium: The team would spend $352 million to sell the stadium proper, while the city and state would put up $275 million for land acquisition and infrastructure. Many in the city, though, warned that the land cost would likely be higher than projected, with the weekly *Boston Phoenix* (whose offices just happened to be in a building marked for demolition for a new Red Sox parking garage) predicting the total price tag could end up being as high as $900 million.

It was not the best time to be asking for public funds. First off, the highway-construction project known as the Big Dig had just blown a $14 billion hole in the state budget. Then there was the presence of Thomas Finneran, the same powerful state house leader who had held the line on funding for a new stadium for the Patriots. Early in 2000 Finneran had remarked about the Sox plan, "I saw the number and was somewhat staggered by the amount. I don't think it's a taxpayer responsibility or obligation to subsidize professional-sports operations. Nor is it an obligation of taxpayers to chase down free agents and pay them extraordinary sums to pay them to come and play ball." If the state were to build the team's parking garages, insisted Finneran, it should get all parking revenues.

As the stadium controversy grew, eight of Boston's thirteen city councilors sent a letter to Governor Cellucci saying they had "grave reservations" about using city money to acquire land for the project. Even Mayor Menino, the project's top backer, felt obliged to begin talking of taxpayers getting a "return on [their] investment," saying, "I'm not going to risk mortgaging the city's future. I want to make sure whatever I invest in the Red Sox comes back to the city. I can't stop building schools and fixing playgrounds." To achieve a "100% return" on the $110 million he was offering toward the project ($30 million less than the team was asking), Menino proposed various solutions, from a special baseball lottery to hotel taxes to a citywide parking surcharge.

With time running out before the state legislature wrapped up its session at the end of July, Cellucci, Menino, Finneran, and state senate leader Tom Birmingham—plus the CEOs of financiers FleetBoston and John Hancock, and high-powered ad exec Jack Connors—huddled with Harrington in the governor's office at the State House on July 25. By late in the evening, the deal was done. The team would put up $352 million for stadium construction, while the state and city would spend $312 million in public money: $100 million from the state for infrastructure, and $212 million from the city to acquire land and construct a 3,000-space parking garage. To meet the mayor's "repayment" requirement, the political leaders cobbled together a mishmash of revenue streams that would be shared with the city, some coming from what would otherwise be team revenues (surcharges on tickets and luxury box sales, and $7 million a year in parking fees), others money that the city would be effectively "repaying" out of its own pockets (sales tax revenue from within the ballpark, plus a commitment of one quarter of 1 percent of the city's hotel tax), and others where it was harder to interpret whose funds they would ultimately tap (a $5 parking surcharge at garages within one mile of the new stadium on game days).

Wrote Bob Ryan in the next day's *Globe*: "Yesterday's announcement represented the necessary go-ahead rally. Messrs. Harrington, Menino, Cellucci, Birmingham, and Finneran are standing together on the mound, signaling for the closer. The Save Fenway types are firing off the e-mails even as we speak, but it's too late now. The countdown will soon begin. The Red Sox will build a new park that will pay homage to baseball tradition while acknowledging a little concept known as progress."

By the end of that week, opponents and supporters of the new stadium had packed a room at the State House on Beacon Hill for a daylong hearing on the $100 million in state funds for the project. The day began with presentations by the team, the mayor, and the governor, all of whom argued that a new stadium was vitally important to the future of the ballclub. When Senator Dianne Wilkerson asked how the thriving Fenway district could be described as "blighted"—a necessary designation in order for the city to seize the land by eminent domain—the mayor responded, "We don't mean 'blight' in the real sense of the word 'blight.'"

Save Fenway and the experts it had brought to testify, meanwhile, cooled their heels for hours as stadium proponents monopolized the podium. "I've been to a lot of these hearings," marveled Rob Sargent of MassPIRG, part of Save Fenway's Coalition against Stadium Subsidies, "and I've never been to one where five hours into it, not one member of the public has gotten a chance to speak."

Before the hearing, Wilkerson had been skeptical of the Sox proposal, telling reporters, "This is a community that has never had a plan formally presented to them. A vetting and an opportunity to ask questions has never occurred. This is hardly a done deal. I'd say we're in the seventh inning." Yet the next morning, Wilkerson joined a majority of the legislature in voting for the Red Sox subsidy. As one of the few "no" voters remarked at the time: "It looks like a deal in progress."

For Save Fenway Park! members who had been meeting regularly with their elected officials to urge them not to provide money for Fenway's demolition, it was a bitter pill to swallow. Tarlin says it was the first time she'd ever made an appointment to visit her state senator in his office. "He assured me there would be no taxpayer money. He would not vote for the $100 million in 'infrastructure' for a stadium. Oh, no, no, no, no."

Just a few days later, Tarlin was sitting in the State House gallery watching as her senator cast his vote to grant state funds for a new stadium. "This huge naivete lifted up," she recalls. "Even when they say they're going to do the right thing, they still don't."

Fenway and Wayfen

Even as the state legislature voted to supply money for a new stadium, Save Fenway and the Fenway Community Development Corporation, which represented Fenway community members angered at the Sox project encroaching on their neighborhood, were already hard at work assembling a charrette, a weeklong gathering of architects and urban planners that would hash out new ideas for reusing the existing site. It would be led by Philip Bess, the erstwhile designer of Chicago's Armour Field, who had brought in several architects he knew from his previous work. Along with the Boston activists, this group would pile into a room at Simmons College's Library Building for nine days in August to develop two proposals, one "reconstruction" plan, where Fenway would be effectively rebuilt in place, and one "preservation" option, which would retain and improve on the existing structure—as Wilson calls them, "a modest proposal, and a less modest proposal."

The charrette began by discarding the Hagenah plan's premise of matching the Red Sox's demands for more seats and luxury boxes. "We realized that probably a better renovation would be a smaller renovation," says Wilson. Instead, the assembled architects prioritized finding a way to retain and enhance Fenway's charms, while being a good neighbor to surrounding residents and businesses.

The reconstruction team was led by Miami architect Rolando Llanes, who'd previously consulted for the Marlins on that team's stadium plans. It proposed a rebuilt Fenway that would seat from 38,200 to 40,000 fans, with at least 4,500 club seats and 67 luxury boxes. The Red Sox could even play at Fenway during the work by using phased construction over several off-seasons, combined with what was dubbed the "Wayfen" option: Home plate would be relocated to the existing right-field corner for a year or two, making the Green Monster the right-field wall, while reconstruction of the third-base grandstand proceeded beyond the new centerfield fence.

"I laughed when he showed that drawing because it was brilliant, and it was perfect," recalls Bess. "It was such a fabulous idea, because it actually made it possible to phase the reconstruction that way, and it would have provided two seasons of statistics that would have just become legendary. People would have talked about that forever."

The preservation plan, put together by a team led by former Illinois Landmarks Preservation Council president Howard Decker, was both more conservative and in some ways more daring. Up to 4,000 new seats would be added, including additional rows in the park's tiny upper deck, along with 2,700 club seats and 75 luxury boxes—all without dramatically altering Fenway's existing structure. Concession and fan circulation space beneath the nine-decade-old grandstand would be dramatically increased by relocating the team's administrative and service facilities to adjacent buildings.

One element that was in both plans was the addition of seats atop the Green Monster, suspended between new pillars running behind the wall along Lansdowne Street. It was an idea that Bess and Llanes had discussed some years earlier, and "a no-brainer," according to Bess. Both plans also would retain the existing field dimensions, the Green Monster itself—and yes, the pillars, which Bess noted kept the seats on Fenway's roof (like the upper-deck seats at the late, lamented Comiskey Park) far closer to the field than in modern stadium designs. Quipped Hartford architect Patrick Pinnell, a charrette participant: "Even in Boston, they can't suspend the law of gravity."

Both plans costed out at far less than the Sox's price tag for a new stadium: Llanes's reconstruction plan came to $266 million, whereas Decker's preservation option would be a mere $165 million to $180 million—some of which, the architect noted, could even be recouped by applying to have Fenway placed on the National Register of Historic Places, making the team eligible for federal tax breaks. Best of all, promised Bess, following the charrette's conclusion: "The Red Sox and their architects could pursue either of our approaches immediately and probably be playing baseball in a renovated Fenway Park well before the first shovel of dirt is turned for their current proposal."

That shovel of dirt appeared much further off than it had the day of the state legislative vote. Even if the mayor's "repayment" demands were less than airtight, they still represented a cap on the amount that the city was willing to spend—any cost overruns on land acquisition, for example, would now fall on the team, not the city. And though the state had committed $100 million to the project, Finneran had made clear the Sox wouldn't be getting a dime more. That left at least $350 million to be covered by the ballclub, an amount that, even as he celebrated the victory at the State House, Harrington had to worry would be too rich for his blood. Wilson noted that in news photos of the stadium announcement, Harrington "looked like he had just lost a child. He knew that it was not going to work."

By October, just three months after the Sox's triumph on Beacon Hill, the *Boston Herald* reported that the team was having trouble finding private bankers willing to loan it its share of the project, and was mulling rebuilding Fenway Park in place. The team denied the report, but it was becoming clear that the momentum was beginning to shift.

Then Harrington dropped a bombshell. The Yawkey Trust, he announced, was putting the Red Sox up for sale. "The team is in strong financial shape; we've had record-breaking attendance this year; we got a ballpark bill passed on Beacon Hill with $312 million in public aid; and the economy is booming," declared Harrington. "It's the right time to sell." On the city council, where nine of thirteen members would need to vote to approve the eminent-domain land takings for the new stadium, even some undecided councilors began backing away from the plan: "It would be irresponsible and reckless to turn around and commit public financing to a new stadium today only to find out tomorrow the team's being purchased by an Internet multibillionaire," councilor Michael Flaherty told the *Globe*. "All bets are off."

Things only got worse for the Sox in December, when the team signed slugger Manny Ramirez to a $160 million, eight-year contract—then promptly declared that it would be seeking more money from the state or city to pay for $60 million in anticipated land-cost overruns. Though team GM Dan Duquette asserted that "the fact we have to compete on the open market for players of this caliber . . .

points to the need for a new ballpark," the rest of Boston didn't see it that way. "Santa Claus is fully engaged right now with schools, health care, and a host of other concerns," snapped Finneran. The *Boston Herald*'s more succinct editorial reply: "The Red Sox have got to be kidding, right?"

The Tide Turns

Thus began a yearlong media circus as focus shifted from the future of Fenway Park to the future of the team itself. A long line of bidders soon formed, with the leading candidates including television producer Tom Werner, who as owner of the San Diego Padres in the 1990s had overseen the team's fire sale of players to cut costs; Cablevision chief Charles Dolan, whose brother Larry owned the Cleveland Indians; Miles Prentice, a Wall Street lawyer who had been blocked in previous attempts to buy the Angels and Royals; Boston developer Frank McCourt; and Boston concessionaire Joseph O'Donnell and mall developer Stephen Karp, widely seen as the "local guys" favored by the mayor and other Boston officials, who were talking of reviving the old idea of a new stadium on the waterfront.

By mid-December, the word was out: The winner would be a group pairing Werner with then-Florida Marlins owner John Henry, which had bid a staggering $700 million. (Henry would also receive $158.5 million for the Marlins from Montreal Expos owner Jeffrey Loria, who would in turn sell his club to the league for $120 million.) Though Henry's group was not the high bidder—Dolan and Prentice had each bid about $90 million more—it was made up of current and former baseball owners who were friendly with MLB commissioner Bud Selig. Harrington explained that he had wanted to ensure that new owners could be in place by 2002, leading to speculation that Selig had indicated that only Henry, a current member of the baseball cabal, would receive quick approval from MLB.

As the losing bidders fumed and the Massachusetts attorney general threatened an investigation, the Save Fenway activists breathed a sigh of relief. "That," says Wilson, "was our first victory." Henry, it had been reported, had been on the verge of joining up with the Karp–O'Donnell team but couldn't agree on who would be in charge of actually running the club. ("If you want me to cook the dinner," O'Donnell told Henry, quoting former New England Patriots coach Bill Parcells, "you've got to let me buy the groceries.") Instead, the "local guys" were locked out, and the fate of the Red Sox—and Fenway—rested in the hands of a billionaire investment banker from Illinois who'd spent most of his life in California and Florida.

Larry Lucchino, who had served as Werner's CEO in San Diego and would take on the same role for the Red Sox, raised hopes when in his inaugural press conference he promised, "We will preserve all that is good about Fenway Park and take that experience to new levels." Save Fenway, always eager to exploit any opportunity, wrote up a 110-page report called "Home Field Advantage" that included both arguments for renovation and the proposals that had been drawn up at the previous summer's charrette. Tarlin hand-delivered it to the Red Sox offices on a Friday afternoon, she says, and "got a handwritten note back on Monday from Larry Lucchino: 'Thank you for taking the time.'" She adds, "And that April we were chatting with Janet Marie Smith."

Janet Marie Smith had first rocketed to fame in the late 1980s, when Lucchino, then president of the Baltimore Orioles, picked her to oversee design and construction of that team's new stadium at Camden Yards. At the time, both she and Lucchino had been explicit in crediting Fenway with inspiring them to demand that designers HOK turn their generic plans for an Orioles stadium into something with a sense of history. Now, her old boss had brought her in to run stadium operations for the Red Sox—but would that mean preserving Fenway, or building a modern facsimile?

In late 2002 Boston got its first hint of what was to come, as Smith revealed that the team was considering adding seats atop the Green Monster and the right-field roof, and moving food-preparation facilities to an adjacent building to create more concourse space under the bleachers. While she dismissed these as "just plain, old-fashioned fix-ups," she also said ownership felt "optimism" about staying at Fenway for the long term. When the new seating proved a huge hit, the team moved ahead with more renovations, getting approval from the Boston Landmarks Commission to increase capacity by 3,700 fans by expanding the existing roof boxes from four rows to eight and adding more standing-room tickets; as part of the construction work, the original pillars holding up the roof would be removed and replaced. The team also applied to have Fenway put on the National Register of Historic Places, which would make it eligible for a federal tax credit equal to 20 percent of the team's renovation costs.

All were adaptations of ideas that had been introduced in the Save Fenway Park! charrette. One of his team members, says Bess, likes to quip that Henry "should be happy that the Save Fenway Park! charrette produced about $500 million of value for the Red Sox— for free." Mostly, though, those involved were pleased just to have helped influence the park's future; as Kim Konrad says, "We aimed to put the ideas in their heads so that they would think they were their own."

On March 23, 2005, Red Sox execs gathered in the soon-to-be-remodeled .406 Club behind home plate to announce that "the Red Sox will remain at Fenway Park for the long term." Declared John Henry: "It is an honor to have the opportunity to protect and preserve Fenway Park. We see how its history and charm attract people from all over the world, and how it helps connect generations within families. We will continue to listen to our fans and make improvements inside the park, at our own private expense, as we have done over these past three years." Lucchino called it a "no-strings-attached commitment" to stay at Fenway indefinitely.

It was as close to a declaration of victory as Save Fenway and its allies were likely to get. "For those of us who've been beating our heads against the wall for fifteen years about neighborhood ballparks, this is as much of a success story as we've been able to muster." says Bess. "I think we've won the argument that ballparks can be parts of cities.

What we haven't won is the idea that they should be neighborhood ballparks instead of parts of entertainment zones. The victory is that we've gotten the ballpark back into the city; the continuing problem is that the city itself is still not viewed by Major League Baseball and developers as being not only a place where people are entertained, but as a place where people live and shop and go to school and go to church."

The Winning Recipe

Looking back, many factors conspired to save Fenway from what once appeared to be a near-certain wrecking ball. If city councilors hadn't balked at additional $212 million in city money; if a subsidy foe hadn't been in command of the state legislature; if Menino hadn't raised the ante on city subsidies just enough to spook the team's bankers; and if John Henry hadn't been baseball's choice to own the team, things could have turned out very differently.

Then there were the pivotal moments that turned on mere chance. The charrette might not have come off if Tarlin hadn't had contacts at Simmons College's library program and if Save Fenway member Randy Divinski hadn't gotten a last-second $4,000 donation out of the blue from someone on his softball team. Wilson also stresses that the importance of Save Fenway's getting the Hagenah plan out first can't be overestimated. "If John Harrington had gotten his plan out three days earlier than he did, we were dead in the water. It would have always been about 'what color do you want the seats in the new stadium, should they be blue or red?'" Instead, he says, "from that moment on, it really was about renovating or building new, and everybody in the Boston area knew that there were two alternatives."

Still, one of Save Fenway Park!'s strengths was that it had the skills and the diverse membership—and the sheer gumption—to take advantage of every opportunity. "Go down the list of the board members, and every person brought something unique to the group," says Tarlin. "You had Kim Konrad, who lives in the neighborhood, totally into working hard to keep this really besmirched community alive. And she's a historic preservationist. Albert Rex was the director of the Boston Preservation Alliance—they gave birth to Save Fenway Park! by providing the seed money for the first box of bumper stickers, our most powerful tool. Andrew Pate: New Yorker, *Yankee fan*. Loves Fenway Park. Loves baseball. Telegenic—he was a good spokesperson. Unlike Paul Shannon, ponytail down his butt, headband. But he worked for American Friends Service Committee and knows about organizing.

"Randy Divinski, huge baseball fan, understands numbers. He could make charts for us. Once we got the numbers in 2001 when they had to release the earnings of Major League Baseball teams, that was *key* for us. Doug Rotundi, huge baseball fan, was our treasurer, kept our books, kept us legal. I'm a librarian, so I keep things organized, I've got the archives. Christine Fry: absolutely meticulous with numbers. Passionate baseball fan, had worked with the Tiger Stadium Fan Club, member of the Society for American Baseball Research. When Doug couldn't keep up with being treasurer and doing the merchandise, Christine stepped in. Jeffrey Harris, another founding member, worked at the time for the National Trust, so he knew how the world of preservation worked, and is a beautiful writer. When we were thinking about nominating the ballpark for national historic landmark status, he and Kim knew how to do it.

"John Valienti, signmaker. Passionate fan. Rallymaster. Who better than the guy who makes signs to make your banner? Michael Governor, another historic preservationist. He did all the press releases in the beginning—he is sharp as a tack, and hilarious. Dan [Wilson] just has the brains and the passion for baseball. His bringing people in, bringing different groups in is what made the whole thing work. Steve Wojnar has got a brain for marketing and presentation—he's someone you can walk into a meeting with the Red Sox, and you don't feel so much like you look like a circus. And because he's a season ticket holder, they would listen to him."

Asked to estimate how many person-hours went into saving Fenway, Tarlin says, "It's immeasurable." Weekly meetings alone ran for four to five hours every Monday over the course of several years—"How many people are doing that once a week, unless they're being paid?" Dan Wilson recalls that when he first joined the BPA's nascent opposition to a new stadium, "I said, 'I've got like five hours a month to put into this cause.' And then of course I wound up spending 60 hours a week."

Mostly, though, the Save Fenway activists had something that no other community opposition group did. "It was Fenway Park," says Wilson. "I said early on, 'The park is going to save itself.' If it had been Three Rivers Stadium, obviously, this never would have happened."

New York vs. Boston

But could the lessons of Fenway be applied elsewhere? In particular, how did Fenway end up saved, when Yankee Stadium, its near-equal in both baseball history and popularity as a tourist destination, was quickly consigned to the scrap heap? Tarlin, who closely followed the Bronx stadium wars, herself wonders: "There are so many parallels: historic stadium, storied team, neighborhood ballpark, eminent-domain issues, city council that has some power." In both cases, the team owners had proposed to pay for construction themselves, while hitting up the public for land and infrastructure costs. There had even been a renovation plan proposed for Yankee Stadium, the 1998 proposal by Bronx borough president Fernando Ferrer with an estimated cost of less than $200 million.

One big difference was that where Fenway had remained largely unaltered since the '30s, Yankee Stadium had been extensively remodeled in the 1970s. This made preservationists far less willing to take up saving the House that Ruth Built as a cause. Bess says that "you could make a case that you could reconstruct Yankee Stadium, to make it economically up to date around the existing playing field." But with a far more radical restoration needed, he notes, "They'd have to do now what they did in the mid-'70s, which is find some-place else to play while that was happening."

The even greater obstacles in the Bronx, though, were tactical and economic. When starting their new-stadium campaign, the Red Sox had tipped their hand, giving the opposition three solid years to or-ganize before the team's stadium plan ever came to a legislative vote. In New York the Yankees devoted years of behind-the-scenes lobby-ing to ensuring that elected officials had signed off on the plan be-fore local residents even knew what was being proposed. Moreover, in a compact city like Boston, Save Fenway activists who worked in central Boston could visit both their city and state legislative offices on their lunch hour; for Bronx residents, on the other hand, it was an hour's subway ride to City Hall, and a four-hour train trip to Al-bany.

Mostly, though, the Yankees had targeted a very different neigh-borhood, one with plenty of outrage and dedication but neither lob-bying expertise nor, crucially, the time to devote sixty hours a week to combating a well-heeled stadium push. "We didn't have the luxury of coming out to every single meeting, and to come out to protest, or to stay on the phone trying to get our elected officials what we want them to do," says Anita Antonetty of Save Our Parks. "If you're working two or three minimum-wage jobs just to put food on your table, you really don't have the time."

How to Fight City Hall

It has now been almost twenty years since SkyDome opened in Toronto, ushering in the era of the modern publicly funded sports facility, loaded with luxury boxes, club seats, ad boards, and food courts—the "mallpark," as ESPN.com baseball columnist Rob Neyer dubbed it. Every week, it seems, brings another news story about how economists see no benefits to using public money to build sports stadiums for private use—no benefits, that is, except for the owner of the team that will play there. Yet the windfalls available from the stadium game are simply too lucrative for any team owner to give up on, even if it takes a decade, as in Minnesota, to find a way past popular opposition.

And popular opposition to stadium subsidies does remain the norm. During the time that Pennsylvania was planning to build four new baseball and football stadiums in Pittsburgh and Philadelphia, one state representative told stadium researchers Kevin Delaney and Rick Eckstein, "Ninety-five percent of the calls we get on this issue are against it." Yet the response among legislators, he continued, was not to respond to constituents' opinions, but to find a way to circumvent them: "For dynamic issues like these that are wildly unpopular, the legislative leaders decide it will happen; and then they decide how many votes each side [Republican and Democratic] will give up and which representatives are least vulnerable—so they don't get taken out."

It was a process, noted Delaney and Eckstein dryly, that "seemed to have little in common with democracy as we conventionally define it."

Jeanette Mott Oxford saw a similar dynamic at work in St. Louis, where she helped lead the Coalition against Public Funding for Stadiums in its battle to prevent the Cardinals from tapping the public purse for a new baseball stadium. A veteran campaigner on welfare and poverty issues, Oxford says that the stadium fight was "the most popular thing [she'd] ever worked on." Fifty-five percent of St. Louis voters approved a referendum in November 2002 requiring a public vote before any city money could be spent on a facility for a private sports team; two years later, 72 percent of St. Louis County voters approved a similar measure for the use of county funds.

Yet Oxford's group ended up winning the battle but losing the war. Since the state legislature had gone ahead and approved funding for the Cardinals stadium in the weeks before the city referendum, state courts ruled, the new law didn't apply to them, and construction moved forward on what would become the third building to bear the name Busch Stadium. Public opposition did force team owners to put up a greater share of construction costs themselves, but hidden subsidies—such as a county loan that the team can effectively forgo repaying—meant taxpayers would still end up footing the bill for about one third of the total cost.

In 2004 Oxford was herself elected to the Missouri state legislature, in part thanks to her popularity for leading the charge against stadium subsidies. Her experience there has only deepened her belief that it's best to avoid putting decisions in the hands of elected officials, whenever possible. "If your city has a petition initiative process, get going on that and put things on the ballot through the power of the people rather than spending a whole lot of time lobbying elected officials," she advises would-be stadium activists. "They're too swayed by the gun held against their head saying, 'We'll move the team if you don't participate.'"

Of course, as the saving of Fenway shows, even without recourse to a voter referendum it's possible to fight off a stadium juggernaut—sometimes. "Save Our Sox lost in Chicago, the Tiger Stadium Fan Club lost in Detroit," notes Bess. "And the Save Fenway Park! people and those of us who worked on the charrette, we were beneficiaries of having witnessed those previous losses." That Save Fenway won, Bess agrees, was due to a combination of factors, but it was mostly that "the Save Fenway Park! people were just tenacious—it's an amazing group of people."

That certainly didn't hurt. Nor did the fact that, as it turned out, they were right in arguing that a renovated Fenway would be best not just for taxpayers, but for fans and the team as well. But as Dan Wilson concludes after seeing his group succeed where so many others failed: "It's not quite enough just to be right."

Acknowledgments

This book contains research compiled over the course of nearly twelve years, from hundreds of interviews, dozens of governmental hearings, newspaper clippings arriving in packages from far-flung corners of the continent, and e-mail traffic on various generations of listservs and bulletin boards. Which is to say that any list of acknowledgments is going to be horrifically incomplete, and we apologize in advance to all those whose contributions will go unrecognized.

That said, among those without which this book would not have been possible:

The list of grassroots activists, academics, and researchers who generously shared their time, wisdom, and expertise with us just keeps growing: Hallie Amey, John Aranza, Roldo Bartimole, Philip Bess, Doug Bukowski, Michael Charney, Jon Commers, John Davids, Judy Davids, Dorothy Dean, Donna Donovan, David R. Elkins, John Fisher, Dan Goldstein, Dan Golub, Brian Hatch, Meryl T. Johnson, Dennis Keating, Bruce Kidd, Norman Krumholtz, Ed Lazere, Greg LeRoy, Bill Marker, Shabnam Merchant, Chris Michaels, Marge Misak, Jeanette Mott Oxford, Shawn Newman, Mary O'Connell, Kevin O'Brien, John Pastier, Frank Rashid, Sheila Radford-Hill, Ricky Rask, Tony Ross, Steven Rubin, John Ryan, Tom Sevigny, Janice Shields, Kim Stroud, Newton Suwe, Hank Trenkle, Chris Van Dyk, and Chris Weiss; also Anita Antonetty, J. J. Brennan, David Gratt, Lukas Herbert, Joyce Hogi, and everyone at Save Our Parks, and Kim Konrad, Albert Rex, Erika Tarlin, Dan Wilson, and everyone at Save Fenway Park! And given that we began this project with just one entry-level economics course between us, we are forever indebted to the numerous economists who have selflessly given their time to school us in the nuances of fiscal number crunching, especially Robert Baade,

Tim Chapin, Rod Fort, Roger Noll, Philip Porter, Allen Sanderson, Andrew Zimbalist, and Dennis Zimmerman.

We are extremely fortunate to have as friends a large number of extremely talented people who were willing to provide their services at small-press rates. (Read: for free.) Jim Naureckas and Mindy Nass, who read every page of the original edition and provided invaluable editorial guidance, returned to reprise their roles for this version. Other friends and colleagues who provided invaluable editorial and research help with specific chapters include Margot Abel, Beth Cagan, Steve Cagan, Pete Cenedella, Stacy Cowley, Eileen Mullin, Nancy Nisselbaum, Andrew Ross, Wendy Roth, Anne Savarese, Christopher Tate, and Michele Tepper. If this book reads smoothly, you have them to thank, far more than us.

This book grew out of our work as journalists, and if writers are nothing without readers, they're also nothing without editors who believe in their work and keep it on the printed (or, these days, electronic) page. Our *Village Voice* editors Miles Seligman, Ward Harkavy, and Laura Conaway never failed to encourage us to stick to the stadium and arena beat, helping make chapter 15 the most extensively researched (and, not coincidentally, the longest) one in the book. Likewise, the gang of baseball smart guys known as Baseball Prospectus enthusiastically turned Neil loose to explore stadium deals both for their Web site and for their excellent book *Baseball between the Numbers*—thanks begin with Maury Brown, Steven Goldman, Derek Jacques, Jay Jaffe, Christina Kahrl, Jonah Keri, and Joe Sheehan, but everyone who's a part of BP deserves a round of applause. Nina Ascoly, Max Freund, Kurt Gottschalk, Bernie McAleer, and Michelle Phipps of the late, lamented zine *Brooklyn Metro Times* helped shepherd our very first investigations into the stadium game to print; Deidre McFadyen, then of *In These Times*, gave our work its first national exposure. We will forever be indebted to Greg Bates of our original publisher, Common Courage Press, who had the vision to give two young journalists a contract to write a book on the doings of the sports industry, even if he admitted that his only exposure to sports was having been to a hockey game once. And, of course, this newly revised and expanded version of the book would not have been possible without the tender loving care of Rob Taylor, Chris Steinke, Jackie Doyle, and everyone at the University of Nebraska Press, whose enthusiasm, professionalism, and attention to detail make us wonder if they perhaps wandered in from some industry other than book publishing.

Likewise, the work of researching this book was far beyond the means of we two alone. Ted Benson, John Cheney, Rob Daviau, Janet Pope, and Wendy Roth were instrumental in providing news clippings of stadium battles in the days before easy Web access to newspapers; since then, that role has been ably filled by readers of fieldofschemes.com and the Field of Schemes e-mail list, including Charles Everett, John Cheney, Bob Trumpbour, Darren Dahl, Mike Marshall, and especially the tireless Erika Tarlin, who has a standing invitation to be the official *Field of Schemes* archivist as soon as we can secure funding. Bettina Damiani, Dan Steinberg, and Stephanie Greenwood of Good Jobs New York were invaluable in helping untangle the thicket of sports subsidies in New York (not to mention the arcane world of Freedom of Information Law requests). We are also indebted to several of our colleagues in the newspaper world: G. R. Anderson of the *Minneapolis City Pages*, Patrick Arden of *Metro NY*, Charles Bagli of the *New York Times*, Matthew Futterman of the *Newark Star-Ledger*, and Jay Weiner of the *Minneapolis Star Tribune*, and our *Village Voice* colleagues Jarrett Murphy and Tom Robbins, who provided aid and assistance both directly and through their reporting; as much as you may hear us complain about the shabby state of journalism these days, these folks are distinct exceptions. Louise Quayle and Anne Savarese provided sage publishing advice and counsel that helped get this new edition from dream to reality. Jim Bouton and Sandy Padwe were relentless in their enthusiasm for this project (and Jim's ever-expanding *Ball Four* was inspiration for a book that keeps growing to include the latest information). And though they may not make an appearance in the book, no acknowledgments would be complete without a shout-out to Morgan Andrews and the Shoddy Puppet Company of Philadelphia, whose play "The Big Bailout" not only performed the seemingly impossible task of translating this book into shadow puppets speaking in rhyming couplets but helped prevent a baseball stadium from landing on the edge of Philadelphia's Chinatown.

Writing a book, especially a collaboration, is a bit like running a marathon, complete with the cramping and self-recriminations that hit about halfway through. We survived only with the tireless enthusiasm and support of friends and family. Joanna's thanks go out to Jennifer Eaton, Miles Seligman, Regina Shields and Jeanette Valentine, for their timely meals and free clipping services, and unwavering faith in this project; the long-distance advice and camaraderie of Susan Snyder and Lisa Tozzi; the constant cheerleading of Jessie and Shauna Cagan; Craig Campanella for an impeccably timed e-mail and Lisa Sklar for her daily enthusiasm; and, finally, to her parents Beth and Steve Cagan—who offered endless advice, patience, humor and compassion. Neil would like to thank: Matthew Amster-Burton, Steve Bernard, Adam Cadre, Stacy Cowley, Liza Daly, David Dyte, Lenny Pitts, Dan Schmidt, and Dan Shiovitz, for online kibitzing at all hours; the members of the echonyc.com writing conference who helped kibitz the title into shape; Dave Cutler, driving partner and research assistant extraordinaire; everyone at Fairness and Accuracy In Reporting, for generosity of both time and resources; the brilliant oral historian (and almost equally brilliant center fielder) Jeff Kisseloff, for the reassurance that all books take forever to write and twice that to rewrite; and, most of all, Mindy Nass, for her wisdom, clarity, humor, and the continued patience for a partner inclined to disappear at odd moments into the computer.

Finally, this expanded edition of *Field of Schemes* almost certainly would not have come about without the encouragement and inspiration of Doug Pappas, the longtime writer for Baseball Prospectus and the Society of American Baseball Research. In his spare time from his day job as a Manhattan attorney, Doug simply redrew the map of baseball business writing, relentlessly questioning official league pronouncements and questionable economic claims with brilliant analysis and his trademark quick humor; Doug's Business of Baseball blog was the first thing Neil read every day in the morning throughout much of the research for this book. Doug died in May 2004, while pursuing his other avocation: hiking in America's national parks. (His travel writings, and his baseball writings, have been preserved at roadsidephotos.sabr.org.) With his passing, the sports world lost not just one of its most brilliant analysts, but one of its nicest, funniest, most humane people. Doug should have been here to write the introduction to this edition of *Field of Schemes*; since he's not, he gets a featured role at the end, instead. Farewell, Doug, and thank you for showing the way.

Notes

All unattributed quotations are taken from interviews and firsthand reporting conducted by the authors between February 1996 and December 2006.

1. A Tale of Two Inner Cities

1. *"It is simply unconscionable."* Peter Richmond, *Ballpark* (New York: Simon & Schuster, 1993), 97.

1. *"It's unbelievable, the callousness."* Robert McG. Thomas Jr., "Colts' Move to Indianapolis Is Announced," *New York Times*, March 30, 1984.

2. *"If the Colts can be moved that way."* Dave Anderson, "12 Vans to Indianapolis," *New York Times*, April 1, 1984.

4. *The local government had already poured more than $400 million.* Jacob V. Lamar Jr. and Don Winbush, "'India-no-place' No More; The Subject of a Joke Gains Major League Attention," *Time*, June 11, 1984.

4. *Construction of the Hoosier Dome was under way by 1982.* Andrew H. Malcolm, "The Colts' Move: For Indianapolis It's a Boon . . . but in Baltimore, It Leaves a Void in the Hearts of the Fans," *New York Times*, April 8, 1984; Kent McDill, "Why Is Indianapolis Building a $75 Million Domed Stadium?" United Press International, June 27, 1982.

4. *By 1982, however, it had become clear.* The Raiders' ultimately successful lawsuit challenged the NFL's right to control franchise movement; until it was resolved, the league put its expansion plans on hold. Mark Fury, "Will Indianapolis' Domed Stadium Become a White Elephant?" *Bond Buyer*, July 28, 1982.

4. *Articles started appearing in financial publications.* Fury, "Will Indianapolis' Domed Stadium Become a White Elephant?"

4. *In 1979, with the Colts floundering on the field.* Charles C. Euchner, *Playing the Field: Why Sports Teams Move and Cities Fight to Keep Them* (Baltimore: Johns Hopkins University Press, 1993), 105.

5. *The Colts, tipped off to the city's plans.* According to Hudnut's chief negotiator, the deal was finalized in just three days because of fears of legal entanglements. "Rushed Negotiations for Colts Revealed," United Press International, April 1, 1984.

6. *"a monument to the progressive spirit of the city's people."* "Most Modern Stadium in the World, and One of Most Beautiful," *Cleveland Plain Dealer,* July 31, 1931.

6. *When eighty thousand fans jammed into Municipal Stadium's wooden seats.* Carol Poh Miller and Robert Wheeler, *Cleveland: A Concise History, 1796–1990* (Bloomington: Indiana University Press, 1990), 143.

7. *Year after cellar-dwelling year.* Local baseball fans, desperately searching for explanations for one of the most ignominious reputations in professional sports history, were willing to turn to any explanation. Besides the stadium's inhospitability, Clevelanders pointed to the legendary "curse" of Rocky Colavito, the popular Indians outfielder who was inexplicably traded before the start of the 1960 season. Terry Pluto, *The Curse of Rocky Colavito* (New York: Simon & Schuster, 1994), 47.

7. *The city, which had lost 23 percent of its population between 1970 and 1980.* Poh Miller and Wheeler, *Cleveland: A Concise History,* 183–84.

8. *The choice of a property tax to fund the initiative.* Mark Rosentraub, *Major League Losers: The Real Cost of Sports and Who's Paying for It* (New York: Basic Books, 1997), 256.

8. *Indeed, Campanella himself would later speculate.* "All it took was a significant proportion of the political elites to contest it," says Elkins, who points out that even Voinovich "had to be persuaded and cajoled." In the course of his own research on the domed saga, Elkins spoke with Campanella and many of the other key figures.

8. *"Cleveland leaders can't ignore a study."* Paul Attner, "For Many Cities, There's No Place Like Dome," *Washington Post,* June 8, 1994.

8. *And although their referendum failed.* Elkins also speculates that there may have been a greater than normal turnout by African American voters on that day in May 1984—it was the same election day that would see Jesse Jackson score significant numbers in the city of Cleveland in his presidential campaign.

8–9. *The Civic Committee would later become.* Poh Miller and Wheeler, *Cleveland: A Concise History*, 189.

9. *"We are not going to be able to do anything."* Richmond, *Ballpark*, 49.

10. *"For as long as the city will support the team."* Richmond, *Ballpark*, 58.

10. *"unless private enterprise builds it, we won't build it."* Euchner, *Playing the Field*, 115.

11. *While Marker sat, several legislators expressed concerns.* Richmond, *Ballpark*, 96.

13. *In a final touch that delighted architectural critics and baseball fans.* That the warehouse was owned by Schaefer's chief fundraiser was, no doubt, merely coincidence. Euchner, *Playing the Field*, 115.

13. *"Baltimore didn't need a new baseball stadium."* Richmond, *Ballpark*, 44.

14. *Significantly, they had made their fortunes in the Cleveland area.* Rosentraub, *Major League Losers*, 256. In Rosentraub's extensive look at stadium financing and the cost to local municipalities, he argues that the Jacobs brothers were seen as the ideal new owners of the beleaguered team. Rebuilding the Indians was part of the brothers' plans for redeveloping downtown Cleveland.

15. *Raising $1 million from private interests.* Rosentraub, *Major League Losers*, 263.

15. *"Who wins with Issue 2? . . ."* Emphasis in original. Newspaper advertisement, *Cleveland Plain Dealer*, May 3, 1990.

15. *"Should this facility not be available in Cleveland . . ."* Roldo Bartimole, "If You Build It," *Progressive*, June 1994.

16. *"Anyone who thinks the Indians."* Rosentraub, *Major League Losers*, 261.

16. *The so-called Gateway initiative won.* Rosentraub, *Major League Losers*, 263.

16. *But that soon turned into a much greater public investment.* Rosentraub, *Major League Losers*, 269–78.

16. *It wasn't until late December 1996.* James F. Sweeney, "Gateway Agrees to Pay Taxes on Jacobs Field, Gund Arena," *Cleveland Plain Dealer*, December 24, 1996.

17. *the future of the Browns was never publicly questioned.* Perhaps it should

have been. In *Ballpark*, Peter Richmond mentions, almost in passing, that in 1984 then Baltimore Mayor William Schaefer "mobilized a secret meeting . . . between [Orioles owner Edward] Williams, Governor Hughes, Cleveland Browns owner Art Modell, and Larry Lucchino. It was Schaefer's idea: the state would donate the land, private capital would be raised, and Art Modell, a friend of Williams, would buy an NFL team, put it in Cleveland, and move his Browns in." Richmond, *Ballpark*, 65.

18. *But Modell had also promised the city in 1994.* Stephen Koff, Timothy Heider, and Evelyn Theiss, "How Cleveland Lost the Browns," *Cleveland Plain Dealer*, November 19, 1995.

18. *It was perhaps the only time.* Malcolm Moran, "Hugs, Tears and a Victory: Browns Say Goodbye," *New York Times*, December 18, 1995.

19. *"As sweetheart [deals] go, call this one."* Tom Cushman, "Maybe S.D. Deal with Chargers Is Not So Bad," *San Diego Union-Tribune*, November 17, 1995.

19. *But when Mayor White met with NFL officials.* Stephen Koff and Tony Grossi, "City May Need New Stadium to Keep a Team, NFL says," *Cleveland Plain Dealer*, January 5, 1996.

19. *White, following negotiations with NFL officials. Cleveland Plain Dealer*, January 5, 1996.

20. *"The best deal possible." Cleveland Plain Dealer*, February 11, 1996.

21. *"the percentage of Clevelanders living in poverty rose."* Norman Krumholtz, "To Fund or Not to Fund?" *Detroit Free Press*, March 12, 1996; W. Dennis Keating, "Cleveland: The Comeback City," in *Reconstructing Urban Regime Theory: Regulating Urban Politics in a Global Economy*, ed. Mickey Lauria (Thousand Oaks CA: Sage, 1997), 192.

21. *The city school system, drained of property taxes.* Sandra Dallas, ed., "Tackling Football, And Oh, Yes, Education," *Business Week*, December 9, 1996.

22. *"in the worst financial shape."* Scott Stephens, "Cleveland Schools to Cut Sports, Teachers," *Cleveland Plain Dealer*, March 8, 1996.

22. *the Camden Yards complex ultimately drew more than $400 million.* According to Jack Lapides, the poorest 25 percent of the state's population buys 63 percent of all lottery tickets. Richmond, *Ballpark*, 98.

23. *And the city did lose many of the one thousand manufacturing jobs.*

Though the Maryland Stadium Authority would later rent out office space in the warehouse to local companies, as a state agency it pays no property taxes. Jack Lapides reports that over his three decades in the state senate, the portion of city land not paying property taxes had nearly doubled, from 20 percent to 37 percent, as a result of the sports stadiums, university and hospital expansion, and other tax-exempt development.

24. *The Orioles, bought by Eli Jacobs for $70 million.* John Helyar, *Lords of the Realm* (New York: Ballantine Books, 1994), 569–72.

25. *The Indians, whose new stadium coincided.* Team-value figures drawn from annual estimates compiled by Michael Ozanian for *Financial World* magazine from 1991 to 1997. Since 1998 Ozanian has compiled similar yearly figures for *Forbes* magazine. All the *Financial World* and *Forbes* team-value estimates are available from economist Rodney Fort's Web site: www .rodneyfort.com/SportsData/BizFrame.htm.

25. *In 2000, the* Cleveland Plain Dealer *put the public's final tab at $470 million.* Alan Achkar and Bill Lubinger, "Gateway's Scorecard; Sports Complex Still Trying for Home Run a Catalyst for Economic Renewal," *Cleveland Plain Dealer*, September 10, 2000.

25. *"I didn't have a clue what this project was going to cost."* Kevin J. Delaney and Rick Eckstein, *Public Dollars, Private Stadiums* (New Brunswick NJ: Rutgers University Press, 2003), 73–74.

25. *"Today, the main streets in and around the Gateway."* George E. Jordan, "Games Cities Play," *Newark Star-Ledger*, December 5, 2004.

26. *"All told, each dollar of extra revenue from the ballpark."* Doug Pappas, "New Stadia: Baltimore, " *Boston Baseball*, May 2000.

2. Stealing Home

27. *"It's amazing what a pretty picture you can draw."* John Williams, "Early Stadium Sketches Unveiled," *Houston Chronicle*, October 12, 1996.

27–28. *The bill for the '90s is expected to exceed $12 billion.* These figures do not include the more than a hundred minor-league ballparks and arenas built during the decade, which could add another billion dollars or two to the numbers. James Quirk and Rodney Fort, *Hard Ball: The Abuse of Power* in *Pro Team Sports* (Princeton NJ: Princeton University Press, 1999), 218–25; Tom Farrey, "New Stadiums, New Fans," ESPN.com, September 18, 1998; John Riley, "Where the Grass Is Always . . . Greener: An $8.1B Building Boom in Pro-Team Stadiums: How Public Money Is Fueling Private Fortunes," *Newsday*, August 18, 1996.

28. *77 percent of stadiums and arenas in use were publicly owned.* James Quirk and Rodney Fort, *Pay Dirt* (Princeton NJ: Princeton University Press, 1992), 127.

29. *What some have called "the economic war among the states."* Kary L. Moss, "The Privatizing of Public Wealth," *Fordham Urban Law Journal* 23 no. 1 (1995): 106.

29. *In 1977 fewer than half of all states.* Greg LeRoy, "No More Candy Store," Federation for Industrial Retention and Renewal and Grassroots Policy Project, 1994, 3.

30. *In his study "No More Candy Store."* LeRoy, "No More Candy Store," 3.

30. *Meanwhile, the automaker BMW.* Phil Bereano and Todd Fedorenko, "High Tech Candy Store," *Seattle Times*, March 23, 1997.

30. *the state of Louisiana handed out $3.7 billion in tax abatements.* Moss, "The Privatizing of Public Wealth," 107.

30. *The city sent thirteen hundred checks.* John Butera, "The Ties That Bind," *Plants, Sites and Parks Magazine*, March/April 1996.

30. *The following year, tiny Rio Rancho, New Mexico.* Janice Shields, "Ending Corporate Welfare," *Business and Society Review*, Summer 1995.

30. *"Despite recurring predictions."* LeRoy, *No More Candy Store*, 2.

31. *The previous year, the L.A. Rams.* Mark Rosentraub, *Major League Losers: The Real Cost of Sports and Who's Paying for Them.* New York: Basic Books, 1997, 66–67.

31. *"the mother of all stadium deals."* Mark Thornton, "Bring Back the Football Cartel," *Free Market*, January 1996.

32. *"It's a wonderful thing for our community."* Andrew H. Malcolm, "The Colts' Move . . . For Indianapolis It's a Boon. . . . but in Baltimore It Leaves a Void in the Hearts of the Fans," *New York Times*, April 8, 1984.

32. *"The Raiders coming to Sacramento."* Charles C. Euchner, *Playing the*

Field: Why Sports Teams Move and Cities Fight to Keep Them (Baltimore: Johns Hopkins University Press, 1993), 55.

32. *"off the charts."* Richard Sandomir, "Mayor Says If Yanks Must Move, West Side Would Be Best," *New York Times*, April 3, 1996.

34. *"professional sports teams generally have no significant impact."* Robert A. Baade, "Stadiums, Professional Sports, and Economic Development: Assessing the Reality," A Heartland Policy Study, April 4, 1984.

34. *"finds no support for the notion."* Baade, "Stadiums, Professional Sports, and Economic Development."

35. *"If you draw larger and larger circles."* Joanna Cagan and Neil deMause, "The great stadium swindle," *In These Times*, August 19, 1996.

35. *"Coors Field is a beautiful place."* Steers, "Bowlen for Dollars."

36. *"How much more food do people eat."* Rosentraub, *Major League Losers*, 151–53.

36. *"dropped out of a helicopter over the Twin Cities."* Terry Fiedler, "Boosters: Ballpark would aid economy," *Minneapolis Star Tribune*, March 4, 1997.

36. *In a study Rosentraub did.* Rosentraub, *Major League Losers*, 138–49.

37. *"One city official estimated."* Euchner, *Playing the Field*, 67.

37. *"economic benefits were overstated by 236 percent."* Dennis Zimmerman, "Tax-Exempt Bonds and the Economics of Professional Sports Stadiums," Congressional Research Service, May 29, 1996.

40. *"Our research suggests that professional sports may be a drain."* Dennis Coates and Brad R. Humphreys, "The Stadium Gambit and Local Economic Development," *Regulation* 23 no. 2 (2000).

40. *"sales tax collection in the city of St. Paul hasn't gone down."* Jay Weiner, "The Economics of Stadiums Look Bad for the Twin Cities," *Minneapolis Star Tribune*, June 19, 2005.

41. *"We really feel it would be in the best interest."* CBC News, August 26, 1994.

41. *"At some global level they are obviously correct."* Dennis Coates, "D.C. Stadium Déjà Vu," *Reason*, December 16, 2005.

3. Ball Barons

42. *"Anyone who quotes profits of a baseball club."* Andrew Zimbalist, *Baseball and Billions*, rev. ed. (New York: Basic Books, 1994), 62.

42. *"The revenues they rake in."* Michael K. Ozanian, "Value Investing, Sports Division," *Financial World*, May 20, 1996, 70.

42. *Topping the magazine's to-buy list.* A year later, Raleigh, North Carolina beat out Nashville, luring the Whalers with a $120 million publicly funded arena.

43. *"about the size of the pork and beans industry."* Charles C. Euchner, *Playing the Field: Why Sports Teams Move and Cities Fight to Keep Them* (Baltimore: Johns Hopkins University Press, 1993), 65.

43. *franchise values in every sport abruptly leaped upward.* James Quirk and Rodney Fort, *Pay Dirt* (Princeton NJ: Princeton University Press, 1992), 56-63.

44. *"It will take a club to go belly up."* Quirk and Fort, *Pay Dirt*, 209.

44. *"You don't make money operating a baseball club."* John Helyar, *Lords of the Realm* (New York: Ballantine Books, 1994), 249.

45. *It's less well known that he also devised a plan.* Bill Veeck, *Veeck as in Wreck* (New York: Ballantine, 1976), 173–78.

47. *Team owners who have their own television stations.* Zimbalist, *Baseball and Billions*, 65.

47. *The list of fiscal shenanigans.* Zimbalist, *Baseball and Billions*, 65, 215.

47. *When Roger Noll was hired.* Helyar, *Lords of the Realm*, 347.

47. *"The balance sheet and the income statement."* Quirk and Fort, *Pay Dirt*, 97.

52. *"In other words," Moynihan would later explain.* Daniel Patrick Moynihan, *Congressional Record*, January 21, 1997.

54. *"We thought as an incentive."* Jeff Wilkinson, "Marketing Guru Upbeat over Seat Applications," *Nashville Banner*, January 1, 1996.

55. *"It has been unfairly reported."* *Nashville Banner*, January 1, 1996.

57. *When the owners of the New York Knicks and Rangers.* Robert Hennelly, "Field of Schemes," *Village Voice*, October 5, 1993.

58. *The "privately built" Fleet Center.* Celeste Hadrick, "Arena Face-Off,"

Newsday, August 21, 1996; Robert Fresca, "Teams Play Hardball," *Newsday*, August 21, 1996.

60. *Total subsidy: $1.07 billion over 30 years.* Because some of the expenditures will be deferred many years, this amounts to roughly $525 million in current dollars.

61. *"about as believable as Enron's September 2001 financial statements."* Doug Pappas, "The Numbers (Part Five): National and Other Local Expenses," *Baseball Prospectus*, January 24, 2002.

61. *Researcher Judith Grant Long has more recently estimated.* Judith Grant Long, "Full Count: The Real Cost of Public Funding for Major League Sports Facilities," *Journal of Sports Economics* (May 2005): 119–43.

61. *The city of San Diego ended up paying the team $36.4 million.* Ronald W. Powell, "City oks New Stadium Lease with Chargers," *San Diego Union-Tribune*, July 13, 2004.

4. The Art of the Steal

62. *"The subsidy they get is totally disproportionate."* John Riley, "Where the Grass Is Always . . . Greener: An $8.1B Building Boom in Pro-Team Stadiums: How Public Money Is Fueling Private Fortunes," *Newsday*, August 18, 1996.

62. *"The result [of not using public funds]."* John Williams, "Users to Pay a Majority of Stadium Costs," *Houston Chronicle*, October 20, 1996.

63. *Lanier commissioned a study.* Riley, "Where the Grass Is Always . . . Greener."

65. *The owners also may have decided.* Michael Betzold and Ethan Casey, *Queen of Diamonds* (West Bloomfield mi: Altwerger & Mandel, 1992), 137–39.

66. *"There is something about a dome."* Paul Attner, "For Many Cities, There's No Place Like a Dome," *Washington Post*, June 8, 1984.

66. *Old Metropolitan Stadium.* Like Comiskey, Metropolitan Stadium for years had been undermaintained; one account called it "the most poorly maintained park in the Majors," where broken railings created a safety hazard in 1981, just before the Twins moved into the Metrodome. See www.ballparks.com.

67. *calling the boxes "spartan" and "claustrophobic."* Christopher Lopez and Jeffrey A. Roberts, "Are New Arenas Worth It? Broncos, Nuggets Are Going on Offensive for New Digs," *Denver Post*, August 14, 1994. As of mid-1997, the Nuggets and their cotenants, the Colorado Avalanche hockey franchise, were awaiting word on their proposed multimillion-dollar publicly financed Pepsi Center.

67. *Next door to the Nuggets.* Stuart Steers, "Bowlen for Dollars," *Denver Westword*, December 20, 1995.

67. *"This is a serious, serious question."* Lopez and Roberts, "Are New Arenas Worth It?"

67. *the stadium could "last indefinitely."* Steers, "Bowlen for Dollars."

67. *The new stadium should be a "35,000-to-37,000-seat park."* John Pastier, "Diamonds in the Rough," *Slate*, July 31, 1996.

68. *"And, with those three little words."* Kevin Mulligan, "Lurie: Birds Staying at Least in the Area," *Philadelphia Daily News*, July 23, 1996.

68. *"I almost shit when I read it."* Phillip Matier and Andrew Ross, "Chastened 49ers Own Up to Unsportsmanlike Conduct," *San Francisco Chronicle*, February 12, 1997.

69. *The undisputed master of the non-threat threat.* Steinbrenner's lawyer in the campaign contribution case: future Orioles owner Edward Bennett Williams. Ed Linn, *Steinbrenner's Yankees* (New York: Holt, Rinehart and Winston, 1982), 48.

70. *"We want to do all we can to first keep a team in Houston."* John Williams, "Baseball Officials Want Houston to Hurry Stadium Plans," *Houston Chronicle*, August 8, 1996.

70. *"if there isn't anything on the horizon."* Jay Weiner, "Bud Selig Addresses Minnesota Legislature on Stadium," *Minneapolis Star Tribune*, May 1, 1997.

70. *"No one is anxious to leave Fenway Park."* Associated Press, May 6, 1997.

71. *The Houston Astros successfully threatened a move.* Alan Truex, "Threat of Astros Moving to Virginia Remains Alive," *Houston Chronicle*, June 19, 1996.

71. *Major League Baseball granted Tampa Bay.* So named because an enter-

prising local registered a trademark to the preferred name, the Stingrays, and refused to let it go for less than a small fortune.

72. *"If you're an owner and thinking, 'What are my options?'"* Jay Weiner, "Few Cities Either Ready or Willing to Adopt Twins," *Minneapolis Star Tribune*, May 12, 1997.

73. *"The economics of professional sports today."* Bill Steigerwald, "Phoenix's Diamond in the Sun," *Pittsburgh Post-Gazette*, June 12, 1997.

74. *the stadium-hungry Astros released an audit.* John Williams, "Astros Debt List Is Huge," *Houston Chronicle*, August 15, 1996.

74. *it's far too easy for a rich team. Financial World*, June 17, 1997.

76. *the project would result in fourteen hundred new jobs and $123 million.* Donald L. Henry, "On the Move," *Business Facilities*, April 1996.

76. *Two separate economic-impact studies.* Edward Epstein and John King, "49ers' Deal Raises Doubts," *San Francisco Chronicle*, February 8, 1997; John King, "Controller's Message to Voters Boosts 49ers Stadium Measure," *San Francisco Chronicle*, March 20, 1997.

77. *"Mr. Collins has made it clear."* John Williams and Terry Blount, "Officials Pitch Idea of Ticket Drive to Save Astros," *Houston Chronicle*, October 20, 1995.

79. *the Ontario public had taken a $262.7 million bath.* For the complete SkyDome saga, see Neil deMause, "Can a Ballpark Figure?" *This*, March/April 1999. See also Mark Rosentraub, *Major League Losers: The Real Cost of Sports and Who's Paying for Them* (New York: Basic Books, 1997), 321, and Betzold and Casey, *Queen of Diamonds*, 214, 242–43.

80. *"one of the fanciest pieces of parliamentary maneuvering."* David Brauer, "Let the Stadium Wars Begin," *Citypages*, April 1996.

80. *Although $40 million would come from the sale of stadium naming rights.* Jonathan D. Silver, "Bombshell Provided New Stadium for Brewers," *Pittsburgh Post-Gazette*, June 2, 1997.

81. *"This does not mean taking one cent more."* Kenneth R. Lamke and Amy Rinard, "Stadium Funding Plan Revived," *Milwaukee Journal Sentinel*, June 10, 1996.

81. *In the end, Selig would be responsible only for.* Kenneth R. Lamke, "As Deals Go, Brewers' Is in Middle," *Milwaukee Journal Sentinel*, August 12, 1996.

81. *And because the state also agreed.* Brauer, "Let the Stadium Wars Begin." In November 1997 the stadium cost estimate was revised upward by an additional $50 million, leaving the state still further in the hole. Jim Chilsen, "Brewers park may cost $50 million more," Associated Press, November 13, 1997.

82. *"Good morning, madam. You have five minutes to do what I say."* Stephanie Salter, "The 49ers Need a New Game Plan," *San Francisco Examiner,* June 1, 1997.

5. Deus Ex Pizza

83. *"I have little patience with people."* Paul Ferrante, "Save Our Stadium!" *Sports Collectors Digest,* September 20, 1996.

84 *As they sat eating pizza.* The Tigers won, 2–1, with rookie catcher Matt Nokes breaking up the opposing team's no-hitter with a two-run single in the bottom of the ninth.

85. *But following the Tigers' 1968 championship.* Michael Betzold and Ethan Casey, *Queen of Diamonds* (West Bloomfield MI: Altwerger & Mandel, 1992), 109–10. Betzold and Casey's history of Tiger Stadium and the first five years of the Tiger Stadium Fan Club is easily the most comprehensive case study of a stadium scam to date and was invaluable in compiling this chapter.

88. *"I'll let them build a new stadium, then I'll cry."* Unobstructed Views: The Tiger Stadium Fan Club Newsletter, February 1988, 1.

88. *Monaghan was telling local politicians.* Betzold and Casey, *Queen of Diamonds,* 126.

88. *"determine the costs of shoring up."* Betzold and Casey, *Queen of Diamonds,* 132.

88. *"Nobody in their wildest dreams expects."* Betzold and Casey, *Queen of Diamonds,* 134.

89. *Instead, HOK proposed a 56,000-seat stadium.* Betzold and Casey, *Queen of Diamonds,* 149–50.

89. *"Should public money be used."* Unobstructed Views, Summer 1988, 1.

90. *When completed in January 1990, the Cochrane Plan.* Betzold and Casey, *Queen of Diamonds,* 154.

91. *Tiger Stadium, which to fit the most seats.* John Pastier, "Diamonds in the Rough," *Slate*, July 31, 1996.

92. *"We were telling people at [the Fan Club] meeting."* Betzold and Casey, *Queen of Diamonds*, 154.

92. *"Yeah, I mentioned it to him."* Betzold and Casey, *Queen of Diamonds*, 155.

92. *Meanwhile, accolades poured in.* Betzold and Casey, *Queen of Diamonds*, 157.

93. *"I'd rather have the old stadium."* Betzold and Casey, *Queen of Diamonds*, 157.

93. *"It's unfair for you to think."* Betzold and Casey, *Queen of Diamonds*, 209–10.

93. *"about to fall down."* Betzold and Casey, *Queen of Diamonds*, 145.

95. *he would augment its modest $20 million in cash reserves. Unobstructed Views*, November 1995, 1.

96. *"not state funds."* Associated Press, March 22, 1996.

96. *The Fan Club raised about $20,000.* Valarie Basheda, Shawn Lewis, and Phil Linsalata, "Voters Like Pitch, OK Stadium Funding," *Detroit News*, March 20, 1996.

96. *One survey found that just 4.8 percent.* Jeffrey Chadiha, "Baseball Struggles to Get Minorities Interested Again," *San Francisco Examiner*, June 15, 1997.

97. *"They want us to renovate the old Tiger Stadium."* V. Lonnie Peek Jr., "Stadium Support Strengthens," *Michigan Chronicle*, February 14–20, 1996.

97. *Down the street a ways sits the Fox Theater.* Tom Henderson, "Chuck Forbes: Mad as Hell but Forced to Take It," *Corporate Detroit*, January 1997. Moten later left city government and went to work for Little Caesar's.

102. *As of 2006, the GM Poletown plant employed about 3,000. workers.* Brian McKenna, "We All Live in Poletown Now," *Counterpunch*, March 9, 2006.

6. Home Field Advantage

103. *"This is not about a very rich guy."* Bill Steigerwald, "Phoenix's Diamond in the Sun," *Pittsburgh Post-Gazette*, June 12, 1997.

105. *San Francisco Mayor Willie Brown declared.* Edward Epstein, "Brown Says 'Trust Me' On Stadium," *San Francisco Chronicle*, February 26, 1997.

105. *"He wasn't close to hysterical."* John Carman, "Radio Gets Mayor's Mouthful," *San Francisco Chronicle*, June 5, 1997.

106. *"It was beyond David vs. Goliath."* Carla Marinucci and Gregory Lewis, "Foes Say Team Spent $33 a Vote to Carpet Bomb City," *San Francisco Examiner*, June 4, 1997.

107. *To that end, Cross brought in.* Murphy also served on the presidential campaigns of George Bush in 1988 and 1992, and Bob Dole in 1996.

109. *"hunker down behind the public opinion polls."* Minneapolis Star Tribune editorial, June 6, 1997.

110. *The next day, the paper ran a front-page story.* Joanna Cagan and Neil deMause, "Root, Root, Root for the Home Team," *Extra!*, August 1996.

110. *"49ers drive toward goal as clock ticks down."* Eric Brazil, "49ers Drive toward Goal as Clock Ticks down," *San Francisco Examiner*, June 1, 1997.

110. *The day before the 49ers referendum.* Scott Ostler, "Brown Wins with His Jabbing," *San Francisco Chronicle*, June 2, 1997.

110. *"Sports editors and writers freely acknowledge."* Beth Hawkins, "Home Field Advantage," *Minneapolis City Pages*, April 2, 1997.

111. *The most egregious example of media self-interest.* Hawkins, "Home Field Advantage."

111. *The* Seattle Times *went so far.* Michael Francher, *Seattle Times*, September 24, 1995.

112. *One of the most insightful looks into the inner workings.* All quotes in this section from California Newsreel's *Fear and Favor in the Newsroom*, 1997.

114. *"The Civic Power Brokers No One Elected."* O. Casey Carr, "The Civic Power Brokers No One Elected," *Seattle Times*, April 2, 1997.

114. *"the king of bondsmakers in Washington State."* Seattle Times, April 2, 1997.

114. *"These guys take council members and 'educate' them."* Seattle Times, April 2, 1997.

115. *The biggest spender of all.* David Schaefer and David Postman, "Stadium Measure Is Passing," *Seattle Times*, June 18, 1997.

117. *"I don't think it was any secret in the Tampa Tribune newsroom."* Neil deMause, "Throwing the Game," *Extra!*, November 1999.

117. *"even [Tiger Stadium's] supporters acknowledge it had to be replaced."* Larry Lage, "Price of Progress," Associated Press, July 10, 2005.

7. Local Heroes

120. *By the mid-1980s, the relatively new owners of the White Sox.* Charles C. Euchner, *Playing the Field: Why Sports Teams Move and Cities Fight to Keep Them* (Baltimore: Johns Hopkins University Press, 1993), 133–59.

123. *"suggest the windows of a church."* Doug Bukowski, *Baseball Palace of the World* (Chicago: Lyceum, 1992), 12.

123. *"One man stood up in a room full of strangers."* Bukowski, *Baseball Palace*, 9.

124. *"Should all of Chicago . . . be in the style of the Loop . . ."* Douglas Bukowski, Mary O'Connell, and John Aranza, "Comiskey Park: A Landmark Proposal," Save Our Sox, Chicago, Illinois, 1987, 16.

124. *At its peak, the group was able to generate.* Bukowski, *Baseball Palace*, 86.

125. *"The ailing mid-South Side."* Bukowski, *Baseball Palace*, 18.

125. *"The value of a professional sports team."* Bukowski, *Baseball Palace*, 4.

126. *The owners of the White Sox had initially hoped to pull their team.* Euchner, *Playing the Field*, 133–59. Euchner cites a market study the new owners had done in the early 1980s, which urged the team to develop a strong suburban fan base; he also looks to the television broadcasting wars with the North Side Cubs and the general trend in the '70s and '80s to locate key parts of Chicago industry away from the inner city and in the area's growing suburban sprawl.

126. *The state would supposedly receive $100 million.* Bukowski, *Baseball Palace*, 4.

126. *But White Sox management ran into strident opposition in Addison.* Bukowski, *Baseball Palace*, 4.

126. *As location after profitable location proved unworkable.* Bukowski, *Baseball Palace*, 4.

127. *Hallie Amey and many other residents.* Bukowski, *Baseball Palace*, 4.

129. *In the end the neighborhood coalition.* John J. Betancur, Michael Leachman, Anne Miller, David Walker, and Patricia A. Wright, "Development Without Displacement," Task Force Background Paper, The Chicago Rehab Network, The Nathalie P. Voorhees Center for Neighborhood and Community Improvement, June 1995. Euchner, *Playing the Field*, 154.

129. *Those residents who stayed filed a class action suit.* Euchner, *Playing the Field*, 154.

130. *Anxious city officials actually flew White Sox executives.* Kenneth L. Shropshire, *The Sports Franchise Game* (Philadelphia: University of Pennsylvania Press, 1995), 11.

131. *"It'll never happen unless people think you are going to leave."* Unobstructed Views, May 1995, 4.

131. *Designed by the rising architecture firm of* HOK. Philip J. Lowry, *Green Cathedrals* (Reading MA: Addison-Wesley, 1992), 49–50.

132. *In a midnight session on June 30, 1988.* Andrew Zimbalist, *Baseball and Billions* (New York: Basic Books, 1992), 129.

132. *In fact, it was an after-midnight session.* John Helyar, *Lords of the Realm* (New York: Ballantine, 1994), 483.

133. *"With the dawn of this new era."* Bukowski, *Baseball Palace*, 17.

135. *"We now know, though certain suits will never admit it."* John McCarron, "Opening Day Blues Go Back to the Days When Baseball Parks Were Baseball Parks," *Chicago Tribune*, April 13, 1998.

8. Bad Neighbors

136. *"To speak logically about the effects."* Philip Bess, "Urban Ballparks and the Future of Cities," *Real Estate Issues*, December 1996.

136. *"The pride and the presence of a professional football team."* Leonard Pitts Jr., "a professional football team is far more important than 30 libraries," *Baltimore Sun*, August 30, 1996.

138. *"For thirty years."* Philip Bess, "City Baseball Magic," *Minneapolis Review of Baseball*, 1989, 25.

139. *Ebbets Field was located in a bustling Brooklyn community.* James Tack-

ach and Joshua B. Stein, *The Fields of Summer* (New York: Crescent, 1992), 67.

139. *The Polo Grounds in Manhattan.* Philip J. Lowry, *Green Cathedrals* (Reading MA: Addison-Wesley, 1992), 11, 191.

141. *In upper deck seats in SkyDome in Toronto.* Lowry, *Green Cathedrals*, 4.

141. *Even the sterile '60s stadiums.* Lowry, *Green Cathedrals*, 4.

142. *This tremendous increase in sheer bulk.* James Quirk and Rodney Fort, *Pay Dirt* (Princeton NJ: Princeton University Press, 1992), 162.

146. *The proposed stadium and adjacent public park.* Charles C. Euchner, *Playing the Field* (Baltimore: Johns Hopkins University Press, 1993), 156–57.

150. *"Disneyland is quintessentially."* M. Christine Boyer, "Cities for Sale: Merchandising History at South Street Seaport," in *Variations on a Theme Park,* ed. Michael Sorkin, (New York: Hill & Wang, 1992), 181–204.

151. *"What Celebration was promising."* Russ Rymer, "Back to the Future," *Harper's,* October 1996.

151. *"What Celebration celebrates, oddly."* Rymer, "Back to the Future."

153. *In fact, a poll by the* Minneapolis Star Tribune. Robert Whereatt, "Public Unmoved by Twins' Proposal," *Minneapolis Star Tribune,* January 26, 1997.

153. *"The result is what has been termed the* dual city." W. Dennis Keating, "Cleveland: The Comeback City," Mickey Lauria, ed., *Reconstructing Urban Regime Theory: Regulating Urban Politics in a Global Economy* (Thousand Oaks CA: Sage, 1997), 192.

153. *Using numbers from the Cuyahoga County Auditor.* "How Much Does It Really Cost," *Critique,* February 1997.

154. *A study conducted by the senate's Economic Development Committee.* Tamar Lewin, "Seeking to Shield Schools from Tax Breaks," *New York Times,* May 21, 1997.

156. *The formula is simple.* There are numerous excellent studies on the policy of structural adjustment and its impact on the developing world. Among them, see Osvaldo Sunkel, "Economic reform and democratic viability" in *The Consolidation of Democracy in Latin America,* ed. Joseph S. Tulchin (Boulder: Lynne Rienner, 1995). He suggests that Latin American democratization is going to be undermined by neoliberal economic re-

form. Also, Isabella Bakker, ed., *The Strategic Silence: Gender and Economic Policy* (London: Zed, 1994). And Kerianne Piester, "Targeting the Poor: The Politics of Social Policy Reforms in Mexico" in *The New Politics of Inequality in Latin America: Rethinking Participation and Representation*, ed. Douglas A. Chalmers, Carlos M. Vilas, Katherine Hite, Scott B. Martin, Kerianne Piester, and Monique Segarra (Oxford: Oxford University Press, 1997).

157. *"Gateway does not represent something new."* Steve Cagan, "Our Stadium," WCPN-FM commentary, May 6, 1997.

9. Repeat Offenders

160. *"Sports is a way of life, like eating."* Robert Whereatt, "Public Unmoved by Twins' Proposal," *Minneapolis Star Tribune*, January 26, 1997.

160. *Saddled with what he claimed were insurmountable debts.* "Chronology: The Long Goodbye," *Seattle Times*, December 15, 1996.

161. *"Every time they put up a dike."* O. Casey Corr, "Ballpark's a Big Pain—and Proud of It," *Seattle Times*, April 2, 1997.

162. *"Recently, after more than three years of work."* "Last Out for Baseball in Seattle, Excerpts of Owners' Statement," *Seattle Times*, December 15, 1996.

163. *"Gorton helped persuade the owners to reconsider."* Ericy Pyrne and O. Casey Corr, "Seattle Holding Firm on Stadium Deal," *Seattle Times*, December 25, 1996.

163. *Under the terms of the new deal. Seattle Times*, December 25, 1996.

164. *By February 1997, Washington Governor Gary Locke.* "Locke: Let State Vote on Stadium Funding Tax Aimed at Aiding Hawks," *Seattle Times*, February 21, 1997.

165. *"I just don't recall ever seeing someone pick up a total tab."* Carey Goldberg, "Billionaire Finances a Vote about Replacing a Stadium," *New York Times*, May 25, 1997.

167. *Wolfenson and Ratner, as part of the deal.* Robert Fresco, "Teams Play Hardball," *Newsday*, August 21, 1996.

167. *The seven-year-old Target Center.* Jay Weiner, "Lessons learned from Target Center," *Minneapolis Star Tribune*, May 7, 1997.

168. *The state responded by passing the Minnesota Corporate Welfare Reform Law.* Janice Shields, "Ending (Corporate) Welfare as We Know It," *Business and Society Review,* Summer 1995.

168. *Pohlad, the billionaire head of a banking empire.* Chris Ison and Paul McEnroe, "Dealing with Carl Pohlad," *Minneapolis Star Tribune,* April 20, 1997.

169. *Proclaiming himself the state's "number one fan."* Jay Weiner, "State's First Fan Talks about Sports and a New Stadium," *Minneapolis Star Tribune,* December 1, 1996.

170. *"Never has the owner of a football or baseball team."* Beth Hawkins, "Home Field Advantage," *Minneapolis City Pages,* April 2, 1997.

170. *On January 26 the first polls came in.* Whereatt, "Public Unmoved by Twins' Proposal."

171. *"it's not unlike when you want to pass the victim's rights bill."* Robert Whereatt, "Twins Legends Make Pitch for Ballpark," *Minneapolis Star Tribune,* March 11, 1997.

171. *"If I invest two thirds of the money."* Jay Weiner, "Citizen Panel Says 'No' to Funding New Twins Stadium," *Minneapolis Star Tribune,* January 23, 1997.

171. *"If ever someone gets around to writing a brochure."* Robert Whereatt, "The Rise (and Fall) of the Twins Ballpark Bill," *Minneapolis Star Tribune,* March 10, 1997.

172. *"The financing of the thing is too screwy."* Michael T. Johnson, post to www.startribune.com, November 10, 1997.

173. *"On November 13, professional baseball died in Minnesota."* Conrad deFiebre, Jay Weiner, Robert Whereatt, and Dane Smith, "Out at Home: Legislators Vote Down 'Final' Stadium Plan," *Minneapolis Star Tribune,* November 14, 1997.

173. *"Everybody says it's dead."* deFiebre, "Out at Home."

173. *"Ten years, five mayors."* John Yewell, "Build It Yourself, Carl," *Twin Cities Reader,* March 5–11, 1997. The Giants chronology that follows is drawn largely from Yewell's article.

176. *"Given the fact that there are many cities."* Phillip Matier and Andrew Ross, "Public Opposes Paying for 49er Stadium," *San Francisco Chronicle,* October 28, 1996.

177. *"For every $4.25 that the 49ers put on the table."* Susan Yoachum and Edward Epstein, "Stadium Poll Holds Lessons For 49ers," *San Francisco Chronicle,* March 11, 1997.

177. *The first member of the public.* Edward Epstein and John King, "49ers' Deal Raises Doubts," *San Francisco Chronicle,* February 8, 1997.

177. *City controller Ed Harrington promptly issued.* John King, "Controller's Message to Voters Boosts 49ers Stadium Measure," *San Francisco Chronicle,* March 20, 1997.

178. *"Opponents call it 'Candlestick Pork.'"* Edward Epstein, "Ballot Satirists Hauled Into Court," *San Francisco Chronicle,* April 2, 1997.

178. *"Once the mayor gets into the posture."* Edward Epstein, "49ers Want Taxpayers to Help Carry the Ball for New Stadium," *San Francisco Chronicle,* September 10, 1996.

179. *"combining [an indigenous culture] with some kind of cheap horror movie."* Michael Dougan and Julie Chao, "Raunchy 'Ritual,'" *San Francisco Examiner,* May 8, 1997.

179. *"Candlestick is almost to the point."* Joan Ryan, "49ers Woo Women's Vote With Wine, Words—and Steve Young," *San Francisco Chronicle,* May 16, 1997.

179. *"Threatening to go to Los Angeles is like."* Rob Morse, "49ers 90210? Like, I'm So Sure," *San Francisco Examiner,* May 22, 1997.

180. *City employees, it was further revealed.* Michael Howerton, "Winning Ugly: How Willie Brown Used City Employees to Win the 49ers Stadium–Mall," *San Francisco Bay Guardian,* June 11, 1997.

180. *After spending more than $2 million.* Carla Marinucci and Gregory Lewis, "Foes Say Team Spent $33 a Vote to Carpet Bomb City," *San Francisco Examiner,* June 4, 1997; Eric Brazil, "Funding the Stadium Fight," *San Francisco Examiner,* May 23, 1997.

180. *"The guy upstairs must really have wanted."* Gwen Knapp, "In the End, Sentiment Led to 'Ugly' Win," *San Francisco Examiner,* June 4, 1997.

180. *In June 1997* Your Money *magazine.* Deborah A. Rogus, "America's Sports Stadiums: How Much Do They Really Cost You?" *Your Money,* June / July 1997.

181. *"If you go into building a new stadium."* Jay Weiner, "Is the Dome Doomed?" *Minneapolis Star Tribune,* April 28, 1997.

181. *"Seattle will now be relegated to a second-tier status."* Stuart Eskenazi, "Voters Support Restriction on Arena Financing," *Seattle Times*, November 7, 2006.

10. The Bucks Stop Here

182. *"The loyal rooters never doubted."* Bill Veeck, *The Hustler's Handbook* (New York: G. P. Putnam's Sons, 1965), 305.

185. *"lobbied to death by the NFL's hired guns."* Jason Vest, "Uproot for the Home Team," *U.S. News and World Report*, March 10, 1997.

186. *In 1997 Minnesota representative David Minge.* Mike Meyers, "Minge Bill Puts Subsidy Debate on National Agenda," *Minneapolis Star Tribune*, December 3, 1997.

188. *The team now has 1,915 stockholders.* Johnette Howard, "Frozen in Time," *Sports Illustrated*, January 13, 1997.

189. *"I don't think the institutionals will touch this."* Larry Lebowitz, "Investors Go for Panthers Shares; Analysts Warn of Potential Losses," *Fort Lauderdale Sun-Sentinel*, November 14, 1996.

189. *"If the pattern of previous publicly traded teams."* Ed Fowler, "Franchise Owners Too Rich for Their Own Good," *Houston Chronicle*, September 29, 1996.

189. *The Celtics, which became the first team.* Ed Fowler, "Franchise Owners Too Rich."

189. *But that initial offering also gave.* Joanna Cagan and Neil deMause, "Buy the Bums Out," *In These Times*, December 9, 1996.

189. *"essentially creating a partnership."* "Twins Announce Plans for New Outdoor Ballpark," January 8, 1997, Minnesota Twins Team News, Minnesota Twins / Major League Baseball Web site.

190. *The California Supreme Court rejected the case.* Cagan and deMause, "Buy the Bums Out."

190. *When Joan Kroc inherited ownership.* Barry Lorge, "Kroc Wanted to Give Padres to City; Owners' Committee Thwarted Philanthropic 1989 Offer," *San Diego Union-Tribune*, July 29, 1990.

190. *It seemed too good to be true.* Lorge, "Kroc Wanted to Give Padres to City."

191. *"If the city owned it."* Lorge, "Kroc Wanted to Give Padres to City."

191. *and in Montreal, where the Expos ownership.* Kenneth L. Shropshire, *The Sports Franchise Game* (Philadelphia: University of Pennsylvania Press, 1995), 62.

191. *no right-thinking for-profit owner.* Major league owners did vote, in September 1997, to allow for public stock offerings in professional baseball teams, but the gesture seems likely to be as ultimately meaningless as it is in the other major sports.

191. *"baseball should be a partnership among owners."* Ross Atkin, "Move Over Major Leaguers, Here Comes the UBL," *Christian Science Monitor*, September 29, 1995.

11. Winning Isn't Everything

196. *"I too never forgot that story."* Leo Rosten, *Captain Newman, M.D.* (New York: Harper & Row, 1961), 331.

12. One Year

198. *"Buying the team, instead of building a stadium."* Scott Stringer press release, December 6, 1998.

198. *"Scott Stringer's proposal is a concept."* Bill Egbert, with Maureen Fan, "Pol Wants City to Take a Swing at Owning Yanks," *Daily News*, December 7, 1998.

198. *"If we don't have a downtown ballpark."* www.fieldofschemes.com/ news.

199. *At 2 p.m. on April 13.* Joe Gergen, "Coming Apart at the Seams," *Newsday*, April 14, 1998, A71.

199. *"The traffic and the parking are horrendous."* Dan Barry, "On Opening Day, Uncertainty about Yankee Stadium," *New York Times*, April 11, 1998.

199. *"unavailable for comment because."* Randy Kennedy, "Suspicious New Yorkers Cultivate Steinbrenner Conspiracy Theories," *New York Times*, April 16, 1998.

200. *The morning after the beam incident.* Grant McCool, "Yankee Stadium Future in Doubt after Collapse," Reuters, April 14, 1998.

200. *"From a structural perspective."* David Seifman, "Ruth Built House to Last," *New York Post*, April 20, 1998, 6.

200. *Giuliani announced that a Manhattan ballpark.* Seifman, "Ruth Built House to Last," 6.

200. *"thousands and thousands and thousands of jobs."* Dan Barry, "City Study Sees Big Revenues If Yankees Play in Manhattan," *New York Times*, April 22, 1998, B1; Robert Hardt Jr., "Yanks' Move to W. Side All Add$ Up, Says City Hall," *New York Post*, April 22, 1998, 4.

200. *The next morning, the* New York Times *revealed.* Charles V. Bagli, "'96 Stadium Study Found Fewer Benefits," *New York Times*, April 23, 1998, B3.

201. *Giuliani declared that he had successfully scared her off.* Frank Lombardi and Luke Cyphers, "Rudy: I Win Yankee Fight," *Daily News*, April 29, 1998.

201. *"I would like New York to have."* Robert Hardt Jr., "Box-Office Bombers?" *New York Post*, May 7, 1998, 3.

201. *even New Jersey residents wanted.* "Poll in New Jersey: Yankees, Stay Put," Associated Press, April 23, 1998.

201. *"If you build a new stadium."* Ray Sánchez and Pete Bowles, "Home Sweet Home," *Newsday*, April 25, 1998, A3.

202. *"I bet if we were playing in Baltimore."* Sánchez and Bowles, "Home Sweet Home," A3.

202. *especially in a city whose schools were literally falling down.* Several critics noted that part of a school in Queens had partially collapsed the same week as the beam incident at Yankee Stadium, forcing the school's closure in an already overcrowded district.

202. *"one of the most fantastic stadiums."* Luke Cyphers, "Double Play for Shea," *Daily News*, April 4, 1998, 5.

203. *"definitely would contribute an unspecified amount."* Bill Madden and Douglas Feiden, "Rudy, Yanks' West Side Story," *Daily News*, April 19, 1998, 5.

203. *the number-one tourist attraction in the entire state.* Save Fenway Park, *Save Fenway Park: An Economic and Planning Analysis*, March 1999.

203. *Though ranked among the top ten baseball teams.* Michael Ozanian, "Selective Accounting," *Forbes*, December 14, 1998.

204. *That city's $238 million collection.* Charolette Aiken and Randy Ellis, "Underestimate Led to Mistake in Ballpark Cost," *Oklahoman*, February 8, 1996.

205. *When Birmingham residents were polled. Birmingham News*, November 16, 1997.

205. *"if we would have voted on that piece by piece."* Steve Lackmeyer and Jack Money, "MAPS Tax Supported, Poll Shows," *Oklahoman*, November 6, 1997.

206. *"It's the voters who make the decisions."* Associated Press, "Alabama Voters Reject Stadium Proposal," August 6, 1998.

206. *"I do not believe the city should build an arena."* Kelley Shannon, "Spurs May Move to Privately Financed Arena," Associated Press, February 8, 1996.

207. *"I'll go out and tell people."* Mark Rosner, "Vote Probably Dooms Spurs' Plans for New Arena," *Austin American-Statesman*, December 15, 1998.

207. *"If you're going to move a team."* www.fieldofschemes.com/news.

208. *An initial plan for restaurant chains.* Scott Maxwell, "Anti-Tax Sentiment the Key," *Greensboro Journal*, May 7, 1998; Justin Catanoso, "Stadium Tax Campaign Loses Restaurant Chain's Support," *Greensboro News and Record*, February 18, 1998.

208. *Plans for a "bottle hanger" promotion.* Justin Catanoso, "Pepsi Won't Be Helping Distribute Information for the Triad Baseball Campaign, but It Still Supports the Effort," *Greensboro News and Record*, March 13, 1998.

208. *"The economics of baseball have gotten."* John A. Nagy, "Commissioners Ask for Rejection of Ball Plan," *Greensboro News and Record*, April 24, 1998.

208. *In the end, Vote Yes.* Lenox Rawlings, "Thumbed Tax," *Greensboro Journal*, May 7, 1998.

208. *In voting more than twice as heavy.* "Tuesday's Vote," *Greensboro Journal*, May 7, 1998.

208. *"The [Winston-Salem] Warthogs."* Rawlings, "Thumbed Tax."

209. *"a victory not only for taxpayers."* Scott Maxwell, "Anti-Tax Sentiment the Key," *Greensboro Journal*, May 7, 1998.

209. *Thirteen days later, the city of Charlotte.* Justin Catanoso, "Charlotte Sized Up Its Appetite for Major League Baseball," *Minneapolis Star Tribune*, May 19, 1998; Jay Weiner, "Charlotte's Next in Line as Twins Home," *Minneapolis Star Tribune*, May 18, 1998.

209. *"It's not a grant."* John Baer, "It's a Go!" *Philadelphia Daily News*, February 4, 1999.

210. *The difference would affect the team's annual rent payment.* Philip J. LaVelle, "City Finds Consolation on Tickets," *San Diego Union-Tribune*, December 25, 1998.

210. *Houston software tycoon John Moores.* Philip J. LaVelle, "Padres Release Ballpark Terms in Public Pitch," *San Diego Union-Tribune*, June 28, 1998.

211. *Included in the $115 million, for example.* Philip J. LaVelle, "Ballpark Approved Decisively," *San Diego Union-Tribune*, November 4, 1998.

211. *"Why should San Diego give $275 million."* Don Bauder, "New Studies Fail to Make the Case for a Ballpark," *San Diego Union-Tribune*, October 15, 1998.

211. *"You don't want to be, five years from now."* Gerry Braun, "Padres Start Ballpark Drive with Rally," *San Diego Union-Tribune*, August 16, 1998.

211. *"If we don't build it."* Nick Canepa, "If We Don't Build It, Padres Will Be Gone," *San Diego Union-Tribune*, August 1, 1998.

211. *"Time running out."* Gerry Braun and Philip J. LaVelle, "All-Night Talks Fail to Sew Up Ballpark Deal; Time Running Out for Mayor, Padres," *San Diego Union-Tribune*, July 31, 1998.

212. *Standard & Poor's, the Wall Street rating agency.* Philip J. LaVelle, "Credit Agency Cautious over Ballpark Debt," *San Diego Union-Tribune*, August 29, 1998.

213. *"We're getting a chance."* Philip J. LaVelle, "Ballpark Approved Decisively," *San Diego Union-Tribune*, November 4, 1998.

213. *A Moores-controlled company. San Diego Reader*, May 6, 1999.

213. *"How do you think the players."* Chris Jenkins, "Vaughn Traded," *San Diego Union-Tribune*, February 3, 1999.

214. *But in 1987, reportedly in need of quick cash.* Jenkins, "Vaughn Traded."

214. *"What I say is, the tax is minimal."* Stuart Seers, "Bowlen for Dollars; Denver's Favorite Canadian Millionaire Wants a Stadium Subsidy. Here's What He Won't Tell You about It," *Denver Westword*, December 20, 1995.

214. *With no apparent irony.* Julia C. Martinez, "City Reaches Stadium Pact," *Denver Post*, August 27, 1998.

215. *"Someone has to take care of our visiting dignitaries."* Peggy Lowe, "Board Gets Own Luxury Box," *Denver Post*, September 5, 1998.

215. *"Incredibly, while our negotiators."* COST press release, September 4, 1998.

215. *filing a federal complaint against Jacor Broadcasting.* Peggy Lowe, "Stadium Foes Blast Radio Chain," *Denver Post*, August 4, 1998.

215. *Pollsters estimated that the team's undefeated record.* Peggy Lowe and Julia C. Martinez, "Voters Agree to Back New Broncos Stadium," *Denver Post*, November 4, 1998.

215. *Bowlen contributed $1.98 million of his own money.* Peggy Lowe, "Bowlen Is Biggest Donor," *Denver Post*, December 2, 1998.

216. *As a result, SkyDome opened with a $300 million mortgage.* Tony Van Alphen, "Skydome 'In Trouble' NDP Finds," *Toronto Star*, October 11, 1990.

216. *Realizing it had been stuck with a fiscal lemon.* Neil deMause, "Can a Ballpark Figure?" *This*, March/April 1999.

217. *"riding a bicycle after driving a Mercedes."* Jim Byers and Geoff Baker, "Debate Rages over the Jays' Move Threat," *Toronto Star*, November 1, 1998.

218. *"the second shot heard round the world."* New York City Independent Budget Office, "Double Play: The Economics and Financing of Stadiums for the Yankees and Mets," April 1998, 17.

219. *An investigation by the New Haven Advocate's Carole Bass revealed.* Carole Bass, "Pigskin Pork," *New Haven Advocate*, December 4, 1998.

220. *A Connecticut Office of Fiscal Analysis study reported.* Stephen Ohlemacher and Dan Haar, "Taxpayers' Bill: $257 Million?" *Hartford Courant*, December 10, 1998.

220. *"For the first time today."* "Pats' Price Shrinks," Associated Press, December 14, 1998.

221. *"Our goal has always been to play."* Greg Garber, "Kraft's Decision Was a Business Decision," *Hartford Courant*, May 1, 1999.

221. *"My goal and the Patriots' goal."* Mike Swift and Greg Garber, "Kraft, Rowland Reassure State Deal Is Still Alive," *Hartford Courant*, April 30, 1999.

222. *"That's bankable money the team could count on."* Meg Vaillancourt, "Patriots Sack Hartford Stadium Deal," *Boston Globe*, May 1, 1999.

222. *several new economic studies had confirmed the findings.* Among those issuing new economic reports: North Carolina State professor Michael Walden (see Michael Walden, "Don't Play Ball," *Carolina Journal*, October/November 1997); University of California–Berkeley graduate student Jack Sylvan (see Charles Burress, "Cities' Economies Not Helped by Sports Teams, Study Says," *San Francisco Chronicle*, August 24, 1998); and the studies contained in Roger G. Noll and Andrew Zimbalist, eds., *Sports, Jobs, and Taxes: The Economic Impact of Sports Teams and Stadiums* (Washington DC: Brookings Institution Press, 1997).

223. *When the city of Phoenix attempted.* John Rofé, "D-Backs Equal Greenbacks," *Sports Business Journal*, August 24-30, 1998.

13. The Art of the Steal Revisited

225. *"We don't want a new building."* Neil deMause, "Cough It Up, Rich!" *Orlando Weekly*, May 3, 2001.

225. *"If I set you up in a business."* deMause, "Cough It Up, Rich!"

226. *An inattentive* Beijing Evening News *editor.* Henry Chu, "U.S. Satire Tricks Beijing Paper," *Los Angeles Times*, June 8, 2002.

226. *"some small American newspapers frequently fabricate offbeat news."* Daniel Terdiman, "*Onion* Taken Seriously, Film at 11," Wired.com, April 14, 2004. Retorted *Onion* editor Carol Kolb: "That's what we do at the *Onion*. We do print lies to make money."

226. *Popular opposition to stadium deals has mounted.* Neil deMause, "How to Win Friends and Influence Voters," SportsJones.com, November 15, 2000. By election day in 2000, teams like the Houston Rockets and Arizona Cardinals were routinely spending more than $1.5 million on pro-funding referendum campaigns, outpacing the opposition by a greater than 100-to-1 margin.

229. *Toronto Blue Jays general manager J. P. Ricciardi declared.* Dave Perkins, "Dome Is No Longer Home Sweet Home," *Toronto Star*, May 20, 2004.

230. *"Some of it is just ego."* An edited version of this quote appeared in deMause, "Cough It Up, Rich!"

230. *"I don't see anything wrong, from an owner's perspective."* An edited version of this quote appeared in deMause, "Cough It Up, Rich!"

230. *"We're not a threatening type of ownership."* Brian Schmitz, "If Magic Must Move, Devos Will Give Up Game," *Orlando Sentinel*, October 12, 2004.

231. *"We want to stay in Seattle."* Chris McGann, "NBA Chief Backs Sonics' Arena Plea," *Seattle Post-Intelligencer*, February 24, 2006.

231. *"It's got me real nervous."* Jeffrey Spivak and Benita Y. Williams, "Chiefs Raise Specter of Moving Team," *Kansas City Star*, May 21, 2005.

231. *"We try to get our ownership not to talk."* Jay Weiner, "Vikings Officials Feel Handicapped by Lease," *Minneapolis Star Tribune*, July 20, 2003.

231. *Carter wrote that although Jones "should pay totally for any stadium."* O. K. Carter, "3 Questions about Cowboys Stadium," *Fort Worth Star-Telegram*, August 5, 2004.

231. *"simply can't use the old 'give us a new stadium or we'll leave.'"* O. K. Carter, *Fort Worth Star-Telegram*, May 3, 2004.

232. *a self-proclaimed "close personal friend" of Bud Selig.* Sid Hartman, "Catching Up on Some Friends," *Minneapolis Star Tribune*, August 8, 2005.

232. *A review of the past decade's Hartmanisms.* Paul Demko, "The Great Sidoni," *Minneapolis City Pages*, May 11, 2005.

232. *"We were coming close to the end."* Sid Hartman, "Selig: Twins Would Be Gone If Vote Failed," *Minneapolis Star Tribune*, May 21, 2006.

233. *"The economics of baseball are such."* Steven Pearlstein, "Subsidized Team May Throw an Economic Curve," *Washington Post*, October 1, 2004. In the baseball postseason that started the week after Pearlstein's column appeared, not a single one of the eight teams involved (the New York Yankees, Boston Red Sox, Minnesota Twins, Oakland A's, Anaheim Angels, St. Louis Cardinals, Chicago Cubs, Los Angeles Dodgers and San Francisco Giants) played in a new taxpayer-funded facility.

233. *An examination of the link between new baseball stadiums and winning*

percentage. Neil deMause, "Are New Stadiums a Good Deal?" in *Baseball between the Numbers*, ed. Jonah Keri (New York: Basic Books, 2006), 221.

234. *"People say, well, new stadiums are not the panacea."* Marc Topkin, "Selig Visits Trop, Sees Need for New Stadium," *St. Petersburg Times*, June 10, 2004.

234. *"It's very frustrating to have to go through this."* Carl Steward, "Wolff's Directive: Get Stadium Constructed for A's," *Oakland Tribune*, November 14, 2003.

235. *"You have to spend money in order to make money."* Sally Claunch, "Stadium Tax Hike Benefits Debated," *Fort Worth Star-Telegram*, August 24, 2004.

235. *"You hire a firm like ERA and say."* Neil deMause, "Error, Comptroller," *Village Voice*, October 20-26, 1999.

237. *"June 30—that's our target goal."* Dave Levinthal, "County Lists Hurdles for Stadium Funding," *Dallas Morning News*, May 5, 2004.

238. *"It's my experience that without a deadline."* "More Ballpark Issues for Marlins," Associated Press, February 20, 2004.

238. *"We're confident that forty-five days from now."* "Architects Say There's Still Time for 2007 Opener," Associated Press, March 15, 2004.

238. *"This is it."* Jayson Stark, ESPN.com, April 26, 2004.

240. *"The lease is like the Energizer bunny."* Cindi Andrews, "Stadium Clause Tosses Turf Cost to Taxpayers," *Cincinnati Enquirer*, February 14, 2004.

240. *"has informed us that it will not, under any circumstances."* Team Seeks Millions to Stay in Sunshine State," ESPN.com, January 21, 2005.

240. *"Let's say for some reason."* Alex Marvez, "Owner Sees an Eventual Turnaround," *South Florida Sun-Sentinel*, March 24, 2005.

244. *"My wife and I have often talked."* Edward Lotterman, "My Tiff with TIF: It's Misleading," *St. Paul Pioneer Press*, March 18, 2004.

14. Youppi! Come Home

247. *"Nobody is better equipped to show people how."* Steve Fainaru, "Selig Plays Hardball on Stadium Deals," *Washington Post*, June 27, 2004, A01.

248. *"it is all but inevitable now."* Jack Todd, "The Grinch Who Stole Baseball," *Montreal Gazette*, March 12, 1999.

249. *Tulane sports-law professor Gary Roberts called the proposal.* Neil deMause, "Send Money or We'll Shoot This Team: Contraction Signals That Baseball's About to Birth Something Ugly," *Village Voice*, November 14–20, 2001.

249. *"Whatever long-term leases these two have."* deMause, "Send Money or We'll Shoot."

250. *"MLB wants to know."* Mark Asher, "MLB Wants to Hear Plans for Financing," *Washington Post*, December 13, 2002.

251. *And thus began what baseball business writer Doug Pappas.* Pappas, a contributing writer to the Baseball Prospectus Web site as well as author of the Business of Baseball Web log, tragically died at the age of forty-two while hiking in a Texas state park in May 2004. Much of this section was compiled with the help of his writings.

251. *Selig himself had called the nation's capital.* Jayson Stark, "D.C. Baseball: Questions and Answers," ESPN.com, March 11, 2002.

252. *$150 million that MLB couldn't extract in sale price.* "If Major League Baseball can 'shnooker' a city into paying 100 percent of the costs of building a new stadium," declared DC councilmember Jack Evans on June 12, 2003, "they can get the maximum amount of money from the potential owner to buy the team." Evans would go on to become one of the prime supporters of a subsidized stadium to lure the Expos.

253. *"Ten years from now."* David King, "Plan Would Serve S.A. Expos Slice," *San Antonio Express-News,* December 16, 2003.

253. *a Florida movie mogul named Craig Marquardo.* Andy Giegerich, "A Baseball Angel from Way out of Left Field?" *Portland Tribune,* May 2, 2003.

254. *"a phrase not likely to inspire confidence."* Doug Pappas, "Officials Crunching Numbers for Proposed Stadium," www.roadsidephotos.com/baseball, February 4, 2004.

254. *"We think we'll have enough support to go to New York."* Dave Fairbank, "Norfolk's Approach to Expos 'Unique,'" *Hampton Roads Daily Press,* April 24, 2004.

254. *"Some of their accomplishments."* Tom Shean, "Pair Embellished Accomplishments," *Virginian-Pilot,* July 29, 2004.

254. *"Ask me that later this year."* Eric Fisher, "Baseball Says Expos May Not Move in 2004," *Washington Times*, January 17, 2003.

255. *"I know [July 15] was the goal."* Eric Fisher, "Decision on Expos Not Likely," *Washington Times*, July 10, 2003.

255. *"Obviously the options are the various cities."* "Expos Future Still Uncertain: Selig," CBC Sports, September 11, 2003.

255. *"I would rather get [the relocation of the Montreal Expos] done."* Mark Asher, "Expos' Relocation to Be Discussed," *Washington Post*, January 14, 2004.

255. *"It is an objective to have a facility."* Thom Loverro, "NLB Won't Budge on Stadium," *Washington Times*, January 15, 2004.

255. *"We'll get it done this year, I promise you."* Hal Bodley, "Expos' Relocation to Be Discussed," *USA Today*, February 5, 2004.

255. *"by the All-Star Game this year."* Tom Verducci, "Q&A with the Commish," SI.com, March 9, 2004.

255. *"I don't know if 'embarrassment' is the right word."* Verducci, "Q&A with the Commish."

256. *"That probably wouldn't build a stadium."* Derek Zumsteg, "Expos Saga Rolls On," Baseballprospectus.com, March 23, 2004.

256. *"We need to get this done sooner rather than later."* Eric Fisher, "Decision on Expos Likely Soon," *Washington Times*, August 26, 2004.

257. *"I'm beyond thrilled."* Eric Fisher, "D.C. Gets Expos; 33-Year Wait Over," *Washington Times*, September 30, 2004.

257. *"Major League Baseball didn't want a team here."* Malcolm Moran, "Baseball No More in Montreal," *USA Today*, September 29, 2004.

258. *In the end, DC taxpayers would be on the hook.* For a more in-depth analysis breaking down the costs of the DC stadium deal, see: Neil deMause, "D.C. at the Bat: Who Would Pay for Washington's New Stadium?" Baseballprospectus.com, September 28, 2004.

258. *"People were amazed that the District."* Peter Whoriskey, "Lucrative Deal On Stadium Won Baseball Over," *Washington Post*, September 29, 2004.

258. *"helped convince the mayor that his only chance."* Thomas Boswell, "Baseball in D.C.? It's Almost Too Good to Be True," *Washington Post*, October 3, 2004.

260. *"vast body of economic research on the impact of baseball stadiums."* "An Open Letter to Mayor Anthony Williams and the DC City Council from 90 Economists on the Likely Impact of a Taxpayer-Financed Baseball Stadium in the District of Columbia," October 21, 2004. The full text of the letter, and signatories, can be found at www.dcfpi.org/?p=50.

260. A Washington Post *poll a few weeks later.* Richard Morin, "Public Financing Opposed, Poll Finds," *Washington Post,* November 9, 2004.

260. *"I'm going to stop this baseball stadium."* S. A. Miller, "Barry to Block Building Pacts," *Washington Times,* October 14, 2004.

260. *"the biggest stick-up since Jesse James."* Eric Fisher, "Baseball Proposal Provokes Anger," *Washington Times,* October 28, 2004.

260. *"We say to this mayor and some members of the city council."* David Nakamura, "Coalition Vows to Fight Stadium," *Washington Post,* October 6, 2004.

261. *"Are you willing to kill baseball?"* Lori Montgomery and Yolanda Woodlee, "Foes of New Stadium Want Team to Stay at RFK," *Washington Post,* October 2, 2004.

261. *"Everybody understands that this occurs."* Lori Montgomery and Yolanda Woodlee, "Stadium Backers in Line for Reward," *Washington Post,* November 10, 2004.

261. *"Our chances, if we had a vote today."* David Nakamura, "Stadium Support Seems Solid," *Washington Post,* October 20, 2004.

261. *"At this point, I don't think that there's going to be enough to stop it."* Nakamura, "Stadium Support Seems Solid."

262. *"How much money does it take."* "Baseball Hearing Ends at 2 a.m.," Associated Press, October 29, 2004.

262. *"This is going to blow the thing up."* Michael Wilbon, "D.C. Baseball in Foul Territory," *Washington Post,* November 6, 2004.

262. Post *sports columnist Michael Wilbon called Cropp.* Wilbon, "D.C. Baseball in Foul Territory."

264. *"My basic belief is that there are too many public dollars."* David Nakamura, "Council Approves Altered Stadium Deal," *Washington Post,* December 15, 2004.

264. *"inconsistent with [the] carefully negotiated agreement."* Thomas Bo-

swell, "Nationals Face an Unhappy New Year," *Washington Post,* December 16, 2004.

264. *"The bits of charred ash and shattered fragments."* Thomas Boswell, "Cropped out of the Picture," *Washington Post,* December 15, 2004.

265. *Tom Knott dubbed Cropp "the Grinch who stole baseball."* Tom Knott, "Remembering the Grinch Who Stole Baseball," *Washington Times,* December 15, 2004.

265. *"Of course it's not the world's greatest deal."* *Outside the Lines,* ESPN, December 16, 2004. The people of Montreal, meanwhile, had lost their team and were set to be left with only an empty stadium for their thirty-five years of fandom. When the province of Quebec proposed to turn over Olympic Stadium to the city of Montreal in 2006, the city wanted no part of it: "Knowing that the government gives grants of $22 million per year to operate the stadium, well, we're not ready to put that kind of money into it; we just don't have it," Montreal executive committee vice-chair Michel Prescott told the CBC.

267. *A DC government source admitted to the Washington Post.* David Nakamura, "True Costs of Stadium Go beyond Budget," *Washington Post,* December 11, 2005.

267. *"They're not going to contract."* Dave Sheinin and Barry Svrluga, "Without Lease, Nats Are on Shaky Ground," *Washington Post,* December 20, 2005.

268. *"give the store away."* Council member Carol Schwartz, "Statement on Ballpark Financing Bill," November 30, 2004, www.dcwatch.com/govern/sports041130.htm.

268. *"It was time to declare victory and move on."* Marc Fisher, "Ballpark Deal's Salvation? Both Sides Chickened Out," *Washington Post,* March 7, 2006.

268. *"trying to be perceived as a team player."* Fisher, "Ballpark Deal's Salvation?"

269. *"Two thirds/one third is fine."* Lori Montgomery, "One Guarantee Sparked Larger Baseball Battle," *Washington Post,* December 19, 2004.

270. *"A savvy negotiator creates leverage."* Edward Kiersh, "Playing Hardball: Jerry Reinsdorf Got Michael Jordan Back Playing Basketball, but the

Federal Courts Stymied His Assault on Baseball's Economics," *Cigar Aficio-nado*, Summer 1995.

270. *"Everyone realizes as soon as the Expos [were] announced."* Barry Jackson, "Marlins to Contend with Free Agency, New Stadium Talks during Off-season," *San Jose Mercury News*, October 2, 2004.

271. *"Even after covering operating losses in Montreal."* "Twins may be a hot commodity: Reggie Jackson's interest is only the beginning." *Minneapolis Star Tribune*, November 9, 2005.

271. *In a long analysis of the stadium designs.* Josh Levin, "Rich Fan, Poor Fan," *Washington City Paper*, October 7–13, 2005.

15. The Perfect Storm

272. *"There are only two things you do not want."* Bill Shaikin, "Economists: Stadiums Are Bad Investments," *Los Angeles Times*, May 11, 2005.

272. *"We make 'investments.' We don't do subsidies."* T. J. Quinn, "New Ballpark's a Winner," *Daily News*, June 16, 2005.

273. *the most-expensive minor-league baseball stadiums in history.* See Neil deMause, "2 STDMS, OCEAN VU, $110M: Minor-League Ball Comes to Coney and Staten Islands," *Village Voice*, June 20–26, 2001. The Coney Island ballpark also claimed a victim by collateral damage, when city demolition crews tore down the Thunderbolt, the seventy-five-year-old wooden rollercoaster featured in Woody Allen's *Annie Hall*. Although Giuliani's Department of Buildings had declared it a "dangerous structure," speculation was that the city decided an ivy-covered, abandoned rollercoaster was not the appropriate backdrop for a new baseball showplace. In a fit of irony, the stadium's prime luxury box was later dubbed the Thunderbolt Suite.

273. *"I know there's a knee-jerk misunderstanding of it."* Bill Madden, Lisa L. Colangelo, and Luke Cyphers, "New Stadiums by '07? Rent Plan Will Aid City, Giuliani Says," *Daily News*, December 27, 2001.

273. *"Given the lack of housing."* Neil deMause, "If You Don't Build It, They Still Will Spend," *Village Voice*, January 16–22, 2002.

274. *"The passion and intensity absolutely floored me."* www.heremagazine.com/sausages.html.

274. *"He wouldn't have picked me."* Lois Weiss and John Lehmann, "New $1B Stadium in Play—May Host Jets, Olympics," *New York Post*, January 10, 2002.

275. *And that was before any of the cost overruns.* Neil deMause, "Athenian Dreams of Trojan Horse? New York's Olympic Bid Could Be Billion-Dollar Boondoggle," *Village Voice*, December 13-19, 2000. Both the Atlanta and Sydney losses would pale in comparison to the 2004 Athens Games, which wound up absorbing more than $4 billion in cost overruns.

277. *Any new taxes from the office buildings.* Depending on how the geographical boundaries of the plan were defined, the West Side property was, according to the city Independent Budget Office, paying anywhere from $24,000. to $60,000. a year into city coffers. Anything above this would be redirected to repay the costs of the stadium and subway line.

277. *"Someone's going to have to guarantee those bonds."* Neil deMause, "West Side Stories: Scrounging Up $3 Billion in 'New' Tax Money? Hey, No Problem," *Village Voice*, January 22-28, 2003.

278. *"the precise structure may be different than a classic TIF."* Neil deMause, "Jockbeat: West Side Stories," *Village Voice*, March 5-11, 2003.

279. *helped lead USA* Today *to rate the arena as the worst facility.* Greg Boeck, "NBA arenas: Fantastic or Not?" *USA Today*, April 12, 2005.

280. *"As a boy, I cried when the Dodgers left."* Bill Farrell, "Boro Courting the Nets," *Daily News*, July 24, 2003.

282. *For MetroTech, which replaced several square blocks.* All figures in this paragraph compiled by Good Jobs New York: www.goodjobsny.org.

282. *"I was never interested in traditional real estate."* Alex Williams, "Back to the Future," *New York*, October 27, 2003.

282. *"We are essentially bailing out this white elephant."* Tom Topousis, "Taxpayers Malled," *New York Post*, November 17, 2003. Montgomery later reported receiving an angry phone call from Ratner in response to her published comments.

283. *Ratner's own figures would show.* Ariella Cohen, "Ratner Jobs Fall Short: Bruce's Malls Haven't Met Projections," *Brooklyn Papers*, November 10, 2006.

283. *"if they came to Brooklyn, [players] would pay $5.5 million."* Jamie Her-

zlich, "Plan for Nets Arena to Get Hard Review," *Newsday*, December 11, 2003.

286. *"It's a huge step forward."* Lee Romney, "Community, Developers Agree on Staples Plan Deal," *Los Angeles Times*, May 31, 2001.

287. *"like an angel sent from God."* John Doyle, "Arena Supporters and Foes Clash at Borough Hall Pro-Ratner Rally," *Brooklyn Eagle*, June 18, 2004.

287. *Even* BUILD'*s office space came courtesy of the developer.* Juan Gonzalez, "Snake in the 'Grassroots,'" *Daily News*, September 29, 2005.

287. *"dead-end, low-wage, non-union, no-benefit jobs."* Katherine Hawkins, "Wage Rage," *City Limits*, November 2000.

287. *"This agreement represents the first time that this concept."* Jess Wisloski, "Sealed with a Kiss," *Brooklyn Papers*, May 28, 2005.

288. *"We're concerned about traffic, hell yeah."* Norman Oder, "ACORN's Lewis Gets Fiery as 'Affordable Housing' Debate Heats Up," *Atlantic Yards Report*, March 1, 2006.

288. *Some also recalled Lewis' previous foray into sports projects.* Neil deMause, "The Battle of Brooklyn," *Here*, #3. The Parade Grounds stadium plan was ultimately scuttled by a lawsuit, and a smaller facility was built for community use.

289. *a poll of Brooklynites conducted by Crain's New York Business.* Norman Oder, "Closer Look at Crain's Poll," *Atlantic Yards Report*, September 8, 2006.

289. *"I think race was used from Day 1."* Nicholas Confessore, "Perspectives on the Atlantic Yards Development through the Prism of Race," *New York Times*, November 12, 2006.

289. *"The devil could bring in a project."* Confessore, "Perspectives on the Atlantic Yards."

289. *"forget the most important mantra."* Michael O'Keeffe, "Color of Money the Real Issue at Atlantic Yards," *Daily News* iTeam Blog, June 7, 2006.

289. *the public spending about $600 million for the rail yards platform and a retractable roof.* While $600 million was the official figure, city public advocate Betsy Gotbaum analyzed other recent stadium deals and projected that an additional $430 million in overruns and inflation costs were likely.

289. *"This is an incredibly complicated jigsaw puzzle."* Charles V. Bagli, "Jets Stadium in Manhattan Moves Closer, but Issues Remain," November 29, 2003.

290. *"providing needed flexibility to our efforts."* Neil deMause, "Where Does Your Garden Go?" *Village Voice*, June 18–24, 2003.

290. the New York Times *reported that the Jets were working on redesigning.* Charles V. Bagli, "To Avoid Competing with Garden, Jets Redraw Plans for Stadium on West Side," *New York Times*, January 28, 2004.

290. *"There is an allegation that one company."* Jennifer Steinhauer, "Garden Backs Ad Opposing New Stadium," *New York Times*, May 28, 2004. The Jets' own figures, meanwhile, projected seven thousand new permanent jobs from the project, for a cost-per-job ratio of nearly $100,000 in public money per new job; using the city Independent Budget Office's estimate of thirty-six hundred jobs created, the per-job figure would jump to nearly $170,000 per job.

291. *In total, according to figures compiled by Common Cause New York.* The final lobbying tally, according to Common Cause–NY: Cablevision $38,964,287, Jets $12,705,136.

291. *"It didn't change my mind."* Charles V. Bagli, "After City Hall Lobbying, Group Postpones Stadium Vote," *New York Times*, May 6, 2004.

291. *"If a client came to me and said."* Ben Smith, "You Can't Buy Mayor—So Give To 2012 Games," *New York Observer*, January 26, 2005.

292. *"I haven't rooted this hard for England, France and Russia."* Mike Vaccaro, "'Doctoroff' Base with Olympics," *New York Post*, August 16, 2004.

292. *"The stadium argument comes down to tax dollars."* Associated Press, July 21, 2004.

292. *"We're not going to cut off our nose."* Michael Saul, "Housing Plan for W. Side," *Daily News*, January 11, 2005.

293. *"Silly me, I thought the state constitution."* Neil deMause, "The Jets' End Run," *Village Voice*, November 16, 2004.

293. *"The State of New York's budget operates like a slush fund."* deMause, "The Jets' End Run."

293. *"we'll take every legislative and other remedy available."* Charles V. Bagli, "City Plans to Use Real Estate Revenue to Finance Stadium," *New York Times*, February 9, 2005.

294. *"There is a reign of terror in this town."* Tom Robbins, "Stadium Fear Factor," *Village Voice*, February 15, 2005.

294. *"We are going to create 20 million square feet."* NY1, December 11, 2004.

295. *"ambivalence [was] driving other politicians slightly batty."* Charles V. Bagli, "Will He Block That Stadium? Speaker Silver Bides His Time," *New York Times*, January 22, 2005.

295. *"the MTA is under a public and moral obligation."* Graham Rayman and Dan Janison, "MSG Makes Bid for West Side Yard," *Newsday*, February 5, 2005.

295. *"used as a shield."* Errol A. Cockfield Jr., "Lawmakers Say No to Stadium," *Newsday*, June 7, 2005.

295. *"let America down."* Cockfield Jr., "Lawmakers Say No."

295. *"It was never alive."* Cockfield Jr., "Lawmakers Say No."

295. *Within an hour of landing on legislators' desks.* Neil deMause, "The Shel Game: Silver and His Albany Pals Mint Hundreds of Millions in Corporate Handouts without Anybody Noticing," *Village Voice*, August 2, 2005.

298. *On one occasion, Steinbrenner had tried to bill the city.* Clyde Haberman, "Millionaires on a Field of Diamonds," *New York Times*, May 4, 2004.

299. *When all was said and done, the new Yankees stadium.* The public tally for the Yankees stadium plan as it was approved: $307 million from the city ($130 million for land and infrastructure, $11 million in added capital funds, $6 million in maintenance funds, $13 million in rent rebates from 2006-8, $144 million in forgone property taxes, $10 million in construction sales tax rebates, $11 million in forgone mortgage recording taxes, $12 million in tax-exempt bond subsidies, and $21 million in forgone rent credits from the old lease, less $43 million in new garage rent money and $10 million in projected memorabilia sales from the old stadium), $119 million from the state ($70 million in garage subsidies, $5 million in maintenance funds, $11 million in construction sales tax rebates, $11 million in forgone mortgage recording taxes, and $22 million in tax-exempt bond subsidies), and $120 million in federal tax-exempt bond subsidies. For the Mets: $256 million from the city ($98 million for land and infrastructure, $6 million in maintenance funds, $13 million in rent rebates from 2006–8, $72 million in forgone property

taxes, $9 million in construction sales tax rebates, $6 million in tax-exempt bond subsidies, and $25 million in forgone rent credits from the old lease, less $31 million in maintenance savings), $97 million from the state ($73 million in infrastructure subsidies, $5 million in maintenance funds, $9 million in construction sales tax rebates, and $10 million in tax-exempt bond subsidies), and $57 million in federal tax-exempt bond subsidies. In February 2007, the city revealed that it was adding an additional $35 million for Yankees stadium infrastructure, and another $90 million in city and state funds was later added for a commuter rail station to serve the new Bronx stadium, bringing the total public subsidies for the two projects to $1.082 billion.

299. *They would get to defray their costs with lucrative naming-rights.* The Mets would ultimately strike a deal with Citigroup to pay a record $20 million a year to have the new stadium dubbed CitiField. The naming-rights payments alone would cover more than two thirds of the Mets' construction costs.

301. *"will leave us with a great sports landmark structurally mauled."* Bill Shannon and George Kalinsky, *The Ballparks* (New York: Hawthorn, 1975), ix.

303. *"New Yorkers need schools and not stadiums."* Bob Kappstatter, "New Bronx Beep: ко Stadium Plans," *Daily News*, January 7, 2002.

308. *"No alienation has moved as fast as the Yankees'"* An abridged version of this quote appeared in Neil deMause, "Two Stadiums. No Waiting," *Village Voice*, March 14, 2006.

312. *"There are no shortcuts."* Patrick Arden, "Parks Law May Trip Up Yankee Stadium," *Metro New York*, March 28, 2006.

312. *The $5 million a year in "stadium planning" rent credits.* See Neil deMause, "Yankee Lobbyists on Taxpayers' Tab: Circling the Bases: Documents Reveal City Paid the Team's Lobbyists and Execs—for Lobbying City and State Officials," *Village Voice*, July 25, 2006, and Neil deMause, "Another Yankee Sweep: How City Officials Snoozed While the Yanks Burned Public Money for Their New Stadium," *Village Voice*, August 29, 2006.

313. *"like padding the expense account."* DeMause, "Another Yankee Sweep."

313. *"You've created this weird circular situation."* DeMause, "Yankee Lobbyists on Taxpayers' Tab."

313. *"$3 billion sports stadium crisis."* Richard Wilner, "A State-of-the-Art Big Apple Complex," *New York Post*, December 7, 2000.

314. *"the worst thing [Bloomberg] has done."* Patrick D. Healy and Marjorie Connelly, "Big Issues Lift Mayor's Rating to a New High." *New York Times*, June 29, 2005.

315. *"We would never have had the access in Albany."* Jarrett Murphy, "Stopping a Stadium: Heroes Had Different Motives, but They Shared Scorn for the Jets Deal," *Village Voice*, June 14, 2005.

315. *novelist Jonathan Lethem brought national attention.* Jonathan Lethem, "Brooklyn's Trojan Horse," *Slate*, June 19, 2006.

317. *"When you walk out of the building."* Neil deMause, "Yankees Build Giant Dustbowl in Bronx," Villagevoice.com, November 21, 2006.

16. Saving Fenway

318. *"If there isn't a new ballpark by 2006."* Bob Ryan, "Fenway Is History—and Belongs in the Past," *Boston Globe*, April 11, 2000.

318. *This, the* Globe *coverage made clear.* This section, including all the quotes within, is adapted from a portion of Neil deMause, "Throwing the Game," *Extra!*, November 1999. Special thanks to the Fund for Investigative Journalism for helping fund the research for that article.

320. *"Fenway is a wonderful ballpark."* Meg Vaillancourt, "Diamond in Rough: Backers of New Fenway Say Renovating a Park Past Its Prime Doesn't Make Economic—or Baseball—Sense," *Boston Globe*, April 2, 1999.

320. *"The All-Star Game is a great opportunity."* Vaillancourt, "Diamond in Rough," 2.

321. *"What we want to do is to preserve the old site."* Vaillancourt, "Diamond in Rough," 2.

323. *"It would be easier to straighten the Leaning Tower of Pisa."* Vaillancourt, "Diamond in Rough," 2.

323. *"You can't renovate Fenway because the footprint is too small."* Vaillancourt, "Diamond in Rough," 2.

323. *"I love Fenway Park and I was an advocate of renovating it."* Vaillancourt, "Diamond in Rough," 2.

323. *"would exceed $500 million."* Meg Vaillancourt, "Analysis Is Cool to a Fenway Overhaul: Study for City Sees a $500 Million Price Tag," *Boston Globe*, September 28, 1999.

324. *"If we could get a 45,000-seat ballpark."* Cosmo Macero Jr., "Sox Blame Ticket Prices on Fenway," *Boston Herald*, April 8, 1999.

325. *"the total price tag could end up being as high as $900 million."* Seth Gitell, "Fenway Neighborhood May Be Too Expensive for the Red Sox," *Boston Phoenix*, May 25, 2000.

325. *"I saw the number and was somewhat staggered."* Jean McMillan, "Fenway Price Tag Shocks Lawmaker," Associated Press, January 12, 2000.

325. *"grave reservations."* Meg Vaillancourt, "Mayor's Aides Consider City-Owned New Fenway," *Boston Globe*, April 28, 2000.

326. *"Yesterday's announcement represented the necessary go-ahead rally."* Bob Ryan, "Raise a Toast—but It's Past Closing Time," *Boston Globe*, July 26, 2000.

327. *"This is a community that has never had a plan formally presented."* Adrian Walker, "Fenway Foes Should Be Heard," *Boston Globe*, July 27, 2000.

329. *"Even in Boston, they can't suspend the law of gravity."* Tom Condon, "No Need for New Fenway," *Hartford Courant*, September 17, 2000.

330. *"The team is in strong financial shape."* Meg Vaillancourt, "For Sale: Olde Towne Team," *Boston Globe*, October 7, 2000.

330. *"It would be irresponsible and reckless."* Tina Cassidy and Stephanie Ebbert, "Announcement Fuels Opposition to New Park," *Boston Globe*, October 7, 2000.

332. *"If you want me to cook the dinner."* Kevin Cullen, "An O'Donnell Combination Comes Apart," *Boston Globe*, December 21, 2001.

332. *"We will preserve all that is good about Fenway Park."* Kevin Paul Dupont, "Lucchino Outlines a Few Goals," *Boston Globe*, December 22, 2001.

338. *"Ninety-five percent of the calls we get on this issue."* Kevin J. Delaney and Rick Eckstein, *Public Dollars, Private Stadiums: The Battle Over Building Sports Stadiums* (New Brunswick NJ: Rutgers University Press, 2003), 184.

338. *"seemed to have little in common with democracy."* Delaney and Eckstein, *Public Dollars, Private Stadiums*, 184.

Index

activists: community, xv, 19–20, 33, 128–29, 157, 166; social-justice, 84

Agnos, Art, 174

Allen, Paul, 44, 115, 163–65, 193

Allen, Sandy, 261

Alou, Felipe, 198

American Basketball Association, 279

American Friends Service Committee, 335

Amey, Hallie, 119–30, 135n1

Anaheim Angels, 199

Anderson, Dave, 2

Angelos, Peter, 71, 74, 252, 256

anti-Ratner rallies, 315

Antonetty, Anita, 302–3, 305, 308, 315–16, 337

Aranza, John, 119–35

Archer, Dennis, 96, 97

Arco Arena (Sacramento), 229

arenas: filling, 58; life cycle of, 229

Arison, Mickey, 106

Arizona Cardinals, 373

Arizona Diamondbacks, 103, 213

Armour Field (Chicago) (proposed), 138, 146, 328

Arrington, Richard, 206

artificial turf, 131, 166, 239; AstroTurf, 137

"as-of-right" tax breaks, 284

Association of Community Organizations for Reform Now (ACORN), 287, 288

Astrodome (Houston), 48, 66

Atlanta, Olympics in, 149

Atlanta Braves, 60n1

Atlantic Yards, 281, 282, 283, 316; affordable housing plan for, 287–88; financing of, 284–85

attendance (MLB), 183–84

Baade, Robert, 34–35, 39, 59, 173

Bagley, Lester, 231

Bagli, Charles, 294

The Ballpark (Arlington TX), 141; as a new "old-time" park, 203

Ballpark (Richmond), 350

Ballpark Agreement, 261

ballpark district, 210–13

"ballpark village," 241–42

Baltimore Colts, 4, 190; relocation of, 1–2

Baltimore Orioles, 5, 9, 52, 71, 74, 252, 332; sale of, 10

Baltimore Ravens, 19, 31, 37, 52

Bank One Ballpark (Phoenix), 53, 223

Barron, Charles, 289

Barron, Ken, 193

Barry, Marion, 260, 267–68

baseball: as entertainment, 124; viewing experience of, 137

Baseball between the Numbers (Keri), 233

Baseball Club of Seattle, 160–61, 162

Baseball for Real Men (Wolff), 253

Baseball Palace of the World (Bukowski), 123

Bass, Carole, 219

Beaver, Don, 172, 207

Beeston, Paul, 42, 46

Behring, Ken, 163

Beijing Evening News, 225, 226

Bell, Jerry, 41n5

Belle, Albert, 182

Bennett, Bruce, 207

Bennett, Clayton, 181n1

Bergman, Lowell, 112

Bess, Philip, 133–34, 136–39, 141–42, 145–49, 328–29, 333, 336, 339

Betzold, Michael, 84, 86, 358

Beyle, Thad, 165

Birmingham AL, building of stadium in, 204–6

Birmingham, Tom, 326

blackmail, sports-franchise, xv

Black Voices for Peace, 260

Blassingame, Mary, 303

Bloomberg, Michael, 272, 273–74, 287, 290–91, 293, 295–96, 301, 313–14; and stadium planning credits, 299

Bloomington Stadium, 243

Blumenauer, Earl, 185

Bobb, Robert, 267

Boggs, Wade, 203

bonds: and influence of lawyers, 114; private activity, 51; tax-exempt, 50–52, 81

book losses, 47

Boston Celtics, 188, 189

Boston Landmarks Commission, 321, 333

Boston Preservation Alliance (BPA), 321, 322, 335, 336

Boston Red Sox, 70, 180, 203, 233, 237, 300, 324; and financing of new park, 325; and lack of new stadium, 318; sale of, 250, 332

Boswell, Thomas, 258, 264, 267

Bowlen, Pat, 35, 67, 214, 215

Boyd, Richard A., 22

Boyer, M. Christine, 150

Bradley Center (Milwaukee), 229

Brendan Byrne Arena (NJ), 279

Brewer, Gale, 310

Bridgeport IL, 120, 146

Brooklyn Dodgers, 2, 182, 183, 202

Brooklyn United for Innovative Local Development (BUILD), 287

Brower, Jordan, 114

Brown, Kevin, 213

Brown, Kwame, 267–68

Brown, Maury, 265, 269, 270

Brown, Willie, 105, 110

Bruenig, Carla, 166

Bruno, Joseph, 291, 294–95

Buchta, Bob, 84, 86

Buckley, John, 324

Budig, Gene, 70

Buffalo Sabres, 230

Bukowski, Doug, 123–25, 131–34; and kids' sight lines, 143

Burns, Joy, 215

Buscemi, Steve, 315

Busch Stadium (St. Louis), 258, 338

business-entertainment deduction, 49

"but-for" problem, 243, 277

Cablevision, 290, 291, 293, 314, 331

Caldwell, James, 287, 289

Camden Yards (Baltimore), 10, 12, 13, 32, 91, 151; cost of, 16, 25n1; and free rent, 52; good points of, 142–43; and less fashionable neighboring areas, 152; neighborhood of, 158; as new "old-fashioned" ballpark, 137, 320; outdoor walkway at, 144; success of, 21, 22

Caminiti, Ken, 213
Campaign to Stop the Giveaway, 106
Campanella, Vincent, 7, 8
Candlestick Park (San Francisco), 53, 64, 173, 176, 179
Captain Newman, M.D. (Rosten), 196
Carey, Drew, 18
Carlson, Arne, 104–5, 169, 171
Carolina Hurricanes, xiii, 217
Carolina Triplets, 207
Carponter, Candace, 285, 286, 288, 289
Carrion, Adolfo, 303, 306, 315
Carroll, Maurice, 292
Carter, O. K., 231
Casey, Ethan, 358
Cashen, Frank, 9
casino gambling, 95
Catania, David, 261, 266, 267
Celebration FL, 150–51
Celeste, Richard, 8
Cellucci, Governor, 325, 326
Central Market, 14–15
Central Market Gateway Project. *See* Gateway Project (Cleveland)
Charlotte Coliseum, 229
Charlotte Hornets, 54, 180, 227, 230
Charney, Michael, 154
"charter seat rights." *See* personal seat license (PSL)
Chema, Tom, 25n1
Chicago, ethnic divisions of, 121
Chicago Bulls, 187; success of, 233
Chicago Cubs, 45, 60n1, 121, 300
Chicago newspapers, and campaign for new stadium, 125
Chicago White Sox, 65, 71, 119, 120, 121, 145, 182, 226, 270; fan base of, 125; as a stadium suitor, 223
Chrétien, Jean, 249

Christison, John, 26n6, 225, 230
Cincinnati Bengals, 20, 239
Cinergy Field (Cincinnati), 53
cities: as entertainment zones, 148–49, 154; stadiums' benefits for, 32
Citi Field (Mets stadium), 385; costs of, 299, 384–85
citizen comments, 308–9
citizen groups, 83, 84
Citizens for a New Stadium, 215
Citizens for More Important Things, 161, 181n1, 194
Citizens Opposing the Stadium Tax (COST), 215
Citizens Union, 313
city council hearings, 309–10
City Planning Commission, 308
City Project, 159n3
Civic Center Arena (St. Paul), 167
"clawback" legislation, 116, 185
CLEAN, 161
Clemens, Roger, 215
Cleveland: downturn of, 6–7; illiteracy of adult population in, 155; poverty in, 21–22, 25n3
stadium proposal for, 7–8
Cleveland Browns, xiii, 25n2, 176; and move to Baltimore, 17–21; public takeover of, 187
Cleveland Cavaliers, 14, 16
Cleveland Indians, xiii, 6, 13, 45, 70, 71, 74, 182, 186–87, 331
Cleveland Teachers Union (CTU), 194, 195
Clinton Special District Coalition, 276
Cluck, Robert, 235
Coalition against Public Funding for Stadiums, 338
Coalition against Stadium Subsidies, 327

Coalition for a Greater Miami, 107

Coates, Dennis, 40n3

Coats, Cari, 225

Cobo Arena (Detroit), 99

Cochrane Plan, 90, 91, 92, 95, 104, 136

Colangelo, Jerry, 38, 73, 103

Colavito, Rocky, 348

Coleman, Leonard, 70

Collins, William, 77

Colorado Avalanche, 356

Colorado Rockies, 35, 214, 249

Comerica Park (Detroit), 102n4

Comiskey Park (Chicago), 45, 65, 84,
    117, 119–35, 141; collective memory
    of, 125; history of, 125–26; nostalgia
    for, 133; protests at, 129

Comiskey Park (Chicago) (new), 91,
    141–42, 223; alternatives to, 136; at-
    tendance at, 134; and emphasis on
    tourists, 156; surrounded by parking
    lots, 145

Commers, Jon, 169

Common Cause New York, 291, 313

community benefits agreement (cba),
    286, 288, 309

Community Board 4, 303, 305, 307, 308,
    315

community groups, 286–87

competitiveness, 73–75, 201

computers, taking of, 238

Cone, David, 216

Coney Island ballpark, 380

configuration of playing fields, 139

Connecticut Office of Fiscal Analysis,
    220

Connors, Jack, 326

contraction, 249, 267

Coors Field (Denver), 32, 35, 146, 151,
    208, 214

CoreStates Center (Philadelphia), 58

corporate ownership, 43

corporate pullouts, 152

corporate subsidies. See government
    subsidies

corporate welfare, xv, 3, 28, 45, 103; and
    activism, 124; and Candlestick Park
    (San Francisco), 178; continuing
    unchecked, 156; and efforts to stop,
    185; local politicians and, 116; and
    Northwest Airlines, 167–68; as a pri-
    ority of public spending, 196; public
    sentiment on, 108; and subsidizing
    of baseball, 132. See also govern-
    ment subsidies; tax abatements; tax
    breaks

cost overruns, 78–81, 258

Cowles, John Jr., 111

Cowles Media, 111

Crain's New York Business, 289

Cropp, Linda, 262–65

Cross, Jay, 69, 106, 107, 108

Cushman, Tom, 19

Dadey, Dick, 313

Dallas Cowboys, 54, 216, 231, 235; and
    "deadlines," 237; economic report
    for, 236; and tax-increment financ-
    ing, 243

Dallas Stars, 167

Daniels, Brett, 237

Darin, Catherine, 101

David, Dilsa, 305

Davids, John, 89–90, 91, 92, 93, 101, 136

Davids, Judy, 89–90, 92, 101, 136

Davis, Al, 56, 72

Davis, Jack, 176, 177; and "The Party,"
    178–79

"Dawg Pound," 17

DC Baseball, 257
DC Fiscal Policy Institute, 259
DC Friends of the Earth, 259
DC stadium: construction costs of,
    262–65; private-financing scheme of,
    264, 265
"deadlines" of sports owners, 237–38
DeBartolo, Edward, Jr., 82n3, 176, 178–80
Decker, Howard, 329
Delaney, Keven, 338
Denver Broncos, 35, 67, 213–15
Denver Nuggets, 67, 356
Denver Post, 214
Department of Environmental Conser-
    vation, 304
depreciation of player contracts, 45–46
depreciation rights, 263
design-change requests, 238–40
Detroit: desperation in, 155–56; deterio-
    ration of, 98–100
Detroit Lions, 64, 78, 85, 97
Detroit Pistons, 99
Detroit Red Wings, 94, 99
Detroit Renaissance, 95
Detroit Tigers, 71, 77–78, 85, 100, 115, 234
Develop Don't Destroy, 281, 285, 286,
    317
DeVos, Rich, 229, 231
DiMaggio, Joe, 301
DiPalermo, Christian, 308
Disney, 43
diversity in sports crowds, 24
Divinski, Randy, 334, 335
Doby, Larry, 45
Doctoroff, Dan, 274, 276–77, 289, 290–
    91, 292–93, 294
Dodge, Richard, 66
Dolan, Charles, 331
Dolan, Larry, 331

Dombrowski, Dave, 44
Domino's Pizza, 87; boycott of, 89
Donovan, Donna, 218, 222, 223
double standard, 316
Dow, Bill, 83, 92, 94, 95, 96, 97, 101; and
    uphill battle, 155
downtown "renaissance," 151–55
"dual city," 153
Duggan, Michael, 78, 93, 94
Duncan, Tim, 206
DuPuy, Bob, 254–56, 264–65, 267, 268;
    and hardball negotiating tactics, 269
Duquette, Dan, 330
Durkee, Alice, 205

East Bay Alliance for a Sustainable
    Economy, 243
Ebbets Field (Brooklyn), 139, 140, 183,
    202
Eckstein, Rick, 338
economic benefits, 260
economic development, 33; and pitfalls,
    236
economic impact of stadiums, 234–37
economic impact study, 283, 308, 309
Economic Policy Institute, 30
economic projections, 235–36
"economic renaissance," 228
Economic Research Associates (ERA),
    234–37
economic studies, 212, 222–23, 226, 373
economic success, 158
Einhorn, Eddie, 65, 120, 126–27, 131
Elkins, David R., 14, 16
Ellis, Michael, 247
eminent domain, 190; and blight, 327;
    principle of, 5
emotional presence of home teams,
    182–83

Empire State Development Corporation, 292
employment, 158–59
Engler, John, 94, 95, 96, 107
Ervin, Sam, 42–43
Euchner, Charles C., 37, 361
Evans, Jack, 261, 264, 376
Evans, Ryan, 277
Exhibition Stadium (Toronto), 217
expansion football teams, 4
expenditure substitution. *See* substitution effect

false crisis, 77–78
Faneuil Hall (Boston), 149
fans, alienation of, 183–84
Fans Advocating Intelligent Spending, 169
Fear and Favor in the Newsroom (California Newsreel), 112
fear of losing team, 228
Fenty, Adrian, 261, 266, 267
Fenway Community Development Corporation, 327–28
"Fenway factor," 321
Fenway Park (Boston), 70, 85, 143–44, 146, 203, 233; maintenance problems of, 324; as old steel-framed ballpark, 300, 320; and preservation/reconstruction charrette, 328–29, 334, 339; saving of, 318–39
Ferrer, Fernando, 306, 336
"50-50" affordable housing plan, 287–88
Figueroa Corridor Coalition for Economic Justice, 286
Finley, Daniel, 105
Finley, Steve, 211, 213
Finneran, Thomas, 218, 325, 326, 330, 331
"fiscal impact," 235

Fisher, John, 275, 276, 291
Fisher, Marc, 268
Flaherty, Michael, 330
Flannery, Tim, 211
Fleet Center (Boston), 58
Florida Marlins, xi, 189, 230, 237, 238, 270, 328, 331; and "ballpark village," 241; and desperate measures, 240; success of, 233; and three-way deal, 250
Florida Panthers, 28, 106, 188
Florida Suncoast Dome. *See* Tropicana Field (Tampa Bay)
food services, 143–46
Forbes Field (Pittsburgh), 67
Forest City Ratner, 279, 285, 287
Fort, Rodney, 42, 43, 46, 47, 351; and competitiveness, 75; and contraction, 249–50; and economic-impact studies, 236; and expansion, 73; and "Huizengaland," 241–42; and movement of franchises, 72, 191; and planned obsolescence, 230; and publicly traded teams, 189
Foster, Helen Diane, 310, 315
Foxboro Stadium, 159n1
Francher, Michael, 111
franchise movement, NFL's right to control, 347
Free, World B, 281
Fry, Christine, 335
Fund Kids First, 169

gag order (Brooklyn), 285
Gandhi, Natwar, 262, 266
Ganis, Marc, 106, 222
Gargano, Charles, 292, 293
Gateway Economic Development Corp., 16

Gateway Project (Cleveland), 14–16, 18, 154
Gehry, Frank, 281
Gephardt, Richard, 225
Giambi, Jason, 234
Giants Stadium (New Jersey), 279
Giuliani, Rudolph W., 32, 70, 198–203, 274, 296, 313; problems of, 272; and stadium planning credits, 298–99
Glendening, Parris, 22, 76
Golding, Susan, 211, 213
Goldstein, Dan, 280, 281, 285, 287, 289
Good Jobs First, 244
Good Jobs New York, 299
Goodman, Oscar, 253
Gorton, Slade, 162, 163, 238
Gotbaum, Betsy, 382
Gottfried, Richard, 315
government subsidies, 29–31, 40n2, 45. *See also* corporate welfare
Governor, Michael, 335
Governor's Strategic Fund, 95
Graham, Jim, 261, 267
Gray, Vincent, 267–68
The Great American Jobs Scam (LeRoy), 118n4
Greater Cleveland Domed Stadium Corporation, 9
Green, Stephen, 263
Green Bay Packers, public ownership of, 187–88, 193n2
Green Monster (Fenway Park), 203; seats atop, 329, 332
Greenwich, Howard, 243, 277
Griffey, Ken Jr., 239
Griggs, Roman, 99
growth centers, urban, 21
Gruber, Mike, 87, 92
Gund, George, 16

Gund, Gordon, 16
Gund Arena (Cleveland), 17, 144, 153
Gwynn, Tony, 211

Hagan, Patti, 280
Hagenah, Charles, 322
Hagenah plan, 322, 323, 328
Hall, Bob, 257
Hamilton, Bruce W., 26n4
Harborplace (Baltimore), 149, 158
Harel, Louise, 248
Harlan, Robert, 193n2
Harrington, Ed, 177
Harrington, John, 320, 323–24, 326, 330–31, 334
Harris, Jeffrey, 335
Hartford Civic Center, 218
Hartford Whalers, xiii, 42, 217
Hartman, Sid, 170, 232, 248
Harwell, Ernie, 93, 102n4
Hawkins, Beth, 110
hearings, public, 326
Heimlich, Phil, 240
Hellmuth Obata Kassebaum architects, 89, 131, 134, 323, 332; and domination of new-stadium construction, 136; and relationship with baseball owners, 145; and use of leftover space, 142
Hell's Kitchen, 276
Henry, John, 237–38, 250, 331–34
Herbert, Lukas, 235, 303–5, 311, 313, 316
Heritage Field, 301
Hess, John, 113
Hlinko, John, 178
Hoffberger, Jerrold, 10
Hogi, Joyce, 305, 309, 317
Hoke, Martin, 185
"holographic replay system," 240

Holt, Peter, 206
"Home Field Advantage," 332
home-field disadvantage, 65–67
home-rule message, 307–8
Hoosier Dome, 3, 4, 347
Horrow, Rick, 204, 205
Houston Astros, 62, 66, 70, 71, 74, 77, 251
Houston Oilers, 62, 63, 176
Houston Rockets, 373; success of, 233
Hubert H. Humphrey Metrodome
    (Minneapolis), 66, 111, 165–66, 226
Hudnut, William H. III, 32
Hudson's building, 101n2
Hudson Yards, 276, 277, 290, 294, 295
Hudson Yards/Hell's Kitchen Alliance,
    315
Hudson Yards Infrastructure Corpora-
    tion, 278, 292
Huizenga, Wayne, 28, 189, 238, 240; and
    "ballpark village," 241
Humphreys, Brad, 40n3
Hunt, Clark, 231
Hunt, Jim, 208
Hutchins, Ray, 215

Ilitch, Mike, 94, 95, 96, 97, 100, 116
Illinois Landmarks Preservation Coun-
    cil, 329
imputed income, 186
incremental tax revenues, 283
Indiana Pacers, 2
Indianapolis Colts, 1, 20, 230
Industrial Development Agency, 293
inequities between haves and have-nots,
    156
infrastructure money, 297
Inner Harbor (Baltimore), 13, 24, 158
Irsay, Jim, 26n7
Irsay, Robert, 1, 2, 4

Jack Murphy Stadium (San Diego), 53,
    58–59, 78, 210
Jackson, Reggie, 310
Jackson, Shoeless Joe, 123
Jacksonville Jaguars, 230
Jacobs, David, 14, 25, 349
Jacobs, Eli, 12, 24
Jacobs, Richard, 14, 17, 25, 349
Jacobs Field (Cleveland), 17, 24–25, 32,
    141, 151, 153; amenities of, 144; as
    new "old-time" park, 203, 320; seat-
    ing distances of, 140–41; success of,
    21; suites in, 48; and tax abatements,
    195
Jacor Broadcasting, 215
James, Letitia, 284, 308
Janis-Aparicio, Madeline, 286
Javits Convention Center, 276, 294
Jennings, Loren, 173
Joe Louis Arena (Detroit), 99
Johnson, Donna, 317
Johnson, Nick, 256
Johnson, Randy, 103
Jones, Jerry, 231, 235

Kahn, Peter, 26n4
Kalikow, Peter, 294
Kalinsky, George, 301
Kansas City A's, 2
Kansas City Chiefs, 230, 231
Kansas City Royals, 131
Karp, Stephen, 331, 332
Kasten, Stan, 269
Kay, Michael, 202
Keating, Dennis, 153
Kernersville NC, 207
KeyArena (Seattle), 231, 236
Kidd, Bruce, 216
Kim, Jung, 284

Kingdome (Seattle), 63, 163; replacement of, 161
Klein, Ed, 52
Klein, Walt, 208
Knott, Tom, 265
Koebele, Bob, 171
Kolb, Carol, 373
Konrad, Kim, 321, 333, 334, 335
Kopp, Quentin, 110
KPMG-Peat Marwick, 200, 219, 220
Kraft, Robert, 218, 220, 221, 222
Kriegel, Jay, 277
Kroc, Joan, 190
Kroc, Ray, 190
Krueger, Liz, 293
Krupa, Gregg, 318

Labatt Breweries, 216
Labatt Park (Montreal), 248
Lage, Larry, 117n3
Lambeau Field (Green Bay), 188, 193n2
landmarks, historic, 138
Lane, Gary, 67
Lanier, Bob, 62, 63
Lapides, Julian (Jack), 1, 11, 12, 23, 24, 351
Larkosh, Dan, 178
Las Vegas, 270; as new home for Expos, 251, 253; and stadium building, 227
Latin America, development investment in, 157
Lazere, Ed, 259, 260, 261, 266, 269
League of Fans, 40n1
leakage, 236–37
lease agreements, lavish, 133
Lee, Tom, 240
Lefkowitz, Stephen, 313
legislation, federal, 184–85
Lemenu, Jerry, 84, 86
Lerner, Ted, 269

LeRoy, Greg, 30, 104, 118n4, 244
LeSuer, Bill, 199
Lethem, Jonathan, 315
Level I enhancements, 239
Levin, Anna, 315
Levin, Carl, 95
Levin, Josh, 271
Levin, Rich, 255
Levine, Randy, 273, 296, 306, 312
Lewis, Bertha, 287, 288, 289
Leyva, Nick, 217
Lindsay, John, 69
Lites, Denise Ilitch, 116
Little Caesar's, 95
Llanes, Rolando, 328, 329
lobbying: big spending on, 291; for stadiums, 228
Locke, Gary, 164
Long, Judith Grant, 40n1, 61n4, 245
Loria, Jeffrey, 237, 248, 250, 331
Los Angeles Alliance for a New Economy, 286
Los Angeles Raiders, 2, 56, 72
Los Angeles Rams, 31, 59, 72
Lotterman, Edward, 244
lottery, as funding for stadiums, 22, 80
Lowell, Mike, 240
Lucchino, Larry, 210, 239, 332, 333
Lurie, Bob, 64, 173, 174
Lurie, Jeffrey, 67–68

Macombs Dam Park, 299, 311, 317; and "alienation" of, 307–8; destruction of, 302–3
MacPhail, Lee, 10
Madison Square Garden, 290; replacement of, 272, 274, 314
Magowan, Peter, 64, 175
Major League Baseball, 15, 60n1, 71;

Major League Baseball (*cont.*)
bringing ballparks into cities, 334;
and contraction, 245–46; and financing of DC stadium, 264; and the
Montreal Expos, 257, 265; owners
committee of, 190–91; and public
ownership of franchises, 170

Major League Losers (Rosentraub), 36

Major League Soccer, 164

Malcynsky, Jay, 218

Malek, Fred, 258

"mallpark," 337

Manion, Clyde, 86

Mantle, Mickey, 301

Maris, Roger, 321

Mark, Stephen, 201

Marker, Bill, 10–12, 22, 25, 152

Markowitz, Marty, 280

Marquardo, Craig, 253

Martin, Billy, 66

Martinez, Pedro, 247, 248

Marty, John, 209, 227, 228

Marylanders for Sports Sanity (MASS), 11

Maryland Sports Authority, 12

MassPIRG, 327

McCarron, John, 135n3

McClaren, Bob, 77

McClatchy, Kevin, 67, 234

McCourt, Frank, 331

McCurdy, James, 39

McDevitt, John, 88

McDougal, Patrick, 217

McGwire, Mark, 209, 321

McLane, Drayton, 77

McMorris, Jerry, 249

McNeill, Deb, 171

McNichols Arena (Denver), 67

media: and coverage of Seattle's stadiums, 162–63; as lobbyists, 111; owner-

friendliness of, 110; and pleasing corporate sponsors, 113; repetition and
impact of news, 109; and stadium
deals, 109–10. *See also* reporters

Memorial Stadium (Baltimore), 4, 9,
23–24, 26n5, 143

Memphis, and stadium building, 227

Mendelson, Phil, 267

Menino, Tom, 323, 325, 326, 334

Menlow, David, 189

Met Center (Bloomington), 166, 167

Metrodome. *See* Hubert H. Humphrey
Metrodome (Minneapolis)

Metropolitan Area Projects Strategy
(MAPS), 204–6

Metropolitan Football Stadium District
Board, 214

Metropolitan Sports Facilities Commission (Minnesota), 115, 169

Metropolitan Stadium (Minneapolis),
66, 355

Metropolitan Transportation Authority
(MTA), 294, 295, 298

MetroTech office complex, 279, 282

Mets stadium. *See* Citi Field (Mets stadium)

Miami Arena, 28, 106, 229

Miami Heat, 28, 69, 106, 108, 115, 177

Michaels, Chris, 212, 213, 223

migration, sports-franchise, 2

Mile High Stadium (Denver), 35, 67, 214

Miller, Gifford, 292, 310

Miller, Reverend Clinton, 289

Miller Park (Milwaukee), 53

Milwaukee Brewers, 46, 70, 79, 145

Milwaukee Bucks, 229

Minge, David, 186, 193n1

Minneapolis North Stars, 166, 167

Minnesota Corporate Welfare Reform
Law (1995), 168

Minnesota Timberwolves, 153, 165, 166, 167, 228

Minnesota Twins, 44, 160; demands of, 75, 230; and domed stadium, 66; and economic development, 41n5; and lobbyists, 228; and move of team, 70, 72, 207; and publicly traded shares, 189; and replacement for Metrodome, 28, 153, 166, 168–73, 226; and signing of Brad Radke, 234; and tax-increment financing, 243; threatened move of, 198; and use of media, 232; and new stadium victory, 227

Minnesota Vikings, 66, 166, 226, 230, 231

Minnesota Wins!, 36

Misak, Marge, 19–20, 33

Mitchell, George, 293

Modell, Art, xiii, 17, 24, 68, 136, 187, 195

Monaghan, Tom, 65, 87, 89, 92, 93, 113; and sale of Tigers, 94

Monterrey, Mexico, as new home for Expos, 251

Montgomery, Velmanette, 282–83, 381

Montreal, and loss of team, 379

Montreal Expos, 44, 82n2, 191, 198, 230, 233, 247–50, 331; disposing of, 250–59; and sale of club, 269; taken over by MLB, 237

Moores, John, 210, 213

Morris, Dick, 205

Morris, Jack, 216

Moss, Richard, 191

Moten, Emmet, 97, 359

moving a struggling team, 271

Moyihan, Daniel Patrick, 52, 184

Muhleman, Max, 54

Mullaly Park: and "alienation" of, 307–8; destruction of, 302–3

Mullin, Stephen, 39

Municipal Issuers' & Sports Franchises' Symposium on Sports Facilities Finance. See Sports Facilities Finance conference (1997)

municipal ownership: of sports teams, 190; of stadiums, 185

Municipal Stadium (Cleveland), 6, 17, 141; renovations, 18

Murphy, Mike, 107, 360

naming rights, 53, 79, 80, 195, 258, 299

NASCAR track, 314

National Football League (NFL), 73, 75

National Park Service, 311, 312

National Register of Historic Places, 329, 333

Naureckas, Jim, 109

Navin Field Consortium, 102n4

Navy Yard Metro station, 263

negotiating tactics, 269

Neighborhood Capital Budget Group (NCBG), 243–44

New England Patriots, 159n1, 198, 325; and move to Connecticut, 218–22

New Jersey Americans, 279

New Jersey Devils, 233

New Jersey Nets, 243, 279; new home for, 314

Newman, Shawn, 161, 163–64, 192

New Orleans Hornets, 227

New Orleans Saints, 230

New York Association for Better Choices, 290

New York Economic Development Corporation, 305–6

New Yorkers for Parks, 308

New York Giants, 300

New York Jets, 276, 289–91, 314; new home for, 272

New York Knicks, 57, 290; new home for, 313

New York Mets, 202, 248, 296; minor league affiliate of, 273; new home for, 272, 313, 314; and paying construction costs, 297

New York Rangers, 57, 290; new home for, 313

New York's City Council, 292

New York Times, 200, 282, 289, 290, 294; poll of, 314; and Regional Plan Association, 291

New York Yankees, xiv, 32, 43, 47, 69, 74, 198, 209–10, 216; annual rent of, 298; minor league affiliate of, 273; new home for, 272, 313, 314; and paying construction costs, 297; and stadium demands, 75

Neyer, Rob, 337

No DC Taxes for Baseball Coalition, 259, 260

Nolan, Patricia, 244

Noll, Roger G., 33–34, 46, 47, 52, 373

"No More Candy Store" (LeRoy), 30

non-threat threat, 68, 69

Norfolk VA, as new home for Expos, 253, 270

Norick, Ron, 205

northern Virginia, 256; as new home for Expos, 252, 253, 270

Northwest Airlines, 167–68

NYC2012, 274, 276, 277

Oakland A's, 2, 230, 234, 241

Oakland Coliseum, 56

Oakland Football Marketing Association, 56

Oakland Raiders, 2, 32, 56, 72, 190

obsolescence, 229; planned, 230

O'Connell, Mary, 121–22, 131, 138

O'Connor, Maureen, 190, 191

O'Donnell, Joseph, 331, 332

O'Keeffe, Michael, 289

Oklahoma City OK: building of stadium in, 204–5; and New Orleans Hornets, 227

Olympics: city losses of, 275, 381; NYC's bid for, 291, 292, 294, 295

Olympic Stadium (Montreal), 79, 248

O'Malley, Walter, 183

O'Neill, Steve, 7, 13

Onion, 226, 373

opposition: to new ballparks, 126, 169, 290; stadium-funding, 106

Orange, Vincent, 261

Oriole Park at Camden Yards. *See* Camden Yards (Baltimore)

Orlando Area Sports Commission, 103

Orlando Arena, 26n6, 229, 230

Orlando Magic, 225, 229, 231

Osborne, Jason, 254

O'Toole, Robert J., 81

overhangs in baseball parks, 124

Oxford, Jeanette Mott, 338, 339

Ozanian, Michael, 351

Pacific Bell Park (San Francisco), 53, 57

PAC spending, 107

Pappas, Doug, xi, 26n4, 60n1, 251, 254, 376

Parade Grounds stadium, 382

Parcells, Bill, 332

parking surcharge, 326

Pascal's Wager, 39

Passafiume, Joseph, 39

Pastier, John, 90–92, 141–42, 144–45, 148

Pataki, George, 291, 292, 293, 294–95, 313

Pate, Andrew, 335

Patrick, Dan, 27
Paul Brown Stadium (Cincinnati), 239
Pay Dirt (Quirk and Fort), 43
payments in lieu of taxes (PILOTS), 278,
    289, 292, 293, 311–12
Pearlstein, Steven, 233
Peebles, Gustav, 284
Peek, V. Lonnie, 97
Penthouse Suites Ltd., 214
Pepsi Center (Denver), 356
Perez, Rosie, 315
permanent-seat licenses. *See* personal
    seat license (PSL)
personal seat license (PSL), 54–57, 195
Petak, George, 80
Petco Park (San Diego), 239
Petrone, Thomas, 209, 242
Philadelphia A's, 2
Philadelphia Eagles, 67–68, 209, 242
Philadelphia Phillies, 45, 209, 242
Phoenix Cardinals, 59
Phoenix Coyotes, 243
Phoenix Suns, 103
Pigtown MD, 152, 158
Pinnell, Patrick, 329
Pioneer Baseball League, 39
Pittsburgh Penguins, 230
Pittsburgh Pirates, 67, 74, 209, 234, 242
Pittsburgh Steelers, 209, 242
player development, costs of, 46
players: spending on, 233; workout
    rooms for, 142
PNC Park (Pittsburgh), 234
Pohlad, Carl, 44, 72, 75, 160, 168–73; and
    possible move of team, 198, 271; and
    publicly traded shares, 189; and sale
    of Twins, 207; and use of media,
    232; and new stadium victory, 227
Policy, Carmen, 68, 176, 178, 180

politicians, self-interest of, 103–4
Polo Grounds (Manhattan), 139, 300
Porter, Philip, 241
Portland OR, 251, 253, 256, 270
Portland Trailblazers, 44
Powers, Bill, 312
Prentice, Miles, 331
PricewaterhouseCoopers, 323
property taxes: exemptions to, 292, 298;
    as unappealing to voters, 15
Public Authorities Control Board
    (PACB), 294–95, 316
Public Facilities District, 161–62
public hearings, 115, 262
public offerings of team shares, 188–89
public ownership of franchise, 170, 171
public takeover, 187
Puckett, Kirby, 170

Qualcomm Stadium at Jack Murphy
    Sports Complex (San Diego), 53,
    58–59, 210
Quattlebaum, Megan, 313
Quinn, Christine, 310, 316
Quirk, James, 43, 72

race: and Atlantic Yards project, 289; as
    issue in Tiger Stadium fight, 96–97;
    and location of stadium, 129
Radford-Hill, Sheila, 127, 128–30
Ramirez, Manny, 330
Rashid, Frank, 65, 78, 83–102, 103, 113,
    115; and desperation in Detroit,
    155–56
Rashid, Kevin, 84, 86
Rask, Ricky, 105, 115, 169, 228
Ratner, Bruce, 279–89, 309, 314, 381
Ratner, Harvey, 166, 167
Rawlings, Lenox, 208

Rawls, Wendell Jr., 113
Real Accountability, Progress, and Solutions (RAPS), 205
referendum(s), 106, 211; binding public, 12; defeat of (Seattle), 161; financing of (Washington), 165, 373; public (San Francisco), 174; and money and public votes, 114–16
Regional Plan Association, 291, 294
Reinsdorf, Jerry, 65, 120, 126–27, 134; as principal White Sox owner, 133, 223; and St. Petersburg offer, 130, 131, 135n2, 269, 270
"relocation committee," 250
Renaissance Center, 98
reporters: and influence of publishers, 112–13. *See also* media
Resolution G-3, 222
revenue sharing, 74, 75
Rex, Albert, 335
RFK Stadium (Washington), 252, 265
Ricciardi, J. P., 229
Richardson, Jerry, 55
Richfield Coliseum, 17
Richmond, Peter, 13, 350
Rider, Richard, 79
Riley, Pat, 107–8
Ringold, May, 23
Rivera, José, 315
Riverfront Stadium (Cincinnati), 53, 137
Roberts, Gary, 249
Robinson, Jackie, 45
Roche, Colleen, 198
Rock and Roll Hall of Fame (Cleveland), 18, 154
Rodriguez, Alex, 239
Rolnick, Arthur, 116, 153, 168, 185–86
Rose, Harvey, 177
Rosentraub, Mark, 36, 39, 181

Ross, Jim, 106
Ross, Stephen, 72
Rosten, Leo, 196
Rotundi, Doug, 335
Rouse, James, 149
Rowland, John, 218, 220, 221
Royals Stadium (Kansas City), 131, 138
Rubin, Steven, 204
Rubinstein, Howard, 199
Ruth, Babe, 203, 300, 302
Ryan, Bob, 318, 319, 326
Ryan, John, 16, 36
Ryan, Timothy, 236
Ryder, Richard, 59
Rymer, Russ, 151

Sacramento Kings, 159n2, 180, 229, 230
Safeco Field (Seattle), 181n2, 238
salary cap, 247, 249
Salter, Stephanie, 81
Samson, David, xi, 237, 238, 240, 250, 270
San Antonio Spurs, 233
San Antonio TX, 206–7, 253
Sanders, James, 277
Sanderson, Allen, 36, 237, 272
San Diego Chargers, 58, 71, 210, 230, 241
San Diego Padres, 180, 190, 210, 239, 331
San Francisco 49ers, 68, 76, 81, 176
San Francisco Giants, 28, 56, 64, 71, 173, 206; sale of, 174–75
San Juan PR, as new home for Expos, 251
Santee, Earl, 323
Sargent, Rob, 327
Sasso, John, 319
Save Fenway Park!, 204, 322–23, 327–28, 333, 339; and diversity of membership, 334
Savelkoul, Henry, 167, 169
Save Our Browns, 83

Save Our Parks, 305, 309, 315, 337

Save Our Sox, 121, 122–26, 128, 130, 134, 138, 339; and loss of core members, 131–32

SBC Center (San Antonio), 224n1

Schaefer, William, 9, 10, 11, 350

Schanberg, Sydney, 112–13

Schembechler, Bo, 93

Schott, Steve, 234, 241

Schramm, Tex, 54

Schultz, Howard, 231

Schwartz, Carol, 267, 268

scoreboard, "exploding," 133

seat guarantees, 210, 219, 220

seating distances, 91, 140–41

"seat options," 54

seat rights, 54

seat size, 140, 271

Seattle Mariners, 28, 63, 109, 114, 145, 160–63, 181n2; and public subsidies, 238, 239

Seattle Pilots, 46

Seattle Seahawks, 44, 163–65, 193

Seattle Sonics, 181n1, 230, 231, 226

Selig, Allan H. (Bud), 46, 70, 232, 247, 331; and contraction, 249; and Milwaukee Brewers stadium, 79–81; and move of Expos to DC, 250–71; on new stadiums, 234; and "stadium extortion" tour, 251

Sevigny, Tom, 219, 221

Shannon, Bill, 301

Shannon, Paul, 335

Sharp-Leadenhall Planning Committee, 23

Shaughnessy, Dan, 318

Shaw, Marc, 294

Shea Stadium (New York), 296, 298; lack of nostalgia for, 300

Sheinkopf, Hank, 205

shopping malls, "historic," 149–50

Silva, Gaston, 200

Silver, Sheldon, 291, 294–95, 315

Silverdome (Pontiac), 85

Simmons College, 328, 334

sin tax, 15, 16, 18, 33

SkyDome (Toronto), 37, 141, 215, 337; attendance at, 217; debt of, 79; as obsolete, 229; sale of, 216, 217

"smart seats," 240

Smith, Damu, 260

Smith, Janet Marie, 332

Smith, Mike, 231

Smulyan, Jeff, 160

social services, cutbacks in, 157

social welfare, 156

Society for American Baseball Research, 335

Somerindyke, William Jr., 254

Sosa, Sammy, 209

South Armour Square, 126–27, 131, 132, 146

South Armour Square Neighborhood Association, 127, 128

South Street Seaport (Manhattan), 149, 150

Spanos, Alex, 210

sports: as entertainment and tradition, 124

sports facilities and isolation from surrounding neighborhoods, 136–37

Sports Facilities Finance conference (1997), 106, 114, 184

sports fans, 83

sports finances, 44–48; and profits of clubs, 42, 43

sports industry, 42–43

Sports, Jobs, and Taxes (Noll), 34

sports teams: sale price of, 44; and threatening to move, 67–73; value of, 24–25, 216

stadiums: amenities of, 48; and backlash against subsidies, 207; benefits of, 75–77; captive audiences at, 145; circular, 137; competitiveness of, 73–75, 201; and configuration of playing fields, 139; construction of, xiii; cost of, 27–28, 31, 40n1, 142, 296–97, 351–52; cost overruns of, 78–81; domed, 7, 66, 85, 216, 348; and driving payroll costs, 234; dual-purpose, 9; economic arguments for, 200; economic impact of, 234–37; food service at, 143–46; free rent for, 19; hidden costs of, 28, 40n1; "honeymoon period" of, 216; impact on cities' economy, 34–35; as imputed income, 186; and integration with urban neighborhoods, 145–46; lottery as funding for, 22, 80; luxury suites of, 48–50; municipal ownership of, 185; need for new, 31–32; new "old-fashioned," 137, 141; obsolescence of, 65, 200; opposition to, 63–64, 226; and parking, 297; as part of entertainment zone, 148–49; and paying own way, 173; payment for, 28–29; and performance of teams, 212, 215; and privately owned facilities, 28; public's lack of desire for, 153; renegotiation of subsidies for, 78–81; rents of, 31, 52; retractable roofs on, 66, 79, 161, 169, 171; and seat guarantees, 210, 219, 220; shelf life of, 229; subsidies on, 184; tax revenues to finance, 171; unique character of, 139–40; volume (overall size) of, 141–43

"stadium self-cleaning machines," 240

Staples Center (Los Angeles), 286

Stark, Jayson, 238

state-of-the-art clauses, 239, 240

Stebbins, John, 117n2

Steinberg, Dan, 299, 300, 307–8, 312, 316

Steinbrenner, George, xiv, 43, 47, 199–203, 296; demands of, 69, 75; and leakage, 237; and purchase of Yankees, 301; and stadium parking, 297; and subsidies, 298

Sterling, John, 202

St. Louis Cardinals, 47, 241, 297; and "deadlines," 237; as a stadium suitor, 223

St. Louis Rams, 31, 6n6; and moving fine, 72

Stone, Mike, 191

Stop Tax-exempt Arena Debt Issuance Act (STADIA), 184–85

Stop the Stadium, 218, 219, 221, 222

St. Petersburg, and new stadium, 130

strike: baseball, 216; players', 44, 247

Strike Three on Proposition C (STOP-C), 212

Stringer, Scott, 198

Stroud, Kim, 78, 101, 102n4, 115, 117n3

structural adjustment, 156–59, 363–64

"studied incompetence," 113

subsidies: and backlash against, 207; hidden, 57, 245–46, 339; stadium, 269, 298, 338. See also government subsidies; tax abatements; tax breaks; tax exemptions

"subsidy abuse," 30

substitution effect, 35, 37, 40n4, 76, 236–37, 258

Sugg, John, 117n2

suites, 48–50

Sullivan, Kevin, 220

Super Bowl: hosting of, 240; and tourism, 241

Suwe, Newton, 123

Swindal, Steve, 296, 297

Sylvan, Jack, 373

Tagliabue, Paul, 177, 240

Tampa Bay Buccaneers, 117n2

Tampa Bay Devil Rays, 71, 251, 270, 314; as a stadium suitor, 223

Target Center (Minneapolis), 165, 166, 167

Tarlin, Erika, 322, 327, 332, 334, 336

Tavares, Daniel, 305

tax abatements, 153–56, 194; limits on, 157. *See also* corporate welfare

tax breaks, 29–31, 45, 50–52. *See also* corporate welfare

taxes, regressive, 148

tax-exempt bonds, 50–52, 81, 311

tax exemptions, 57–58, 298

tax-increment financing (TIF), 172, 175, 206, 242–44, 277

Tax Reform Act of 1986, 47, 51, 52, 184, 311

tax revenues to finance stadiums, 171

Taylor, Glen, 228

Taylor, John, 320

team owners, demands of, 27

T. E. Brown apartments, 130, 133

Teflon roof, 166, 248

Tejada, Miguel, 234

ten-percent solution, 50–52

Texas Rangers, 71, 72, 191

Texas Stadium (Dallas), 54

Thompson, Jim, 131

Thompson, Tommy, 80, 107, 260

Thornton, Bill, 206

3Com Park, 53

Three Rivers Stadium (Pittsburgh), 67, 137, 336

ticket guarantees, 58–59

ticket pricing, 26n6

ticket surcharge, 55

Tiger Stadium (Detroit), 64, 65, 84, 101, 143, 234; engineering study for, 88–89; as fan-friendly ballpark, 90; on the National Register of Historic Places, 92–93; renovation of, 85; saving, 86–94

Tiger Stadium Fan Club, 65, 83–84, 87–94, 102n4, 115, 335, 339, 358; and correcting reports, 117n3; and new reporters, 113; small-scale plans of, 104; and uphill battle, 155

Time-Warner, 43

Todd, Jack, 248

Toronto Blue Jays, 46, 215, 216, 229, 314

tourists, emphasis on, 156

Tower City, 195

town hall meeting, 306

tradition of sports, 124

Trenkle, Hank, 134

Tropicana Field (Tampa Bay), 71

TV commercials, 107–8

TV revenue, 175

TWA Dome (St. Louis), 59, 60

"unanticipated capital costs," 239

"undervalued" franchises, 42

Uniform Land Use Review Process, 306

United Artists theater, 97, 101n1

United Baseball League (UBL), 191, 192

United Center (Chicago), 187

Updike, John, 324

"urban homesteaders," 158

urban planning, 33

urban priorities, 152
urban renaissance, 157
U.S. Olympic Committee, 164

Vaillancourt, Meg, 318
Valienti, John, 335
Vallone, Peter, 202, 274
Vancouver Grizzlies, 229, 230
Vander Weide, Bob, 231
Van Dyk, Chris, 161, 165, 181n1, 194, 196
Vaughn, Greg, 213
Veeck, Bill, 44, 45–46, 182; and sale of
    White Sox, 65, 120
Vennocchi, Joan, 319
Ventresca, Joel, 177
Ventura, Jesse, 250
Verducci, Tom, 255
Veterans Stadium (Philadelphia), 48, 137
Vincent, Fay, 15–16, 70
Virginia Baseball Stadium Authority,
    254
Voinovich, George, 8, 348
voter turnout by African Americans,
    348
Vote Yes for Major League Baseball, 208

Walden, Michael, 373
Walt Disney Company, 150–51
Ward, Lloyd, 275
Washington, Harold, 131
Washington DC, as new home for Ex-
    pos, 251, 270
Washington Nationals, 265
Washington Redskins, 57
Washington Senators, 251, 256
Wasynczuk, Andy, 159n1
"Wayfen" option, 328
Weiner, Jay, 40n4
Weiss, Chris, 259, 268, 271

Wentworth Gardens, 119, 127
Wentworth Residents United for Sur-
    vival, 127, 130
Werner, Tom, 331, 332
White, Michael, 18, 19, 20, 21, 33, 105,
    195, 350
Whitman, Christine Todd, 107, 201
Wilbon, Michael, 262
Wilkerson, Dianne, 327
Williams, Anthony, 252, 256–71
Williams, Edward Bennett, 10, 11, 105,
    356
Williams, Ted, 203
Wilner, Richard, 313
Wilpon, Fred, 202, 203, 298
Wilpon, Jeff, 298
Wilson, Dan, 321, 322, 323, 324, 328, 330,
    332, 334, 335, 336, 339
Winfree, Chuck, 208
Wojnar, Steve, 335
Wolfenson, Marv, 166, 167
Wolff, Lew, 241
Wolff, Nelson, 253
Woodward, Denni, 178–79
World Series, cancellation of, 247
Wrigley Field (Chicago), 92; and its
    neighborhood, 147; as old steel-
    framed ballpark, 300

Yankee Stadium, 32, 198–203, 296, 298;
    cost of, 384–85; and fall of roof, 199;
    inadequacies of, 306; nostalgia for,
    300; rally for, 305; renovation of, 69,
    301, 336
Yankee Stadium (new), 299
Yaro, Robert, 294
Yastrzemski, Carl, 203
Yawkey, Jean, 324
Yawkey, Tom, 320, 324

Yawkey Trust, 324; putting Red Sox up
  for sale, 330
Young, Coleman, 88, 93

Zimbalist, Andrew, 191, 192, 220, 373;
and hiring by Ratner, 283; report
  of, 284
Zimmerman, Dennis, 37
Zurnsteg, Derek, 256

CPSIA information can be obtained
at www.ICGtesting.com
Printed in the USA
LVOW01s1804180716

496784LV00014B/91/P